Transmedia Character

Transmedia Character Studies provides a range of methodological tools and foundational vocabulary for the analysis of characters across and between various forms of multimodal, interactive, and even non-narrative or non-fictional media.

This highly innovative work offers new perspectives on how to interrelate production discourses, media texts, and reception discourses, and how to select a suitable research corpus for the discussion of characters whose serial appearances stretch across years, decades, or even centuries. Each chapter starts from a different notion of how fictional characters can be considered, tracing character theories and models to approach character representations from perspectives developed in various disciplines and fields.

This book will enable graduate students and scholars of transmedia studies, film, television, comics studies, video game studies, popular culture studies, fandom studies, narratology, and creative industries to conduct comprehensive, media-conscious analyses of characters across a variety of media.

Tobias Kunz holds an MA in Cross-Media Culture from the University of Amsterdam, the Netherlands. He works as an editorial assistant for the peer-reviewed journal *Connotations*.

Lukas R.A. Wilde is Associate Professor in the Department of Art and Media Studies at the Norwegian University of Science and Technology (NTNU) in Trondheim. His monograph *Im Reich der Figuren* (*Kingdom of Characters*) was awarded with the Roland Faelske for the best dissertation in Comics and Animation Studies 2018 as well as with the GIB Dissertation Award 2021 of the Society for the Interdisciplinary Study of Pictures (GiB). He is Vice President of the German Society for Comic Studies (ComFor).

Routledge Advances in Transmedia Studies
Series Editor: Matthew Freeman

This series publishes monographs and edited collections that sit at the cutting-edge of today's interdisciplinary cross-platform media landscape. Topics should consider emerging transmedia applications in and across industries, cultures, arts, practices, or research methodologies. The series is especially interested in research exploring the future possibilities of an interconnected media landscape that looks beyond the field of media studies, notably broadening to include socio-political contexts, education, experience design, mixed-reality, journalism, the proliferation of screens, as well as art- and writing-based dimensions to do with the role of digital platforms like VR, apps and iDocs to tell new stories and express new ideas across multiple platforms in ways that join up with the social world.

Transmedia Practices in the Long Nineteenth Century
Edited by Christina Meyer and Monika Pietrzak-Franger

Transmedia Change
Pedagogy and Practice for Socially-Concerned Transmedia Stories
Edited by Kevin Moloney

Transmedia Narratives for Cultural Heritage
Remixing History
Nicole Basaraba

Multiplicity and Cultural Representation in Transmedia Storytelling
Superhero Narratives
Natalie Underberg-Goode

Transmedia Character Studies
Tobias Kunz and Lukas R.A. Wilde

For more information about this series, please visit: www.routledge.com/ Routledge-Advances-in-Transmedia-Studies/book-series/RATMS

Transmedia Character Studies

**Tobias Kunz and
Lukas R.A. Wilde**

Routledge
Taylor & Francis Group

LONDON AND NEW YORK

First published 2023
by Routledge
4 Park Square, Milton Park, Abingdon, Oxon OX14 4RN

and by Routledge
605 Third Avenue, New York, NY 10158

Routledge is an imprint of the Taylor & Francis Group, an informa business

British Library Cataloguing-in-Publication Data
A catalogue record for this book is available from the British Library

ISBN: 978-1-032-28507-8 (hbk)
ISBN: 978-1-032-28848-2 (pbk)
ISBN: 978-1-003-29879-3 (ebk)

DOI: 10.4324/9781003298793

Typeset in Baskerville
by codeMantra

Contents

Figures

Preface and Acknowledgments

This volume on a potential Transmedia Character Studies as a developing interdisciplinary field of research has emerged out of teaching and research at the University of Tuebingen's (Germany) Department of Media Studies. Lukas R.A. Wilde organized a first Winter School on "De/Recontextualizing Characters: Media Convergence and Pre-/Meta-Narrative Character Circulation" in February/March 2018 as well as a second one with a somewhat broader scope on "Transmedia Character Studies: Interdisciplinary and Media-comparative Approaches" in March/April 2022, both generously funded by the Federal Ministry of Education and Research (BMBF) and the Baden-Württemberg Ministry of Science as part of the Excellence Strategy of the German Federal and State Governments. Between the summer term 2020 and the winter term 2021/2022, there have also been three BA seminars titled "Transmedia Character Studies: An Introduction" for Tuebingen University's students of media studies together with international exchange students and visitors from other disciplines such as Interdisciplinary American Studies, English Literatures and Cultures, or Korean Studies, introducing them to the topic of transmediality through a shared focus on fictional and fictionalized characters in contemporary media culture. During the first installment of the seminar, Lukas Wilde was mainly working with the existing research literature that is referenced and discussed in this volume in detail. Striking differences in terminology and methodology, however, continued to provide huge challenges for students. Researchers from fields as different as media studies, literature studies, game studies, anthropology, cognitive sciences, gender studies, and many more certainly brought invaluable perspectives into discussions of transmedia characters in recent decades; the methodological orientation as well as even the most foundational terminology in these works, however, varied greatly. In the seminars, students kept getting back to the question of what the respective authors *meant* by even (or perhaps especially) the use of the word "character" one session after the other. Beyond matters of terminology, there seemed to be no agreement at all where fictional or fictionalized protagonists could even be "located" between textual representations, mental models, abstract meanings, or public discourses and discussions. In the end, Tobias Kunz and Lukas R.A. Wilde started to provide more and more chapters of this book on their own to students, offering a concise and unified terminology and a shared methodological framework. Participants in the seminars were encouraged to apply these tools, questions, and approaches on their own to media texts and artifacts of their choices – frequently, students had already accumulated lots of interest and (fan) knowledge about specific characters and franchises they were following for years, now viewing them from new, critical perspectives offered in the following pages. The authors of this volume are proud to have learned from them as well as the other way round. During the second Winter School in March/April 2022, exemplary students even presented their own research and findings from their resulting term papers and BA theses in front of an international audience of leading experts in the field, bringing teaching and research together in a way that is, unfortunately, still rather rare in universities.

This "secret origin" of the resulting present volume explains two things that a reader might find surprising at first and which we would make transparent here. Since most of the examples in class were chosen by the students themselves, drawn from media texts and characters they were familiar with or interested in, we are mostly keeping away from the usual "canon" of works in, say, film studies or comic book studies. Although certain established "test cases" for character theory like HAL 9000 from the film *2001: A Space Odyssey* or Vladek from the graphic novel *Maus: A Survivor's Tale* will be mentioned, most of the examples under discussion – from films, TV shows, comic books, manga, anime, or video games – are taken from popular franchises and texts of the last five to ten years. There is also a strong predominance of Anglo-American works on the one hand and Japanese ones on the other, as well as – to our shame – of works by male, white authors. We have tried in the seminars and will try in the following pages to continuously reflect on the limitations as well as on the political implications of our selective, certainly problematic corpus of works (as well as of the media industries that foster such an overrepresentation of privileged creators over other groups in the public awareness). Perhaps more surprisingly, however, although most of the students in the Transmedia Character Studies classes were German (with maybe only every fifth an international exchange student), the media texts chosen were predominantly either of American or Japanese origins (with Korean works steadily rising in popularity). Since this might be similar in many other countries today, the examples discussed in this volume should at least be prominent enough across the globe to make the discussions easily accessible. Incidentally, the two authors of this volume also have backgrounds in English/American Studies and Japanese Studies, adding some cultural knowledge as well as familiarity with the respective research literature. In conclusion, we'd like to thank our students who have contributed enormously to the perspectives and samples presented here, through discussions, questions, and critical voices in class as well as through particularly outstanding term papers and even their own contributions in the Winter School. We'd especially like to mention Shama Alam, Christina Anagnostoudi, Antonia Bangemann, Sophia Bauer, Eleanor Brockwell, Mara Brune, Stephanie Harenbrock, Lena Herrmann, Kilian Huber, Helen Keller, Hannah Krämer, Fabian Lenhardt, Louis Lory, Lisa Müller, Frederike Myhsok, Clara von Obernitz, Lara Proß, Carlota Pizá Ramos, Fabian Runkel, Annkatrin

Voos, and Lei Wang, whose thoughts and interests permeate some of the following discussions. We would also like to thank Vanessa Ossa, Philip Dreher, and Nicolle Lamerichs for their critical remarks, as well as Stephan Packard and the participants of his research colloquium at the University of Cologne where we had the pleasure to discuss early versions of chapters. Of equal importance to this book were Johanna Blom and Espen Aarseth who organized a highly stimulating Character Seminar at the IT University of Copenhagen in October 2019. Finally, we are very grateful to Klaus Sachs-Hombach for his continuous support of the project as well as to our assistant Marcel Lemmes for his tireless efforts in putting the results together and adding many of his perspectives.

Trondheim & Amsterdam,
August 2022

0 Transmedia Character Studies – An Introduction

A discipline of Transmedia Character Studies does not exist to date. Yet, contemporary media cultures around the globe are saturated with popular characters such as James Bond, Daenerys Targaryen (*Game of Thrones/A Song of Ice and Fire*), Harley Quinn, Donald Duck, Rick Grimes (*The Walking Dead*), Tanjirō Kamado (*Demon Slayer*) or Lara Croft (*Tomb Raider*). They cut across all boundaries of different media forms such as novels, films, TV shows, comic books, manga, anime, or video games. In a way, such transmedial worlds have permeated every aspect of everyday life from workplace decoration to marriage ceremonies, as media studies scholars Susana Tosca and Lisbeth Klastrup have demonstrated recently (2019). The fictional protagonists of such works seem to share many attributes with human beings, but everyone would most certainly agree that they do not "really" exist. Usually, the term *character* is reserved for such *fictional* (or *fictionalized*) protagonists and accordingly opposed to the term *person*: We are only able to "meet" the former through media texts. However, as English literature scholar John Frow has argued, fictional and fictionalized characters are not only modeled after real persons – the reverse relationship exists as well and has historically developed mutually: "Social personhood works as a kind of fiction" (Frow 2014, vii). The interplay between literary, cinematic, or other sorts of medial characters and what we colloquially call the "character" of a politician, an athlete, or other figures of public life – their personalities – is undoubtedly extraordinarily complex (see Garber 2020, 3–22). In any case, it would be hard to find media texts that do *not* feature or even center around one or several human-like protagonists, informing and often negotiating our understanding of "actual" people. Media studies scholar Rainer Leschke thus considered characters to be "medial forms migrating through media systems," "intermediary categories between medium, work, and sign" (Leschke 2010, 12f., our translations). In a way, characters can then be regarded as the "currency of media [...], their universal means of exchange" (11, our translation). This is especially true for today's "franchise era" (see Fleury et al. 2019) in which media content is produced and distributed in complex industrial practices across interconnected digital platforms. In many ways, characters do not even seem restricted to narrative media but are found everywhere around us on material objects, in bodily performances, in

DOI: 10.4324/9781003298793-1

adopted figures of speech – in our *Umwelt*, our Lifeworld, as English literature scholar Rita Felski put it aptly:

> The world would look very different without Jekyll and Hyde, Faust, Antigone, Mary Poppins, Norman Bates, Dracula, Nancy Drew, Don Juan, Spock, Hedda Gabler, Oedipus, Winnie the Pooh, Scrooge, Darth Vader, Hercule Poirot, HAL, Mickey Mouse, the Simpsons, Alice, Medea, Scrooge, Gandalf, Sam Spade, Anna Karenina. These figures are not just bundles of signifiers; they are worldly actors haloed with affective and existential force.
>
> (Felski 2019, 87)

Surprisingly, however, characters are still a rather under-theorized topic in the humanities. Jens Eder, a media studies scholar who dedicated considerable parts of his work to the research of characters in film, found that "many have written only a little and only a few have written much on characters" (Eder 2008a: 40, our translation).

0.1 Where Are Transmedia Character Studies Located?

Analyzing characters – and comparing the various media-specific means of their construction, reception, and circulation – can be an ideal starting point to reflect on the material-technological, semiotic-generic, and social-institutional affordances, as well as on the representational strategies used in different popular media forms and media texts to tell stories or comment upon real or imaginary events. The importance of characters as entry points into cultural reflections, or as nodes in discussions thereof, has long been noted by literary studies and cultural anthropology. Not by accident, many important narratives within human history have been named after their protagonists: Gilgamesh or Don Quixote, Tristram Shandy or Anna Karenina. This tradition continues within many contemporary, transmedial narratives – especially those based on comic books and animated films – centered around, and often directly named after popular heroes such as Tintin, Tom and Jerry, Superman, or Wonder Woman. The centrality of their names announces that these stories focus on characters' behaviors, their fates, their struggles, and experiences.

Even more importantly, many characters seem to exist "across" different medial works, so we can follow their adventures in countless stories and texts. In many cases, most people will not even be familiar with some kind of "original" from which all other versions are derived. In this sense, transmedia characters are much like the protagonists of ancient myths, "authorless" narratives that belong to anybody and everybody, thousands of iterations partly contradicting, partly confirming each other: King Arthur, Robin Hood, or the heroes from Greek mythology. Figures from myths, folklore, and fairy tales often *are* used as modern transmedia characters in every sense of the word: A version of Hercules has not only been portrayed by Dwayne "The Rock" Johnson in *Hercules* (Ratner 2014) and by dozens of other film actors over the years but also drawn by cartoonists in Disney's animated *Hercules* film (Clements and Musker 1997) and employed as the computer-generated protagonist in the Nintendo Switch game *The 12 Labours of Hercules* (JetDogs 2019). Another version has even become a recurrent superhero within the Marvel comic book universe (first appearing in *Avengers* #10, Lee and Heck 1964, then solidified in *Journey into Mystery Annual* #1, Lee and Kirby 1965). From antiquity on, Hercules had been used as a motif for statues, vases, classical paintings, and poetry. Not surprisingly, comic book superhero narratives are often considered the descendants of ancient myths (see Eco 1972, or, more recently, Wood 2021), precisely for the fact that their protagonists are used and re-used without any claim to an "original" or "definite" version.

The term *series character* (see Denson and Mayer 2018) has been offered for protagonists that appear recurrently within a larger series (as, for instance, *The Simpsons* animated show, Brooks et al. 1989–present). If the same characters (or, at least, what *appears* to be the same characters by name) appear in texts that are *not* perceived as a continuous series – but a range of individual works by varying authors – they are also referred to as *transtextual characters* (see Richardson 2010). Sometimes, a character of the same name even seems to star in heterogeneous fictional worlds. For such contradictory transtextual appearances, the term *transfictional character* is used as well, as they seem to traverse across mutually exclusive fictional worlds (see Ryan 2013; Haugtvedt 2017). The canonical example for this would be Sherlock Holmes (see Pearson 2018a). To phrase it with narratologist Jan-Noël Thon:

> Indeed, there can be little doubt that the Victorian master detective Sherlock Holmes represented by Sir Arthur Conan Doyle's 1892–1927 short stories and novels, the 21st-century Sherlock Holmes represented by *BBC's Sherlock* (2010–2017), and the 21st-century American immigrant Sherlock Holmes represented by CBS's *Elementary* (2012–present), the 21st-century African-American Sherlock Holmes in Boller, Leonardi, and Stroman's comics series *Watson and Holmes* (2013–present), the canine master detective in the Italian-Japanese anime series *Sherlock Hound* (1984–1985), or the rodent master detective in Walt Disney's animated film *The Great Mouse Detective* (1986) do not – and do not seem to be intended to – coalesce into a single transmedia character.
>
> (Thon 2019, 188)

A transtextual/transfictional character's identity thus remains highly malleable, not only when it comes to context and setting, but also in terms of age, gender, ethnicity, or even species. This is especially true for "transformational" fan fiction, often engaged with the reimagination of popular characters in partly different identities (see Stein and Busse 2012, 15–16; Coppa 2017). For cases where many appearances of a transtextual character occur in different forms of media, each with their respective affordances and constraints, the overarching term *transmedia characters* has gained wide circulation in recent years. While the designation "intermedia" or "crossmedia" focuses on the relationship or the contact between individual media forms or texts from different media, the prefix "trans-" signifies a (perceived) transcendence of, a relative autonomy from any individual media of origin (see Rajewsky 2005; Thon 2014). Transmedia characters are part of our *cultural* vocabularies rather than confined to texts or (individual) media forms. A field of research concerned with such dynamics has been emerging under the umbrella of transmedia studies within the last couple of years (see Freeman and Gambarato 2019).

Character theories – and means to their analysis – did not originate within this relatively contemporary field of research, but first developed in literary studies. Human-like protagonists are a key component of literature and drama, after all. Aristotle in 335 b.c. (see 2018) and Horace in 15 b.c. (see 1972) already developed a rather detailed theory of characters in drama. To recount the innumerable approaches that have been taken toward their theory and function ever since would amount to no less than summarizing the theory of literature and the history of narrative theory itself, as Fotis Jannidis rightfully remarked (2004, 85). Descriptive rather than normative approaches first emerged in the 19th century and developed in the 20th century interconnectedly for literature (see Harvey 1965; Phelan 1989), theater (see Pfister 1977), and film (see Tomasi 1988; Smith 1995). Traditionally, these approaches were first and foremost concerned with "realistic" narratives. But, as Felski has pointed out,

> [a]udiences identify with figures from fairy tales, comic strips, melodramas, parables, and superhero movies, not to mention *Star Trek*, *The Texas Chain Saw Massacre*, or *Blood and Guts in High School*. The draw of character has far less to do with realism than with qualities of vividness and distinctiveness.
>
> (2019, 78)

A range of recent book-length studies by scholars such as Henry Jenkins (2006), Kristin Thompson (2007), Robert A. Brookey (2010), Elizabeth Evans (2011), Mark J. P. Wolf (2012), Marc Steinberg (2012), Derek Johnson (2013), Colin B. Harvey (2015), Matthew Freeman (2016), or Dan Hassler-Forest (2016) examined the most important functions of the production, aesthetics, and reception of popular, generic characters in convergent media culture. However, while the semiotics, aesthetics, and economics of serial and transmedial narratives, in general, have been the focus of many research projects, also from historical perspectives (see, e.g., Freeman 2014; Scolari et al. 2014a; Meyer 2019), less attention has been paid to the crucial role fulfilled by characters as "nodal points" or "currencies" between converging and diverging storyworlds (important contributions include Kelleter 2017; Thon and Wilde 2019; Riis and Taylor 2019; Aarseth and Blom 2022). "So far nobody has devised a theory that is meant to cover fictional characters exhaustively," Henriette Heidbrink judged in her survey on the state of research in 2010 (67), which has not changed significantly to this day.

The most exhaustive approaches to the analysis of characters are certainly derived from semiotic and structuralist traditions (see Barthes 1975; Propp

1984; Greimas 1984, as well as Bertetti and Thibault 2022 for a survey). Many of these authors objected strongly to the commonsensical assumption that represented characters should be treated as analogues to human beings (persons) or that they could be analyzed with related psychoanalytic or hermeneutic methods. After all, we "encounter" (fictional and fictionalized) characters exclusively in medial representations consisting of multimodal sign configurations (words, images, sounds, etc.). These scholars declared that characters could be understood as mere textual functions, for which specialized technical terms such as "agents" (Barthes), or "actors" and "actants" (Greimas) were offered. These are then entirely composed of "semes" (ascribed semantic properties), which can only be interpreted as human-like characteristics – "character traits" (Chatman 1978, 127) – on the level of what is represented: The *storyworld*, also called the *diegesis* of a given text. In semiotic film theory, Edward Branigan likewise regarded a character as a mere "surface feature of discourse" (1984, 12), i.e., as a semiotic network of represented character traits. Fotis Jannidis, arguing from literary theory, defined characterization as the process of "ascribing information to an agent in the text so as to provide a character in the storyworld with a certain property or properties" (2014, 37). These traits could then be analyzed according to parameters such as their relative "complexity" (the number of traits), their "development" (static vs. dynamic traits), or their "penetration of the inner life" (objective-outside vs. subjective-inside traits) (see also Rimmon-Kenan 1993, 40). According to Gerard Genette, the founder of modern narratology, characterization should likewise be primarily considered the semantic effect of a textual structure (one of many such effects). After all, our knowledge of a character's intentions, experiences, worldviews, and other traits is revealed only through certain literary (or, more generally, *narrative*) techniques: direct and indirect speech, focalization, or description. We should hence focus on the study of these techniques rather than on their results (the "character effect").

In contrast to these earlier semiotic traditions, more recent cognitive theories try to provide answers as to how the undeniable resemblance of characters to actual persons can be explained from the side of audiences. For Uri Margolin, who first attempted to integrate questions of reception into existing textual approaches with a series of groundbreaking articles (1990a; 1990b; 1995; 1996), the "character effect" would be situated on two different levels. Only the first one ("the ascription of individual properties," Margolin 2007, 71) could be analyzed within the text. A second "site" of the character, however, must be localized in reception, where audiences engage in some kind of "make-believe." In cognitivist approaches, this second domain is understood as a kind of "spark of life" (Varis 2019, 72), through which the signs and textual structures are fused within a "cognitive second creation" (75) in the minds of audiences. Only then can higher-level symbolic meanings or cultural connotations be assigned to these imaginary entities. In James Phelan's (1987) influential model of literary protagonists, these different dimensions correspond to a triadic model of the "synthetic" (the semiotic materials of representation and their textual structures), the "mimetic" (the character as a fictional or imagined individual), and finally the "thematic" (the character as a representation of ideas or concepts).

Following Margolin's fundamental work, media studies scholar Jens Eder has certainly compiled the most comprehensive cross-disciplinary comparisons of character theories and methods to their analysis in numerous publications (2008a; 2008b; 2010). Even though his starting point for reflection is based on film, his considerations (especially 2008a) are decidedly media-comparative. In the last few decades, various additional media-specific theories of characters have also been developed. We now have theories for literary characters (see, e.g., Schneider 2001; Jannidis 2004; Frow 2014), film and TV characters (Tomasi 1988; Smith 1995; Eder 2008), comic book characters (Mikkonen 2017, 174–200; Varis 2019; D'Arcy 2020, 57–92), and video game characters (Vella 2015; Blom 2019; Schröter 2021). Often, these approaches developed independently from each other, although many aspects of characters – for instance, that media will usually grant some access to their "inner life" – are transmedial, that is: They apply across media. It is not surprising, then, that there have been many foundations for a truly transmedial character theory in recent years that do not take *specific* media as their starting point (see Pearson 2019). Jan-Noël Thon, for instance, expanded Eder's assumptions into a transmedia character theory (2019) against the background of his transmedia narratology (2016), while Paolo Bertetti developed similar foundations within the tradition of semiotics (2014; 2019).

0.2 Dimensions and Aspects Relevant to the Construction, Reception, and Circulation of Transmedia Characters

This book is not so much about characters, media-specific or transmedial, but about what a potential Transmedia Characters Studies could look like as an interdisciplinary field of research. It is then mostly about methodology, presenting a "toolbox" of analytical concepts and methods derived from the various fields mentioned above that are concerned with characters across media. The most important question it asks is: If characters are essentially "ontologically hybrid beings" (Frow 2018, 109) between the synthetic, the mimetic, and the thematic, or in other words: between material signs arranged into textual structures, represented individuals, and abstract topics and themes, where do we have to look for characters "as such"? How do these dimensions interrelate? To address this question, we first turn to comprehensive models by scholars such as Phelan, Margolin, or Eder, who tried to synthesize the various dimensions to investigate their interrelations. Margolin combined a range of different disciplinary perspectives: from structuralism and semiotics to the theory of possible worlds to cognitive reception studies. Eder later developed a model for the analysis of characters in film, which was at least intended to be applied in a transmedial fashion. According to Margolin, a character is first and foremost "an artistic product or artifice constructed by an author for some purpose" (2007, 66). This corresponds to the semiotic or structuralist perspective, according to which characters are primarily "bundle[s] of qualities (character traits)" (Müller 1991, 103) ascribed to them by medial artifacts. In Jonathan Culler's words, characters are nothing but "sets of predicates grouped under a proper name" (1981, 5). Some narratives – and their characters – might be body-centered (slapstick, cartoons), while others might be mind-centered (psychological narratives or crime dramas); others again might be social-centered (melodramas or sitcoms). Character traits can then be either (1) physical (what characters look like), (2) mental: We are granted some sort of access to their "inner life," their subjectivity; as well as (3) social: What relations they share with other protagonists and how they are positioned within their world. This becomes clear if we look at a media text like David Mitchell's novel *Utopia Avenue* (2020). It begins by telling us that "Dean hurries past the Phoenix Theatre" (3), a phrase which introduces us to a fictional (presumably male) individual named Dean, who is apparently in a hurry. Starting with this single detail, the novel goes on to add more and more attributes and information to the name of "Dean": We learn that, for him, "Friday morning is rent-paying morning, and Mrs. Nevitt is waiting in her parlour" (3), which not only explains the hurry Dean is in but also identifies him as the rentier of property, and as a not particularly wealthy man. As we continue reading, the text discloses that Dean is a struggling musician; it introduces his friends and tells us about his complicated attitude toward his working-class background. All these individual traits slowly accumulate to a detailed fictional representation – and probably to some sort of mental model in the minds of readers – of and about "Dean."

Pictorial media, by contrast, always seem to depict a fictional or fictionalized character "as a whole," whether there was an actor in front of a camera or whether some cartoonist created a colorful illustration. We will look at different pictorial modes of character representations in more detail later, but it should be noted early on that pictures must be considered "signs close to perception" (see Sachs-Hombach 2011; see Wilde 2018b). Any individual picture always contains more predicates – perceivable properties legible as character traits – than we could ever explicate verbally, or only with the greatest difficulty. Pictures are hence said to possess a "presence" that seems to transcend deliberate representation: Watching a film like *Birds of Prey: The Emancipation of Harley Quinn* (Yan 2020), we seem to perceive its protagonist Harley somehow "directly," including all her mannerisms, facial expressions, and gestures, even when we are keenly aware that it was the actress Margot Robbie who was in front of the camera. While the pictorial representations are "here" with us while the represented scenes were shot in Downtown Los Angeles and at Warner Bros. Studios in Burbank, Harley is supposed to exist in the purely fictional domain of Gotham City. Her backstory within the film is additionally presented in animated sequences showing *the same character* in a completely different pictoriality. The black outlines enclosing her animated body are also perceivable, but we readily attribute them to the medial format, not the character herself. Where does Margot Robbie stop, then, and Harley begin? While we are going to look at some of the representational peculiarities of "real life" and cartoonish media formats in more detail later on (chapters 4/5), it should have become clear from these examples already that even in pictorial media, characters themselves – supposed to exist within their own, fictional domains – must not be confused with the materials of their medial representations (neither from the recording/producing situation nor from the text we actually watch and read). In James Phelan's triadic model of character dimensions (see Phelan 2022), this corresponds to the "synthetic level" of a character, "the material out of which the character is made" (Phelan 1987, 285). Eder addresses this as "the primary perception of the images and sounds of the film" (2010, 19). In this view, transmedia characters first appear to be material signs in various media and formats: written or spoken words, drawn, photographic, or computer-generated imagery, bodily performances by actors, and so on. Often, our fascination with characters is clearly deeply entangled with their synthetic side: "[C]haracters cannot be separated from their aesthetic mediations: Identifying with a character can also be a matter of cathecting onto a plot, a situation, a mise-en-scène, a setting, a style" (Felski 2019, 85). (We are going to take a look at some of these synthetic aspects, including aesthetic affordances within different media forms, in more detail in chapters 4–6).

Usually, however, our attention as audiences is not immediately directed at this level, but rather at what it represents. This corresponds to Phelan's "mimetic side" of characters, the character as a fictional or fictionalized individual. In order for these to exist, however, there must be a text-based construct or mental image in the reader's mind first. Comic studies scholar Essi Varis (2019) offers a fitting analogy between a character's mode of existence and the creation of "Frankenstein's Monster." First, characters are nothing but "a pile of 'materials,' […] an idealized vision of humanness" (75). Like Frankenstein's Monster, they are *nothing* like actual, living persons, but mere semiotic structures constructed in a way to *resemble* a human being. But, as actual audiences approach the text, they infuse these "dead" traits with the "spark of life": Characters then emerge as complete, autonomous entities in audiences' minds. Their creations are thus a process of being "sewn together" – but the "needle" is wielded by the audiences. To Eder, this is simply "the formation of mental character models" (2010, 19). The core of this process is this: "We are willingly engaging in a game of make-believe in which we pretend that there is a spatio-temporal domain in which [characters] exist and act independently of and prior to any narrative about them" (Margolin 2007, 71). This spatio-temporal domain is, again, the storyworld (or diegesis), understood as a possible – imaginable – world of interrelated situations (see Thon 2016, 35–71). In other words, a storyworld consists not only of places and locations but also of the continuous timeline audiences can construct out of these fragments.

Margolin (2007) accordingly defines a character as a "non-actual but well-specified individual presumed to exist in some hypothetical, fictional domain – in other words, character as an individual within a possible world" (66). He refers to the "possible world theory" that developed during the 1970s in analytical philosophy (see Ronen 1994). It tried to answer several logical questions, for instance, how a fictional text can be *about* something when this something does not exist, or how statements about fictional worlds can be "wrong" and others "right" when, again, their objects do not exist. Put in simple terms, possible world theory states that fictional worlds are not "actual" (existing), but only *possible*. We could say, for instance, that if Hillary Clinton *had* acquired 53.000 more votes in the 2016 US elections, Donald Trump never would have been president of the United States. Even though that is not the actual course of history, only a possible one, statements like these can be right or wrong. In the same way, stating that Donald Duck is the "richest man/duck in the world" is not only wrong in "our" world where there is no such person, but also according to the narrated world that he is living in (where this position is already taken by his uncle, Scrooge). "Possible," then, does not claim that talking ducks could possibly exist (which does not seem to be the case, for all we know), but that they are consistently imaginable according to media texts such as Disney comics. Once a media text *has* established – and a reader *has* imagined – that there *is* a character, their identity can be enriched by ongoing characterizations with additional character traits, as outlined above. Media texts thus ascribe properties or attributes to them and produce "fictional facts" by which audiences' statements about characters can sometimes indeed be "true" or "false."

Within a story, some of these properties will change during the course of events, while others will stay relatively stable. More "static" characters (like Mickey Mouse) do not change many of their traits, at least not from one story to the next, so they will always be "set back" to their core definition – at least in their officially sanctioned versions (see Levin 2003). By contrast, Batman has transformed quite a bit over the years, although a specific set of core properties has remained the same throughout (see Brooker 2013): He has a dark, brooding personality, a brilliant mind, and superior physical abilities (note that the goofy 1960s *Batman* TV show, however, as well as many comic book stories from that period, deviated considerably from what we now consider his canonical "core definition" – more about that in chapter 7). Characterization does not only serve to differentiate characters from others within their world, but also aligns them with some established, preexisting character type (the superhero, the femme fatale, or the mad scientist, for instance), as well as to social categories: From binary options such as "male" vs. "female" (which have begun to be expanded even in transmedia franchises such as *Star Wars* or *He-Man*, which have both recently introduced fluid and/or non-binary gender identities; see Brown 2019; Bacon 2021) to very specific distinctions such as "White, middle-class intellectuals with a college degree." These higher levels of categorization open them up to symbolic readings that correspond to Phelan's "thematic level" of a character (1987, 282). If characters are taken to belong to a certain social category, they might also be said to represent that category and thus *be about it* in a thematic sense.

A character then appears to be a "carrier" of various immaterial meanings. Narrative texts are usually *about* something: Topics, conflicts, and ideas, that can be reconstructed – and criticized – in analysis. Usually, these topics are also enacted through characters, but here we enter the difficult realm of textual interpretation. It is fairly established that Godzilla, for example, is representing (the Japanese post-war fear of) the atomic bombing of Hiroshima and Nagasaki (and the destruction caused by it) on a thematic level. *American Gods* (both Neil Gaiman's 2001 novel and the Starz TV show released from 2017 to 2021) pits the old gods of ancient mythology against the "new gods" of technology and media. The latter, serving as the "villains" of these works, are certainly thematic (and personalized, anthropomorphic) symbols for these themes that can be regarded as "hidden" subtexts within the respective narratives. (Sub)textual interpretation, however, has been one of the most complicated domains of literary studies, film studies, and many other fields of the humanities. It goes far beyond the scope of this volume to even outline the many ways media texts, whether seen as "root[s] or source[s] of all possible meanings" or merely as "system[s] of restrictions that limit the spectrum of possible interpretations" (Pisanty 2015, 39), generate such subtexts in this broad sense or how they offer a variety of heterogeneous subtexts for different audiences. For transmedia characters, this becomes even more complicated, since any analysis of narrative meaning will certainly have to resort to a "close reading" of specific, individual texts. Can there then be an overarching thematic meaning or an overarching subtext of "the" James Bond or "the" Batman? Transmedia characters have been addressed as "free-floating signifiers" (Uricchio and Pearson 1991, 186) for precisely the fact that they remain forever malleable and ambiguous within seriality, where their most persistent attribute is their durability (see Klein and Palmer 2016; Herbert 2020). Any definitive judgment will then either have to resort to the broadest generalizations or look for commonalities between *all* similar iterations of a specific character (what we will address in chapter 7 with Thon, 2019, as the transmedia character template) or even of general character types. The American superhero, as one such character type, has been described as essentially conservative and capitalist, for instance (see Hassler-Forest 2012). They are mostly upholding the given status quo, their formidable powers rarely introducing any structural societal change. In generalizing terms, superheroes could be said to accommodate a recurring subtext of the "American dream" in which crime is a problem rooted in the individual, not in social conditions such as the unequal distribution of wealth. "Criminals are a superstitious cowardly lot," as it says in Batman's origin story reiterated over decades. "[E]vil assumes only the form of an offense to private property," Umberto Eco wrote about Superman as early as 1962 (1972, 22). Such a subtextual interpretation would certainly be all the more plausible for Batman or Iron Man, billionaire playboy tycoons who spend their money on expensive gadgets and costumes rather than on fighting climate change. Then again, Superman *did* mostly fight lobbyists and corrupt politicians in his earliest pre-war adventures, so he was much more a response to the Great Depression and the plights of the American working class in the 1940s (see Gordon 2017). And there are other superheroes like the X-Men who have been taken as symbols or icons for social outcasts and their continuing struggles for equality and citizens' rights on the thematic, subtextual level (see Fawaz 2011). Differences matter, then, and transmedia characters can be charged with countless, often contradictory differences.

Looking at Japanese popular culture of manga and anime, too, many main protagonists of action franchises aimed at a young, male audience (called "*shōnen*") like *Dragon Ball* (Toriyama 1984–1995; Tsuchiya et al. 1992–1994), *Naruto* (Kishimoto 1999–2014; Date 2002–2007), or *Demon Slayer* (Fujio et al. 2019–present; Gotouge 2016–2020) might be characterized by a recurring *shōnen* subtextual ethos: It includes a continued desire for learning and self-improvement, of never giving up in the face of obstacles, of saving the world (or one's social surroundings) through an unshakable belief in values like friendship and responsibility. These are generally considered *masculine* values that are undoubtedly fueled by the Japanese "Ganbatte Kudasai!," "give it your all!," one of the backbones of the Japanese post-war economy (see Drummond-Mathews 2010). Then again, *Demon Slayer's* Tanjirō Kamado is quite different from *Dragon Ball's* Son Goku in that he embodies values traditionally seen as more feminine, too, such as his care and love toward his sister, who is a powerful demon fighter herself (see Borlaza 2021). Differences, once again, matter!

To avoid broad generalizations, we are going to approach the "meaning" of transmedia characters quite modestly in this volume. We will largely ignore subtexts on the broad textual level and instead offer only the first, foundational tools to unravel characters' meanings. In the first six chapters, we are advocating approaches to characters *within individual texts* where a "close reading" is indeed possible. Transmedial perspectives can only be assumed against a background of specific books, specific films, or specific video games in order to get hold of salient differences *between* character versions bearing the same name. Within the thematic approach to characters in specific texts (chapter 3), we are going to limit our perspective considerably as well. Yes, characters are essential for all kinds of abstract topics, conflicts, and ideas negotiated within narrative texts; we will nevertheless confine our analysis to what characters represent *about themselves* as human-like figures (see Bacon 2019). In Phelan's words: Any character's "attribute can be viewed as typical of a class of people" (1986, 285). Certainly, James Bond could be seen as a symbol of Western fascinations and fears during the Cold War era, where spies and agents were assumed to protect our freedom against the looming threats of Communism. We could thus consider him as the subtextual embodiment of an idealized, extra-governmental agency not bound by laws and regulations (see Funnell and Dodds 2017). Bond, however, has long outlived the Cold War in his newest instantiation portrayed by Daniel Craig (2006–2021), so the character has again proven highly malleable, if perhaps not entirely free-floating, on a thematic level. More congruently, however, we could also see Bond representing a specific ideal of British masculinity, a notion involving style and class, as well as sexual and physical prowess (see Chapman 2021). While the obsession with ideas of masculinity did stay remarkably constant in all his adventures throughout media, its specific expression has changed significantly since the 1960s, which can easily be seen in the striking difference between the respective performances of Sean Connery and Craig:

> If one compares the individual James Bond films with each other, then it can be stated that the character 'James Bond' always remains 'James Bond,' but the way in which dominant discourses are inserted into the protagonists or

cross each other differs. Bond is thus not only a sign of his time(s) but a sign moving in time (and changing, embodying different cultural values).

(Liebrand 2012, 311, our translation; see also Omry 2013)

Not only have the demands on Bond's physique increased, but his medial representations have also changed. When Craig rises from the surf in *Casino Royale* (2006) the scene knowingly echoes Honey Ryder doing the same in *Dr. No* (1962). "This is a male body *on show*," film scholar Edward Ross comments (2015, 38), "purely for the spectacle of it, shot in the same slow motion manner that women have been for years." Popular media's obsession with gendered and sexualized bodies, especially female ones, can thus be a "site" to investigate changing as well as persisting notions of "(ir)regular" bodies and power relations between people represented as male vs. female, White vs. Black, able-bodied vs. disabled – something that will be the focus in chapter 3. For now, it is worth noting that, to a certain degree, "all fictional plots are body plots," as Frow remarked aptly, "stories about birth and death, sexual desire, pain, aging, struggle, eating, touching, excreting, blushing, speaking, seeing and being seen, feeling, becoming" (2018, 114).

If a critical perspective on characters is as much about revealing and criticizing hidden, ostensibly "natural" and hence *ideological* notions of "normality" or "regularity" – that heroes are mostly male, White, heterosexual, and able-bodied, for instance – we could nevertheless hardly call this a character's "thematic" meaning: It is precisely *not* thematized within some books, films, or games, but rather problematically presented *as default*. Eder proposes a helpful fourth, "symptomatic" dimension of characters alongside Phelan's third, thematic one that connects them back to "our" world of actual production and reception: "[C]haracters are taken to be symptoms, that is, causal factors or consequences of real elements of communication; for example, as the outcome of the work of the filmmakers or as role models for viewers" (Eder 2018, 22). This often amounts to a distinction in terms of intended vs. unintended, or more precisely *highlighted* vs. *invisible* meanings. Within the world of the *Smurfs* comic books (Culliford 1963–1992) and animated show (Barbera et al. 1981–1989), every protagonist of the species is presented as *male*, additionally defined by one specific character trait (Clumsy Smurf is clumsy, Brainy Smurf smart, Hefty Smurf strong). "Smurfette," by contrast, is entirely defined as "being female" – with highly problematic and quite stereotypical connotations – as if this was an attribute that leaves room for no other. No more female Smurfs are in existence, she was even introduced as an artificial creation by the evil wizard Gargamel (see Barbera et al. S01E27, 1981). Addressing this gender subtext as Smurfette's "thematic" meaning would render the *Smurf* comics and cartoons as a criticism or a parody of existing gender stereotypes when, in truth, it might just reflect or betray the ideological world the authors and their intended audiences live(d) in, in which "women" are entirely comprised by their "essential" nature of being female. Smurfette, in our sad reality, is thus more a *symptom* of the actual communicational context in which *Smurf* comics and cartoons were produced, rather than a willful symbol for restrictive gender roles. In this respect, she *betrays* something about the authors and their cultural contexts instead of being deliberately designed as a vehicle for commentary. Granted, deciding whether something is "intended" may be difficult and even impossible in many cases. This is particularly true, for example, for the popular animated sitcom *South Park* (Parker et al. 1997–present), whose portrayal of Arab characters and those of Middle Eastern descent both satirizes and reproduces racist stereotypes. At the same time, the ostensibly ironic tone of the show can serve to shield it from any criticism for these depictions (see Hughey and Muradi 2009). Nevertheless, drawing a conceptual distinction between characters as symptoms vs. thematic symbols highlights the ideological contexts of media productions. Eder's distinction between symbol and symptom *within the thematic level* thus draws our attention to the fact that intended and unintended meanings may be equally relevant – and often entangled. Chapter 3 will offer a clearer understanding of how symptomatic meanings can be distinguished from symbolic ones without recourse to authorial intentions which we can never truly know on the one hand, while they might not even be decisive for that question on the other.

In summary, the four dimensions of characters (synthetic, mimetic, symbolic, and symptomatic) might always be entangled, but our attention can be deliberately directed. While many popular media texts highlight the mimetic side of characters as fictional beings, more experimental works exhibit their constructedness and artificiality. An example of this would be Superhot Team's eponymous first-person shooter video game *Superhot* (2016), in which the player fights reddish human silhouettes in desaturated, almost abstract environments, foreclosing any imagination of "actual people" in a coherent world. "Allegoric" works such as political cartoons strongly highlight characters' thematic meaning, while we cannot approach propaganda films (or other texts we consider "problematic" for various reasons) without accounting for characters' symptomatic meaning, i.e., that they conceal a specific symbolism by normalizing it without making it thematically explicit. Which of these meanings are only subjective, or: open to interpretation? How "objectively" can we talk about a character's meaning if they are entirely based on the interaction of texts and specific audiences (and their *inaccessible* mental models) (see Pisanty 2015)? This brings us back to the questions of methodology within a potential Transmedia Character Studies.

0.3 Notes on Methodology: Intersubjectivity, Rules of Imagination, and Incomplete Epistemology

The four dimensions of characters (synthetic, mimetic, symbolic, and symptomatic) can only emerge, in any case, if actual people are reading these books, watching these films, and playing these games. How much of what is "going on in their heads" is purely subjective, however? This is a serious problem for the analysis of characters since, after all, even as scholars we are first confined to our own, personal interpretations and associations. There must be a level of cognitive processing for each audience member where characters emerge as some sort of individual "mental image." This is something that we might certainly research empirically: We could be talking to actual audiences, and we might be doing eye-tracking studies exploring the perception of films. If that is not possible – for instance, because both original authors and audiences have passed away decades or centuries ago – we must reconstruct by what material and textual cues, by what patterns of narrative information the media texts in question enable audiences to construct, enrich, alter, and modify their mental models of characters piece by piece in a "process of continuous mental activity" (Eder 2010, 78). How is a text *communicating a character* by offering cues that we can draw inferences from? Literary scholar Ralf Schneider (2001), for instance, developed a complex, empirically informed model of cognitive character comprehension that outlines in great detail how readers are able to construct characters as imaginary, autonomous agents within a story. The resulting mental models seem at least partly accessible by public discussions *about* these characters and their meanings. This is what can be addressed as *discourse*. Some of our personal associations might be shared by others, while some will remain purely private. Sometimes fans have heated arguments about the "right" interpretation of a character or about the question of whether a new version is a "wrong" one. Looking at these discourses as recurring patterns of discussion, we can study what people (authors as well as audiences, including other scholars) are stating *about* characters and their meanings, often in what is addressed as the *fantext*: "The entirety of stories and critical commentary written in a fandom (or even in a pairing or genre), [which] offers an ever-growing, ever-expanding version of characters" (Hellekson and Busse 2006, 7). Fan texts not only contribute in written or spoken forms to characters and their discourses but also through pictorial media forms – such as fan art or cosplay – that continue to reinterpret them. They contribute to consolidating a specific character image, a certain iconography, or a distinct interpretation in opposition to others: "This canvas of variations is a work in progress insofar as it remains open and is constantly increasing; every new addition changes the entirety of interpretations" (7). Any "source" text is thus layered with the constantly developing interpretations of its audiences (see Derecho 2006).

A key term within this volume will be the notion of *intersubjectivity*. If it is true that there can be no characters without media texts, nor without people's mental models of their represented contents, are characters located within media texts or mental representation? Eder, Thon, and many others have stressed that neither is the case. What else is there, then? No character exists "objectively," without human comprehension and interpretation, nor materially or "actually" – only possibly, as imaginable beings. There must be media texts within a culture so that actual audiences will form individual, private models. These mental models will certainly be different for each person, as they bring their specific associations, memories, biases, and interpretations to these texts. But once they start engaging with others about them, once discourse patterns emerge, one usually realizes that *some* claims will overlap, while others will not. There is then "a public image or notion" (Margolin 2007, 67) of a character that is *not* subjective or private, and far from random – this is what the term intersubjectivity entails. Audiences' many subjectivities comprise countless individual experiences, assumptions, and claims about characters, but these are bridged or *mediated* by something "in-between" – hence *inter*subjectivity – namely media texts. According to Margolin, characters exist "[i]n the sphere of our individual imagination as an object of thought, and in the sphere of public communication as an object of discourse" (2007, 67). Whether or not Batman's parents were murdered – in a specific media text like Frank Miller and David Mazzucchelli's comic *Batman: Year One* (1987), as well as in many other typical iterations of the character – is then *not* up to the individual! Thematic meanings are certainly much more open to interpretation, by contrast, but they will not be random, either.

One can observe this "zone of intersubjectivity" most clearly at its thresholds and borders, where it *does* become contested and disputed, when people *do* start arguing passionately about characters and their meanings. This would be pointless if there were simply as many individual, private "mental versions" as there were people and audiences. For many popular franchises today, fans go to great lengths to prove or disprove a specific point, analyzing the available texts like forensic evidence, and publishing the results online to inspire discussions in comments and boards. Practices of meaning-making in which audiences do take the smallest of cues as intended messages (hinting at hidden connections and diegetic facts) are what Henry Jenkins defined as "poaching" (1992): In contrast to mere "consumers" who are enjoying texts for what they state (or don't), "textual poachers" actively create new connections and transcribe them into fantexts such as essays and fan videos. From a pragmatic point of view, Jonathan Culpeper and Carolina Fernandez-Quintanilla (2017) have argued, poaching must be based on the implicit assumption that every narrative information given about a fictional character must be *relevant* to our understanding, and not merely accidental. This distinguishes our interpretation of characters and their behaviors fundamentally from actual people. Culpeper and Fernandez-Quintanilla give the following illuminating example:

> To illustrate briefly, a man was observed by one of the authors of this chapter reversing out of a car parking space and nearly colliding with his partner. The event was attributed to a moment of distraction, a non-correspondent inference. Within a fictional work, the same event might have triggered more interpretative effort and have led to correspondence inferences, such as "he is an evil man with murderous intentions", especially when the act is deemed consistent with other behaviours and/or there is a supporting context (e.g. it is a work of crime fiction).
>
> (Culpeper and Fernandez-Quintanilla 2017, 97)

YouTube channels such as "Alt Shift X" (2012–present) or "Preston Jacobs" (Jacobs 2013–present), each followed by hundreds of thousands of viewers, present analytical essay videos for popular TV shows, films, and novels such as *Game of Thrones/A Song of Ice and Fire*, *Westworld*, or *Watchmen*, connecting "hidden" evidence in order to construct elaborate theories about characters and their motivations that are never explicitly stated within the original works. On boards and forums found on platforms like Reddit and Quora, audiences speculate daily on narrative facts like "[i]n the MCU, why couldn't Doctor Strange do the whole 'knocking the soul out' thing that The Ancient One did to him and Hulk but do it on Thanos?" to come up with "a theory that I believe had been overlooked entirely" (J.J. Fortune 2020, n.pag.). Importantly, these discussions are not even necessarily concerned with disputed thematic meanings but often focused on ambiguous aspects of the mimetic dimension, on "what was the case" within characters' storyworlds, and their motivations. Many of these fan theories go to extreme lengths, digging out facts that point to inconsistencies to reveal "hidden" conspiracies, connections, or backstories. In a video essay about *A Song of Ice and Fire* – which, at the time of writing, has close to a million views – Preston Jacobs wonders why the actions of a certain group of side characters (the "Dornish" ruling house) do not really make sense, only to propose a ridiculously complicated theory of over 40 minutes that explains how all of his findings *would* add up – by cross-referencing dates, travel distances, and character relations of events that happened decades before the diegetic present (see Jacobs 2014).

All of these assumptions are based on the intuition – an implied "rule of imagination" which author George R.R. Martin is expected to honor – that no pieces of information provided in the books are random, but rather a *relevant* part of a storyworld merely touched upon at the surface level in the actual texts. Every public statement of Martin in interviews and at conventions is thus scrutinized by fans and taken into account. Roland Barthes' (1977) thesis of the "death of the author" – that authors have become insignificant and all agency over a text rests solely with the readers – thus seems "increasingly outdated" to Felski (2019, 89) and others. Authors "become ever more visible, voluble, and inescapable. They give interviews, hold forth on blogs or Twitter, opine on the latest political events, talk back to prize committees, appear in full or half-empty auditoriums – not titans to be worshipped but promoters of their work and participants in numerous networks" (89). Audiences thus often attribute paramount relevance to the stated or purely hypothetical intentions of prominent author figures, including directors and showrunners (for a newer narratological conception of authors and their hypothetical intentions see Patron 2021; on their overall role within transmedia franchises see Salter and Stanfill 2020). In cases where pieces of narrative information are clearly unintended, audiences will readily disregard them: Such is the case for "goofs" in films or "bugs" in video games. In *Lord of the Rings: The Return of the King* (Jackson 2003), for instance, Gandalf is seen with a modern wristwatch on his left hand in the final battle. No audience member would take this as a "hidden clue" that the wizard was secretly a time traveler from the present day – it is simply taken as an unintended mistake, revealing again that this distinction is continuously drawn.

The "poaching" form of engagement has been cultivated by authors and companies over long periods of time within specific media and genre traditions. Jenkins addressed this sort of "additive comprehension" (2006, 123) from a historical perspective as well. To him, forensic modes of meaning-making – drawing inferences from little cues by assuming that they were intentional, rather than accidental – are especially encouraged by and reliant on two new media developments: The increase of transmedia storytelling practices where franchises, stories, and worlds are distributed over countless iterations and installments each claiming to represent only fragments from the same, overarching whole on the one hand; and on interconnected communities of fans working together on digital platforms and forums, each eager to "connect the dots" within collective efforts of interpretation on the other hand. Shared diegetic universes that allow (or, at least, promise) narrative consistency between all "diegetic facts" developed rapidly within superhero comics from the 1960s on, and many earlier "bottom-up" or "grassroots" examples exist (see Friedenthal 2017). The fictional universe attributed to the works of H.P. Lovecraft, for instance, inspired many other writers and fans to situate their stories and characters within the same world. In other media and genres (such as three-panel comic strips or humoristic animated cartoons), a similar "forensic reading" would hardly be plausible. Audiences are usually well aware of which reading conventions are established between creators and fans, and, in many cases, inconsistencies are merely inconsistencies that can be ignored conveniently instead of giving reasons for diegetic arguments.

What we can see from this is that some "rules of imagination" guide our understanding of fictional narratives and characters toward intersubjectivity, otherwise there would be no point in any such engagement. Maybe the most foundational, transmedial convention of narrative meaning-making is what media narratologist Mary Laure-Ryan called "the principle of minimal departure" (1991b, 51). It states that readers will apply most of their "regular" world knowledge to any text as long as the story does not dictate otherwise. Audiences can thus rely on their own experiences to "fill out" the limited information provided by a text. Film scholar Murray Smith, for instance, states that "we assume – until cued otherwise – that a character will have one body, individuated by a particular set of physical features, just as a person does" (1995, 19). When a novel informs us that "the servant returned with a short note from the doctor" (Mitchell 2014: 229), both the servant and the doctor are still to be imagined as "complete" human beings, although their description remains intersubjectively "empty" (unspecified) except for their belonging to our species and practicing specific professions. This is relevant for a number of reasons, not least for our initial question of what a character "is." In some first-person video games such as *Half-Life* (1998), for instance, we never get to see more of the protagonist (Gordon Freeman) than his hands (as we assume their point of view throughout the game). In a material sense, the hands are the only parts of the character that *do* exist within the game's 3D models (see Aarseth 2022). We would nevertheless feel justified to state that the *character* has a body and a face the same as other people do, as the game does not indicate that he is part of a strange species which does not. Whether the medial representation – the 3D model – showcases these elements is not particularly important for this question, for the same reason that we also imagine the hands to possess infinitely more elements that we still won't "see" directly (such as a bone structure underneath). Additional pictorial material (on the game's box, as well as in advertisements) in fact *does* represent Gordon Freeman's face (thus "filling" his incompleteness with more information: that he wears glasses and has a beard), as do fans in their artwork interpretations. But even if no picture of his face existed within any "official material" at all, we could still feel right to imagine him having one according to the principle of minimal departure. This gap-filling activity also, or maybe especially, applies to characters' inner lives: Even Pac-Man, due to his mandated behavior in the video games, apparently *desires* pills and fruit very much and might be *afraid* or *weary* of ghosts.

The principle of minimal departure can be understood as the most foundational, general rule guiding our meaning-making of characters. Many additional conventions are much more specific to media forms and genres. If in an anime like *March Comes In like a Lion* (Yodo et al. 2016–2018) a character is depicted with a cruciform or triskelion sign in the upper head region (initially an exaggerated visual shorthand for throbbing veins), this serves as a conventional expression for the diegetic fact *that* the character is experiencing anger or irritation. In a video game like the *Metal Gear Solid* series, flashing exclamation marks over enemies' heads – accompanied by recognizable sound effects – represent the fact (the "mental event") that Solid Snake has drawn their attention. Mainstream US comic books such as *Saga* (Vaughan and Staples 2012–present) use boldened text to indicate which words a character emphasizes in speaking. In films like *Sherlock Holmes* (Ritchie 2009) and TV shows like *Babylon 5* (Straczynski 1993–1998) or *Veronica Mars* (Ruggiero et al. 2004–2007), monochrome filters represent flashbacks to moments that took place before the diegetic present, while manga like *Fullmetal Alchemist* (Arakawa 2001–2010) indicate the same by black (instead of white) panel backgrounds ("gutters").

Countless media- and genre-specific traditions for narrative conventions exist, so the study of characters must always be concerned with media- and genre-specific rules of imagination that allow specific inferences to anyone versed ("literate") in these traditions. The reasons why certain character traits and "diegetic facts" are often only implied can be manyfold. Sometimes, this is due to regulations of what can be explicitly stated – or what can only be implied – due to moral or legal considerations. For instance, under the American Motion Picture Production Code's regulations prohibiting "excessive and lustful kissing, lustful embraces, suggestive postures and gestures" (Doherty 1999, 363), it was impossible for films released between 1934 and the 1960s to depict sexual relationships. This did not prevent filmic metaphors to emerge as creative workarounds. Linda Williams (2006) has found that, during the code era, on-screen kisses, followed by narrative ellipses, frequently served as stand-ins for more explicit sex acts. But more inventive visualizations were also developed: When Roger Thornhill (played by Cary Grant) and Eve Kendall (played by Eva Marie Saint) climb into their sleeping compartment in Alfred Hitchcock's *North by Northwest* (1959), a shot of the train entering a tunnel indicates what could not be depicted more directly. The metaphor of a steam train has been used untold times to substitute intimate relationships throughout the decades, even in the adaptation of *Anna Karenina* (Wright 2012) 50 years later where the metaphor lingers as a creative resource. Familiarity with this conventional shorthand enables audiences to justify that, yes, the characters can and maybe should be said to entertain an intimate affair (and sometimes this is even "proven" by the narration when it later reveals that one of the protagonists got pregnant). The intersubjectivity of diegetic facts and character traits can thus be differently "durable" for varying audiences, as these metaphorical substitutions are intentionally designed to avoid some responsibility. Producers can always claim that respective readings were "left to the imagination," in other words: merely private games of make-believe and *not* part of the intersubjective construct. As respective "cues" and "signposts" are part of the communicative process, however, the resulting interpretations are not at all random, revealing a deliberate interrelation of storyworld/character construction and implicit rules of the imagination (see Walton 1993).

It should have become clear by now that the works and media texts this volume is mainly concerned with are part of "popular culture(s)," openly embracing repetitious practices of conventionality in some way. A much longer tradition in the humanities was mostly concerned with the examination of "high art" that specifically valorizes works bringing our attention to their uniqueness and to their defiance of established "rules" of narrative and artistic expression. Popular transmedia characters, by contrast, are not necessarily created to "stand out" due to their distance from common conventions employed in other works. On the contrary, a familiarity with generic conventions is what makes them enjoyable more often than not – this is something that will be discussed in chapter 2 concerning narrative structures and repetitive tropes in more detail. It does not mean that everything is repetitive within genre traditions: Often, we find playful approaches to repetition (and audiences' familiarity therewith) on the one hand and surprising variations on the other. In order to see these negotiations, however, we have to familiarize ourselves with the respective conventions – fans as much as scholars analyzing these works – to fully appreciate the achievements and constraints of specific works that are in constant dialogue with preexisting traditions. These "reading conventions" – always in the background, as a handy resource for situated surprises – form the basis for intersubjective rules of imagination.

In what way does a transmedia character "exist" then, concludingly, if we try to think all these aspects – the four dimensions of the synthetic, the mimetic, the symbolic, and the symptomatic, as well as their intersubjective side founded on public discourses and rules of imagination – together? It is helpful to compare transmedia characters to other parts of the social world that do not exist materially but are nevertheless "real" in a very strong sense of the word: Laws, prices, or musical compositions. A law exists not exactly because it was written down somewhere – it could also be enforced verbally in a given society – but because someone with the necessary authority declared it so and people act accordingly. It is no use arguing with a police officer that the speeding limit "does not really exist." Laws exercise no power without humans, but they are a part of our social world and thus exist intersubjectively and irrespectively of individual human beings. Prices in the supermarket are likewise not up to the individual. Beethoven's Fifth would still "exist" if all the papers where it was written down were burnt, as long as there were people remembering – or even performing – the piece.

A musical composition exists then in a way that is not identical to its material representations (all the sheets available in libraries, stores, and private homes). Eder addresses all of these abstract social agreements and negotiations as *communicative constructs* (2008a, 61–69; 2010, 18; see also Thon 2016, 56–70). These constructs, socially shared models of meaning-making, emerge only while we are communicating them – not as private mental images but within social communities that form patterns of discourses agreeing upon (or passionately disagreeing over) them. Margolin (2007, 67) accordingly speaks about a character as "a contingently created, abstract cultural entity." *Contingently* here means that characters are not an autonomous, independent part of the physical world that would be "there" without humans like a mountain range would. Characters are dependent on actual human people writing and reading texts, producing and watching movies, creating and playing games – and discussing all of these experiences with recourse to "good arguments" (based on textual information as well as on implicit or explicit rules of imagination). Then, however, characters gain an intersubjective *social* quality that is independent of texts – and of individuals. This intersubjective side of characters is mostly what we will be focusing on when we approach characters within this volume. That means that we are continuously trying to separate what makes aspects and meanings of (as well as claims and judgments about) characters *intersubjective*, more than just private and personal, by relating textual information to public discourses, and vice versa, "triangulating" the character as a communicative construct emerging in between both.

Due to characters' complicated ontology outlined here – their "mode of being" as intersubjective communicative constructs – there are crucial differences between characters and actual persons that every character theory acknowledges in some way or the other. This will be at the center of the concluding chapter 10 of this volume, but the most important distinction should be made clear from the beginning. Fictional and fictionalized characters are often considered "ontologically incomplete" (see Doležel 1995). As they intersubjectively only possess those properties that media texts (including artworks, cosplay, and other fan works) *ascribe* to them, or imply for them through implicit or explicit rules of the imagination, many of their aspects are *not defined* at all – neither positively nor negatively. Since transmedial appearances of characters complicate matters quite a bit, let us focus on characters as they appear within a specific narrative text (a novel, a film, a comic book) for now. The two canonical examples for this argument within literary studies are that we *do not know* whether Lady Macbeth had children (and, if so, how many) and that we do not know whether Sherlock Holmes has a certain birthmark or not. For any real person, it must be the case that they either have these properties or not, even though it might not be possible for us to gain actual knowledge about it. But if no film, no book, and no video game mentions or depicts anything about these traits, then characters are ontologically *incomplete* in this sense.

Usually, protagonists' presentations are always incomplete in temporal terms, to begin with: We "meet" them only within segments of their lifetimes when they are already of a certain age, and we leave them at the end of the story where we imagine them to go on with their lives (if they did not die). What has happened before the beginning will often only be revealed in a piecemeal fashion, through flashbacks, recounts, or summaries. Characters are usually also represented discontinuously *within* any given story: We rarely "follow" protagonists to the bathroom, and comic books have "gutters" (gaps) between any two panels. According to the principle of minimal departure, we nevertheless suppose that there *is* a continuous timespan in between our "encounters" (as small or big as they might be), although we can usually not say what has happened there, exactly. Probably we can imagine *something*, however. To say that characters are "incomplete" only makes sense then if we consider the intersubjective aspect of the character the object of our study, the "discourse object," the part everyone *should* agree upon. "Even though we assume in our game of make-believe that non-actual individuals are as complete in their world as we are in ours, only a limited subset of their properties can ever be specified" (Margolin 2007, 73). The intersubjective part, the character that people exchange arguments about in fan forums, is only ever partially defined. Within our private imagination, however, we experience characters as possible (imaginable) and thus *complete* beings. If a character does not really exist, and only media texts, imaginations, and social rules of the imagination do, then it is not so much the character that is "incomplete" but the rightful claims we can make about them and accept in some sort of social agreement. This is the domain not of ontology but epistemology: what we can know and accept as "true" or "false" in a given social context. In the natural sciences, some things may be proven to be "objectively" the case, whereas claims about characters can only be intersubjectively acceptable (or unacceptable) to a certain community that bases its judgments on media texts and media literacy. That is why we can now rephrase that characters are *epistemically incomplete*: "Rightful" (acceptable) claims about them (in a given medial context, and to a given community) will always leave blind spots that we can continue to fill within our private, subjective imaginations. In other words, if characters exist only as normative abstractions about actual meaning-making, then it is the social constraints to uphold and defend *certain* imaginations – and not others – that are at stake. Ontologically, only "rules of what is to be imagined" *exist*, not abstract objects within a Platonic sphere of ideas; in the same way as we would subscribe to Ludwig Wittgenstein's (1986 [1953]) or Ernst Tugendhat's (1982 [1975]) assumptions that no linguistic universals, no abstract objects like "redness" *exist*, only rules of language use. We have learned how to use a linguistic predicate like "red," and we need no independently existing redness to account for that. "The meaning of a word is what is explained by the explanation of the meaning," as Wittgenstein (1986, 148) put it aphoristically. Rules, in turn, can never be complete (or incomplete for that matter), just as individual "games of the imagination" (actual reception processes) can never be entirely, or not even predominantly regulated, and neither can the affects and emotions connected to them. The threshold between both is certainly continuously negotiated. If this is true, then studying characters must always take public discourse into account where we can observe uncontested as well as contested rules of the imagination "in action" – especially where controversies arise.

To avoid misunderstandings here, "intersubjective" must not be confused with "rational." Quite to the contrary, as we will see, affects and passions toward characters are often an especially salient aspect of their intersubjective affordances (see Lamerichs 2018). These affects are often far from private and personal, too, as Sara Ahmed (2010), Brian Massumi (2015), and many others have taught from different perspectives. We shall find ample support for that in the chapters of this volume tracing countless "sites" of collective affects surrounding transmedia characters. Affects and passions can also never be completely, or maybe not even particularly firmly controlled by their actual authors and creators. They "happen" within the public domain of their circulation which we can observe as discourses.

0.4 Outlines of a Potential Transmedia Character Studies

The character models by Margolin or Eder have specific limits for their application to transmedia characters. They are strongly oriented toward the analysis of individual texts (novels, films). Originating from literary and film studies, their point of departure are works by specific authors or author collectives (in film). If a book creates a character with a specific name and another author reuses the same name, we could understand the result to be a different entity, a "same-name entity" (see Müller 1991). "[L]iterary characters are text-bound and cannot be detached from the text or storyworld(s) in which they occur" (Margolin 2007, 70). If they are taken to do so, Margolin goes on, then only "as long as texts by the same authors are concerned" (70). This does not take us too far for transmedia characters like Batman or Donald Duck, where there often is no "ur-text," no "arch-text" to begin with, where – just like with myths – most people would not even be able to name any "original." Transmedia franchises are instead built around the idea that characters exist "outside" or "beyond" any single work. Margolin later introduced the term "intertextual super or mega character," such as "the" Quixote, or "the" Don Juan, "which both synthesizes and transcends any individual figure of this name" (70). This intertextual super or mega character, he elaborates, is "based on a set of core-properties ascribed to the figure in all of the works in which it occurs" (70). Transmedia characters seem to be *based* on this plane, even right from their invention. This becomes even more pronounced if we also take "pre-narrative characters" (or mere "figures," see Denson and Meyer 2018) into account, for which no relevant narrative even exists. Examples include company mascots or merchandise figures such as Hello Kitty. While, in Margolin's thinking, a "super or mega character" can only be synthesized from a great number of texts, many transmedia mascots "start right there," without any ur-text or a long series of narrative instances to begin with (see Wilde 2018b). It should come as no surprise then that there are many unresolved questions regarding the outlines and scopes of a transmedia character theory – and the methodology of their study. To indicate the range of controversies, three especially poignant questions on which there is not yet any consensus can be given.

First, if we go back to the many contradictory cases of transmedial "character versions," it remains highly contested whether the different "Sherlocks" or "Batmen" should be considered representations of *the same character,* as we would for non-contradictory versions whose stories can be related to the same, coherent fictional biography. Some authors, especially from narratology, argue that characters are "first and foremost elements of the constructed narrative world" (Eder et al. 2010, 9), rendering their "overall" contradictory versions (who seem to appear across works and worlds) something different – a "second-order original," a "network of character versions," or a mere "cultural icon" (see Thon 2019 for this position). Other scholars, especially from anthropology and cultural studies, take these broader, inherently contradictory "icons" as their starting point ("*the* James Bond"), assigning storyworld-specific instances to a lower-level category – "character versions," for instance (see Wilde 2019 for a more detailed discussion). This volume is not intended to settle these debates but rather to point out the most salient insights and distinctions from such ongoing debates for a refined understanding of character canonicity, character continuity, and character appropriation, especially in chapters 7/8.

Second, for *some* transmedia characters, the very distinction between "contradicting" and "non-contradicting" instances does not seem to apply very well, since the media they circulate in provide no stories and few "narrative facts" about them to begin with. We have addressed those as pre-narrative characters/figures before, and we are going to dedicate the better part of chapters 8 and 9 to their conceptualization and discussion: Protagonists of political cartoons such as Uncle Sam, "virtual idols" such as Hatsune Miku, political icons such as Pepe the Frog, or product placement figures such as Hello Kitty, which all seem to exist without any (relevant) narrative media texts about them. Is there a minimum threshold of "characterhood" to begin with – in other words, can and should anthropomorphic figures, logos, or design products be considered "characters" in the same sense as the protagonists of a novel or a film? How about emoji or pictogrammatic street signs, such as the "Helvetica Man" perpetually running for some door on the international Exit Sign? Are the automated voices of Siri and Alexa (minimal traces of) characters, specifically employed to achieve such a resemblance? By connecting narrative character theories with non-narrative approaches (especially from Japanese studies and semiotics), this volume tries to expand the transmedial foundations for the analyses of characters to non-narrative media and objects such as coffee cups, T-shirts, merchandising, or interface design, especially in chapter 9.

Third, are "characters" and "real persons" in fact mutually exclusive terms? For one thing, even media texts that are usually *not* considered "fictional" – such as autobiographies, documentaries, or journalistic reports – are mostly centered around representations of human beings. These works are constructed and interpreted in similar ways as fictional ones would be. In narratology, it is fairly established that factional (or non-fictional) storytelling is of equal relevance as its fictional counterpart, both being distinguished not primarily or principally by their contents but by their surrounding "truth claims" (see Fludernik and Ryan

2020). Is Donald Trump a "non-fictional character" then, one who we encounter in news reports and on Twitter? How about the countless appearances of historical figures and real-life politicians in fictional TV shows, comic books, and cartoons? Fictionalizations of existing persons have been discussed extensively in literary studies, philosophy, and narratology. They are epitomized by the "Napoleon problem" (see Gallagher 2011). Napoleon really existed, yet protagonists bearing his name appear in historical fictions (such as Tolstoy's 1869 novel *War and Peace*, 2020). If we nevertheless distinguish between fictional characters and "actual" persons – if not by name, then by the respective contexts of fictional vs. non-fictional *claims* attached to specific texts – our knowledge about actual public figures is usually still entirely mediated. In some cases ("mockumentaries" or fictionalized biographical works) an audience might even be mistaken about the claims and scopes of a represented being's fictional vs. non-fictional "status." The relation between transmedia characters and fictionality is thus more complicated and challenging than it first might seem. The final chapter 10 of this volume introduces theories of fiction, outlining the potentials of Transmedia Character Studies for our understanding of an increasingly mediated world.

What finally brings all these approaches together, distinguishing a potential Transmedia Character Studies most saliently from more "traditional" literary approaches, is a focus on problems of pictoriality (see also Hanly and Rowney 2020). Character representations in film, comic books, video games, or material objects alike are all based on – and constructed by – *pictures* (within multimodal configurations of other semiotic resources) as much as by verbal texts. Whereas traditional literary approaches to characters consider a *proper name* the most important element to generate and reiterate a specific fictional or fictionalized entity, "Superman" is as much known from, for, and by his iconic costume and logo. The respective pictoriality will be of a different kind in the hand-drawn images of comic books, in the recorded images taken from actors such as Christopher Reeve or Henry Cavill, or in the computer-generated imagery of video games such as *DC Universe Online* (Dimensional Ink Games 2011). Audiences and players are nevertheless able to identify and recognize him by iconography alone: his costume, a specific arrangement of primary colors, the famous crest, as well as the immediately recognizable gesture when he takes off his glasses and tears off his shirt to reveal his secret identity. Many appearances of transmedia characters on material objects (T-shirts, coffee cups, stationery) do not even feature any verbal references. Within this volume, the pictoriality of multimodal media will thus be continuously foregrounded, providing a vocabulary for the description of transmedia characters' visuality. Taken together, this volume traces the most relevant positions and theories about transmedia characters to provide several methodological tools, as well as a foundational vocabulary for the analysis of characters between and across media.

The first section – "Foundations of Characters across Media" – will focus on characters as they appear within the contexts of individual, non-contradictory stories and storyworlds. These approaches are hence going to be restricted to narrative media texts such as a novel, a film, a continuous narrative within a

TV show or of a comic book series – video games occupy a somewhat special position (discussed in detail later in chapter 6), but their protagonists can also be discussed in these terms up to a point. In all these forms and formats of media, characters will first be considered mimetically as subjective consciousness frames, then synthetically as actants in relation to plot, and finally thematically as social representations concerning the "real world." Taken together, this section is thus going to establish a basic vocabulary for the analysis of characters across media. The first chapter is going to ask how we are able to recognize a character and what separates them from other elements of fictional texts; it investigates how media can give access to a character's "inner life," their subjectivity, and what it means to "identify" with a character and their worldview. The second chapter is then going to explore the relation between characters and the stories surrounding them, plots of narrative events. This relation has been studied extensively in semiotic and structuralist approaches, which treated characters – in stark contrast to "actual" persons – as mere "actants" or "agents" of the story in which they operate. We will see that characters-as-actants have different degrees of narrative agency depending on the medial, generic, and historical contexts these stories operate in. The third chapter is finally looking at characters in terms of actual social contexts, treating them as representations of intersectional categories such as race, class, gender, or dis/ability. As we are surrounded by stories of human-like figures, these categories will not only be reflected by media texts; media texts can also be said to contribute to our image of the world we live in – especially of its human inhabitants. Characters in and across media thus often influence, reinforce, or negotiate our understanding of social relations and power structures between people.

While all of these foundations are valid and useful for analyses across media, specific media forms and formats offer different affordances to employ them. The second section, "Characters in Different Narrative Media," is thus looking into relevant affordances of character representations across media. The fourth chapter is introducing problems related to embodiment in real-life films, TV shows, and cosplay performances where characters are represented through actual people and their corporeality. In what ways can we distinguish – and interrelate – actors, their "star personas," and the characters they portray? The fifth chapter is going to look at the drawn and animated characters of animated films and comic books. They are often assembled from a variety of signs; their cartoonish bodies are abstracted and exaggerated in comparison with "actual" people. Are audiences nevertheless likely to imagine them in accordance with "our world," or do cartoonish characters themselves – and not just their medial representations – fundamentally differ from "realistic" entities? The sixth chapter is then going to look at characters in video games that usually also function as "game pieces" and, sometimes, as avatars for the players in social interactions. Due to the non-linear stories of many video games, this chapter is also introducing questions of character multiplicity: What happens to the intersubjective rules of imagination when two different players of the same game may not only have different interpretations of that game's narrative but actually experience significantly different "paths" of branching storylines?

The third section, "Foundations of Transmedia Character Analysis," will then investigate characters that seem to exist across and beyond individual media texts and media forms. The seventh chapter is going to investigate cases in which character versions seem to be in clear contradiction to each other. Differences between characters of the same name – such as the many "Batmen" across the decades, often rebooted and retconned – can then be analyzed as networks of (partly contradictory) character versions. As this is often a question of continuity and canonicity management, this chapter is also going to explore the notion of authorship in more detail. The subsequent eighth chapter is then going to take a look at characters that seem to exist "outside" any consistent fictional biography in a "dreamlike state" where their appearances can be read, watched, or played in any order. They seem either "trapped" in a continuous loop of repetition where no lasting progress, change, or memory is involved for their serial appearances; or, for some anthropomorphic beings whose most prominent representations circulate outside of narrative context to begin with, the term "character" might even be misleading as they seem to "exist" in entirely contradictory storyworld contexts without any need for continuity management or differentiation. Such entities discussed as pre-narrative or even meta-narrative figures entail protagonists of and in political cartoons, memes, or company logos.

The concluding fourth section, "Characters and Non-Fiction," is finally investigating some of the conceptual tensions between characters and various aspects of media texts that are generally considered non-fictional, i.e., inherently related to "our" world. Chapter 9 is first going to explore how transmedia characters – or rather, building on the previous chapter, transmedia figures – are often used on street signs and other domains of everyday life where they fulfill useful functions; how mascots are employed in theme parks and public events where audiences seem to be able to interact with them "directly." In these cases, character representations are strategically employed to bridge the gap between fiction and real-live settings – at least in some imaginary frame of reference that includes actual audiences as much as their fictional protagonists. Chapter 10 is turning this perspective around, discussing the many instances in which actual people (historical figures, politicians, or celebrities) appear as fictionalized protagonists in films, TV shows, or comic books. This chapter also provides a critical vocabulary to assess the aesthetic and political potentials of media forms to engage with actual people and events. While such rhetorics of fictionalization are fairly established within narratological accounts, the concluding section of this last chapter is also looking at medial representations of "characters" that *are* non-fictional for all accounts: To what respect can we still apply some of our earlier approaches to representations which claim complete faithfulness to unmediated reality? A final postscript then serves as a concluding reflection on the potentials and limitations of a Transmedia Character Studies for our understanding of an increasingly mediated world.

Section 1

Foundations of Characters across Media

1 Characters as Subjective Consciousness Frames

This chapter will first focus on the mimetic dimension of characters, that is, approaching and interpreting them as (primarily) fictional individuals structurally resembling actual persons within our real world. Often, audiences form strong attachments and emotional responses towards characters, as they would to actual persons. This is also where many moral or ethical dimensions come into play, "as though [characters] were acquaintances whose virtues and shortcomings one were dissecting: They have faults and admirable qualities, perhaps a 'fatal flaw,' they do foolish and wise things, they show different sides of their personality" (Frow 2018, 108). Such a "realist" view should be surprising for several reasons: There are countless examples for protagonists in novels, film, comic books, and video games that are *not* human at all, or that don't even have any sort of body – e.g., *The Lord of The Rings*' Sauron who is only ever present as a hovering orange eye on top of his tower, and perhaps as a powerful "mind." The overall question remains, then, what distinguishes a "character" – in any medial context – from other parts of represented worlds and stories? This is also an important methodological issue for a potential Transmedia Character Studies: How *can* we justify addressing phenomena that operate not only in different media forms but also in different semiotic, material, technological, and social contexts with similar assumptions and terminologies? This chapter (1) first outlines some fundamental assumptions from cognitive sciences and anthropology to give a clearer picture of how the *subjective consciousness* of someone different from ourselves is constituted in everyday life and in media representations. This also forms the core of character recognition. It then (2) describes in more detail how media texts cue audiences to (re)identify such *continuous consciousness frames* and how to maintain them. The third part (3) is introducing some basic narratological vocabulary to describe in more detail how media texts grant different *sorts of access* to represented, subjective minds, while the fourth part (4) investigates different *emotional stances* toward them, their worldviews, and their values; it also discusses fundamental questions of how to analyze these essentially subjective states intersubjectively.

1.1 Agency, Personality, and Intentionality

As has been outlined in the previous chapter, more recent approaches toward characters are strongly informed by cognitive reception studies. They have

DOI: 10.4324/9781003298793-3

highlighted the "cognitive second creation" (Varis 2019, 75) of characters not within the realms of materials, texts, and multimodal sign configurations, but within the minds of actual audiences. More precisely, readers process media texts by relating them to cognitive schemata that we also rely on in our everyday meaning-making of the social world surrounding us. Psychologists such as Jerome Bruner (1990) or Lee Roy Beach (2010) argued for a "narrative psychology" that first investigates actual, real word orientation with recourse to "narrative hypotheses" that we cannot help but to rely on in everyday life (see Bruner 1991; Dewey and Knoblich 2016). Confronted with situations in our lifeworlds, we *infer* earlier events, speculate about causes and motivations, and predict probable outcomes and consequences. Memory, too, lends a narrative structure to one's self-image, as people construct their personal biographies in the form of causally and logically interconnected episodes of experienced behaviors. Both can be understood as the construction of micro-narratives, of narrative situation models that help us to structure events, places, and people in terms of temporality, causality, and intentionality. Within narratology – concerned not primarily with reasoning in the "real world," but with the comprehension and interpretation of media texts – this approach has been integrated by what has been called a "natural narratology." English literature scholar Monika Fludernik (1996; 2003) redefined narrativity in respective terms: To understand a narrative – in any medial context – does not merely, and maybe not even primarily, rely on the codes and conventions of literature, theatre, film, etc. Instead, the argument goes, we have to ask how *regular habits* of meaning-making can be activated, instrumentalized, and maybe also modified by media texts.

There is ample support for this from various fields: One can argue, for instance, that any form of communication would be impossible if we knew only the lexical meanings of words; instead, we need to be able to comprehend our interlocutor *as another human being* whose "interior" is in some way similar to our own. Whether we conceptualize this as a largely subconscious process in which our cognitive system keeps "running simulations" of other people's assumed inner lives (see Davies and Stoney 1995), or whether we understand this in a way similar to the "theory of mind" (see Zunshine 2006; Herman 2011; Leverage et al. 2011), as a partly rational process in which we continuously draw inferences from probable assumptions about each other's intentions; for both approaches, we take other people's minds to be fundamentally "like ours," as having memories, desires, and fears like ourselves, in order to make sense of conversations and communicative artifacts. If a pair of fictional entities described as "Mr. and Mrs. Dursley, of number four, Privet Drive" (Rowling 1997, 1) is instantaneously understood as two human beings, each of them with two arms, one head, and interior organs, it is because we can accept it as probable that an author using these words (in this case Joanne K. Rowling) is not only relying on the same understanding of the English language as we are, but also anticipating our understanding as similar to theirs. They are thus taken to rely on the same, implicit theory of mind to anticipate and guide *our* reasoning so that we first take any "Mr. and Mrs." as regular human beings – until specified otherwise (they could be revealed as a cyborg or alien couple, for instance). This is another way to substantiate Marie-Laure Ryan's (1991b) principle of minimal departure introduced in the previous chapter. Its unwritten rules of the imagination form the foundation of intersubjective meaning-making – not only between authors and audiences but also between groups of audiences reading the same text, watching the same film, or playing the same game. Character construction thus continuously oscillates "between top-down knowledge from the reader/perceiver's head and bottom-up information from the text" (Culpeper and Fernandez-Quintanilla 2017, 93).

Our understanding of "subjective minds" – minds equipped with a "subjective life" and personal intentions – is thus not the result, but a prerequisite for meaning-making of communication. One of the most important, mostly innate cognitive schemas for humans is the so-called "person schema" (Smith 1995, 20–24). It serves to distinguish animate from inanimate objects, and we acquire it at a very early age. It should come as no surprise then that many or most medial representations are not about purely abstract thoughts or possible states of the world or of society, but also *about* subjective minds and other people's consciousnesses. Obviously, the problem of what defines a *human* being or *human* consciousness is far from universal and will be answered differently by members of different cultures or across historical contexts. However, as Murray Smith (1995, 22) has argued for characters in film, it makes sense to distinguish between two complementary levels of thought and comprehension, which he conceptualizes with anthropologist Robin Horton (1982) as "primary" and "secondary theories" guiding our reasoning. The latter contain culture-specific scripts, roles, and concepts such as "a mail man" (implicating specific knowledge about the institution of postal services) or "an honorable woman" (entailing gendered moral and ethical judgments specific to a given society, see Geertz 2006, 360–411). Such secondary theories also contain highly malleable cultural notions of "regularity," of acceptable or "normal" behavior for various sorts of people that are influenced by media texts and must remain open to negotiation and criticism – these questions will be at the center of chapter 3 about characters as social representations. On a more foundational level, however, secondary, *cultural* notions must be based on an earlier, more immediate understanding of the everyday physical world which varies little from culture to culture. The two major distinctions offered to us by such innate "primary theories," which are of major importance to character studies, are first those between animate and inanimate objects: We attribute individual or personal *agency* to some "objects" surrounding us, and not to others. A character is sometimes defined in exactly this way in literary studies: "A character is an entity in the story that has agency, that is, who is able to act in the environment of the storyworld" (Ribó 2019, 47). The second major distinction acquired at a very early age is that between self and others. Human bodies – their assumed identity as well their inner lives – are thus involuntarily distinguished from each other as discrete and continuous, and they have a special saliency within our recognition of immediate physical environments (primary theory) before higher levels of meanings, cultural codes, and classifications enter the picture (secondary theory). If this is true, then the recognition or even anticipation of human-like entities within narrative accounts (fictional, non-fictional, or ones unclear in that respect) would also precede medial conventions by activating the same person schema that we rely on in our daily encounters with other human beings in the bus or at the supermarket.

> The fact that in real life humans ascribe a spatio-temporal continuity to bodies and assume that persons continue to exist even if they cannot be seen or heard anymore, is a precondition for this ability to identify characters. Fictional worlds constructed in the media can rely on our willingness to keep characters existent if they are not shown or mentioned.
>
> (Eder et al. 2010, 28)

Necessary for media texts to activate this innate ability are merely some minimal cues that we can relate to such a transcultural and transhistorical *person schema*.

The resulting conception of "represented personhood" is not so much reliant on "human-like" qualities but rather, on the one hand, on a notion of *intentionality*. Possessing intentionality means having an inner, subjective life that is directed toward the same "outside" reality inhabited by and shared with others. On the other hand, it is based on *personal agency*: Possessing some sort of ability to introduce changes within the intersubjective world and being responsible for these acts. Taken together, intentionality and agency entail that *someone* is capable of self-initiated action and planning for its outcomes, which necessitates some sort of past recollection and future-orientedness, and that this someone should also be considered responsible for these actions by others. This nodal point of intentionality, agency, and memory (and, optionally, a discrete body), has been addressed as the *basic type* of characters by literature study scholar Fotis Jannidis (2014). A common denominator for all sorts of characters, then, is what narratologist Alan Palmer (2010, 10) addressed as their "continuous consciousness frame." They carry their memories of earlier experiences with them and anticipate upcoming events, integrating past, present, and future into one continuous "fictional biography" of evolving character traits. To Palmer, the core of any narrative is then mostly "the description of fictional mental functioning" (12). As audiences, we use our "ability to take a reference to a character in the text and attach it to a presumed consciousness that exists continuously within the storyworld between the various, more or less intermittent references to that character" (10).

Although the person schema indexing a consciousness frame of mental processing is most frequently established through representations of human bodies, characters must not be confused with bodies, and especially not with human ones. Characters that are clearly *not* human (animals, robots, aliens, monsters, all kinds of animated objects) are made legible for audiences precisely when the person schema derived from human interaction is applied to them. They are then not necessarily humanized, but certainly *personalized* when we understand their consciousnesses as human-like. Disney animated movies, for instance, feature countless "characterized/personalized objects" such as most protagonists in

Beauty and the Beast (Trousdale and Wise 1991) (humans magically transformed into household objects) or the flying carpet in *Aladdin* (Clements and Musker 1992) – the latter without any sort of face and not even capable of language, but clearly able to perceive and to comprehend, to act and to react. Characters may not be human-like in the sense that they think, feel, or act (and certainly not look) *like us* – but that they are *able to* think, feel, or act in general (see Langkjær and Jensen 2019).

Animals are especially interesting here, as fictional texts can present them in various ways closer or further away from a human sort of consciousness (see Wells 2009; José 2020). The protagonists in Brian K. Vaughan and Niko Henrichon's graphic novel *Pride of Baghdad* (2006), fictionalized versions of four actual lions that escaped the zoo of Baghdad after the US invasion of Iraq in 2003, are presented as complex personalities imbued with conflicting memories, responsibility for their actions, and, above all, human-like thought processes and linguistic skills expressed in thought balloon speech bubbles. While these lions – or, rather, their minds – are clearly humanized, Grant Morrison's and Frank Quitely's Sci-Fi comic *WE3* (2004) presents three cybernetically enhanced animal protagonists whose "more realistic" animal minds and cognitive processes remain entirely different from human ones. Despite their terrifying abilities to use lethal combat weapons, the dog, the cat, and the rabbit only understand the simplest of linguistic commands (like "friend" and "good boy") and their desires and drives remain animal ones (fight vs. flight, food, shelter). They are thus considerably further away from the basic type; remaining unfamiliar and strange, they invite the audience to consider a consciousness different from human ones and different from more prototypical characters. In other texts, animals might be presented as mere human possessions, objects among other objects, which have little in common with characters. In the James Bond Film *For Your Eyes Only* (Glen 1981), for instance, a parrot is decisive to the plot by repeating secret information to Bond and Melina Havelock (the parrot is thus an actant in the plot, as will be discussed in chapter 2), but it is not a character in any meaningful way. Comics and cartoons feature various additional anthropomorphized animals (see Herman 2017) – perhaps humans only represented as animals, like Donald Duck or Mickey Mouse – that we will look at more closely in chapter 5.

Rarely do we encounter bodies that are not perceived as characters – zombies might constitute particularly good examples for this, as they are not taken to possess any sort of consciousness in comics or shows like *The Walking Dead* (they are only actants, but not characters, as we will see in the next chapter). Conversely, we encounter many characters in media texts that are not only entirely dissimilar from humans but might not even possess any discrete body. Aside from Sauron's hovering eye mentioned above, the canonical example in film history is HAL 9000, the supercomputer from *2001: A Space Odyssey* (Kubrick 1968), whose consciousness seems distributed all over the spaceship Discovery One (an influential inspiration towards the conception and development of actual, ubiquitous cloud computing decades later). In contrast to actual "artificial intelligence," however, HAL 9000 is presented to have personal responsibility for "his" actions as one of the most fascinating antagonists in film history. In the story's resolution, HAL is even presented to experience emotions like fear when he is gradually switched off ("Stop, Dave. I'm afraid"). In the *Doom Patrol,* vol. 2 comic book series (Morrison et al. 1987–1995) and its recent TV adaptation (Carver et al. 2019–present), we encounter a "sentient street" called Danny. On a perceptional level, Danny cannot be distinguished from regular urban geometry (blocks of buildings, shops, and window fronts), except for the fact that they (Danny is described as a "gender-fluid, sentient street") communicate through various forms of visual printing within their proximity (street signs, ads, graffiti). These expressions are all attributed to the same disembodied consciousness that clearly has a sense of memory, strategic thinking, and even humor. They are therefore presented as a fictional *personality* while we succinctly interpret everything happening on Danny the Street as "character traits" experienced, controlled, and recalled by their continuous consciousness. "Skynet," the artificial machine consciousness responsible for the human apocalypse in the *Terminator* franchise, is not even shown in any sort of embodiment or materiality: It is merely a network controlling millions of machines but nevertheless described as some sort of unified, strategic consciousness that has *awakened* when scientists created a disastrous singularity event. Aside from characters that do not possess any sort of body, fictional texts frequently feature bodies "inhabited" by more than one character. The Hulk in the Marvel Cinematic Universe is not presented as another "side" of Dr. Bruce Banner that he can turn into (such as the schoolgirl Usagi Tsukino who can turn into Sailor Moon in the respective manga [Takeuchi 1991–1997] and anime series [Azuma et al. 1992–1997], or the boy Billy Batson who can transform into the superhero Shazam through a magic word in the film *Shazam!* [Sandberg 2019]; see TV Tropes, "Henshin Hero" for more examples). From the first *The Incredible Hulk* film (Leterrier 2008) onwards (and especially in comic book versions like Mark Millar and Bryan Hitch's *The Ultimates,* 2002–2004), the Hulk is presented as a separate consciousness living within Banner and sometimes taking over, possessing his private agendas, desires, and drives. More recent examples include the "symbiont" Venom sharing one body with Eddie Brock in the *Venom* movies (Fleischer 2018; Serkis 2021), or the demon Sukuna inhabiting the body of high school student Yuji Itadori in the *Jujutsu Kaisen* anime (Matsutani et al. 2020–present) and manga series (Akutami 2018–present) (see more examples listed under TV Tropes, "Sharing a Body").

Although all kinds of natural, social, or entirely abstract occurrences can be represented in media texts – the coming of a storm, the incitement of a revolution, the decline of a country's economy – it is usually only characters that we "feel with" or "identify with": not with the justice system, the functioning of a construction site, or even with a bicycle. If we *do,* however, it is because we understand these entities as characters – we apply the person schema onto them – when the media texts in question personalize them. Examples include the personifications of Death or Dream in the *Sandman* (1989–1996) comic books, audio plays (2020–present), or the TV show (2022–present) by Neil Gaiman and others, the anthropomorphic computer programs in the transmedial *TRON* or *The Matrix* franchise, the personalized emotions Joy, Sadness, Fear, Anger, and Disgust in the Pixar animated Film *Inside Out* (Docter 2015), and countless others.

In any case, including characters in any medial representation, even if they are not human at all as the examples above show, always generates a moral and ethical dimension: Someone – and not merely *something* – could have chosen to *act differently* (see Aldama 2010, 319f.). Giving a name, a race, a gender, and a social status to a character distinguishes them from others, yet only when they start acting and reacting do they become interesting within the narration as they can influence occurrences – and be held accountable for it. Once any basic type is activated within a text, it can continually be expanded and updated through textual cues of characterization. Character representations will usually not merely activate this foundational schema embedded within our primary theory, after all, but also have us applying more culture-specific or even media- and genre-specific schemata of knowledge. There are many generic character types that we find *only* in fictional narratives, after all, not in the "real world" (such as the "superhero," the "mad scientist," or the "kaiju monster"). For now, it is important to note that even characters highly specific to certain medial and genre traditions will still conform to the basic type. Despite all those important differences, a common feature remains their continuous consciousness frame that a media text has to establish and maintain and which we, as audiences, have to (re)identify amongst all other sorts of narrative information.

1.2 Establishing and Maintaining a Continuous Consciousness Frame

"Identification" has two very different meanings: The identification *of* a character precedes the identification *with* a character. This section will deal with the former aspect first (while the last part of this chapter will look into the latter). In literary narratives, the person schema – necessary to generate a character – is activated by three primary means: A text can (1) contain a verbal description that entails the attributes of humanness or, rather, personhood – such as "the gunslinger" (King 1982, 1) or "the one-armed man" (Martin 1963–1967; Davis 1993). Within individual languages, the available options for respective terms are huge, and most of these descriptions entail further character traits such as gender, age, profession, or social standing. A text may avoid that by using only (2) proper names. These, however, can also carry certain associations of gender or sociality. The name "Ezio Auditore da Firenze" from the *Assassin's Creed* game series (e.g., *Assassin's Creed II*, Ubisoft Montréal 2009), for example, implies both masculinity ("Ezio" being a traditionally male Italian name) and high social class (indicated by the addition of "da Firenze" – of Florence – to the family name). Proper names and descriptions can also blend into each other: Memorable characters like "Agent 355" from the *Y: The Last Man* comics (Vaughan et al. 2002–2008) and TV adaption (Vaughan et al. 2021), the "Cigarette Smoking Man" from *The X-Files* TV show (Carter et al. 1993–2002), the "High Sparrow" from the *Game of Thrones* show (Benioff et al. 2011–2019), "L" from the manga/anime *Death Note*

(Ohba and Obata 2003–2006; Nakatani et al. 2006–2007), or simply "the Guy" from the comedy-drama show *High Maintenance* (Blichfeld and Sinclair 2012–2020) are *only* known by these pseudonyms used like proper names. Finally, a text (3) may simply describe actions that are reserved for intelligent, or at least *intentional* beings, such as "[i]n a hole in the ground there *lived* a hobbit" (Tolkien 1937, 1) or "[t]here is a thing she will *think* over and over in the days to come" (Jemisin 2015, 1) (emphases added).

Within structuralist approaches to literary narratives, the proper name (or a pseudonym used like one) has been considered *the* essential nodal point – the point of convergence – to which all further attributes attach in order to become legible as character traits. In novels, we often have no other grounds to decide whether two represented beings introduced by descriptions ("one knight" and another "one knight") or by their actions ("someone opens a door" and "someone talks on the phone") are meant to refer to *the same character* except by name. Distinctness and identity over time are two of the most important aspects of the person schema, however. When George R.R. Martin introduced a telepathic collective of hive-minded consciousnesses in his science fiction novel *Tuf Voyaging* ("[T]hey lived side by side in the billions, each linked with all the others, each an individual and each a part of the great racial whole. In a sense, they were deathless, for all shared the experiences of each..." [Martin 1986, 18]), we are so far away from the prototypical core of the basic type that one might argue we are not even dealing with characters anymore – only with actants in the sense introduced in the next chapter.

Within pictorial media, this problem presents itself differently. In principle, there are not too many films, TV shows, or comic books that withhold the names of their protagonist. Quite a lot of them nevertheless *do*, however, such as the unnamed stranger portrayed by Clint Eastwood in *A Fistful of Dollars* (Leone 1964), the main protagonist in the TV show *Fleabag* (Waller-Bridge et al. 2016–2019) portrayed by Phoebe Waller-Bridge, the memorable narrator-character with the huge mustache played by Sam Elliot in *The Big Lebowski* (Coen 1998), or Ryan Gosling's unnamed protagonist in *Drive* (Refn 2011). An even greater number of video games regularly employ only nameless soldiers, for example in *Halo 3: ODST* (Bungie 2009), or invisible racecar drivers, as in *Gran Turismo 5* (Polyphony Digital 2010). Even for characters in pictorial media that *are* named, the audience will not always care to remember their names. This is because in pictorial media, as Smith has argued for film (1995, 30), images of *human bodies* – either shown in continuous shots or recognizable throughout montages – take the place of the proper name as the primary nodal point to activate the person schema and to assemble all subsequent character traits. The same is true for comic books, animated films, or video games where a recognizable iconography – a "pictorial code" – replaces the likeness of a specific actor. Pictures presenting a body or a face precede proper names in all these cases, because they can be understood to offer a correspondence to a large number of "descriptions," i.e., visible character traits that one can recognize, remember, and compare to each other in order to *re-identify* the same character throughout different representations (see Potysch and Wilde 2018). At the same time, representations of bodies immediately open up a range of thematic meanings, "the boundaries between the inside and the outside, between the self and the other, between male and female, between the clean and the polluted, and between the living and the dead" (Frow 2018, 114).

The recognition of characters thus strongly depends on a perceived or inferred continuity of identity. When high school detective Shinichi Kudo, the main protagonist of the manga and anime *Detective Conan* (Aoyama 1994–present; Suwa 1996–present), is rejuvenated into a six-year-old through the experimental drug Apoptoxin 4869, we consider him *the same individual*, since he is able to keep all his previous memories and most aspects of his personality: He experiences this transformation within the same frame of consciousness. When writer David Mitchell uses protagonists' names such as "Marinus" recurrently throughout his novels *The Thousand Autumns of Jacob de Zoet* (2010), *The Bone Clocks* (2014), *Slade House* (2015), and *Utopia Avenue* (2020) – set across different times, spaces, and in different genres – the assumption that this is, in fact, *the same character*, even though they are sometimes described as a man, sometimes as a woman, implies that their consciousness has a continued existence as Marinus is a supernatural being literally reincarnated into different bodies and thus able to recall earlier events and retain experiences (see Lesser 2014). We understand the motivations and actions of *Utopia Avenue*'s Dr. Yu Marinus-Li fully *only* if we take character traits and earlier experiences from *Slade House*'s Dr. Iris Marinus-Fenby and *The Bone Clocks*' many other Marinus incarnations into account. Characters thus have to retain several stable traits and not change significantly without explanations: If they are brave and fearless in one appearance, but shy and humble in the next, we will search for explanations in "life-changing" occurrences and narrative events (which were maybe "only omitted" by the actual narration).

> In making *Dr. No*, for example, [actor Sean] Connery had to work in an original way to establish [James Bond] as a charming, manipulative, witty, physically skillful, and knowledgeable man of the world. By the time he made *From Russia with Love*, all these character traits, painstakingly constructed for original audiences, could be taken as read.
>
> (Pomerance 2016, 178)

The *different* actors playing James Bond, however, are hence often treated as different Bond characters because the character traits of the Connery version are seen at odds with Craig's brute and often vulgar ones (and there are also conflicts in continuity – more about that in chapter 7). *Casino Royale* (Campbell 2006) provided a strong textual cue for such a differentiation when the new Bond, asked whether he liked his Vodka Martini "shaken or stirred," brusquely replied "Do I look like I give a damn?" The preference for Vodka Martini, "shaken, not stirred," was such a prominent character trait for earlier versions that it became a recognizable catchphrase for the character. By contrast, Luke Skywalker in *The Last Jedi* (Johnson 2017) is presented as a solitary, grumpy hermit very different from the optimistic hero in the original *Star Wars* trilogy, but still intended to be the same character. The text tries to make that plausible by the fact that so much diegetic time has passed between the trilogies that he has changed accordingly over implied traumatic events. In the next chapter, concerned with plot and eventfulness, we will look in more detail at narrative events maintaining continuity precisely by introducing changes to characters and their traits.

An interesting border case is presented by the TV show *Severance* (Erickson et al. 2022–present) built on the Sci-Fi premise that characters like Mark (played by Adam Scott) or Helly (Britt Lower) separate their consciousnesses into a private version and a work version, unable to carry any memories from one "side" of their life into the other: Their "work personages" thus experience their whole existences in their office. While their bodies are continuous – physical character traits like a head injury from work are "imported" into their private life without them knowing the causes – Mark's opposing "personage" is addressed as "the other one" (S01E01) in informal conversations as if they both were, in fact, two different characters hosted in a shared body. In later episodes, they both communicate through video messages and even plot against each other (S01E04). It also turns out that the process is reversible (at a cost) so that people undergoing the severance procedure can become *one* consciousness frame again.

All the objects, entities, and events within a storyworld are then not only related in temporal, spatial, and causal terms but also within subjective experiences and perceptions *of the characters themselves*. Protagonists in narrative media do not "stick out," exactly, because they seem "life-like." On the contrary, philosopher Brigitte Hilmer has argued (2009) that their impression of "aliveness" is rather the consequence of the fact that their consciousnesses are ontologically distinguished from their surroundings. They often have to draw inferences about the storyworld themselves, and they can be mistaken doing so: Keanu Reeve's Neo only believes to inhabit a large US city in *The Matrix* (Wachowski and Wachowski 1999), while he is actually trapped within a virtual reality; John Nash, Russel Crowe's protagonist in *A Beautiful Mind* (Howard 2002), believes to be blackmailed into government black-op missions which are later revealed to be nothing but paranoid, schizophrenic delusions. Tyler Durden (portrayed by Brad Pitt), who recruits the unnamed main character of *Fight Club* (Fincher 1999) for his rebellion against society, exists merely in the protagonist's imagination.

"Carrying" their personal subjective consciousnesses with them, characters thus multiply the storyworld into distinguished *subjective versions*, into states of the world they desire or fear, long for, or try to avoid, and states of the world they remember (correctly or falsely). The intersubjective storyworld or diegesis must hence be distinguished from characters' *hypo-diegeses* (embedded storyworlds), their subjective worlds within that world (feelings, memories, imaginations, anticipations). By introducing characters into any representation, the multiplicity of different modal states of affairs (intended ones, desired ones, dreaded ones) thus establishes a distinction between the "possible" and the "actual." A storyworld – and, as such, any represented situation – has been defined as a *possible* world/ situation before, in the sense that they are imaginable from our perspective. If part of audiences' imagination, however, includes characters, then, *to them*, the represented state of affairs is not merely possible, but actual again: It has "real" consequences for all participants, while they imagine additional, once again merely possible situations. According to philosopher Gregory Currie, "[n]arratives represent things as existing, and circumstances as being so" (2010, 7). At the same time, *different* states of affairs become possible (imaginable). By introducing characters and subjectivities, media texts' authors and audiences then necessarily reiterate the distinction between the actual and the possible *within the realm of the possible*. Narrative actuality – what is sometimes called the "basic facts domain" (Margolin 2007, 71) of a storyworld – is that which is *not up to the characters* to change at will. To them, it is a "brute fact," reality. Experientiality, a key term for character studies introduced by Fludernik (1996, 12), refers to the fact that worlds filled with characters are always worlds *for someone*, experienced "from within" (see Caracciolo 2014). Each and every consciousness has, as philosopher John Searle has put it, a "first-person ontology" (1999, 42). They carry, by definition, a certain point of view, a worldview.

Narratives such as those presented in the films *Rashomon* (Kurosawa 1950) or *The Last Duel* (Scott 2021) even build their whole plot around different characters' contradicting viewpoints on the same course of events, while some transmedia franchises add a "perspective flip" in later installments like *Maleficent*'s (Stromberg 2014) and *Cruella*'s (Gillespie 2021) live-action "retelling" of the Disney animated films *Sleeping Beauty* (Geronimi 1959) and *101 Dalmatians* (Geronimi et al. 1961) from the point of view of the respective villains. Both strategies invite audiences to reflect upon given situations from different (ethical, social, political) perspectives (for more transmedial examples see TV Tropes, "'Rashomon'-Style"). Audiences following and comprehending characters' represented consciousnesses perform a kind of "fictional recentering," to use another term by Ryan (1991b, 13). We *mentally relocate* to the fictional world that the characters inhabit and adopt their perspective, merely by following the narration. This lends characters an *emotional realism* (Ang 1982, 47; see also Lamerichs 2018, 67–102), irrespective of how fantastic or otherworldly the stories and narrative events are that they undergo. Smith argues accordingly that "our 'entry into' narrative structures is mediated by character" (1995, 18). While there is some dispute over whether the theory of mind is productive for the analysis of all sorts of narratives (see Grethlein 2015), it is certainly *one* valuable starting point to approach represented characters (complementary ones will be presented in the next two chapters). How, then, does a narrative media text grant us access to characters' minds?

1.3 Access to Character's Subjectivity: Alignment, Narrators, Perceptual Overlays

One of the most important questions concerning representations of characters is how media texts are able to grant us access to their subjectivity, to their continuous consciousness frame. Certainly, a simple drawing of a face might already be enough to indicate an intelligent consciousness that "comes to life" in audiences' minds and imaginations. Just as we presuppose that other people we encounter on the street have a mind similar to ours, literary scholar Lisa Zunshine (2006) argued that we employ the same "mindreading" abilities (Zunshine 2020, 257) in the same way to interpret fictional and fictionalized characters. David Bordwell, a film scholar who consolidated cognitivist approaches for the analysis of fictional films, gave the following related account for meaning-making in film which evidently rests strongly on characters: "Filmic storytelling usually relies on our everyday assumptions about why people act as they do, how they will respond to others, and how they come to decisions" (Bordwell 2013, 30).

Most inferences we draw about characters' subjectivities are hence based indirectly on the way that they *behave* within the presented plots. In order to explain characters' actions, we construct – and continuously revise – working hypotheses about their supposed motivations and beliefs, about their continuous consciousness frames. As a basis for that, the plot has to provide information about them and their actions. Smith (1995, 81–96) addresses this correlation between plot and characters as *alignment* (often also addressed as *focalization* in narrative theory, see Hühn et al. 2009). Two major forms can be distinguished as external vs. internal alignment. External forms generate a spatio-temporal proximity, or an attachment, to the characters within their physical storyworld, following their actions and behaviors (including dialogue). Narrative proximity, however, is always a matter of degree. No film shows the whole timespan that a character is lying in bed, sleeping, going to the bathroom, eating dinner, and so on (except for experimental works such as Andy Warhol's *Sleep*, 1964, showing 5 hours and 20 minutes of John Giorno sleeping). Films that approach a real-time coupling of narrating time and narrated time by minimizing cuts, such as *Locke* (Knight 2013), *1917* (Mendes 2019), or *Oxygen* (Aja 2021), are extremely rare. In video games, it is more common that we follow the characters continuously as we maneuver them in "real-time" through their adventures – except for ellipses in between levels or during cut scenes. Usually, however, we also have little information about what has occurred before the game has started.

Relevant to our engagement with characters are also differences of alignment *between* protagonists, as heroes are usually fleshed out with more information than side characters. Many popular narratives are centered around one or two main protagonists, whereas ensemble casts in sitcoms or superhero team stories are centered around a whole group. Network narratives in TV shows like *The Wire* (Simon et al. 2002–2008) or *Watchmen* (Lindelof et al. 2019), or in films like *City of God* (Meirelles and Lund 2002) or *Contagion* (Sonderbergh 2011) follow a larger cast which does not interact as a group at all (spread around the storyworld and only occasionally interlinking), in which no single character can be said to serve as "hero" of the story. Typically, protagonist-centered works are what Carl Plantinga (2010, 35) called "sympathetic narratives": they encourage audience engagement with and emotional attachment to their heroes, whereas "distanced narratives" favor a cool, critical, or ironic stance towards their protagonists. The latter is typical for interlinked network narratives, although some of them are clearly intended as sympathetic (e.g., the 2012 film *Cloud Atlas* by Wachowski et al.), while others that *do* feature a central protagonist must be seen as distanced in emotional terms (like Martin Scorsese's 2013 film *The Wolf of Wall Street*). In any case, a close analysis of how a plot aligns audiences with characters (as a basis to draw inferences about their supposed inner life) is always a good starting point for reflection on them. Alex Woloch (2003) has aptly addressed characterization – plot information aligning with characters – as a limited resource in the novel so that characters always have to compete with each other in their "narrative ecology." Transmediality and seriality can provide a possible solution here, when a side character like Saul Goodman from the show *Breaking Bad* (Gilligan et al. 2008–2013) is provided with a spin-off show of his own, *Better Call Saul* (Gilligan et al. 2015–2022), fleshing out his adventures, motivations, and desires in more detail. In literature, there has long been the subgenre of "minor character" explorations, imagining the fates of *Ahab's Wife* (Naslund 1999) or some *Mr. Dalloway* (Lippincott 1999) (see Rosen 2016). The interconnected "shared universes" of comic books – or transmedial expansions like Marvel's MCU – are certainly interesting in this respect as well (see chapter 7).

Aside from such indirect means of providing access to characters' inner lives by aligning plots with their actions, media texts have developed various ways to grant a more "direct access" to their consciousnesses. While it may be true that we, as humans, will never be able to understand "what is it like to be a bat" (Nagel 2016), our imagination is certainly able to "simulate" experiences that are entirely alien to us – other minds' feelings and perceptions, thoughts, and beliefs (see Reinerth and Thon 2017). If these imaginations are "externalized" in the form of media texts, we are able to approach them, again, intersubjectively. Unlike other forms of the imagination such as daydreaming, our engagement with characters is guided and constrained by multimodal texts, after all. Maike Sarah Reinerth and Jan-Noël Thon (2017, 3) proposed the somewhat paradoxical phrasing of an "intersubjective subjectivity" made accessible by narrative media. Eder (2008, 584) distinguishes between five aspects of represented subjective states that are helpful for our understanding: (1) Perceptual perspective represents the way a character sees, listens, smells, etc. in a given context – this is obviously especially relevant for pictorial and audiovisual media which, more so than literature, can directly simulate the perceptual states of characters' conscious experiences; (2) epistemic perspective represents what a character thinks, knows, or beliefs in a given context; (3) evaluative perspective represents how a character judges a given situation according to aesthetic or moral criteria; (4) emotional perspective represents the feelings or moods of a character in a given context; finally, (5) motivational perspective represents what a character wants, wishes, desires, or fears. This is where the diegetic context shown as actual (within the basic fact domain of the storyworld) is multiplied into branching alternatives of possible states of affairs (hypo-diegeses or embedded diegeses) most clearly.

Different forms of media have developed a range of strategies to grant access to characters' subjectivities. Comic books, especially humoristic ones, often employ thought balloons to indicate what characters are thinking – entailing all of Eder's five categories – quite directly. One of the most common transmedial strategies to grant access to characters' subjectivities is derived from literature: An "omniscient" narrator simply *tells* audiences about a character's inner life and their subjective experiences. We can find this not only in novels but also in other forms of media, each with specific traditions and aesthetics. Film and TV, as well as some video games, usually rely on a voiceover narration spoken by actors, while comic books often insert narration into "caption boxes." A character is also not only present as an experiencing self within the diegetic world but also as a *narrator* themselves, commenting upon their own experiences by communicating them verbally. Suzanne Collins' *The Hunger Games* trilogy, for instance, opens up with the words "When I wake up, the other side of the bed is cold. My fingers stretch out, seeking Prim's warmth but finding only the rough canvas cover of the mattress" (Collins 2008, 1). It is the book's protagonist, Katniss Everdeen, to whom these words can be attributed, as she is granting access to her sensory experience of heat perception, touch, and feel. Such a self-narrating narrator is called a "homodiegetic" one, in contrast to a "heterodiegetic" narrator who seems not to be part of the presented storyworld at all. The narrator of the TV show *13 Reasons Why* (Gomez et al. 2017–2020) is Hannah Baker (played by Katherine Langford) who has committed suicide before the diegetic present, leaving her voice on 13 audio tapes that the show overlays as narration over the whole first season. As a narrator, she is thus homodiegetic, since her narrating situation actually exists within the storyworld (albeit in a past that is not directly shown). Some texts *do* generate (and sometimes dissolve) ambiguities and uncertainties surrounding the diegetic status of their narrating instances. In Frank Miller's comic *300* (1998), for instance, the verbal account (presented in caption boxes in the comic and by a voiceover narrator in the 2007 film directed by Zack Snyder) turns out to be a campfire story – not written nor thought, but actually spoken – recounted at a later time within the same storyworld.

Introducing a homodiegetic narrator – whose mind we can "listen in to" like a thought balloon in comics – always involves specific stylistic choices: We necessarily form judgments of how the character expresses themselves, what words they use, what they are paying attention to and what not – something addressed as "mind style" by Roger Fowler (1977, 103). Whether we should trust these narrating characters is another question altogether: The butler in Ishiguro's novel *The Remains of the Day* (1989) has been discussed extensively for his unreliability that is, at its core, self-deceiving. *Fight Club* has been mentioned before as a film that employs unreliable narration, other filmic examples include *The Usual Suspects* (Singer 1996) or *Gone Girl* (Fincher 2014), on TV *You* (Siega et al. 2018–present) and *Mr. Robot* (Esmail et al. 2015–2019), or in anime *Ghost in the Shell: Stand Alone Complex* (Matsuya et al. 2002–2005) or *Death Note* (Nakatani et al. 2006–2007). Usually, however, we attribute only the verbal accounts to homodiegetic (in-world) sources, to characters, while the audiovisual parts of representations are not shown to originate from in-world filmmakers, comic book artists, or game producers. The film and TV examples above only "illustrate" the accounts of the unreliable voiceover narration, but their pictures and audio tracks do not exist within the world. This difference becomes especially striking in changes of media forms. The prequel novel to George R.E. Martin's *A Song of Ice and Fire* series, *Fire & Blood* (Martin 2018), is presented as in in-world account from one of its inhabitants, Archmaster Gyldayn. A book called "Fire & Blood" thus exists within the storyworld itself. In it, Gyldayn himself admits to rely on "historical sources" often contradicting themselves. He thus presents the events in alternative versions (mainly attributed to two other characters, the cleric Eustace and a court jester called Mushroom), leaving it to the (in-world as well as actual) readers to decide which accounts of events actually transpired. Gyldayn, as well as Eustace and Mushroom, certainly have their own intentions, motivations, and political reasonings to tell the story one way or another. When the book was adapted into the TV show *House of the Dragon* (Condal et al. 2022), it only shows *one* version of the events in its audiovisual representations, and the audience has no reason to doubt that what we see is what happened: There simply is no medium of film in this fantasy world, after all.

Regardless of whether homodiegetic characters-as-narrators are truthfully reporting facts as they are perceiving them or not, their presence always leads to a duplication of the character into an "experiencing I" and a "telling/thinking I" that both contribute to our understanding of the character as the overall fictional being. N.K. Jemisin's and Jamal Campbell's comic book series *Far Sector* (2021–present), for instance, does not merely show its protagonist, Green Lantern Sojourner Mullein, in the diegetic present. Lantern Mullein is also commenting upon herself through narration in caption boxes: "Yep, that's me. You're probably wondering how this happened" (#10, 2). The comic specifies neither the identity of this "you" that Mullein is addressing, nor the time and space when her narration takes place – it also remains undefined whether the words are supposed to be spoken, written, or perhaps only thought. Her "narrating I" remains entirely outside of the primary storyworld, which is quite typical for this literary convention. While she is looking back at herself from a temporal distance in the former example, the narration at other times approximates a more immediate internal stream of consciousness ("Need to go faster. Damn it," #2, 2). In both cases, Mullein's specific choice of words certainly serves to characterize her overall personality through "mind style" – dry inserts like "But what else is new?" (#1, 2) or humorous comments like "*Syzn of the Cliffs, By the Streaking Ice.* Yes, all of that is her name. Can't get over this place. It's mad wild" (#1, 6).

All of these strategies have in common that they employ verbal language for access to characters' minds. The use of words always activates the person schema, at least to the extent that a verbal narrator – whether realized by a novel's main text, through a filmic voiceover, or in a comic's caption boxes – is usually sharply distinguished from the actual author(s) of the work, especially if they are collectives of countless individuals like in film, TV shows, or video games. A heterodiegetic narrating voice from "outside" the storyworld – often equipped with knowledge that no entity within the diegesis could ever acquire – remains in a disembodied, highly artificial state and can thus be described as "extradiegetic narration" when it cannot be traced back to any tempo-spatial situation within the storyworld. J.R.R. Tolkien opened the first chapter of *The Fellowship of the Ring* (1954, 1), for instance, with the following extradiegetic, heterodiegetic account: "When Mr. Bilbo Baggins of Bag End announced that he would shortly be celebrating his eleventy-first birthday..." The "narrating character" does not seem to be part of the storyworld and the narrating situation (was this written down or told, and, if the latter, when and to whom?) is never explicated – and thus not part of the basic fact domain of *Lord of the Rings*. By contrast, the film adaptation (Jackson 2001) opens with another voiceover narration retelling the storyworld's history in a first-person account ("The world has changed. I feel it in the water, I feel it in the earth, I smell it in the air. Much was once what is now lost, for none now live who remember it"). Here, however, it is the voice of Cate Blanchett who will appear as the elven queen Galadriel later in the story. We can thus infer that director Peter Jackson had "recast" Galadriel as the film's homodiegetic, extradiegetic narrator – she *is* part of the storyworld, after all, although we do not know anything about this precise narrating situation (was it actually told to someone or merely thought?).

As already mentioned above, other forms of subjective representations do not rely on verbal means at all, but instead, use pictoriality or an audio track to simulate perceptual experiences more directly. When James Bond sets off a bomb in *No Time to Die*'s (Fukunaga 2021) opening sequence, the audio track mimics his immediate lack of hearing and the loud ringing in his ears. A point-of-view shot in film may be the most common of these techniques. Pictorial methods of subjectivation could be distinguished on a gradual scale: A perceptual point of view assumes a specific position within a represented space that is otherwise intersubjective within the diegetic world. This is sometimes addressed as *ocularization*, a term describing "the relation between what the camera shows and what the characters are presumed to be seeing" (Jost 2004, 74) if both are in alignment. All other characters will also be able to perceive the same situation, although from different angles or directions. Perceptional points of view (ocularization on the visual track, or *auricularization* on the auditory) can nevertheless entail epistemic (knowledge-related), evaluative, emotional, and motivational character information. In the Netflix teen drama series *Grand Army* (Cappiello et al. 2020–present), we track the aftermath of a suspected Islamist terrorist attack from the perspective of high school student Siddhartha "Sid" Pakam (played by Amir Bageria). Although he grew up in the Bronx and is not Muslim, he painfully experiences countless hostile and suspicious glances from White Americans on the subway the following day (S01E02). The series simulates these experiences visually and auditorily (through ocularization/auricularization) by adopting his point of view – *of being looked at* warily on the train. As audiences, we can easily assume his frame of consciousness where he assumes that he is taken as a Muslim merely for his appearances and judged as potentially hostile and foreign; that this causes him embarrassment and distress; and that he wishes to arrive at his location quickly without incident. A "dream sequence," by contrast, presents memories or hallucinations that are *only* accessible to the subjective minds of one specific character (if the narrative does not establish fantastic powers to enter dreams, as in Neil Gaiman's and other's comic book series *The Sandman*, 1989–1996 or the recent Netflix TV adaptation, Gaiman et al. 2022–present). An intermediate strategy between both has been called a "quasi-perceptual overlay" by Thon (2016, 293–298): The overall situation and most objects within it are intersubjective for all the characters, but their perception is "filtered" or modified by aspects that are *not* accessible to other minds: When Katniss Everdeen is stung by poisonous "Tracker Jacker" wasps in the first *Hunger Games* (Ross 2012) film, visual effects are overlaying the otherwise intersubjective representation of the storyworld that mimic her distorted, erratic visual perception (and the audio track simulates her constrained hearing in similar ways). Likewise, when the character Wallace from Frank Miller's *Sin City: Hell and Back* (1999–2000) comic book is hallucinating from drugs, colorful pictures of little fairies are inserted into the otherwise monochromatic representation of the storyworld: The black and white background is thus intersubjectively "valid" to other characters as well, while the overlay remains accessible only to Wallace (see again Thon 2016, 291–298). Other forms and formats of media, like video games, have again developed their distinct means of representing subjective experiences that align audiences with characters' minds.

1.4 Different Emotional Stances Toward Characters

Although (external and internal) alignment forms the basis for all kinds of attachments and emotional responses, audiences' reactions to characters are far from determined by the *amount* and *depth* of information given. In narratives in which alignment is dispersed more or less equally among many characters, we will still develop stronger sympathies for some characters than for others. The superhero satire TV show *The Boys* (Kripke et al. 2019–present), for instance, employs alignment equally between morally corrupt superbeings such as Homelander or Stormfront and their opposition circled around Hughie Campbell and Billy Butcher. When Stormfront gets brutally mutilated in season 2's finale, audiences are likely to celebrate that, since the character was shown as racist and sadistic, as well as being a literal Nazi superweapon from World War II experiments. Some kinds of sympathy may be better comprised by the term *fascination* when they apply to villains such as Heath Ledger's Joker in *The Dark Knight* (Nolan 2008), who was universally appreciated by audiences and critics alike. Parts of this fascination are certainly based on an appreciation of Heath Ledger's acting (see chapter 4), so audiences' engagements are often triggered by their recognition of a character's synthetic dimension, distinguished from – but intertwined with – their mimetic side: "We can be drawn to fictional figures [...] whose real-world equivalents we would run miles to avoid" (Felski 2019, 84).

The ability of narrative media to elicit emotional attachments towards fictional and fictionalized characters is certainly a key factor in their aesthetic and economic success, as well as in questions of moral and ideological impact. If producers somehow manage to inspire "pro" and "con" attitudes toward protagonists or antagonists – many popular franchises are in fact intended to elicit clear allegiances and oppositions (heroes vs. villains) – they are able to manipulate audiences with desires for specific outcomes and the adoption of moral values and attitudes which characters exemplify on a thematic, perhaps even unintended (symptomatic) level. "Fiction serves as an ethical laboratory that allows for all kinds of experimentation with values" (Felski 2019, 100). Related ethical and rhetorical dimensions of characters inspired the most extensive discussions regarding narrative and fiction, ranging back to the philosophies of Plato and Aristotle. Our moral judgment towards characters, however, is influenced and shaped by myriad factors that no single theory can hope to cover. It will, for instance, often be relative to the *contrasting* options available within one media text, so that even a cannibal like Hannibal Lecter (played by Anthony Hopkins) appears somewhat relatable in a story such as *Silence of the Lambs* (Demme 1991) where there is an even more cruel – and considerably less eloquent and sophisticated – serial killer named "Buffalo Bill" (played by Ted Levine). Batman's moral code of "never to kill" is not shared by other superheroes such as Wolverine or the Punisher, so the same deed may be evaluated very differently for these protagonists. Generic conventions also come into play, so that using violence – if perhaps only against enemies classified as "evil" – is seen as acceptable in battle manga and anime like *Demon Slayer* (Gotouge 2016–2020; Fujio 2019–present), but reserved for villains in Disney animated films.

As we have discussed in the introductory chapter, a potential Transmedia Character Studies should be focused on intersubjectivity (and its limits): Character assessments that transcend the personal and the private. Nowhere does this seem more difficult than where it concerns sympathies for characters, which can be highly unstable from one audience member to the next, and often surprising. A good example of this is the character Rorschach from Alan Moore's and Dave Gibbons' 1986/1987 comic book series *Watchmen* (2014). The anti-hero, whose "uncompromising sense of justice" is rooted in anti-social, sexist, and racist worldviews, was apparently intended as a critique of superheroes like Batman, at least according to the writer himself:

> I wanted to kind of make this like, 'Yeah, this is what Batman would be in the real world.' But I had forgotten that actually to a lot of comic fans that smelling, not having a girlfriend – these are actually kind of heroic. So actually, sort of, Rorschach became the most popular character in Watchmen. I meant him to be a bad example, but I have people come up to me in the street saying, 'I am Rorschach! That is my story!'
> (Quoted after Surman 2015, n.pag.; see also AlanMooreVids 2007)

It is easy to see why many people seem to have sympathized with Rorschach. The comic grants privileged access to his point of view, as he features prominently as the story's narrator through his journal (even though the actual wording there, Rorschach's "mind style," was clearly embedded in xenophobic and homophobic thinking: "Meeting with Veidt left bad taste in mouth. He is pampered and decadent, betraying even his own shallow, liberal affections. Possibly homosexual? Must remember to investigate further," Moore and Gibbons 2014, #1, 19). The attractiveness of identifying with Rorschach despite his reactionary and appalling views is evidenced by the fact that even American politician Alexandria Ocasio-Cortez from the US-American Democratic Party's left-wing – quite unsuspicious of entertaining alt-right fantasies – quoted the character on Twitter when she entered American congress in November 2019: "None of you understand. I'm not locked up in here with YOU. You're locked up in here with ME" (Ocasio-Cortez 2019, n.pag.) – a sentence uttered by Rorschach after he is locked up in prison with villains he brought to justice earlier on, only to brutally maim and murder some of them within the institutional confines. The transmedial expansion of *Watchmen*, HBO's series of the same name from 2019 (Lindelof et al.), critically commented on the Rorschach discourse in an interesting way. While many of the original characters reappear 20 in-universe years later in the show, Rorschach's legacy – the character died at the end of the original series – is only addressed through White supremacist terrorists (the "Seventh Cavalry") who continue wearing his mask. This not only "spells out" the racist implications of his journal more openly, but the Rorschach-terrorists also serve as the show's primary villains.

From a methodological point of view, how *can* we assess characters' potential to elicit sympathies or "identification" if this proves highly unstable from one individual to the next; if "bad fans" can always fail to honor any authorial (stated or claimed) intention (see Nussbaum 2014)? "Audiences become attached to fiction in an abundance of ways; these ties can be ironic as well as sentimental, ethical as well as emotional," Felski noted (2019, 77). The methods described in the introductory chapter to approach characters intersubjectively still hold. On the one hand, we have public discourses *about* characters at our disposal that we can point to: People – including the actual authors – *do* have conflicting opinions about Rorschach and others, and these assessments are accessible through public discourse. On the other hand, not all emotional responses elicited by media texts are accidental and purely subjective, so we can retrace these statements back to the actual media texts: Most assessments *are* clearly guided and constrained by narrative strategies and cues. While, again, the aspects relevant to our sympathies are far too many to give a full view on (see Coplan 2004; Gallagher 2012), we can nevertheless distinguish different *levels* of audience engagements partly independent from, but partly controlled by media texts. Philosopher Carl Plantinga (2010) proposed related but distinct emotional stances that together comprise a "structure of sympathy" surrounding characters (see also Felski 2019 as well as Plantinga 2019). The weakest and certainly most subjective form of engagement is addressed as *liking*. We may "like" fictional protagonists for all sorts of reasons that remain outside any intersubjective analysis: Some forms may be based on personal preferences for certain character traits (attractive, witty, or entertaining), or tribal associations of similarity when they share an audience member's gender, age, ethnicity, or religion.

A stronger form of engagement, however, is more deeply rooted within the plot of the narrative itself and called *sympathy*. Plantinga characterizes it as a "sensitivity to another person's situation along with concern for [them]" (2010, 38). Sympathy, just as liking, is not granted for moral or good behavior (although both forms of engagement can be strengthened or weakened by respective judgments), but rather to those who *need* care and concern. It is thus rooted in the representation of suffering and misfortune and accordingly dependent on specific narrative situations in which characters experience bad things – if we are sufficiently aligned with their plight. Whereas liking is more subjective, sympathy can be generated and manipulated by narrative tools and techniques with much precision. Director Alfred Hitchcock (see American Film Institute 2008; as well as Truffaut 2017, 105–125) is endlessly quoted for a famous example of a hidden bomb suddenly exploding under a table where several people were having breakfast. This is perhaps a shock of 20 seconds for the audience. When they see the fuse burning for some time in advance, however, while the characters are still unaware of it, they cannot help but sympathize with and worry for them in such a situation until the narrative event (see next chapter) is resolved in one way or another. This is an example of "narrative suspense," as we, as audiences, are given anticipating information about the possible fate of a character that we are aligned with, preparing for alternative outcomes. Audiences may thus experience sympathy for characters they do not even like (such as Howard Ratner, portrayed by Adam Sandler in the film *Uncut Gems*, Safdie and Safdie 2019). We should clearly distinguish sympathy from empathy, however: The latter is understood as a *joint feeling* that we may share, while the former only requires concern and understanding for the individual. Empathy is then, at its core, the more subjective experience of sympathy, while the latter is based on "narrative facts" in a more intersubjective fashion (see Keen 2006 for more detail).

While liking and sympathy can both be short-term, scene-based, and independent of moral evaluations, a stronger form of engagement can be found in what Smith called *allegiances* with characters. He defined this as a strong and lasting "pro" stance that is governed by moral judgments of, or rather *agreements* with characters. Audiences are then able to understand the reasons for a character's actions by evaluating their motives and aims favorably. Allegiances are distinguished from both previously mentioned forms of engagement not only in strength and duration but also in their causes and roots. Our "allying ourselves with, focusing on, rooting for a character" (Smith 1995, 41) is only established after appropriate character development that we can base our evaluation on. While likings and sympathies may seem more "emotional," Plantinga warns against the notion that allegiances are, in fact, "rational" or free from manipulations – quite to the contrary. Instead of judgments or evaluations, we should rather speak of *agreements* with characters and their actions. Moral reasoning might even serve to rationalize our intuitive judgments. The "codes of conduct" for acceptable behavior are often subject to specific genre traditions and settings. What might be morally acceptable in one storyworld (or genre) would be despised in another: Within a fantasy novel, we may look up to "heroes" we would find abhorrent in a contemporary setting. We must take into account that every storyworld (set in a specific genre) has a distinct *ethos*, as media scholars Lisbeth Klastrup and Susanna Tosca have proposed:

> How does the good and the bad behave, and what behaviour can be accepted as "in character" or rejected as "out of character" in that world. Thus ethos is the form of knowledge required in order to *know how to behave* in the world.
> (Klastrup and Tosca 2004, n.pag.; original emphasis)

We should remain critical of such justifications, however. *Game of Thrones* has been condemned strongly for its treatment of female characters, and the excuse "it's just fantasy" is rather weak for its normalization of sexualized violence, although it could be stated that (the novels certainly more so than) the show's later seasons at least attempt to criticize and deconstruct such a worldview: In the sixth season, most of Westeros' great houses are represented by strong female leaders after countless male protagonists have died in unglamorous wars and horrors incited by misleading ideas of (male) superiority and heroism. Whether this exonerates the show as a whole would be up to a more detailed discussion that could perhaps produce different results for different characters and their developments.

Our allegiances are also subject to rhetorical effects such as priming: Once established, character behavior becomes normalized and is altered only by dramatic turns of events. Serial narratives such as *Breaking Bad* (Gilligan et al. 2008–2013), in which the protagonist Walter White (played by Bryan Cranston) slowly develops from a family father and schoolteacher into a criminal mastermind whose acts become more and more despicable, employ this mechanic *against* audience expectations when we gradually learn that our allegiances might be misplaced (see Plantinga 2019). Allegiances with characters are thus subject to emotional manipulation, just as likings and sympathies are. This is what makes characters seductive, as Plantinga summarizes: "[S]pectator attitudes toward characters are not fully rooted in moral criteria, but audiences tend to interpret their judgements as having legitimate moral force" (2010, 48). Some media texts at least lend themselves to moral ambiguities while others do not, and there are controversies and discussions surrounding specific characters – and not others.

All three forms of positive engagements naturally have their opposing, negative counterparts, which are often of equal relevance to audiences: There are protagonists we emphatically *dislike* (for their appearances, quirks of behavior, etc.); those that we experience *antipathy* for (a "con" stance expressed in the desire to have them experience bad things within specific narrative situations – the "just revenge!" experienced at the death of a despicable villain like Joffrey Baratheon in *Game of Thrones*); and those we form *oppositions* against because we fundamentally disagree with some of their lasting character traits and values. We can see from this heuristic typology that the narrativity of media plays a central part in modulating audiences' engagements. While we may "like" non-narrative characters such as mascots or Hello Kitty for their attractive character design, we have no basis to form an allegiance with them rooted in moral evaluations – as there are no character developments that we might agree or disagree with.

Taken together, the importance of characters rests in part on what they "teach" us about how to respond to various situations they find themselves in. Put differently, a crucial feature of narratives is that they offer ways to understand and value the world within characters' continuous frame of consciousness. The animated show *Avatar: The Last Airbender* (DiMartino et al. 2005–2008) clearly deviates from the more typical ethos of other action shows in that its protagonist Aang firmly subscribes to values of non-violence, pacifism, and redemption: The show's finale is not only comprised by an epic fight against Firelord Ozai, but also by Aang's inner conflict to find a way *not* to kill the show's villain even when all his friends advocate for it as justified and necessary. The ideological implications of such narratives can hardly be overstated. A protagonist such as *Dirty Harry*'s

(Siegel 1971) Callahan (played by Clint Eastwood) had generations of cinema audiences rooting for the police officer's "take no prisoners" approach that does not "follow the rules." Within the framework of the fictional film – which aligns itself strongly with Callahan's point of view – it is strongly suggested to find this ethical framework acceptable and form allegiances with the fact that Harry kills the criminal Scorpio with a '44 Magnum in cold blood. This seems highly troubling in hindsight when police violence and institutional racism cannot be overlooked in real life. Similar concerns were brought up with respect to torture as a "necessary" procedure to gain information in post-9/11 culture when TV shows like *24* (Surnow et al. 2001–2010) normalized such forms of violent "interrogation" through fictional scenarios in which the deeds of its protagonist Jack Bauer seem justified (see O'Mathúna 2010; Kearns and Young 2018).

A more recent example of a comic book character that their rights holders actively tried to disentangle from misplaced allegiances is Marvel's The Punisher (e.g., Baron 1987–2018), Frank Castle, whose logo had become a symbol for right-wing extremists for years: Just like Harry Callahan, The Punisher – an "anti-hero" and ex-soldier who brutally murders criminals – represented a White supremacist ethos and worldview for some audience members. We could state that one (perhaps unintended, but nevertheless far from accidental) interpretation of the character's thematic dimension gained too much prominence in his public perception for the publisher. When his iconic skull logo appeared more and more in White supremacist contexts and was even worn by rioters during the January 6, 2021, insurrection at the US Capitol, the publisher rebranded the character in early 2022 through a new logo and more strongly fictionalized plotlines (see McGuire 2022). Whether this was effective is certainly another question (comic author Erik Larsen commented on social media that the stronger move to alienate hate groups among the characters' fans would have been to rewrite him as a queer hero, thereby completely altering his thematic affordances, see ErikLarsen 2022).

Another angle of criticism concerns how "good vs. evil" are often linked to unrelated properties within the symptomatic dimension of characters' meanings, such as physical attributes of conventional "beauty" vs. "ugliness." Disney's animated films have a notorious history of "queer coding" villains, for instance. *The Little Mermaid*'s (Clements and Musker 1989) Ursula, *Aladdin*'s (Clements and Musker 1992) Jafar, or *The Lion King*'s (Allers and Minkoff 1994) Scar are all represented with character traits linked to the opposite gender (see Putnam 2013). Jafar, for instance, has a slender body, a high voice, eyeshadow, and wears more feminine clothes than the "straight" protagonists. Queer people are thus intrinsically linked to characters that audiences are likely to form oppositions to, which is hardly subjective within *Aladdin*'s plot. These implicit character traits are clearly coupled with villainy and other negative attributes such as cowardice. In order to get a clearer picture of how characters and their attributes are dependent on plot and narrative events, however, we will have to analyze them on the synthetic level as actants in the next chapter.

2 Characters as Actants in Narrative Events

The present chapter is going to return to one of the most prominent approaches to the analysis of characters, considering them primarily in relation to the *plot* of a given narrative media text. As we have pointed out in our introduction, structuralist scholars sharply criticized the commonplace notion to approach fictional or fictionalized characters in the same ways as actual persons. Instead, they advised to regard them entirely as bundles of semantic information (legible as character traits) ascribed to them by the plot – the narrative information as it is provided by the media text. Roland Barthes (1975) addressed these "hubs" or "nodal points" of semantic information as "agents," Algirdas Julien Greimas (1983) as "actors" or "actants." The idea behind both approaches is that plots and characters can only be determined in relation to each other. Discussing characters in terms of plot, however, goes back to Aristotle (2018), to whom protagonists in drama were only understandable as "agents" or "performers" of the dramatic action as well (see Rimmon-Kenan 1993, 34; Bertetti and Thibault 2022). As a technical term devoid of misunderstandings in regular language use, *actant* remains a highly useful concept, although in the present chapter we will use it in a slightly different way than Greimas to remain compatible with our earlier approaches.

Addressing transmedia characters from the perspective of specific plots poses many challenges, however, since an almost indeterminate number of media texts – each with their specific structures of plots and narrative events – may exist. A lens on characters as actants nevertheless remains highly valuable in this regard, as most transmedia characters appear in recurring actantial roles (see Hogan 2011) throughout their many (trans)medial appearances: Peter Parker will usually be fighting crime as Spider-Man while struggling to manage his job(s) at the same time, while Lara Croft is perpetually chasing after artifacts and buried treasures whether we encounter her in computer games, films, or comic books. Transmedia characters are thus especially shaped by regularity, standardization, and repetition, determining them perhaps more than any assumed inner life. Only then can their established actantial roles, as well as their narrative trajectories and their respective narrative agency in specific scenes, be punctuated by unexpected variations. Thus, after 35 years of being depicted as a threatening villain with great regularity, Darth Vader eventually appeared in a series of picture

DOI: 10.4324/9781003298793-4

books showing his struggles as a father (see Brown 2012; 2013; 2014). Actantial variations such as these are noteworthy and interesting, precisely because they undermine the established role of a character in new contexts. Similar strategies are frequently employed in fan fiction through the construction of alternate universes in which the characters of a "gritty, realistic" fantasy franchise like *Game of Thrones*, for instance, might be cast in the actantial roles of traditional fairy tales (see Kustritz 2016).

Naturally, the construction of plots and the distribution of narrative information will differ drastically between heterogeneous media forms and their affordances – being mono-modal or multimodal (as in novels vs. TV), linear or interactive (as in films vs. video games), or serialized or self-contained (cartoon strips vs. graphic novels). Chapters 4–8 will address some of these media-specific affordances and constraints in more detail. Sophisticated narratologies for all of these media forms and formats are well suited to analyzing their narrative structures and comparing their overlapping as well as diverging affordances for constructing complex plots (see Thon 2016). It has also become clear, however, that many aspects of narrative events and plots are transmedial as well. The most basic components of narratives discussed in the following will be the concept of *narrative events* and their constitutive participants – *actants*. If both are related to each other, it will become clear that characters have different degrees and types of narrative agency in different medial, generic, and historical contexts. A basic understanding of these dimensions is then refined by a closer look at narrative conventions – tropes – shaped by these circumstances. A final section will then provide examples of how actantial roles and characters' respective narrative agency can be negotiated within individual works for surprising effects.

2.1 Narrative Events

Starting with a very basic definition, an actant in a narrative text is everything that influences, conditions, or changes the flow of events, especially at "moments of risk (when things can go 'either way')" (see also Prince 1996, 98; Toolan 2001, 24). Such points in the narrative, which Seymour Chatman addressed as "kernels of narration" (1978, 50–56) or Umberto Eco as "disjunctions of probability" (1995, 31) generate a network of alternative, unrealized courses of actions, an "underlying system of purely virtual embedded narratives" (Ryan 1991b, 156). Probability disjunctions can be seen most clearly in plots when characters are presented with distinct either/or choices. Such is certainly the case when Morpheus in *The Matrix* (Wachowski and Wachowski 1999) offers Neo the (by now almost proverbial) alternative between a blue pill – remaining oblivious but comfortable within his everyday reality – and a red pill – deciding for an uncertain future in which his perception of the world is sure to crumble. Only the red pill is driving the plot of the film forward through subsequent narrative events, while the blue one represents an uneventful life that would likely also be pointless to follow as audiences. Hence, even though we might not be particularly surprised by Neo's decision – we *are* expecting 136 minutes of plot-driven excitement, after all – we understand that it is a serious, perhaps irreversible choice for the character, which makes the event decisive as we assume Neo's consciousness frame.

The notion of *narrative events*, moments within a story that indicate a relevant, irreversible change of states – the death of a character being one of the most drastic ones – is hence a foundational one in narratology (see Hühn 2014). Christian Kock defined narrativity itself in these very terms: "By narrative I understand a text about a state of affairs in which characters are subject to events" (Kock 1978, 203). Narrative events are thus characterized by certain features such as unexpectedness, singularity, and unusualness (see Schmid 2003; Herman 2005), or in the most general terms: *Relevance* to the audience since they consider them relevant to a character respectively. A "microcosm" for analyzing narrative structures can be found in comic strips consisting of three to four panels only, analyzed extensively by comic book scholars such as Neil Cohn (2013). Traditional serialized comic strips like Charles Schultz' *Peanuts* (1950–2000), Bill Watterson's *Calvin & Hobbes* (1985–1995), or Jim Davis' *Garfield* (1978–present) can be read in any order, meaning that the individual strips rarely retain relevant information from one episode to the next. The three to four available panels must thus contain the bare elements of narrative in themselves, usually employed to construct some kind of humorous or witty punchline. Many or most contemporary webcomic strips such as Jerry Holkins' *Penny Arcade* (1998–present), Rob DenBleyker and others' *Cyanide and Happiness* (2005–present), or Tim Buckley's *Ctrl+Alt+Del* (2002–present) still follow this pattern.

Cohn points out that the bare narrative grammar of these strips consists of up to four elements, which are distributed over the available panels, as in one example from *Calvin & Hobbes* from November 22, 1985 (Watterson n.d.). In the first panel, Calvin's father says "Good night, Calvin" to his son and his plush animal, the tiger Hobbes, Calvin responding with "Night, dad!" The second panel shows only Calvin and his tiger, the boy apparently still addressing his father: "Hey! Aren't you going to say goodnight to Hobbes?!" In the third panel, the father merely dispassionately repeats "Good night, Hobbes," followed, in the final panel, by Calvin's imagined response of Hobbes (the series recurrently represents Calvin's subjective worldview in which his imaginary friend is an actual character): "That's IT?! No Story? No Smooch??" According to Cohn's structure, the first panel usually works as an "establisher," setting up the scene and giving readers all the necessary information about the characters (a boy – Calvin –, his father, and his stuffed tiger Hobbes), a setting (a bedroom at an unspecified point in time near the present day), and a situation (bed-time for Calvin). An "initial" then introduces some kind of conflict or tension – the anticipation of a narrative event – which could be resolved in distinct ways. In this example, Calvin's question directly expresses the probability disjunction at play here: Will his father say good night to Hobbes, or will he refuse? The "peak" then features the actual narrative event that the strip is all about, answering the dramaturgical (and, in this example, literal) question: The father (somewhat reluctantly) *does* say good night to Hobbes. The fact that this is rather a non-event feeds into the strip's punchline, undermining the audiences' regular expectation for the final panel:

Instead of a "release," establishing some sort of conclusion or showing the consequences of the preceding event, this strip directly comments upon the (non-)event humorously: "That's it?"

Within longer narratives of more complex media formats such as novels, films, TV shows, narrative video games, or longer comic books, narrative events cannot be identified as clearly and are usually overlapping and interwoven. "Eventful" moments are especially visible when they are as distinct as possible from each other. The TV show *Squid Game* (Dong-hyuk 2021–present), for instance, reiterates a game-like event structure familiar from progenitors like the franchises *Battle Royale* (e.g., Takami 1999), *Hunger Games* (e.g., Collins 2008; Ross 2012); or *Alice in Borderland* (e.g., Aso 2010–2016) (it is a *recurring trope*, as we will discuss later). Protagonists such as *Squid Game*'s Seong Gi-Hun (portrayed by Lee Jung-jae) find themselves in a death match where all 456 initial participants have to compete for survival. In each of the six rounds, unnamed as well as established characters die by the dozens. Their survival would have given the entire series of subsequent games a different outcome. The six games can be considered distinct events for the characters, containing their (realized or unrealized potential) individual deaths as even more distinct narrative events. Granted, most narrative events are much more subtle, their evaluation a matter of interpretation. Narratologists often distinguish between "ordinary events" and those relevant to the overall narration, the "point" of the story that would be part of any summary or recap (see Kock 1978, 222), for instance, on Wikipedia or in episode guides. On the global level of narrative texts as a whole, such events are often characterized by the literal or metaphorical (semantic) "border crossings" of actants, as Juri Lotman (2005) has elaborated: characters moving from a stable, "safe" zone into a hostile one, or from the realm of the living into the realm of the dead. On the most foundational level, most plots are then triggered either by "a person goes on a journey" (leaving the confines of their ordinary world) or the other way around, when "a stranger comes to town" (someone entering the ordinary world who introduces uncertainty) (see Gardner 1984, 203). But just as the global thematic meaning of a text is beyond the scope of this volume, we will also address narrative events primarily with regard to the characters themselves. These then either drastically *alter* important character traits, or they *obstruct* imminent changes (that *could* have taken place).

We can distinguish different kinds of eventful changes to a character by mapping them onto the three fundamental dimensions of the person schema, or the *basic type* (see chapter 1), as identified by Eder et al. (2010, 13; see also Kunz 2019, 68–69): corporeality (attributes of a character's body), psyche (mental states ascribed to the character), and sociality (all qualities emerging from their social roles and interactions within the storyworld). Events can thus alter (a) a character's corporeality: When Bran Stark is thrown out of a tower at the beginning of *Game of Thrones* (Benioff et al. 2011–2019) to remain paraplegic from that point on (Se01E01), it drastically changes the character, as it not only massively limits his ability to (inter)act within a storyworld focused on physical prowess – he is also seen as "broken" in the violently ableist world of Westeros. Interrelated to this, but often independently, events might then alter (b) a character's psyche, as when Walter White, the protagonist of the TV series *Breaking Bad* (Gilligan et al. 2008–2013), learns that he has terminal lung cancer (Se01E01), causing him to commit increasingly ruthless crimes as a drug boss, or when, in the season one finale of CBS's *The Good Place* (Schur et al. 2016–2020, Se01E013), it is revealed to the main characters that they are not actually in heaven, forcing them to re-evaluate their lives. Often, the first two types of events are again connected to alterations in (c) a character's sociality, for example, when Bruce Wayne's parents are murdered, which causes not only a psychological trauma that will create his later persona as Batman but also turns him into an orphan to be raised by his butler. Some narrative events are mainly social, however, as when Rob Stark is proclaimed "King in the North" in episode ten of *Game of Thrones'* first season, something that other aspirants to the throne of Westeros cannot be expected to tolerate (initiating many more narrative events to resolve the ineluctable conflicts in the ensuing "war of the five kings").

What these initial cases show is that whatever counts as "extraordinary" or "eventful" in longer forms of narratives must remain not only a matter of interpretation and context but can only ever be a *relative* feature of any plot: Some events – such as a character's death – are more eventful than others (see Hühn 2008). Judgments about eventfulness are also open to revision as the plot progresses within a series. When Luke Skywalker loses his hand in *The Empire Strikes Back* (Kershner 1980), at first, this certainly seems like an irreversible event that drastically alters his abilities to act and interact in future events. It turns out, however, that he shall receive a technological prosthesis immediately afterward so that the impact of this impairment is softened to a degree that would not have any lasting consequences for the plot – and neither on his fighting abilities or his psyche from that point on. Even characters' deaths are far from irreversible in the realm of fantastic storyworlds: Superhero comics are notorious for bringing dead characters back to life (such as the second Robin, Jason Todd, or the second Flash, Barry Allen, in DC's titles) through supernatural means (often, this counts as a "retcon," as we will discuss in chapters 7–8). This saliently distinguishes serial forms of storytelling from more closed forms of narration like non-serialized (graphic) novels or standalone films, since the former can always be revised so that no event's outcomes are ever truly final.

More generally, however, eventfulness cannot be judged with respect to "reality" exclusively or even primarily, but remains subject to the respective storyworld and its (often generic) ethos as discussed in the preceding chapter. The introduction of magic and supernatural beings, for example, counts as eventful in *The Chronicles of Narnia* novels by C. S. Lewis and their film adaptations (Adamson 2005; 2008; Apted 2010), while being entirely humdrum in Terry Pratchett's *Discworld* novels and their adaptations or in the comic book series *Saga* (2012–present) by Brian K. Vaughan and Fiona Staples. Being physically assaulted is traumatic in many coming-of-age films such as *The Perks of Being a Wallflower* (Chbosky 2012), while physical conflicts are presented as ordinary in many superhero narratives (at least for the heroes themselves). The storyworld of the manga (ONE and Murata 2012–present) and anime (Matsui et al. 2015–2019) series *One-Punch Man* is subject to world-threatening invasions by monsters and aliens on a daily basis, while the "Battle of New York" in the initial *The Avengers* (Whedon 2012) movie comprises the first global alien attack in the Marvel Cinematic Universe that alters the (self-)perception of regular human beings substantially for all following narratives (or, at least, it was initially referred to as such). Events are thus always related to specific characters whose perspectives – their consciousness frames – we once again have to adopt in order to evaluate plots. It must also be said that audiences can always be in disagreement about these qualifications: The revelation that Batman's third Robin (Tim Drake) identifies as bisexual in *Batman: Urban Legends #6* (Zdarsky et al. 2021) when he discovers he is developing romantic feelings for his male friend Bernard was lamented as "merely political" by certain commentators who demanded from writers to "stick to" adventurous stories – to what they saw as "actual" narrative events befitting the character (see Hutton 2021). To others, however, Tim's coming out was precisely a major psychic as well as a social event for him, especially with regard to his earlier, mostly unsuccessful relationships with female partners in previous comics. Whatever our interpretation of specific narrative situations will be, however, plots essentially *do* consist of a range of changing states and transitions from one relevant situation to another.

Pictorial media, by necessity, contain a plethora of details that *could* be considered eventful, but most will be irrelevant to the development of the plot (future events). In the opening of Disney's animated film *Soul* (Docter 2020), for instance, the unsuccessful musician Joe Gardner is told that he gets the chance to participate in a jazz concert with a famous singer – a major social event he is hoping will change his life. When he tells friends on the phone about this while walking down the streets, a variety of things are shown to happen in rapid succession: He dodges a father with his stroller, passes a construction site where a rope breaks, crosses a busy street, and avoids a barking dog. All of these are seemingly irrelevant to the plot (and to Gardner) until a consequential narrative event takes place as he accidentally stumbles into an open manhole – and dies. The story does not end there, however, it follows his soul into the afterlife, which forms the overall trajectory of the film. If the audience cares about Gardner, they might consider different outcomes – probability disjunctions – even before that. When the rope breaks at the construction site, this is an event already in that it does *not* already result in Gardner's death or injury – thus preventing imminent change for the protagonist. The repetition of avoided dangers to his life *foreshadows* the major accident which *does* kill him later, adding narrative suspense and anticipation.

2.2 Recurring Narrative Structures

Characters are able to anticipate different states of their surrounding storyworld themselves, due to their intentionality (their inner life), as has been discussed in the previous chapter. Some of these states they strive toward, and some of them they seek to prevent. Characters thus have an awareness of the forking "train tracks" of plot connected via (realized and unrealized) narrative events. Kai

Mikkonen, a comic book narratologist, summarized the reciprocal relationship between events and characters as follows:

> The characters' actions create events and move the plot forward, and the meaning of an event is typically filtered through what we know about the participants and how they perceive the events. The events that are related in the story, in turn, can reveal and illustrate the agents' properties.
>
> (Mikkonen 2017, 179)

A narrative's plot structure is then comprised of a series of narrative events, each of which will have a certain *tellability*: Together, they make up the "point" of a story that we would give in a summary. The tellability of narrative events often functions as a "hinge" or a "relay" to a story's thematic meaning. The story of Brian K. Vaughan's comic book series (together with Pia Guerra and others, 2002–2008, as well as the recent TV adaption, Vaughan et al. 2021) *Y: The Last Man* is initiated by a global event that kills every human and animal with a Y-chromosome except for the protagonist Yorick and his male monkey Ampersand. Not surprisingly, the series is then thematically concerned with issues of gender, exploring in detail how global politics, arts, religion, or other aspects of culture(s) are changing through the sudden absence of men. Yorick, who hardly lives up to hegemonic expectations of masculinity, embodies many of these topics throughout his journeys. The narrative trajectory of the TV show *Sex Education* (Nunn et al. 2019–present), to take up another example, is initiated when Otis Milburn, a student at Moordale Secondary School, sets up an informal "sex therapy clinic" together with his friend Maeve to help the students with the confusions of puberty. This narrative event does not only change Otis' social status considerably, since he was a rather shy boy before, only able to advise other students about their suppressed problems and unresolved relationship issues because his mother is a professional sex therapist. This development also signposts in no uncertain terms the overall thematic concern of *Sex Education*: The show's sex-positive focus on frustrations, disappointments, and the many taboos surrounding school education set it apart from other high school comedies, and many of these topics and contradictions are again epitomized by Otis himself who starts the whole "sex clinic" business only in order to get closer to Maeve whom he seems unable to communicate with in any regular setting. Characters participating in major narrative events can thus be described by their "thematic roles," as Greimas has put it (1982, 344), and their function with respect to the overall thematic meaning of the plot.

Many media texts, especially in genre fiction, feature recurring narrative structures across works and storyworlds. Drawing on prototypes in myth, anthropologist Joseph Campbell (2008) developed the "universal" model of *the hero's journey*, which he identified as the basic structure for myths and popular stories in most cultures. Even though Campbell's claims on the model's universality have since been disputed (see Dundes 2016, 395–401), the basic structure of the "hero's journey" is still used exceedingly in contemporary popular culture.

Campbell's model includes 12 stations that heroes have to complete. An unusual incident or traumatic event initiates a call to adventure. The departure from everyday mundanity is followed by a path of trials and concludes with the return of the hero with valuable experiences that have fundamentally changed *him* in response (for Campbell, the hero is invariably male, a limitation that has led to the development of multiple models of the heroine's journey, e.g., Murdock 1990; Schmidt 2001; Frankel 2017). Campbell's model enjoys popularity not only as a structural pattern for countless works such as *The Lord of the Rings*, the *Star Wars* saga, *The Matrix*, *Harry Potter*, or *The Lion King*. It can also be identified in super-hero comics or many popular manga and anime. Game designers have similarly been advised to arrange the tasks their protagonists must perform into a similar "hero's journey" of physical and spiritual ordeals (see Dunniway 2000). Many narrative formats, often situated within specific genres, have developed distinct prototypical narrative structures. What is called the "Classical Hollywood Cinema" (see Bordwell 2015), for instance, usually revolves around *two* complimentary plotlines (or event structures): one features the main character as a hero who is to overcome external struggles or to defeat a villain (introducing or resisting changes for their social world), and one revolving around a (usually heterosexual) love interest, thereby changing their social/romantic/sexual relationship status. Such films then end with a danger avoided and a couple united. While many such generalizations are perhaps too abstract to deepen our understanding of individual media texts or their characters profoundly, a view of stories as chains of probability disjunctions (of narrative structures) may reveal surprising similarities between characters that seem entirely unrelated in terms of character traits, narrative settings, or storyworld contexts. We are instead able to describe in great detail how plot structures are adapted across medial, generic, and historical contexts. Clint Eastwood's unnamed Western protagonist in *A Fistful of Dollars* (Leone 1964), for instance, undergoes the same narrative journey as the samurai hero in *Yojimbo* (1961) played by Toshiro Mifune, a plot structure both films mirrored from Dashiell Hammett's 1929 noir novel *Red Harvest* (2003). The basic chain of narrative events could equally be summarized as "a stranger comes to a place where a violent conflict between two parties takes place, both parties hire the hero alternatively, but the hero plays them against each other." The same series of narrative events was later reprised in the film *Last Man Standing* (Hill 1996) starring Bruce Willis, in Brian Azzarello's and Richard Corben's comic *Cage* (2002) featuring the protagonist Luke Cage, in Anthony Bourdan's, Joel Rose's, and Langdon Foss' graphic novel *Get Jiro!* (2012), and in many more – even though all these works showcase protagonists in entirely unrelated story-worlds, generic and historical settings. In the same vein, Disney's *The Lion King* (Allers and Minkoff 1994) closely follows Shakespeare's *Hamlet* in the play's most salient plot structures ("A king gets murdered by his brother, the young heir is undecided whether he should avenge his father or abdicate the throne, leaves the kingdom, but later returns for revenge"). Similarities between these texts and their characters emerge only when viewed in terms of actantial semiotics. We can now also describe in more detail how many serial forms of narrative put their protagonists in recurring actantial roles from one episode to the next. Procedurals like *Law & Order* (Wolf et al. 1990–2010) or *CSI: Crime Scene Investigation* (Zuiker et al. 2000–2015) feature another case to be solved every episode, while in *House* (Shore et al. 2004–2012) or *Grey's Anatomy* (Rhimes et al. 2005–present) a different type of sickness or disease serves as a recurring "culprit-actant" every episode. Fantasy or Sci-Fi shows like *The X-Files* (Carter et al. 1993–2002), *Smallville* (Gough et al. 2001–2011), or *Supernatural* (Kripke et al. 2005–2020) in turn often present a different "monster of the week" every episode (see TV Tropes, "Monster of the Week") – more about this in chapter 8 on seriality!

If narrative events consist of various participating entities, however, some of them are clearly *not* (individual) characters. This is what the term actant addresses on a more general level. Vladimir Propp (1984) was the first to describe seven general roles for characters within Russian folk tales (such as the hero, the villain, the helper). In a given folk tale, however, the same character can perform more than one of these and thus assume a number of actantial roles, just like multiple characters can assume one of these roles together (in the film adaptation of Agatha Christie's *Murder in the Orient Express*, Branagh 2017, for instance, it turns out that all of the passengers except the detective assumed the role of the murderer). Greimas applied this model to literary narratives in general and posited six broad actantial roles on an even more abstract level (sender, receiver, object, subject, helper, opponent, see 1982, 5). He assumed a kind of "narrative grammar" that is as fixed as the grammatical structure of subject, object, etc. within linguistic sentences. These roles can then be filled by specific characters which Greimas dubbed "actors" (1982, 7): The "actant" of the opponent is thus filled by the "actors" Jafar in *Aladdin* (Clements and Musker 1992), by Scar in *The Lion King* (Allers and Minkoff 1994), or by Gaston in *Beauty and the Beast* (Trousdale and Wise 1991). Not only has Greimas' terminology often led to some confusion, his fixed set of actantial roles also does hardly do justice to the great variety of stories and plots throughout media. We will hence be using the term *actant* in a wider sense, neglecting the distinction from "actors" (a term retained here for real-life performers playing characters). An actant in the following will be any entity that is a necessary participant in a specific narrative event opening up distinct, but contradictory outcomes (probability disjunctions) (see Bertetti 2019 for transmedia characters).

2.3 Non-human Actants and Composite Identity

An actant in these terms can obviously not be conflated with a character who is always imagined as a (usually fictional) individual with intentional thought. The radioactive or genetically altered spider that bites Peter Parker to turn him into Spider-Man could hardly be considered a character – it fosters no salient interior motivation and we don't need to attribute any kind of consciousness frame to it in order to follow the story – but it certainly is a decisive participant to get the plot moving. Actants can also be comprised of larger collectives – such as a "crowd of people" whose individual identities are never even revealed to the audiences.

In other words, while some actants *are* individuated as characters, others are collective or even non-figurative and entirely invisible (such as the deadly Kalavirus in the *12 Monkeys* TV show [Suckle et al. 2015–2018] or the Tree-Rush virus in *One Piece* [Oda 1997–present]). Zombies in shows like *The Walking Dead* (Darabont et al. 2010–2022) are an entirely unindividuated actant, as are many other hostile collectives like the Orcs in the *Lord of the Rings* books and films. A more mundane collective (and largely only ever implied) actant within the *Hunger Games* books and films is certainly "the public" following Katniss Everdeen and her trials via the storyworld's equivalent of live TV. This public is only ever shown partially and in glimpses, for example, in the form of spectators during the opening ceremony of the first book/film's games, or through the results of its collective actions, such as the additional supplies Katniss receives from private sponsors. Another, slightly different type of collective actant would be political factions and institutions: In James S.A. Corey's *The Expanse* series of science fiction novels (e.g., 2011), as well as its TV adaptation of the same name (Fergus et al. 2015–2022), multiple factions are competing for power in the solar system. These factions – the United Nations of Earth and Luna, the Martian Congressional Republic, and the Outer Planets Alliance – are sometimes represented by individual characters, but also act as units, declaring war or recognizing each other's sovereignty. Some actants are even entirely abstract and impersonal to begin with, like "The Force" in the *Star Wars* franchise, the "One Power" in the *Wheel of Time* books (e.g., Jordan 1990) and TV show (Judkins et al. 2021–present), or the "Speed Force" of DC's Flash character (see, e.g., the TV show by Berlanti et al. 2014–present).

What does it mean that actants are almost always hybrid entities? Most characters are able to fulfill their actantial role within the plot – triggering events and being influenced by them – only due to specific objects that form salient parts of their actantial identity. The classic example is the "knight" who can only influence the narrative the way he does by virtue of a "horse," a "sword," a "shield," and so on. Tony Stark would not be Iron Man – or, indeed, any sort of superhero – without his armor suit. Within the *Demon Slayer* manga (Gotouge 2016–2020) and anime series (Fujio et al. 2019–present), a special kind of sword is needed to kill demons. Only after protagonist Tanjiro receives his Ichinin sword is he able to introduce "lethal events" for demons, thereby "unlocking" countless fight scenes with distinct possible outcomes (Tanjiro *could* die himself in any of these battles after all). Not surprisingly, some fictional artifacts are as well-known and iconic as the heroes that use them, and many characters are recognized by these items: Indiana Jones by his whip, Batman by his Batarangs, Cloud Strife from *Final Fantasy VII* (Square 1997) by his Buster Sword. Characters-as-actants are thus always hybrids of human and non-human entities, and objects can even be considered actants – but not characters – in isolation (see Langkjær and Jensen 2019). If a door is locked, a key is needed. The key is then another participant needed for the event of unlocking an originally closed entrance, as in one of the final trials of *Harry Potter and the Philosopher's Stone* (Rowling 1997) (in which the key's ability to fly further emphasizes its role as an actant in its own right). The same goes for all kinds of (narratively relevant) artifacts such as Sauron's ring (in *The Lord of the Rings*), which motivates the fellowship to walk to Mordor to destroy it, or the Infinity Stones that Thanos collects to alter the fate of the universe within the *Avengers* movies. Actants can even be abstract music pieces such as Kate Bush's song "Running up that Hill" which, in *Stranger Things* (Duffer et al. 2016–present, Se04E04), has the power to break a powerful spell by a demon and protect the character Max from an evil, potentially lethal enchantment. Actants-as-objects that are central to the plot, motivating characters to hunt for them, to obtain them, or to destroy them, are often referred to as "MacGuffins," a term attributed to writer Angus MacPhail and director Alfred Hitchcock (see IGN staff 2012). A classic example is the Holy Grail in the Arthurian legend, more contemporary ones include the "Maltese Falcon" statuette from the film of the same name, the plans for the Death Star in *Star Wars: A New Hope* (Lucas 1977), or the briefcase in *Pulp Fiction* (Tarantino 1994). In fantasy and Sci-Fi stories, there has been use of the made-up term "phlebotinum" (attributed to writer Joss Whedon) for any fictional material or substance that alters the laws of physics or the world to achieve a similar effect (see Tropedia, "Applied Phlebotinum"): Kryptonite is thus needed to paralyze Superman, while all the major narrative events in *The Expanse* revolve around the emergence of a mysterious "protomolecule" of extraterrestrial origin. We can now distinguish actants that are characters more clearly from actants that are not according to two different types of events: *Actions* and *occurrences*. "Actions are events resulting from acts of volition, while occurrences are events not resulting from acts of volition" (Elleström 2019, 81). This distinction is crucial in Lars Elleström's transmedial account of narration, regardless of what media we apply it to: "[T]here is a substantial difference between things that happen by themselves, because of physical forces freely operating in the universe, and things that happen because of cerebral processes" (Elleström 2019, 80).

What is *neither* a character *nor* an actant, then…? Many elements within a media text do not contribute to any narrative event within the storyworld, merely serving as a form of "decoration" or "backdrop" specifying the setting. In literary narratives, this function is fulfilled by descriptions (which can be longer or shorter without altering the plot). Such relevance is sometimes revealed in hindsight only, although audiences are often encouraged to anticipate the actantial roles of objects. A transmedial convention often addressed as "Chekhov's Gun" refers to the expectation (attributed to writer Anton Chekhov) that, if a playwright introduces a "gun" within a drama or a novel, it will likely be used at some later point in the plot (see TV Tropes, "Chekhov's Gun"). If such foreshadowing turns out to be correct, the gun is revealed to be an actant. When the character Annie in *Attack on Titan* (Kinoshita et al. 2013–2022) conspicuously puts on a plain metal ring before embarking on an adventure (Se01E23), this detail seems entirely irrelevant to the narrative progression at first. Not surprisingly to many viewers, however, the ring turns out to be of major importance later as it contains a secret device that enables her to transform into an evil titan, even when she is chained and gagged. The ring is thus granted an actantial role that some audience members might have anticipated. As Birger Langkjær and Charlotte

Sun Jensen have shown, however, the narrative agency of action heroes and heroines often consists precisely in their "explorative and inventive approach to the physical environment which is skillfully used as an often surprising resource to eliminate and kill adversaries" (2019, 267). In other words, turning background objects into part of their actantial identity in surprising ways – a ballpen becoming a deadly weapon in the hands of film hero Jason Bourne (Liman 2002) – not only defines many characters' ability to act within represented situations but also shapes the narrative as a physical, action-driven one in turn.

Different media and genre traditions have cultivated specific conventions to "signpost" what might be relevant as an actant later in the plot. Savvy members of the audience are literate in these codes. In comic books and animated films, for instance, the scenery and setting are often drawn in a completely different style than the characters and the objects they interact with (only the latter shaping their possibilities to introduce events within the storyworld). In the Disney animated film *Mulan* (Cook and Bancroft 1998), the supernatural guardian spirit Mushu is represented in the style of cel-animation: His body consists of flat colors and clear outlines, easily repeated and modified in up to 24 frames per second. Backgrounds, however, are usually static, so they are painted in more detail and continuous color transitions when the slides remain static against the foreground (see LaMarre 2009). When Mushu is sent to awaken "the great stone dragon," this creature could be an important character-as-actant later on. As audiences get to see the "stone dragon," however, he is drawn in the style of backgrounds, clearly distinguished from characters. It is thus easy to predict that Mushu will *not* be able to "awaken" him: He remains a piece of inanimate architecture. Instead of introducing the Stone Dragon as an actant able to protect Mulan in the future, Mushu then has to fill that actantial role himself. By contrast, manga frequently depict objects in a realistic style in order to single them out as actants in their own right, but as inanimate objects to be looked at, in contrast to the abstracted cartoon style employed for objects as extensions of characters – as hybrid actants (McCloud 1993, 44). Actantial roles are thus often coupled with different aesthetics and pictorial styles in "cartoonish" media. This includes video games, where backgrounds are often clearly distinguished from items that characters can use to influence events. Jürgen Sorg (2009) has addressed this as the inherent "agential structure" of a given video game (see also Christensen 2022). One of the most salient examples of the visibility of such a structure would be the *Lego Star Wars* series of games (2005–2022), in which objects consisting of virtual Lego bricks can be used, destroyed, or re-built, whereas all other parts of the game world are largely static.

The composite nature of actants also becomes evident in video games when it can be astonishingly hard to differentiate between characters and the items they use after they have collected them. The main character of the game *Portal* (Valve 2007) is Chell, a human being we know very little about. The whole plot of the game, as well as the actual game mechanics – something we will analyze in more detail in chapter 6 – both rest on Chell's most prominent item, the

Aperture Science Handheld Portal Device enabling her to open up portals and solve complex spatial puzzles with it. Without the portal gun, none of the potential outcomes of *Portal's* storyworld could be realized. As an actant, Chell is thus a composite of Chell, the character, and her device (as well as the countless other items she can use within the storyworld). In video game theory, the "racecar problem" poses this question differently for the countless racing games in which we never get a name or a picture of any human controlling the car (see Backe 2022). Is the character in a game like *TrackMania* (Nadeo 2020) thus the "car," or an unspecified driver? Researchers such as Rune Klevjer posit that we experience ourselves driving the car directly, without any recourse to characters (see Klevjer 2006, 116–117, as well as Klevjer 2022). Cognitive narratology and the principle of minimal departure would maintain, by contrast, that we are able to "fill out" the invisible driver as easily as we are able to imagine a complete human being from a simple description such as "one politician" (see also Vella 2015, 366). The difference to actually showing – and ascribing the specific character traits to – any representation of a human being would thus be only a matter of salience, or of highlighting their otherwise only "implied" features: Any racecar can be expected to contain an "implicit" driver-as-character, even if we know nothing about this being. Looking at racing games in terms of actantial semiotics solves this problem differently, as actants are *always* hybrid entities, defined only by their ability to participate in narrative events within the constructed world: Racecar and driver are then one hybrid actant (or, in Hans-Joachim Backe's terms, a "composite avatar," Backe 2022, 241) to begin with. Both views are complimentary anyways: If we look at characters as continuous conscious frames, we consider them as analogs of human beings. We then sharply distinguish their bodies and minds (as "containers" of personality) from their surroundings and objects. If we look at characters as actants, they appear as necessarily hybrid "nodal points" within the event structures of the plot – en par with other actants that are *not* characters. "Faced with the same composite avatar, different players might not only gravitate towards one view or another. Their focus might shift regularly during play" (241). Nevertheless, we could name a huge number of non-character-actants within any one story, but it would be hard to find a story that has *only* non-character-actants – we'd then be in the realm of representations about whole peoples, abstract social developments, or natural processes. In pictorial media, this is mainly the domain of essay films or essay comics like Godfrey Reggio's poetic and abstract film *Koyaanisqatsi* (1982) or Nick Sousanis' comic book PhD thesis *Unflattening* (2015) about the interrelation of language, thought, and pictoriality.

2.4 Narrative Tropes and Narrative Agency

A central idea of actantial semiotics is that there is not an infinite number of actantial roles, but a range of *recurring* ones that characters assume again and again within similar (often generic) plots. On a sufficient level of abstraction, the "hero's journey" undertaken by Frodo, Luke Skywalker, Neo, Harry Potter, or Simba could thus be analyzed as the same (or, at least, a similar) actantial role. If we consider characters as actants, we first ask for the most prominent roles that they assume within a plot – especially in relation to others: Main characters, side characters, or villains are the most general ones, which can be further distinguished in specific genre contexts. A romance or love story will need a "lover" and one or more "love interests" (two to generate romantic conflict and some eventful decision between both). A detective story often features some "investigator/detective" and a "culprit," maybe a "victim." Actantial roles thus usually come in clusters of recurring patterns that are subject to medial, generic, and historical conventions. Often, actantial roles within specific narrative events are also associated with recurring places and settings. Train tracks in the desert are connected to Western plots with their recurring actantial roles of the lone gunslinger, the sheriff, and the outlaw. Such settings signposting recurring narrative situations are sometimes addressed as "chronotopes" (Bakhtin 1981): An open-country crossroad is a chronotope that affords encounters between strangers (some of which might be hostile). A dark alleyway in New York City could be part of a noir/crime narrative like the comic book series and the film *Sin City*, but also of the superhero genre. In both generic contexts, the alleyway is associated with the narrative event of an attempted robbery by goons that can be prevented by a hero – and this can be anticipated by the audience. Many of these tropes are genre-specific: In a zombie storyworld such as that of the *Dawn of the Dead* film (Romero 1978), of the *Walking Dead* show (Darabont et al. 2010–2022) and comic (Kirkman et al. 2003–2019), or of the *I Am a Hero* manga (Hanazawa 2009–2017), for instance, a *bite* by an undead is an established trope (event type) that will turn characters into zombies themselves, equaling a delayed death – except if a zombie narrative like the *Resident Evil* videogame series (e.g., Capcom 1996) breaks with these conventions and depicts the bite as a much more negligible danger (see Perron 2016). Such recurring, often genre-specific event types also include specific moral codes, and a generic ethos, that will be different in a present-day legal drama in contrast to a fantasy novel. This ethos, mediated through the consciousness frame of the participating characters, once again contributes to the interpretation and evaluation of eventfulness to begin with. In the context of a Western, for example in Quentin Tarantino's *The Hateful Eight* (2015), killing another human being (if they are "outlaws") is not considered an event that might set the character apart from society. The opposite is true in murder mysteries like *Knives Out* (Johnson 2019), where identifying and determining the guilt of killers is central to the plot.

Narrative events – and the respective actantial roles of characters involved – are often repeated by media texts, turning them from elements of specific plots into stable *tropes* – recurring types of events, actantial roles, and possible outcomes that audiences can recognize and anticipate. The 1993 film *Groundhog Day* (Ramis), primarily a romantic comedy revolving around a vain, selfish character on a quest for redemption to find true love, introduced a supernatural trope into its plot: The protagonist Phil Connors is trapped in a time-loop, doomed to experience the same day over and over again. The narrative situation of someone trapped in a repeated segment of time has been used in a wide variety of generic contexts (see TV Tropes "'Groundhog Day' Loop"): In action manga and comic books such as *All You Need is Kill* (Takeuchi and Obata 2014), adapted as *Edge of Tomorrow* (Liman 2014), in the detective film *Source Code* (Jones 2011), in the Netflix drama show *Russian Doll* (Lyonne et al. 2019–present), in episodes of *Star Trek: The Next Generation* (Roddenberry et al. 1987–1994, Se05E18 "Cause and Effect"), *The X-Files* (Carter and Goodwin 1993–2002, Se06E14 "Monday"), or *Legends of Tomorrow* (Berlanti et al. 2016–2022, Se03E11 "Here I Go Again"); in the 2003 Doctor Who audio drama *Flip-Flop* written by Jonathan Morris, and also in video games such as *P.T.* (Kojima Productions 2014) or The *Legend of Zelda: Majora's Mask* (Nintendo EAD 2000). This shows that tropes can unexpectedly traverse generic contexts. In *Groundhog Day*, the "trapped in a loop" situation is resolved through another trope listed as "Epiphanic Prison" on TV Trope: After Phil accepts that he was a vain and selfish person before, he is set free from his fate without further explanation.

> [T]he only way to escape an Epiphanic Prison is to have an epiphany. The nature of the enlightenment varies. Sometimes it's self enlightenment, and understanding and mastering one's own fears lets one escape the Ontological Mystery. Sometimes it's understanding of one's surrounding, of *why* one is trapped, and thus what must be done to escape.
>
> (TV Tropes, "Epiphanic Prison," n.pag.)

Examples for Epiphanic Prisons listed on the page, spanning again across media forms and genres, include the films *The Truman Show* (Weir 1998), *The Matrix Reloaded* (Wachowski and Wachowski 2003a), or *Isn't it Romantic* (2019), the anime shows *Neon Genesis Evangelion* (Se01E25, Sadamoto 1994–2013) and *Naruto* (Se01E338, Date 2002–2007), or the comic books *The Sandman* (#4, 4, Gaiman et al. 1989–1996) and *Green Lantern Corps Annual* (#2, Venditti et al. 2014).

Audiences are often highly aware of these patterns, as can be seen on collaborative online platforms such as *TV Tropes*, *All The Tropes*, or *Tropedia* which are collecting and cataloging recurring popular tropes across media. Although these databases are not intended as academic resources – the different categories of tropes are often overlapping and the descriptions are humorous – they remain important indicators for audiences' awareness of recurring narrative patterns. *TV Tropes* list countless examples across narratives in film, TV, manga, anime, comic books, and video games for each recurring event type, such as the "Hannibal Lecture" (in which a captured or interrogated villain turns the tables around by proving to the hero that they both are "not so different" from each other), or the "Logic Bomb" (in which a computer or an artificial intelligence can only be defeated by paradoxical questions that force it to self-destruct).

Some media texts explicitly reflect on the tropes and roles included in their plots. The Marvel streaming series *Loki* (Waldron et al. 2021–present) could be said to revolve almost entirely around its eponymous protagonist's struggle with his actantial role: In the first episode, Loki learns that his destiny has so far been controlled by a supernatural bureaucratic institution, the time variance authority

(TVA), which has predestined him to "cause pain and suffering and death [...] all so that others can achieve their best versions of themselves" (Se01E01). This institution (again a non-human actant), and the characters responsible for its formation, become the main antagonists of the series, destroying all characters who deviate from their set roles. While the ending of the show's first season is unclear on whether Loki has actually managed to escape his actantial role as an archetypal villain, it does make a metanarrative argument for the diversification of actantial roles and tropes through subversion, or at least variation.

Variation can be an interesting means of modifying tropes or charging them with new meanings. The horror show *Lovecraft Country* (Green et al. 2020–present), based on a novel by Matt Ruff of the same name (2016), uses each of its episodes to place characters in a series of stable horror tropes adopted to surprising effects. The title refers to the writer H.P. Lovecraft whose novels and short stories invented a range of tropes and conventions, sometimes codified as "Cosmic Horror Stories" (see TV Tropes, "Cosmic Horror Story"). Lovecraft's writing was also permeated with racism, sexism, and ableism so that the inconceivable horrors of ancient evil and dark gods were systematically equated with a racialized "other" of non-White protagonists. *Lovecraft Country* addresses this tension thematically as it is set in the 1950s with a cast of mostly Black actors. In this setting, Atticus Freeman's quest (played by Jonathan Majors) to find his missing father somewhere in New England becomes extremely dangerous simply because people of color have to move extremely careful not to fall prey to members of the Ku-Klux-Clan, racist shopkeepers who deny them service, or trigger-happy police officers who run them out of town simply for being there. In the series' pilot, Atticus and his two Black friends have to find lodging in open country but are soon informed by a sheriff they were in a "sundown country" now where Black people will be shot if they are found outside after curfew – an all too real, actual horror not only in the South of the United States in the 50s. As Atticus makes a desperate run for the county line before the sun sets, slowly and menacingly sinking toward the horizon, horror tropes like "Nice Day, Deadly Night" (TV Tropes) or "Darkness Equals Death" (TV Tropes) come to mind: In films like *Aliens* (Cameron 1986), *Pitch Black* (Twohy 2000), or *I Am Legend* (Lawrence 2007), as well as in video games like *Don't Starve* (Klei Entertainment 2013) or *Alan Wake* (Remedy Entertainment 2010), the setting of the sun is equated with a horrifying evil. The moment of nightfall is thus codified as a generic narrative event that can mean death (or, at least, heightened risk) for the heroes. *Lovecraft Country* fuels these tropes with new political meaning, as the horrors are entirely represented by sadist sheriff Eustace Hunt (played by Jamie Harris). The actantial role of the supernatural monster is thus filled by all too human actants – within the conventionalized, but here defamiliarized type of narrative event. The blending of tropes and actantial roles charges the represented historical situation with the affective appeal of the horror genre. When actual Lovecraftian monsters *do* appear later on, it is almost a relief as they attack cops and heroes without discrimination ("Humans Are the Real Monsters" is in fact codified by TV Tropes as a new trope again, although not many of the listed examples are as explicitly political).

In manga and anime studies especially, the term "database consumption" has gained wide currency. According to the works of cultural critics Eiji Ōtsuka (2003) or Hiroki Azuma (2009), "narrative consumption" – when audiences turn to manga, anime, or video games in order to construct coherent narrative worlds – is increasingly accompanied or even replaced by a form of "database consumption" in which audiences enjoy popular media primarily to recognize, interrelate, and enjoy such recurring narratives tropes and patterns independently from (or alongside to) the individual story that they appear in (see Steinberg 2007; 2010). These patterns and tropes can be mixed and sampled, as has been shown, so audiences' pleasure is mostly derived from the recognition of "database elements" of conventionalized tropes and recurring actantial roles. Often, these recurring elements revolve entirely around characters: A "tsundere" character, for instance, is an (often female) protagonist who first appears hostile and hotheaded, only to gradually reveal a warmer, friendlier side over time ("hard on the outside, soft on the inside"). Examples include Asuka Langley in *Neon Genesis Evangelion* (Sadamoto 1994–2013), Kagura in *Gintama* (Sorachi 2003–2019), or Hitagi Senjougahara of *Bakemonogatari* (Isin and Oh! great 2018–present) (see TV Tropes, "Tsundere"). In the terms given above, we could say that a character who conforms to the actantial role of *tsundere* can be expected to participate in narrative events that will change their relationship with the main protagonist from an antagonistic to a benevolent or even loving one.

Characters-as-actants thus have different levels of narrative agency over scenes that are, to a certain degree, predefined by tropes that can be anticipated by audiences. Many conventions for specific types of characters and tropes – including different sorts of narrative agency – vary greatly from one medial, social, or historical context to the next. The vampire protagonists from the mockumentary sitcom *What We Do in The Shadows* (Clement et al. 2019–present) are a good example of this. Their supernatural abilities would make them immensely powerful in actantial roles of any superhero narrative: They are immortal, can transform into bats, possess superhuman strength and flight, and can hypnotize any human being into complete mental submission. In combat events known from other ("serious") vampire narratives such as *Blade* (Norrington 1998), *Underworld* (Wiseman 2003), *Twilight* (Hardwicke 2008), or *True Blood* (Ball et al. 2008–2014), they would be nearly unbeatable. *What We Do in The Shadows*, however, focuses entirely on social events, as the three vampire protagonists are presented as absolutely clueless about modern times and entirely helpless without their human "familiar," Guillermo. In the episode "The Curse" (Se02E14), for instance, Nandor the Relentless decides to check his e-mail for the first time in ten years, a technology he does not understand at all. Startled by an old chain e-mail stating that he'd be "cursed" if he did not pass on the e-mail to ten more people, he takes the content of the mail literal and spends the rest of the episode frantically trying to find out the e-mail addresses of other people in order to "lift the curse." His supernatural abilities as a fictional being, in other words, may far surpass those of vampires in other shows; his narrative agency over situations is entirely different, however, as audiences are familiar with the fact that decisive narrative events in the show – as well as within individual episodes – are not determined by physical conflicts to begin with but by the protagonists' unsuspecting struggles with modern life and their social tensions within a shared flat apartment. The show thus cleverly combines settings, tropes, and narrative agencies of the heterogeneous generic contexts "sitcom" and "supernatural horror."

These different tonalities are regularly and conventionally combined in *shōnen* manga and anime, Japanese media texts aiming at a youthful, male readership between the ages of 12 and 18 (see Drummond-Mathews 2010). In simple terms, *shōnen* are action-oriented plots following a most frequently male hero (or a group of heroes) on an adventurous journey. On a global textual level, most *shōnen* works are focused on the *physical* agency of their protagonists who experience inner maturation through external challenges. In contrast to American superheroes, they have not already finished learning but remain in perpetual development. Often, these stories are fantastic, so that not only a private problem but the salvation of the entire world is at stake. Typical for *shōnen* plots, however, are also recurring switches between dramatic and comedic events, alternating between pathos-laden and goofy tropes. From a European or North American perspective not accustomed to these narrative conventions, these switches can be irritating, as the respective actantial roles are conceived of as mutually exclusive. For *shōnen* plots, however, a sudden alternation is quite typical for characters: While one event of *Demon Slayer* (Fujio et al. 2019–present) is entirely decided by slapstick – characters have narrative agency only over outcomes like social embarrassment vs. "saving face"–, the next scene might put them in a life-and-death situation (accompanied by dramatic inner monologue) that is only settled through physical spectacle. The narrative agency characters possess in both kinds of situations and the likely outcomes are thus entirely different, determined by either their physical abilities and inner motivations or by their social ability to "save face." Like many other anime shows, *Demon Slayer* also signals this distinction aesthetically: Every time the dramatic narration is interrupted for comic relief, the characters turn into static, super deformed, "dwarf" (*chibi*) versions of themselves accompanied by manga-typical pictograms and "visual morphemes" (sweat drops or throbbing veins) (see Berndt 2021). In humorous scenes like these, violence is of no consequence, while the dramatic fights – rendered in fluently animated, colorful 3D spaces and simulated camera movements – are all about irreversible life-and-death results.

While these switches in tonalities, where the same protagonists alternate between starkly different actantial roles, are entirely conventional (and thus expected) for *shōnen* heroes, other media texts are intentionally designed around playful breaches of narrative (medial, generic, and historical) conventions and characters' expected narrative agencies. An interesting example is provided by the Disney+ show *WandaVision* (Schaeffer et al. 2021), featuring established protagonists from Marvel's Cinematic Universe in an entirely unfamiliar setting.

Wanda and Vision, first appearing in the second Avengers movie *Avengers: Age of Ultron* (Whedon 2015), are established action heroes whose narrative agency is usually defined by epic battles against world-threatening enemies. In *Avengers: Endgame* (Russo and Russo 2019), however, Vision is killed in the film's finale, much to the dismay of his partner Wanda. The first episode of the *WandaVision* series now has both characters (re)appearing within a 1950s black-and-white sitcom. Wanda and Vision are both shown as the "new neighbors" moving into a stereotypical, middle-class suburban family house. Vision is shown to have a regular office job while Wanda is responsible for the household. Audiences will likely be startled by this "alternate reality," since all MCU stories usually take place within the exact same fictional world (see chapter 7), which does not allow for the characters' unexplained appearances in an earlier era – let alone the fact that Vision should not even be alive. The sitcom setting is invoked on the level of style, too, so that each episode includes a laugh track, distanced, largely static camera views, and special effects as they would have been possible at the time referenced by the show. These stylistic choices are also connected to typical spatial settings, narrative tropes, and actantial roles: Instead of urban New York City or locations in outer space, most of the scenes take place in the suburban family home and in Vision's office. Narrative events within the plot of the first episode accordingly consist of Wanda trying to prepare the "perfect dinner" for Vision's visiting boss and his wife, or of the couple participating in a charity fundraiser for neighborhood kids in the second episode. The resulting narrative agency for both protagonists does not cast them in the actantial roles to fight world-shaking battles. They must rather use their superpowers – which they *do* retain from the movies – to *conceal* their superhuman abilities, which generates many humorous situations.

Within the next few episodes, it becomes clear that each installment takes place in a sitcom era ten years later, in terms of special effects and TV style as well as in terms of fashion (Wanda is starting to wear trousers instead of skirts in the 1960s, the third episode set in the 1970s is suddenly shot in full color). Their actantial roles and narrative agency follow this time-shift as well: The 1960s episode hints at the fact that the couple is having sex, something not part of the expected tropes of the 1950s episode. The respective narrative event itself – resulting in the decisive outcome of Wanda's pregnancy with two little boys – still remains only implied (under the blankets of their marriage bed and cut before the scene actually starts), in accordance with the rules of imagination of the respective times. Social representation also varies drastically, so that audiences encounter a Black character, Herb, not earlier than 1960. He appears only as comic relief even then, pointing to the structural racism underpinning the denial of narrative agency to PoC characters that has only gradually improved over the years. Settings, tropes, and actantial roles are thus revealed as strongly entangled and subject to historical change. The fourth episode ("We Interrupt This Program") finally resolves the whole puzzle when the entire setup is revealed to be some kind of alternate reality that Wanda has created with magical powers in order to suppress the trauma of her husband's demise. As this example makes clear, generic actantial roles and notions of narrative agency cannot be separated from gender, ethnicity, and other intersectional identity markers. The actantial roles of female characters or of people of color in many plots are problematic even before explicit stereotypes come into play. Irrespective of what might be explicitly stated *about* such characters, they can be – and frequently are – denied narrative agency over the progress of the overall plot. The following chapter is going to look at such questions of social representation in more detail.

3 Characters as Social Representation

As we have laid out in the preceding chapters, characters can be regarded as actants in plots (synthetic dimension) that, at the same time, activate a "person schema" and are therefore interpreted as individuals situated within a storyworld that "carry" with them a continuous consciousness frame (mimetic dimension). This also implies, however, that characters and their actions are partly determined by – and in constant dialogue with – the same social categories that are imposed onto real-world persons, such as gender, race, dis/ability, and many others. This aspect can be discussed as their *thematic dimension* within which we have further distinguished between (possibly intended) symbolic vs. (possibly unintended) symptomatic meanings (see our introduction). The latter differentiation is certainly often unclear and perhaps not too important in the end. Creators may state noble intentions in interviews or press releases, but media texts generate meanings themselves, and they remain open to interpretation and criticism. This is, after all, what Roland Barthes' (1977) assessment of the "death of the author" was primarily concerned with: Writers and creators are not – and, more importantly, should not be seen as – the ultimate authority on what their texts mean. Still, some thematic meanings of characters are highlighted more strongly than others, and more in line with the overall political message a text is taken to transport. In the introductory chapter, drawing on Jens Eder (2010), we have thus distinguished, within the thematic dimension, between a *symbolic* and a *symptomatic* axis, representing also two different traditions within the humanities: While literary studies or art history have developed many approaches to interpreting the complex meanings of any "work of art" mostly favorably ("when the film is in one way or another 'stating' abstract meaning," Bordwell 1989, 8), critical theory, postcolonial studies, or gender studies have trained us to unravel potentially hidden meanings critically ("repressed or symptomatic meanings that the work divulges 'involuntarily,'" 9). In this chapter, we will try to develop a clearer understanding of how both thematic dimensions can be distinguished and interrelated more clearly with respect to transmedia characters as social representation.

The TV adaptation of Margaret Atwood's *The Handmaid's Tale* (Atwood 1985 and Miller et al. 2017–present respectively) is a particularly good example of a media text that is certainly intended to address urgent political issues on its thematic level. Both the novel and the show present a dystopian, futuristic United

DOI: 10.4324/9781003298793-5

States in which Christian fanaticism, environmental collapse, and plummeting birth rates have created a savage totalitarian state (called Gilead) in which women are horridly subjugated to male rule. World infertility has led to the enslavement of fertile, "adulterous" women (called "handmaids") forced to submit to ritualized rape by their male masters in order to be impregnated and bear children for their infertile wives. The handmaids are literally objectified as mere possessions of their masters, justified by a cruel ideology of Christian fundamentalism. The narrative strongly aligns with June "Offred" Osborne (played by Elisabeth Moss in the TV adaption), clearly a symbol of the atrocities of a patriarchal society, loss of female agency and individuality, and the rise of Christian fanaticism in contemporary American politics. Offred's iconic costume – a red cloak and dress, worn with a white bonnet – has quickly become a political symbol in the real world worn by actual women protesting the erasure of female rights and bodily autonomy in countless protests and rallies since 2017 (see Sutherland 2019).

By contrast, we could point to Frank Miller's comic book *300* (1998) and its later movie adaptation (Snyder 2007), retelling a fictionalized account of the Spartan resistance against the invading Persian army of King Xerxes in 480 AD. The film, released in 2007, received harsh criticism for its political undertones in a post-9/11 media culture. Its strongly fictionalized account of the Battle of Thermopylae has been interpreted as a polemic allegory about militaristic, straight, White men like King Leonidas (played by Gerard Butler) as the last resistance against a savage, orc-like horde of racialized "Others" representing the Middle East (see Stevens 2007). The Spartan's lambda emblem, popularized by the film where Leonidas and his soldiers proudly present it on all their shields, has in fact become the very logo for Identitarianism, a racist, anti-muslim, and anti-immigrant movement originating in France and spreading across Europe and back to the United States: "Some of the [identitarian] 'movement's' videos, which are critical communication channels and mobilisation tools, borrow heavily from the film's visual aesthetics, particularly in their depiction of excitement, courage and peril" (Šima 2021, 79). Whether or not this was intended – or favorably looked upon – by either Frank Miller or film director Zack Snyder (the latter claiming that no parallels between the film and the modern world were intended, see Silverman 2007) should not concern us as much as the fact that these media texts apparently do afford these readings. Many additional interpretations are equally troublesome, such as the thematic coupling of the "barbarous Persians" with disabled and queer bodies (see Chemers 2007): Those who do not conform to a White, able-bodied, heterosexual notion of "manliness" are frequently equated with decadence, vice, and corruption in the story (although the film introduces at least one female heroine, Queen Gorgo, played by Lena Headey, in contrast to the comic's exclusively male protagonists). Reviewer Dana Stevens expressed an opinion shared by many that the film served "as a textbook example of how race-baiting fantasy and nationalist myth can serve as an incitement to total war" (Stevens 2007, n.pag.). For identitarians and other audiences of the far right, these may in fact be the *symbolic* meanings of characters (like Leonidas and Xerxes). Uncovered in a critical analysis (and partly denounced by their authors), these meanings are perhaps better addressed as symptomatic – betraying political ideologies of "regularity" and "manliness," rather than being *about* them in the same way *The Handmaid's Tale* is about the horrors of a totalitarian, patriarchal society. In *300*, in contrast, we are *aligned* with Leonidas, after all, and thus likely to *sympathize* with him in his battle against overwhelming odds, and encouraged to form *allegiances* with his explicitly stated moral value of "freedom" which is tacitly coupled with other, more problematic notions of regularity, militarism, and straight, White, male superiority. In Atwood's text, by contrast, we are invited to adopt the consciousness frame of Offred, portrayed as suffering due to similar ideologies.

The present chapter is concerned with categories of social identity and, perhaps more importantly, of social *difference* as a fundamental structural aspect of our perception of the world and of media texts. Social categories such as "male/female," "White/PoC," or "able-bodied/disabled" are connected to complex clusters of traits that are considered typical or even "natural" for individuals within a given culture: how to look, how to dress, how to behave, and how (and when) to talk, or more generally, which positions to assume within a given society *as well as* within narrative plots. As cultural theorist Stuart Hall has pointed out, the presence of an "Other" is crucial to the formation of semiotic and cultural meaning, as well as to our very sense of self (1997, 234–238). At the same time, social categories of identity and difference are always bound up in cultural and political relations of power, with one pole of the binary "includ[ing] the other in its field of operations" (235). The value *not* considered dominant in a society is then often tied to reductive and marginalizing representations. Transmedia characters are especially prominent embodiments of gendered, racialized, and other dichotomies, a site of negotiation of cultural power relations. On the symptomatic level, they can be analyzed as (perhaps unintended) cultural expressions of preferences, assumptions, and stereotypes. On the symbolic level, by contrast, characters can be used to address these social categories and their structural relations reflexively. Ambiguous cases complicate this relationship, challenging us to look minutely at media texts on the one hand and listen closely to arguments and debates on the other. Before we go into detail on how characters are made legible as belonging to specific social categories, this chapter is first going to introduce three foundational terms concerned with such relations: *Hegemoniality*, *othering*, and *performativity*. The overarching conceptional framework is that of *intersectionality*, the assumption that social categories like race, class, gender, or dis/ability intersect in various, often unexpected ways. This chapter is inspired by Véronique Sina's work in Packard et al. 2019, 151–184 (see also Sina 2016).

3.1 The Conceptional Framework of Intersectionality

In recent decades, the analysis of structural interrelations between social categories of identity and difference has been established as an independent field of research within the humanities. It is often discussed under the paradigm of *intersectionality*, which developed simultaneously in disciplines ranging from sociology, political science, philosophy, anthropology, literary and media studies, to gender and queer studies (see Cho et al. 2013). The term was initially proposed by Kimberlé Crenshaw in her groundbreaking article "Demarginalizing the Intersection of Race and Sex: A Black Feminist Critique of Antidiscrimination Doctrine, Feminist Theory and Antiracist Policy" (1989). Crenshaw demonstrated that structures of exclusion and hierarchization between the categories "gender" and "race" are not merely powerful in isolation, but that they often modulate, reinforce, or sometimes contradict each other. Further powerful social distinctions can be found in terms of class, age, religion, dis/ability, sexuality, or nationality. Within all of these distinctions, the respective categorization for any individual is usually not merely "neutral." Some people are granted privileges and treated favorably within a society, while those who "deviate" from this former position are then marginalized. The term *heteronormativity*, for instance, encapsulates the notion that even today it is considered "normal" or "natural" in many contexts that there are two sexes mapping exactly onto two genders that must be mutually attracted to each other, thereby not only excluding non-heterosexual orientations but also intersex, non-binary and/or trans people. While same-sex marriage may finally be possible in many (but far from all) countries around the world and countless other forms of legal discrimination are gradually removed (while many others remain in place or are even reinstated), traditional cultural preferences still prevail. Nowhere can this be seen better than in popular culture.

Disney animated films, for instance, can be put into critical focus with regard to the representation of diversity (see Cheu 2013). Not earlier than 2020 did Disney announce the first officially queer character within its Pixar animated production *Onward* (Scanlon 2020), introducing the first self-identifying lesbian character named Officer Specter (voiced by Lena Waithe). Before that, princess Elsa of Arendelle – the main protagonist of *Frozen* (Buck and Lee 2013) and *Frozen 2* (Buck and Lee 2019) – was already celebrated as, possibly, the first queer Disney protagonist, although this was only ever *implied* within the two films: Elsa has no love interest at all in both films, so queer readings were mostly based on the thematic subtext: Elsa is forced by her parents to suppress and hide her true, magical nature that she was born with. In the sequel, Elsa's female companion Honeymaren is introduced and positioned in a similar actantial role as a "significant other" would be in a heterosexual context. While the producers allowed a more conservative audience to comfortably ignore this thematic subtext by never making it explicit, this was not possible for *Onward*, which was immediately banned in multiple Middle Eastern countries such as Kuwait, Oman, Qatar, and Saudi Arabia. Russian authorities censored the respective scene to ensure a different, heterosexual characterization of Officer Specter (see McNary 2020). An even larger media outrage occurred in June 2022 when Pixar's *Lightyear* (MacLane), a spin-off from the *Toy Story* franchise, included the first narratively meaningful same-sex kiss between the character Alisha and another female researcher scientist (see Allen 2022). All of this is revealing as it betrays the ideological "rules of imagination" for this media format, according to which a general audience can assume a Disney character whose sexual orientation is undefined can be taken, *by default*, to follow heteronormative notions of gender and sexuality. A non-binary Disney character – a character who is not presented as *either* male *or* female, or as not identifying with either gender – was only introduced with Raine Whispers (voiced by queer actor Avi Roque) in the rather minor animated show *The Owl House* (Se02E07) in 2021 (Terrace and Wisinski 2020–present). As has been mentioned in chapter 1 already, Disney is also notorious for the company's decade-spanning "queer coding": Presenting villains like the *Little Mermaid*'s (Clements 1989) Ursula, *Aladdin*'s (Clements 1992) Jafar, or *The Lion King*'s (Allers and Minkoff 1994) Scar in such a way as to conflict with heteronormative, straight, gender norms in terms of their physical characteristics, costumes, non-verbal gestures, body positions, and speech patterns (see Putnam 2013). Media texts intended for young audiences or children (among others) are thus an especially important site for intersectional negotiations: Deviations from established power relations are immediately branded "political" within these contexts, concealing that a male, White, heterosexual, able-bodied protagonist is no less ideologically positioned than characters who deviate from this (or rather *his*) unquestioned norm.

As stated at the beginning of this chapter, three key terms for intersectional analyses of characters are *hegemoniality, othering,* and *performativity.* Hegemony is a sociological concept derived from Marxist philosopher Antonio Gramsci's (1971) idea of cultural hegemony, the observation that a dominant class in any given society is likely to impose its beliefs, perceptions, and values – its worldviews – on others to become the accepted cultural norm. The term was quickly adopted in gender studies, queer studies, and postcolonial studies: *Hegemonic masculinity,* for instance, legitimizes men's dominant position in society and governs who is regarded as a "real" man (see Connell 2005). In broader intersectional contexts, hegemoniality implies that certain ("intersections" of) social categories are treated as "normal," as "regular," or plainly as *unmarked* in a given cultural context. This is also of paramount importance for questions of fictional representations in media texts. One immediate functional mechanism of hegemoniality is that works deviating from these imposed norms will immediately be branded "political" or "ideological" as a result, while those conforming to them generally conceal their own biases, preferences, and implied power relations. Narratives about cisgender, White, heterosexual men are then seen as "normal," while stories about other kinds of characters are accused of "having an agenda." When the newest *Star Wars* film trilogy introduced the female heroine Rey (played by Daisy Ridley), as well as the Black protagonist Finn (played by John Boyega) in *The Force Awakens* (Abrams 2015), the film was met with critical backlash from right-wing media and reactionary fans accusing the producers of putting "politics over narration" (see Golding 2019). After two consecutive sequels, however, actor Boyega spoke out in disappointment on Twitter that the company Lucasfilm/Disney *did* sideline all characters of color and their developments – like Finn's or Rose Tico's, played by the second-generation Vietnamese-American Kelly Marie Tran – once again in favor of full-fledged character arcs for White protagonists and antagonists like Rey and Kylo Ren (see Watercutter 2020). The same happened when Marvel Comics started to "recast" more and more "legacy characters" with a more socially diverse array of protagonists around 2015 (see Trent 2021). The Black character Samuel Wilson took on the costume and name of Captain America, Iron Man was replaced by a Black teenage girl called Riri Williams, and even Thor was incarnated as a female version (whereby Marvel explicitly declared her not as a "female Thor" but as the current, official representation of Thor on Earth) (see Brown 2021). The outcry from reactionary fans and some artists revealed, if nothing else, that the traditional focus on straight White cis men as protagonists was just as ideological as a (somewhat) reversed stance that represents people beyond the perceived dominant group. The working mechanism of hegemoniality is then not only, and maybe not even primarily, about the representation of certain social categories as *superior* within narratives, but as *"regular"* and non-political, thereby naturalizing, normalizing, and hiding their own political biases.

Central for this structure to successfully operate is the reverse mechanism of "Othering": While *some* characters – and the social categories they represent – are displayed as the "neutral" group, those who do not conform must be "others." The verb "Othering," introduced by literary scholar Gayatri C. Spivak (1985), indicates that this distinction is not something given or "found" within the world but that it is *made* and reproduced by society. When conventional physical beauty and heterosexuality, for instance, are coupled with moral qualities represented by heroes while physical disabilities or homosexuality are reserved for villains, people *not* conforming to these norms are *othered*. They are presented as not forming part of the imagined community of "us" (see Anderson 1983). We are then likely to not form allegiances with them in fictional narratives, as they often also have considerably less narrative agency in terms of their actantial role: Disabled or trans characters, for instance, are only represented as minorities – and often not in a very positive light (see, for example, Reitz 2017) – while able-bodied, heterosexual characters are again reaffirmed as the imaginary majority group. As many narrative structures involve some sort of heterosexual romance by default (consisting of a series of relevant narrative events and tropes like "falling in love," "the first kiss,"), it shows that characters' *desires* are also normed, expected to be aimed at the "opposite" gender unless advertised otherwise. It is thus quite significant when recent TV shows like *Severance* (Erickson et al. 2022) or *Our Flag Means Death* (Jenkins et al. 2022–present) include queer love interest subplots that are not about the characters' homosexuality at all, but rather about the unattainability of *any* emotional relationship within their working environment (*Severance*) or about the casual, everyday fluidity of romantic and sexual desires on a ship of (mostly) male pirates (*Our Flag Means Death*). In the same way, a sitcom with an overall White cast is accordingly seen as "neutral" and "for everyone," while shows with more than one protagonist of Middle Eastern or Asian family background like *Fresh Off the Boat* (Khan et al. 2015–2020), *Ramy* (Youssef et al. 2019– present), or even *Ms. Marvel* (Ali 2022) are still often discussed as "minority programs." Othering thereby works in both directions: It marginalizes some, in order to reaffirm the identity of those who benefit from it.

A third key term to analyze these relations is *performativity*. It is meant to capture the fact that the very distinctions between male/female, White/PoC, able-bodied/disabled, and so on, as well as all of the invisible norms and social expectations attached to them, *are not static*. They need to be produced and maintained by continuous repetitions. Whatever counts as "male" behavior is a *performance* that has to be learned, internalized, and repeatedly staged in order to uphold a distinction from (performances associated with being) "female" or "queer" (see Butler 1990). Often, performative standardizations are hard to notice, as this is precisely how hegemonic ideologies work: Compulsive, almost automatic repetition renders itself invisible as "that-which-we-do-not-see" – because it is accepted as "natural." Repetition, however, also affords subversion. This becomes especially clear within parodies that break with restrictive norms in order to ridicule and thus expose them. The "Hawkeye Initiative" (The Hawkeye Initiative 2012–present) for example, a satirical collaborative Tumblr page established in 2012, accumulates fan art of the Marvel character Hawkeye (Clint Barton) in ridiculous poses usually reserved for female characters (see Avery-Natale 2013): Black Widow, for instance, is often shown in sexually provocative and physically impossible postures that we are trained to overlook, but which we can easily recognize as absurd if applied to a male character such as Hawkeye. Another informative example is a fan-produced Batman video of 2018 that quickly went viral. It was based on the computer game *Batman: Arkham Knight* (Rocksteady Studios 2015), but a savvy gamer named "sn0sh00" modified the game by swapping the digital character models for Batman and Catwoman (see Carter 2019). Not only were the recorded voices of both characters exchanged, but also the digital body acting. Looking only at the resulting parody of Catwoman, we might perhaps miss the editing, as she is mostly standing around in a firm, steady, almost expressionless pose: It is just "regular standing." Batman, by contrast, was assigned *her* body language data, which suddenly appears ridiculous. He swings his hips in an overacted manner, smiles manically, and thrusts out his chest; every aspect of his performance is "feminized" and, above all, sexualized. Reversing the medial conditions for male ("neutral") and female ("gendered") body language – which we are *trained* to overlook by hegemonic culture – exposes their astonishing artificiality and conventionality. As we can see from these examples, an intersectional perspective on characters can not only be applied to criticize specific texts for reproducing stereotypes and hegemonial power structures of norm and "Other." Characters can also help us to uncover, expose, or at the very least question otherwise "invisible" social norms and conventions within the real world.

The following three segments will provide more examples for both analytical stances with regard to the social categories of gender, race, and dis/ability within media texts. One preliminary conclusion from these considerations should be repeated as clearly as possible beforehand: From a structural perspective on social power relations outlined above, it follows that sexism, racism, ableism, or other interplays of cultural *hegemoniality* and *othering* are not at all about the respective creators' intentions – and not even necessarily about whether marginalized groups are represented in a "negative" or stereotypical fashion. The crucial question remains instead whether a *structural marginalization* is systematically re-produced and maintained. We will now discuss in more detail how this may work within different "intersections of identity," how we are accustomed to overlook it, and how characters can be a site to access, reflect, and criticize these relations.

3.2 Gender

While the term "gender" was first introduced in distinction to "sex" – designated to highlight the social constructedness of social roles against "biological reality" – the apparent "naturalness" of sexually dimorphic human bodies has also been criticized from various perspectives within the humanities and empirical sciences (see Butler 1997). It should be uncontroversial by now that it is not possible to infer a particular social identity, "normal" forms of behavior, or a "natural" sexual desire from male or female body attributes. Looking at characters from a gender studies perspective first means to investigate how protagonists coded as "male" or "female" (as well as neither, as rare as examples of this still are) are still assigned very different actantial roles within narratives. One indicator of hegemonic, sexist structures within conventional narratives can be found in the so-called Bechdel-Wallace test. Named after cartoonist Alison Bechdel, who popularized it after an idea from her friend Liz Wallace, the Bechdel-Wallace test asks whether a story features at least two female characters who talk to each other about something other than a man. As Carolyn Cocca remarked for superhero narratives, "[t]his is a very low bar, but most superhero works fail it" (2020, 8; see also Cocca 2016; De Dauw 2021). The same goes for a majority of Hollywood blockbusters (even though the test was itself criticized for oversimplifying mat-ters, see Abdullaeva 2021). Female characters are still far too often employed in one of two prototypical actantial roles: The first is the "damsel in distress," wait-ing to be rescued by a strong, male protagonist (often also her love interest). She is thus denied narrative agency within the plot by acting as a mere motivation or an object of desire for the male hero. Women cast in this actantial role can then be expected to be shy, restrained, and seemingly without sexual desires of their own. The one domain where such desires are expressed is within the actantial role embodied by the "femme fatale," a mysterious and hypersexualized woman seducing the protagonist, thus coupling female sexuality firmly to vice, villainy, and corruption. The femme fatale exemplifies the untamed, "wild" side of female subjectivity which is at the same time *othered* once again: Characters in this role are exoticized, stereotyped, and put on display for male characters – and male audiences. In both cases, that of the damsel in distress as well as of the femme fa-tale, the narrative does not align with its female protagonists but represents them from a heterosexual, male perspective – both in narrative terms (as discussed in chapter 1), as well as in purely visual ones. The term "gaze" was first intro-duced by art critic and poet John Berger in his episodic film documentary *Ways of Seeing* (produced by Mike Dibb in 1972) to describe the reductive visual rep-resentation of women in advertising and classical painting. As *male gaze*, it quickly became a foundational concept in film studies introduced by feminist critic and philosopher Laura Mulvey (2006). The male gaze implies that it is "natural and normal" within patriarchal societies that women *are looked at* – often in slow motion, close-ups, or silhouettes – while men *are looking*, an ideological "grammar" deeply embedded into films (and other visual media like comic books) which often pause narration primarily to present the visual spectacle of sexualized female protagonists for an imagined male, heterosexual audience. Women's "visual presence tends to work against the development of a storyline, to freeze the flow of action in moments of erotic contemplation" (Mulvey 2006, 20). Male bodies, by contrast, are mostly shown in action, emphasizing their actantial ability to change the flow of narrative through physical prowess.

Other actantial roles of female protagonists besides damsels in distress or femme fatales are even less favorable: One of the most problematic ones is epitomized by the "women in refrigerator" trope. Coined by comic book writer Gail Simone (1999), it refers to *Green Lantern* Vol. 3, issue #54 (Marz et al. 1994), in which the titular protagonist Kyle Rayner finds his murdered girlfriend hidden in his refrigerator (see Nelson 2015). This horrible act of violence against her subsequently serves as a mere plot device for Rayner to provide motivation for becoming a "better hero." The "fridge test" can be applied to detect many similar instances of gendered, and often sexualized acts of violence against female protagonists who are murdered, maimed, or otherwise silenced only to guide male heroes throughout their journeys (Catheryne M. Valente's 2017 novel *The Refrigerator Monologues* turns this perspective around, retelling the stories of female comic book characters from their perspectives). As activist-writer Ellen Kirkpatrick (2022, n.pag.) has recently put it aptly: "Fridging is a dehumanizing process, depriving one persona of their individuality by subordinating them, and their story, to another. Female characters, here, become non-subjects, non-agents – mere things." In other words, female characters are reduced to actants that are not characters – their subjective consciousness frames do not need to be taken into account. This misogynistic trope is transmedial as well: HBO's *Game of Thrones* (Benioff et al. 2011–2019), for instance, was repeatedly criticized for its many scenes of sexualized violence against and/or rape of women (see Robinson 2015). While many of them are characters we *are* aligned with and whose perspective we are invited to take – certainly a deviation from more conventional fantasy settings like *The Lord of the Rings* which leave no actantial roles for heroines at all – especially problematic are those scenes that, in line with the "refrigerator" trope, display sexualized forms of violence once again from an entirely male perspective: The character Theon Greyjoy, for instance, is made to watch how the villain Ramsey Snow sexually abuses Theon's stepsister Sansa (Se05E06) while the audience is watching Theon. The scene does not even grant Sansa attention as a victim, she is merely suffering for the audience to "learn" something about the male protagonist.

Disney movies are especially interesting for their reductive gender roles even when they *do* present female titular main characters. *Snow White and the Seven Dwarfs* (Hand 1937) and *Cinderella* (Luske et al. 1950) are both dependent on a handsome prince to rescue them in the films' conclusions. Even in more recent female-led films, male characters are disturbingly dominant. Men speak 71% of all the dialogue in *Beauty and the Beast* (Trousdale and Wise 1991) and 76% in *Pocahontas* (Gabriel and Goldberg 1995) (see Beaudoux 2017). For decades, Disney's female characters have also been among the worst examples of beauty ideals centered around conventionally attractive, thin body types (see Cheu 2013). While male protagonists such as *Robin Hood* (Reitherman 1973), *Aladdin* (Clements and Musker 1992), or *Hercules* (Clements and Musker 1997) are mostly defined by their heroism toward others or society – the main narrative events of these films revolve around heroic deeds and struggles – many female heroines are defined by their aspiration toward (heterosexual) romance and marriage. The most infamous example is certainly Arielle, the titular protagonist of *The Little Mermaid* (1989) who literally decides to give up her voice, her powers of expression and opinion, to please her male suitor, Prince Eric. The more young girls identify with Disney's "princess culture," a recent empirical study found (Coyne et al. 2016), the more they are prone to exhibit patterns of stereotypically "female" behavior – considering themselves more "emotional" than boys their age, considering beauty, sweetness, and obedience their most valuable assets, or accepting leadership and public visibility as "male" qualities.

Not even Disney's filmography remains entirely static, however, so a comparative view on 1998s animated *Mulan* (Cook and Bancroft) proves insightful. This reimagination of a classical Chinese folk-tale about a cross-dressing female warrior who saved the Empire features a strong female protagonist engaging in battle and defying her family's wishes for her to find a handsome, wealthy husband. Not only is the film's female protagonist disobedient and resolutely vocal in her defiance of social conventions reserved for "girls," but she also proves herself as a skilled martial artist and a military strategist. The film's narrative also revolves around the arbitrary and constructed nature of acceptable "male" and "female" behavior and their respective roles within society. Power structures that remain invisible within earlier films are thus constantly highlighted. One of *Mulan's* many songs, "I'll Make a Man Out of You," can in part be seen as a thematic comment on the protagonist's attempts to pass as male within a military training camp. Sung by Captain Li Shang, however, the lines are actually directed toward male cadets who are not yet "manly" enough to pass as real heroes in the coming war. The category "man" is thus not presented as an essential, innate category but rather as a *performance* that the male characters, too, are not (yet) able to master and uphold. Part of this performance – the adoption of the "correct" male behavior for a soldier and hero – consists precisely of questionable views on women as objects to be conquered: The very next musical interlude, "A Girl Worth Fighting For," expresses the soldiers' determination to ultimately possess desirable women through marriage. It is only fitting that the heroine's impersonation of the opposite gender role is then once more reversed in the film's climax when her male companions dress up as concubines in order to infiltrate enemy ranks. Masculinity and femininity are thus both exposed as elaborate, often hilarious play-acts. In the end, even humorous side characters like Mulan's magical helper dragon Mushu seem confused about the relation of gender, action, and the resulting social identity when he praises Mulan's heroic deeds in battle with the spontaneous exclamation "I knew you could do it, you are the MAN!... well, sorta...." Playful and self-aware as these scenes might be in their acknowledgment of socially constructed, often repressive gender norms – especially in contrast to earlier Disney films – *Mulan* has not remained free of criticism either. Not only does the overall binary structure of male vs. female remain largely unquestioned, the protagonist literally has to *become invisible as a woman* and appear "boylike" in order to be accepted as heroic (see Labi 2001). At the end of the film, Mulan is offered a leadership position within the Emperor's council, but she rejects it in order to return to a quiet, private life with her family.

Mulan's modest criticism of limited female agency is also embedded in different sorts of binary structures that an intersectional perspective can reveal: The worst expression of rigid gender norms (and their correlation to social power structures) was put in the mouth of one of the films' antagonists, advisor Chi Fu: "She is a woman, she will never be worth anything!" That such notions are exposed as re-actionary and sexist – they are uttered by a highly unlikable character, after all – might seem progressive from one perspective. Disney criticizes these views not only within a fantastic storyworld of dragons and ancestrial spirits, however, but also in the "exotic" (*othered*) country of China. Western societies, it seems then, are excluded from similar prejudices. Edward Said (2014) prominently discussed "orientalism" as yet another binary system permeating Western thoughts on geo-politics: "The East" or "the Orient" – a crude generalization of regions as diverse as North Africa, the Middle East, and East Asia – is a romanticized construct that reaffirms "Western" (i.e., European and North American) identity as ra-tional, educated, and enlightened. This identity must continuously be reinforced by its opposing other (the "Orient") which remains perpetually ahistorical, magi-cal, and sensual. Other oppositions within such colonial perspectives are directed toward the "idealized savage" of the Americas, and toward the terrifyingly "evil savage" of the African continent (see Mitchell 1998). All these binarisms con-tribute to a *colonial gaze* in which "non-Western" societies are seen as backward and less educated while their stories, storyworlds, and characters are ready to be exploited for spectacle and amusement at the same time (kimono-like clothing and fire-breathing dragons in Western animation like *Mulan*). The addition of Mushu, the dragon, as a magical comedy character (voiced by Eddie Murphy), who was not part of the original Chinese myth, has also been criticized by Chi-nese viewers as a trivialization of their culture. That Mushu is *not* part of Disney's live-action *Mulan* remake of 2020 (Caro) is as much a concession to Chinese audi-ences as the remake's all-Chinese cast (see Campbell 2020; arguments have been made, however, that poking fun at "lower-tier" dragons like Mushu happens to be a common theme in the Chinese storytelling tradition, too, so maybe there are even more cultural misconceptions at play here; see Yi 2020). Again, it becomes clear that intersectional categories of representation must always be investigated in complex relations to each other.

3.3 Race

As we have seen, the category of "race" is as much a political *construct* as gender. While labels like "Black" or "White" are frequently used as if they were simple descriptive statements about a person's skin color, a cursory glance at actual people can easily refute this: As Richard Dyer (1997, 42) observed, the skin tone of Japanese or Chinese people has often been called "yellow" in Anglo-American contexts, even though there is, in most cases, no clear difference from "White" Europeans' complexion. Rather, categorizations like this are the result of "a quite complicated interaction of elements, of which flesh tones [...] are only one: The shape of nose, eyes, and lips, the colour and set of hair, even body shape may all be mobilised to determine someone's 'colour'" (42). However, the assignment of racial identity extends far beyond the realm of physiognomy, with factors like body language, clothing choices, or preferences for certain genres of media all being used as "indicators" for someone's race, if other markers do not yield a sufficiently clear "result" (see Jensen 2011). Also, categorizations can change drastically over time. Italian or Jewish people, for instance, were not considered "White" in the 19th-century United States, revealing once again that respective markers are social – and not physiological – concepts (see Ignatiev 2008; Pascoe 2010). The term "race" is thus often substituted by "ethnicity" to highlight its historical, political, and sociocultural constructedness, as well as its interplay between hegemoniality and othering (see Hall 1996, 446). A good example to show how racial othering often works connected to other intersectional categories, even despite stated or actual best intentions, can be found in the 2004 movie *Catwoman* (Comar 2004). When female superheroes are as underrepresented in popular culture as PoC protagonists are (see Frankel 2020; Guynes and Lund 2020), the idea to cast Black actress Halle Barry as the titular protagonist – in contrast to comic book versions and (most) earlier screen adaptations in which Catwoman is a *White* master thief – might seem like a progressive idea. However, not only was the movie considered a major financial and critical disappointment (earning various "Golden Strawberries" for the worst filmic achievements of 2004), but its treatment of both femininity and Blackness is also far from unproblematic. Breaking with established comic canon for the character – her civic identity Selina Kyle earned her abilities by physical training – the film's protagonist Patience Phillips is killed and reborn as Catwoman, literally *possessed* by the spirit of cats. The resulting (anti)hero amounts almost to a caricature of the "femme fatale," with a marked lack of interior depth, a strongly sexualized performance, and an outfit that is very saliently catering to a male gaze. Her body language, the way she prances around like a pole dancer in almost every scene, might even be the implicit "template" for *Batman: Arkham Knight*'s Catwoman that was later parodied in the role reversal.

What is even more problematic is the fact that this *Black* Catwoman is presented as a literal human/beast-hybrid who uncontrollably gobbles down cat food and is driven by base animal instincts. The character thus taps into a long tradition of Black heroes such as Marvel's Storm or DC's Vixen whose powers are introduced as nature-based and animalistic. These images reinforce the stereotype of Blackness as a promiscuous, primitive, less "enlightened" subcategory of the human species. What is more, *Catwoman* directly connects this to orientalist thinking as well by linking the protagonist's powers to Egyptian feline goddesses in the film's opening. The title sequence shows "ancient scrolls" and "wall reliefs" of pyramids, sarcophaguses, and mummies. Halle Berry's totem animal is a mystical creature of fantasies about Middle Eastern magic, whereas the cat serves as a symbol for urban independence on the thematic level for a White Catwoman such as Michelle Pfeiffer in *Batman Returns* (Burton 1992). Applying our distinctions from before, we might say that the intended thematic symbolism of the cat carries connotations that can be more properly addressed as *symptoms* of a larger cultural discourse. This discourse, and the real-world power structures that it facilitates and reflects, enable the attribution of highly questionable thematic positions to PoC characters such as Berry's Catwoman. Again, whether this was in fact "intended" – and whether we should believe statements to the contrary – is not so much relevant as that the text certainly affords respective readings that an intersectional analysis can uncover. The distinction between symbol and symptom can then be applied to discern between thematic meanings on the level of the single text – that cats are connected to Egyptian gods by the film's opening – and on the level of broader cultural discourses like those identified by Said – that "the Orient" is opposed to the "enlightened" West, or that Black superheroes are inherently connected to nature and instinct.

A more nuanced and complex approach to PoC superheroes can be found in HBO's 2019 show *Watchmen* (Lindelof et al.), which works both as a continuation and a critique of the seminal 1986/1987 comic book series of the same name created by Alan Moore and Dave Gibbons. It is in part due to this doubled relationship with its "original" that the *Watchmen* show can address issues of race in two different ways. On a surface level, it can be read as a direct examination of actual-world racism through an established storyworld. A major real-life event, the so-called "Tulsa Race Massacre" of 1921, was incorporated into the show as a central background for the story. On May 31 and June 1, 1921, more than 800 Black residents of Tulsa, Oklahoma (at that time the wealthiest Black community in the United States) were hospitalized by a mob of White Americans equipped with weapons by city officials. As many as 6,000 Black residents were interned for days, with the death toll estimated between 75 and 300. The show not only explores the implications of these rarely medially represented historical events, thereby turning racial tensions and racism into its central themes (thus replacing Cold War fears about an impending nuclear war as the central topic in the earlier comic book). It also interrogates the symptomatic meanings attached to racially "othered" characters in media texts of the past.

Both aspects of the show's interest in race and racism are most clearly on display in the series' sixth episode, "This Extraordinary Being." The episode mainly consists of extended flashbacks covering the life of William Reeves, who previously appears as an old man in the show's fictional present of 2019 North America. In the late 1930s, Reeves, a survivor of the Tulsa massacre, is recruited into the NYPD as the only Black cadet of his year. As such, he is frequently confronted with the hegemoniality of Whiteness and the resulting othering of and discrimination against people of color: At his graduation ceremony, his superior officer – a White man – refuses to hand him his medal. Later, an arsonist he catches is set free by Reeves' White colleagues; and when a Ku-Klux Klan plot causes a riot in a cinema frequented by Black people, Reeves is sent into the building because, as another officer says, he "speaks [the] language" of the "animals" inside. Eventually, after almost being lynched by a group of White policemen, William becomes the first masked vigilante of the *Watchmen* story-world, adopting the moniker "Hooded Justice." Hooded Justice did appear as a side character in the original comics, where his identity was never revealed. Due to his masquerade, readers could not even make out his skin color, but the text (back) material at least implied that he was a White man of German descent.

William's transformation in the show highlights several key aspects of race as a construct: Perhaps most prominently, his secret identity depends on a capability for *passing*. This term describes "the phenomenon in which a person gains acceptance as a member of social groups other than his or her own" (Dawkins 2012, xii). In the context of race, this means that the ethnicity attributed to an individual, and any notions of "otherness" associated with it, may vary with the context said individual is perceived in. For example, during the first half of the twentieth century, many people in the Southern United States whose birth certificates marked them as "colored" were light-skinned enough to be accepted in social spaces reserved for White people under Jim Crow laws (see Hobbs 2014). An excellent historical example of this is the biography of George Herriman, a US cartoonist most famous for his comic strips starring the titular *Krazy Kat* (1913–1944). Born in 1880 to mixed-race parents, Herriman's legal racial status was "colored," but as an adult he repeatedly stated his identity as White, even to authorities (see Tisserand 2016). In a comparable vein, William actively makes himself pass in *Watchmen* by wearing light make-up under his mask, creating a "Whiteness" for the Hooded Justice persona that is never questioned by any of the other characters who do not know about his actual ethnicity. This draws attention to the constructedness of race as a social category once again: There is no "innate Blackness" that differentiates William from his fellow human beings. All of the cultural meanings attached to a person's ethnicity, such as the animalism and exoticism mentioned above, exist primarily as discursive attributions and consequentially fall away as soon as the configuration of ethnic markers (such as skin color) is changed.

The series makes it very clear that, for Will, this double masking is necessary if he wants to keep fighting crime. As June, his wife, puts it: "You ain't gonna get justice with a badge, Will Reeves. You're gonna get it with that hood. And if you wanna stay a hero, [White] townsfolk gonna need to think one of their own's under it." Will's perceived "otherness" as a Black man bars him from being accepted in the role of a crime-fighter. He cannot succeed as a policeman because policemen need to show their faces, whereas vigilantism allows him to pass as White, fostering acceptance and even admiration from others. Again, the implicit criticism here addresses both the actual world and media artifacts: On the one hand, people of color continue to be significantly underrepresented in the US police force today (see Data USA 2022), with Black police officers often facing discrimination (see Bolton and Feagin 2004). On the other hand, superhero comics (and more recently, films), like most entertainment media in the anglophone world, have historically reserved the actantial role of the "heroic, just protagonist" mostly for White men, relegating people of color to sidekick status or exoticizing them in problematic ways (see Goodrum et al. 2018). Thus, the kinds of heroic deeds associated with superheroes are discursively tied to Whiteness. Viewed through the lens of performativity, this points to a potential problem of Will's passing: By fighting crime in the role of a White man, he necessarily repeats and reiterates a performance of "White" behavior. Instead of subverting and possibly changing the norms governing race to allow for a Black crime-fighter, the Hooded Justice persona potentially strengthens the impression (within the narrated world of *Watchmen*) that Black superheroes do not and cannot exist.

This is, again, tied back into the show's criticism of other superhero media: The episode "This Extraordinary Being" opens with a scene from a fictional show-within-the-show called "American Hero Story," which purports to represent the "real" story of the 1940s vigilantes from a 2019 perspective. In the scene, two policemen blackmail a re-enacted "Hooded Justice" into unmasking himself, revealing him to be a conventionally attractive White man. Within the world of *Watchmen*, the producers of "American Hero Story" may well believe that Hooded Justice was White since his identity is never actually revealed to the public. However, since the show's actual-world audience knows the "truth" as shown in the flashbacks, this can also be read as a criticism of Western media's frequent "White-washing" of characters who were historically (or, in the case of adaptations of fictional works, originally) Black or otherwise racialized. The show's approach can also be read as a comment on White appropriation of Black culture in general. Like many musical achievements such as jazz or hip hop that were "stolen" – made popular in the wider public sphere only when White people adopted them – Hooded Justice "invented" superheroes in *Watchmen*'s revised storyworld without being recognized for it.

Furthermore, the same fictitious documentary also seems to make an interesting point regarding intersectionality. The reason the two policemen were able to put any pressure on the White-washed "Hooded Justice" is that they know of his sexual relationship with fellow vigilante Captain Metropolis. Clearly, in *Watchmen*'s fictional 2019 (as in the actual world), mainstream television shows do offer the actantial role of "secretly gay or bisexual hero" – but again, this role is filled by a White man. The "reality" shown in the flashbacks is more complicated: William Reeves does indeed have an affair with Nelson Gardner, a.k.a. Captain Metropolis, but it becomes clear that, as a Black queer man, he faces problems different from both straight Black and White gay men. While Gardner initially professes solidarity with William and invites him into the superhero group of "Minutemen," it is shown that his own "otherness" in terms of sexuality does not cancel out his hegemonic "belonging" in terms of ethnicity: When William asks him for help foiling the mass murder of Black people by the KKK, Nelson dismisses his concerns and betrays his own racist bias, stating that "the residents of Harlem cause riots all on their own." Once again, intersecting categories of social identity and difference cannot be viewed independently from one another.

3.4 Dis/ability

A consideration of disability as another crucial identity category hinges on a move away from the so-called "medical model" of disability, which regards physical impairments as individual problems of the body to be medically "fixed." Starting in the 1960s, academic and activist accounts of disability shifted toward a social model, conceptualizing disability as stemming from discursive and social practices which hinder impaired people from fully participating in society. In this model, it is not the impairment itself that disables people but the excluding manner in which the social world is organized (see Shakespeare 2006, 9–28). Historically, this paradigm shift allowed disabled people to articulate their demands for equal rights and inclusion as a collective instead of the more fragmented social movements that preceded it (see Krentz 2018, 348–350). While the social model does distinguish between impairment (individual physical limitation) and disability (structural oppression), one important focus of disability studies remains the interrogation of how notions of "normal" and "disabled" bodies are (re)produced through cultural representations (see Garland-Thomson 2005; Davis 2017).

As mentioned above, fictional narratives often cater to the notorious tradition of attributing villains with physical impairments and shortcomings, linking negative personality traits to "conventional ugliness": From Shakespeare's infamous Richard the Third, described as "deformed" and often represented in theatrical performances with a hump, a limp, or an immobilized arm (see Williams 2009), to the long list of James Bond villains with physical disfigurements, the one-eyed Emilio Largo in *Thunderball* (Young 1965), the scarred Alec Trevelyan in *Goldeneye* (Campbell 1995), the facially disfigured Zhao in *Die Another Day* (Tamahori 2002), Raoul Silva with his prosthetic upper jaw in *Spectre* (Mendes 2015), or the two disfigured villains Blofeld and Safin in *No Time To Die* (Fukunaga 2021). The "disfigurement-villainy trope" refers to the visual shorthand of showing the audience that a person is a "bad guy" (see Leary 2017; TV Tropes, "Evil Makes You Ugly"). Countless supervillain origin stories like those of Marvel's Dr. Doom or Red Skull, and DC's Two-Face or Dr. Poison, also establish a physical impairment as an outward sign of these characters' inner moral corruption.

Even when characters presented with impairments *are* the main protagonists, the plotlines they are embedded in are often (intentionally or unintentionally) ableist. Netflix's transmedia adaptation (Hissrich et al. 2019–present) of *The Witcher* video games focuses not only on the titular Geralt of Rivia (played by Henry Cavill) but also on Yennefer of Vengerberg (played by Anya Chalotra). During her childhood, she is repeatedly abused because of her "mixed racial origin" (half Elf, half Human) as well as her resulting physical disabilities, a "hunchback," and severe jaw deformities impairing her speech. Over the course of the first season, she seeks out the help of a powerful sorcerer who heals her impairments and transforms her into a conventionally beautiful woman conforming to modern standards. Afterward, she is also granted magical powers. Overall, her narrative trajectory might perhaps be intended as a story about female empowerment within a deeply misogynist "medieval" society (an analogy to 14th/15th-century central Europe). Her plotline, nevertheless, reinforces the harmful notion that people must "erase" their physical disabilities in order to succeed within society. Power, self-assurance, and narrative agency within the plot thus cannot be achieved while she is physically "imperfect." This is also embedded within sexist structures since male protagonists (such as Tyrion Lannister in *Game of Thrones*) sometimes *can* remain physically disabled and still showcase powers over others. It also does not help that the audience potentially knows about Anya Chalotra being cast as Yennefer beforehand, so it is clear from the beginning that she will either transform into her "beautiful self" over the course of the show or, at worst, that an able-bodied actress is going to imitate a disabled person (a practice addressed as "cripping up" that is criticized as similarly problematic to Blackface discussed in the next chapter; see Lee 2021).

Particularly interesting examples for more complex negotiations of dis/ability are once again provided by various superheroes (see Haslem et al. 2019). As José Alaniz has remarked, superheroes, who are frequently defined by physical prowess and simultaneously posited as role models, make for an excellent "entry point for interrogating the social construction of the (male) body, disability [...] and 'normality'" (Alaniz 2014, 13). In fact, disabilities are at the heart of various superheroes' origin stories, from Tony Stark/Iron Man (heart injury) and Charles Xavier/Professor X (paralysis) to slightly less well-known figures such as Barbara Gordon/Oracle (also paralysis) or Donald Blake, the human alter ego of Marvel's original iteration of Thor (who has an impaired leg). Another such superhero is Daredevil, whose various medial incarnations have occasioned public discussion of disability and its representation (see Perry 2015 or Daleyna 2022). Originally created by Stan Lee and Bill Everett for *Daredevil* #1 (1964), the character is also the protagonist of a feature film (Johnson 2003) and a Netflix series (Goddard et al. 2015–2019) of the same name, as well as appearing in the live-action crossover miniseries *The Defenders* (Petrie et al. 2017), the feature film *Spider-Man: No Way Home* (Watts 2021), and a number of animated films and TV shows. Daredevil is the vigilante persona of defense attorney Matt Murdock who lost his eyesight in an accident when he was a child. At the same time, his remaining senses function with superhuman accuracy, allowing him to perform impressive acrobatic feats as he fights crime in the Hell's Kitchen neighborhood of New York City. From this description alone, we can easily identify him as what disability scholars have called a "supercrip" (see Schalk 2016): A hero who can (over)compensate for the disadvantages of disability, potentially giving "the able-bodied the false impression that anyone can 'overcome' a disability" (Wendell 1996, 116), when in fact it is only due to the extraordinary (often fantastic and supernatural) resources they are provided by fictional narratives. In the case of Daredevil, this includes not only rigorous martial arts training but a degree of heightened perception that is simply unattainable for any actual human being. However, the depiction of Murdock's blindness in the Netflix series *Daredevil* offers insights beyond its reproduction of a questionable stereotype.

In one of the 2015 series' first scenes (Se01E01), Murdock (played by Charlie Cox) and his best friend and business partner Franklin "Foggy" Nelson (played by Elden Henson) meet with real estate agent Susan Harris, who shows them around an office they intend to rent for their newly set-up law firm. When Murdock arrives, Harris introduces herself and offers him a handshake, which he cannot see and therefore ignores, simply stating his name. After a moment of hesitation, Harris curtsies awkwardly, which is promptly described to Matt by an amused Foggy: "She just curtsied. It was adorable." Matt's suave reply – "Well it's nice to know chivalry isn't dead" – glosses over the real estate agent's faux pas but at the same time makes clear that the overall awkwardness of the moment does not result from his blindness. Rather, it is Harris who causes friction here by unthinkingly adhering to a specific social script, even though she already knows that Murdock is blind. When the routine of "name-handshake-name" breaks down, the outdatedness of her curtsy (emphasized by Matt evoking "chivalry") makes apparent that modes of introduction are historically and socially contingent. The narrative representation of the entire exchange can be read as a small-scale affirmation of a social model of disability: If the real estate agent had not insisted on a greeting that required visual cues, there would have been no perceptible difference between this introduction and her prior interaction with Foggy. Thus, the "otherness" of Matt as a disabled person is produced through normative forms of behavior.

Matt's half-serious description of Harris' behavior as "chivalrous" points to an interesting intersection of disability with gendered codes of conduct, as "chivalry" is an ethos usually ascribed exclusively to men. This intersection is explored further in a later scene of the same episode, in which Karen Page (Foggy and Matt's first client, played by Deborah Ann Woll), whose life is being threatened, stays at Matt's apartment overnight. The scene's set-up reproduces a hegemonic order of gender relations, with Matt fulfilling the role of the selfless, "chivalrous" protector offering shelter to a woman who is dependent on his help. This point is driven home when he offers one of his shirts to Karen to replace her soaked top. Realizing that she can change clothes without worrying about Matt looking, Karen briefly exposes her naked torso. His blindness makes Matt the perfect "knight in shining armor," providing protection while being exempt from the potentially threatening male gaze. Of course, this is not true for the show's intended (heterosexual, male) audience, whose voyeuristic gaze is clearly being catered to by the depiction of a half-naked, conventionally attractive woman (even though the show refrains from showing full-frontal nudity). Up to this point, Matt is consistently framed as possessing a high level of narrative agency, whereas Karen is the largely passive object of both his help and the camera's exhibition of her body. However, this distribution of roles begins to shift in the ensuing conversation.

"Can I ask a personal question?", Karen begins, only for Matt to anticipate said question: "I haven't always been blind." As she asks him about his relationship to his blindness, it becomes apparent that Karen pities Matt for his situation. At the same time, the intensity with which she looks at him, in combination with the romantic overtones of the scene as a whole, suggests her romantic and/or sexual interest in him. Matt now becomes the *object* in a double sense: He is reduced to his blindness by Karen's questions (she never touches on any other aspect of his life), while at the same time being the object of a desiring gaze that he can neither perceive nor reciprocate. The complex overlap of roles Matt fulfills in this scene – the desired, but not desiring, the pitiful, yet protective hero – cannot be sufficiently explained by the axis of gender or dis/ability alone, but only by considering the intersection of these categories.

In conclusion, the difficult distinction between symbolic and symptomatic meanings of media texts is not so much about favorable vs. critical interpretations and neither about actual vs. involuntary/absent authorial intentions (although we might take statements of creators into account, as regular audience members surely will, too). Rather, what is at stake here is whether a media text reproduces existing hegemonic structures (including all "regular" narrative conventions connected to specific social identities and tropes), or whether it manages to destabilize and disrupt the established and usually *invisible* categorization of "normal" vs. "other" (identities, values, modes of behavior, etc.). By inviting audiences to assume different consciousness frames of characters, a media text is able to actively create symbolic meanings, instead of merely working ("symptomatically") with and within the lines of power we are embedded in as it is. The difference is thus not one of positive/negative evaluation but of resistance against hegemonic "regularity" which is far from subjective.

On a final note, it is always worth reflecting on our own positionality when approaching characters as social representation. As many of the cases and discussions in this chapter have shown, not only are popular media texts rarely univocally sensitive *or* problematic in their treatment of characters' social categorization; often, it also remains a matter of debate whether certain sexist, racist, or ableist (among others) tropes are reinforced rather than critically displayed by a media text. As researchers, it cannot be our task to "settle" these debates on textual grounds "objectively," but rather listen to arguments brought forth by people actually affected by social categorizations in continuously shifting contexts and discourses. As Donna Haraway has argued most prominently (1988), the idea that knowledge can ever be "objective" (socially unmarked or unrelated to power structures) is itself a fantastically distorted, irrational, and at its core ideological notion. Our *situated knowledge* – that the authors of this volume are both male, White, and "able-bodied," in our case – provides the overall imperative to strive not for "objectivity," but – at best – for intersubjectivity in complex social negotiations. Luckily, the means to educate ourselves not only through academic reflection but especially in terms of public, critical discourses on characters and their perceived (mis)representation have become increasingly accessible in recent decades through articles and discussions in social media, blogs, or popular online magazines (for the changing awareness on racial issues in and for fandom, see Pande 2020). A potential Transmedia Character Studies would then be, above all, deeply embedded in cultural studies and should not dismiss critical perspectives from outside academia – a bias itself susceptible to classism, ignorant of the fact that commentators within university institutions occupy a rather privileged position not available to everyone for various reasons. Embracing these discourses and controversies instead, especially where they are articulated by people sensitive to hegemonic structures necessarily invisible to ourselves, provides the best chance to hone our instruments and tools far beyond the cursory remarks provided in this chapter. Various forms and formats of media, as well as generic traditions and cultural or historical contexts, can then become subject to different critical examinations. Live-action film, for instance, introduces questions of embodiment into character debates that are entirely or partially absent from comics and animated films. This is why the next three chapters are dedicated to three heterogeneous medial contexts of characters and their representations: Recorded "live-action" media forms like film and television, cartoonish media forms like comic books or animated films, and interactive and participatory media forms like digital and analog games.

Section 2

Characters in Different Narrative Media

4 Embodied Characters in Film, TV Shows, and Cosplay

Characters in "real-life media" such as theater performances, films, or TV shows are usually *embodied* by human actors. In cosplay performances, audiences employ their own bodies together with costumes and props to represent characters themselves. Images in film and TV shows are produced by light bouncing off bodies and other physical objects, registering on the photographic emulsion, leaving a trace or an "index" of actual people in front of the cameras. Our cognitive person schema, which activates all other aspects of character recognition (such as their assumed personal agency and, above all, their continuous consciousness frame), is strongly connected to our innate intuition that a person primarily has, or even *is*, a human body. Pictures of recorded actors elicit this schema, as well as our corresponding understanding of these actors as (non-fictional) persons and/or (fictional) characters, even before a single word is uttered. As audiences, we can immediately perceive more character traits from (recordings of) actors than could be specified by any written text: the precise qualities and patterns of their looks and movements, their facial expressions and gestures, as well as their specific ways of speaking. Part of the basic appeal of film and TV is indeed "the delight in bodies and expressive movement," James Naremore (1988, 2) found. These forms of medial representation thus contain a "sensory specificity that [...] diminishes the range of individual imaginations by the recipients" (Eder et al. 2010, 18). Within the vocabulary offered before, embodied characters are rather "dense" intersubjective communicative constructs as we can immediately make – and uphold – countless claims about them that would remain unspecified in literature at first, at least with regard to their outward appearances. At the same time, we always seem to perceive not only the characters but also the actors themselves. In that way, all fictional characters portrayed by a specific actor will also contribute to our mental model of the same celebrity (see Turner 2004).

The present chapter is going to look deeper into the complicated relationship between actors and characters and offer some basic categories and distinctions for analysis. In the first section, we will try to differentiate between actual persons, star personas, and the characters they portray, touching on the question of how all three dimensions are often entangled and interrelated. The second section is then looking at actor-character-relations in more detail, discussing many examples in

DOI: 10.4324/9781003298793-7

which a one-to-one correlation is abandoned in favor of one actor representing different characters in the same media text or, the other way round when the same character is portrayed by different actors. We will also discuss to what degree actors can be considered co-authors of the characters they portray, or at least whether they represent a privileged source of information about them. This will lead to the introduction of *representational correspondence*, a highly useful concept capturing the fact that audiences have to distinguish – more often than we might think – between the visible and audible character traits recorded from actors on the one hand and the mimetic, intersubjective construct of the storyworld on the other. The final section is referring back to sociopolitical issues of embodiment, especially with regard to problematic traditions of Blackface and Whitewashing.

4.1 Actors as Persons, Personas, and Characters

"[P]eople in a film can be regarded in at least three different senses," Naremore (1988, 15) found, "as actors playing personages [characters], as public figures playing theatrical versions of themselves, and as documentary evidence." We will distinguish these dimensions as characters, star personas, and actual persons (see Hagener 2013; as well as Nannicelli 2019). The action star Dwayne "The Rock" Johnson – who even carries something akin to a "character trait" within his established actor name, being "like a rock" – certainly contributes to a continuous image of himself throughout all of his movies. Intuitively, we are certainly aware that this image, this *persona*, will be different from the "actual person" off-screen as it is to a certain degree a highly artificial, controlled construct (see Garber 2020, 43–56). The actor Cary Grant is said to have put this tension between himself and the public image he needed to uphold in the humorous words "Everybody wants to be Cary Grant. Even I want to be Cary Grant" (Wikiquotes, "Cary Grant"). Celebrities will thus always experience a specific split between their private and their public self, sociologist Chris Rojek (2016) found. When Johnny Depp was involved in a series of controversies and scandals revolving around his rather public divorce from Amber Heard and accusations of drug abuse and domestic violence, audiences came to differentiate between the likable persona (image) of the star and the person behind it (see Sawant 2020). An even more notorious "public unmasking" was that of actor-comedian Bill Cosby who represented a role model for Black, middle-class family men in the sitcom *The Cosby Show* (Carsey et al. 1984–1992) until he was convicted for drugging and sexually assaulting women (see Begley 2015; Garber 2020, 55). The stance toward actors and their personas can thus be, in various ways, entirely different than toward the characters they portray. Studies going back to the 1940s revealed that audiences often emphasized the utter *remoteness* and the unattainable glamor of Hollywood celebrities like Rita Hayworth who were "out of this world" – in contrast to the many mundane protagonists they embodied (see Stacey 1994, 126). This relationship might have changed somewhat since fans can now follow actors on social media and since paparazzi capture them in unflattering moments every minute of the day. On platforms such as Twitter, where thousands of people comment on new articulations of vocal celebrities (the most followed celebrity as of May 12, 2022, has been Justin Bieber with over 114 million followers, while Rihanna leads the count with 106.6 million with respect to those also appearing as actors), we increasingly seem to interact more directly with them (see Clark 2015). This is sometimes addressed as a *parasocial relationship* between audiences and stars, the imagination to count celebrities to one's circle of personal friends, even though this relationship is entirely mediated and one-directional (see Giles 2002; Rojek 2016).

Personas can sometimes be connected to specific media formats, genres, or franchises themselves. Coming from professional WWF wrestling, "The Rock" could be understood as a strongly fictionalized persona who engaged in some-times pre-constructed, sometimes improvised stories within his wrestling stage appearances, even though no overarching fictional WWF storyworld is estab-lished (see Reinhard and Olson 2019). The difference between such "WWF char-acters" and other "on-stage personas" in non-fictional TV formats (such as John Oliver in *Last Week Tonight*, Oliver et al. 2014–present, or Hannah Gadsby in stand-up comedy shows like *Nanette*, Parry and Olb 2018) might thus be more one of *degree* than of category. Sometimes, on-stage personas might use specific names (aliases, pen names, or artist names) distinguishing them from their "civil identities" (private individuals). This is by no means bound to actors, however, but to all persons of public interest, so that politicians, too, can be expected to perform a certain persona in public. Journalistic media and the tabloid press re-porting on the private lives of celebrities promise a more immediate access to the person "behind the image," precisely because their reports are not authorized or controlled by the celebrities themselves. From TV shows like *UnREAL* (Noxon et al. 2015–2018) or *The Morning Show* (Aniston et al. 2019–present) to comic books like *Everyone Is Tulip* (Baker et al. 2021), many media texts *about media* tell stories concerned with the very relationship between persona and person, effectively "re-introducing" that distinction within their storyworld. This can even become a major topic in strongly fictionalized narratives such as the superhero satire comic book (Ennis et al. 2006–2012) and TV show (Kripke et al. 2019–present) *The Boys* or the *Hunger Games* books (e.g., Collins 2008) and films (e.g., Ross 2012) where the protagonists are likewise subject to tensions between their actual lives and personalities in contrast to their media personas, continuously judged and evaluated by the powerful, mostly invisible actant of "the public." The adoption of changing social roles, however, is by no means exclusive to actors or even to figures of public interest. Within sociological research, it is fairly established even for private individuals that all of us are performing *different roles* in different social contexts, varying greatly between a professional environment, in sports clubs, or together with family members and friends (see Goffman 1976). By contrast, however, most of us do not try to uphold a *unified*, intentionally controlled pub-lic persona. To make things more confusing, many address these social roles as "characters," too, like philosopher Alasdair MacIntyre (1981, 33): "[T]he culture of Victorian England was partially defined by the characters of the Public School Headmaster, the Explorer, and the Engineer."

What distinguishes actors perhaps most saliently from other public figures is that, for some of them, their personas can seem especially tied to a specific character (or a character type) they portray(ed) – because they are mostly known – and famous – for that very role. Murray Pomerance (2016, 166) addressed this relationship as the (varying) "degree of tenuousness between actors and the characters they play." Leonard Nimoy, the actor playing Mr. Spock in the original *Star Trek* (Roddenberry 1966–1969) series, for instance, struggled for decades to be disentangled from this role (see his first autobiography *I am not Spock* from 1975). The web series *Con Man* (Tudyk et al. 2015–2017) presents a more current negotiation of these tensions. It was created, written, and directed by Alan Tudyk, who also plays the titular character, a struggling fictional actor named Wray Nerely famous for a discontinued (likewise fictional, intra-diegetic) Sci-Fi cult show named "Spectrum" where he represented the pilot "Cash Wayne." The character Wray in the storyworld earns his living by traveling Sci-Fi conventions and making appearances at comic book stores. *Con Man* addresses his love/hate relationship toward fans who forever see him as the character ("Cash") he portrayed, rather than a human being *or* a serious actor able to play other roles as well. Adding a crucial layer of meaning and interpretation to the show is the fact that Alan Tudyk *did* play a role just like "Cash" in the real world, the pilot Hoban "Wash" Washburne in the actual cult Sci-Fi series *Firefly* (Whedon and Minear 2002) and the film sequel *Serenity* (Whedon 2005). Since many other *Firefly/Serenity* actors also make their appearance in *Con Man* besides Tudyk, it becomes clear that "Spectrum" is a humorous stand-in for the actual series *Firefly* – and for Tudyk's real biography as an actor/persona who *does* appear at fan conventions regularly. In much the same way, Michael Keaton's casting in *Birdman or (The Unexpected Virtue of Ignorance)* (Iñárritu 2014) is essential to the film's plot surrounding the fictional protagonist Riggan Thomson – best known within the storyworld for playing the (likewise fictional) Hollywood superhero "Birdman" before. Just as with Tudyk/Nerely/Cash/Wash, "Birdman" is a stand-in for Keaton's actual casting as the titular protagonist in the films *Batman* (Burton 1989) and *Batman Returns* (Burton 1992).

Actors often carry such "traces" of earlier roles with them that add additional meaning to new characters. In the cases of *Con Man* or *Birdman*, it is specific roles and characters that we need to be familiar with while other media texts merely build upon the character *types* usually embodied by an actor ("John Wayne as indomitable cowboy – essentially a category; Marilyn Monroe as sex kitten; Mickey Rooney as irrepressible teen; Marlene Dietrich as naughty underdog," Pomerance 2016, 167). The *Expendables* franchise, for instance, is built around the idea of bringing together "faded" action heroes of the past as an aged military squad. The premise of the films (e.g., Stallone 2010) – paying homage to blockbuster action films of the 1980s and 1990s – could not be appreciated without the casting of names like Sylvester Stallone (who also co-wrote the scripts), Arnold Schwarzenegger, Bruce Willis, or Mickey Rourke who "carry" their earlier roles of 1980s and 1990s action heroes with their star persona. In the terminology proposed earlier, we could say that the synthetic levels of characters – their existence as a medial artifact, co-constructed by actors in the real world who have previously played other characters that "merged" with their star personas – is inventively exploited by such media texts. Actors' personas can also communicate audience expectations about likely actantial roles of certain characters: When we recognize a famous celebrity like Awkwafina in one of *Shang-Chi and the Legend of the Ten Rings'* (Cretton 2021) first scenes, we can be sure that her character (Katy) will be of major importance to the plot later – with the exception of so-called "cameo" appearances that only serve as a sort of "inside joke" for a small part of the audience (like actor Bruce Campbell's short appearance as a pizza vendor in Sam Raimi's *Doctor Strange in the Multiverse of Madness*, Raimi 2022; Campbell is mainly famous for his main role in Raimi's earlier cult film *Army of Darkness*, 1992).

The final chapter within this volume is going to look in more detail at the question of whether transmedia character studies can help us to get a clearer understanding of personas and non-fictional, yet mediated celebrities as well. Confusingly, personas are sometimes also called "character" in the press: "Every presidential candidate plays a character, whether he or she admits it or not [...]. The character Mr. Trump plays may be more honest than of any of his rivals: He's the ambitious businessman who cares only about winning" (Roller 2016, n.pag.). For starters, though, fictional characters portrayed by actors should be sharply distinguished from their personas (although there might be transitional media domains like in professional wrestling). While no one would doubt that Trump's public image will be somehow different from the "actual" human being, this is a tension of attributed and contested "personality traits" (like "smartness" or "straight-forwardness") but not of bodily and psychological continuity. Differences between persona and human being thus entail no *ontological* contradiction. Harrison Ford certainly behaves differently in public and in private, but these social roles remain linked through an identical body and a continuous consciousness frame that unites all appearances and experiences of the actor. Indiana Jones, by contrast, never "turns" into Harrison Ford at any time or in any context, and he also has no recollection of anything that Ford has ever experienced (in another character-role or as himself on set), for the simple fact that the actor does not even exist within Indiana Jones' storyworld set right after Ford was only just born (in 1942). Jones and Ford are thus separated by an ontological barrier owed to the fictionality of any Indiana Jones story within films, TV shows, comic books, or video games. These fictional worlds and their inhabitants exist exclusively as intersubjective communicative constructs (even though they are *represented* by actual people, things, and events). The dozens of fictional characters portrayed by Johnson or "The Rock" – such as Luke Hobbs from the *The Fast and the Furious* series (his first appearance being in *Fast & Furious 6*, Lin 2013), Hercules from the eponymous film (Ratner 2014), or Dr. Smolder Bravestone from *Jumanji: Welcome to the Jungle* (Kasdan 2017) – can also be sharply distinguished from each other as well as from the actor himself in ontological terms: Their existences in the mimetic dimension are mutually exclusive.

4.2 Actor-Character-Relations

To what degree actors can be seen as *authors* of the characters they portray in all their roles is a difficult question. For audiences, actors certainly provide some sort of privileged access to characters. In appearances at conventions, actors not only frequently adopt or "quote" their character-roles or merge them with their personas (the character will nevertheless not be expected to remember these appearances as they didn't take place within their actual, "canonical" stories), actors are also understood as a privileged source of information about a character's feelings, intentions, or motivations. The term "extended television" has emerged to address the fact that audiences can now easily follow their favorite shows and actors on various platforms, forums, and apps, sometimes at the same time as they are watching on a "second screen" (see Evans 2011). *The Talking Dead* (Davies et al. 2011–2022), a live TV chat show that discusses episodes of *The Walking Dead* (Darabont et al. 2010–2022) and its various spin-off series with cast and crew members, is a prime example of a format presenting the actors of these fictional shows (see Freeman 2019). They are interviewed as privileged *sources* on the production process, as well as on the characters they portray, often giving personal opinions about their motivation. Frequently, they also help audiences make sense of characters in emotional terms, offering different forms of evaluation. At the same time, it becomes clear within these formats that the actors are not at all in control of whether their characters behave a certain way or die within the storyworld, commonly being as surprised or conflicted about these creative choices as their fans. John Boyega might strongly disagree with Disney's portrayal of Finn (played by himself) in *Star Wars*, but there is not much he can do to alter the character's fate as a fictional being (see Watercutter 2020). By contrast, Scarlett Johansson did not only *play* Black Widow in her 2021 standalone film (Shortland) – like she did in *Iron Man 2* (Favreau 2010) or *The Avengers* (Whedon 2012) – but was also an executive producer on the movie. This means that she had a say in most decisions regarding the film, trying to ensure the character was not portrayed as a mere "piece of ass" again (Johansson as quoted in Robinson 2021). Johansson could thus choose the *female* director of the movie, Cate Shortland, who, in turn, would construct the character less from a male perspective. Authorship over characters is thus always distributed throughout their synthetic dimension and, as this example shows, often entangled (see chapter 7).

Beyond the simple fact that actors are usually not responsible for the script and the lines they perform, their authorship over character-building remains limited even with respect to their perceived expressions. Early theatrical theories of acting – from directors and actors such as Konstantin Stanislavski, Antonin Artaud, or Jerzy Grotowski – could indeed be characterized as "production-oriented" as they developed a strong orientation toward actors. They were asking about the means of actors to *appropriate* a character adequately in order to achieve a desired expression (see Butler 1991; Sternagel et al. 2012). Accordingly, it was seen as the task of actors to find the most adequate bodily expressions mirroring (or indicating) inner states and emotions, for example, by self-suggestively imagining the fictional situation their character was supposed to be placed in. Such approaches (called "method acting"), deeming the actor the final authority on their portrayed characters (or, at least, their emotions and expressions), could be called *holistic*. In *synthetic* approaches, by contrast, the meaning of any film sequence emerges only through editing and montage. The "Kuleshov effect" serves as a poignant example of this, although it is more of a film historical myth than a reliable experiment (see Prince and Hensley 1992). Soviet filmmaker Lev Kuleshov was said to contrast an identical shot of the actor Ivan Mosjoukine with alternating images of a bowl of soup, a girl in a coffin, and a woman on a divan, and the audience allegedly described Mosjoukine's (identical) facial expression alternately as "hungry," "grieving," and "full of desire." An actor's bodily performance, seen in such a way, is then nothing but raw material for generating meaning in editing – and as such no different from any other prop in front of a camera, whether it is a scenery, an animal, or a coffee cup.

Speaking more generally, material-based or synthetic theories of acting identified three sources of deviation from actor-based, holistic approaches to characters (see Hickethier 1999). First, shooting is usually discontinuous. In contrast to theater performances where an actor might "live through" the emotional trajectory their character is supposed to experience, film and TV scenes are often shot in a different order, in different parts of the world – the actors might not even possess full knowledge about the whole story. In *Game of Thrones*' (Benioff 2011–2019) final season, the ending was kept secret from the actors (see Chapman 2019). In *Avengers: Endgame* (Russo and Russo 2019), the cast was even given wrong information during the shooting of the final funeral scene: According to actors Mark Ruffalo and Tom Holland, they were told they were filming a wedding scene in order to keep the ending a secret. The actors therefore couldn't even guess the emotions of the characters they were portraying, but audiences would deduct those easily from the overall plot and context (see Fitzpatrick 2019). Second, the recorded images of actors are *fragmented* into close-ups (twitching hands, a little smile, a wrinkling of the eyebrows) that only attain meaning as character traits within edited versions later. Finally, the acting style on film can be highly reduced – in contrast to theater performances – as the camera can expand, enlarge, or amplify any recorded fragment. In some cases, this can lead to a desired *underacting*, attributing little authorship to actors over their character in contrast to other filmic means of characterization (such as their depicted actions or a voice-over narration). Taken together, discontinuity, fragmentation, and reduction all point to the fact that authorship over characters is highly distributed between various agents of film and TV productions (see Caldwell 2008). Contemporary motion capturing technologies perhaps provide the clearest example for acting in which performers like Andy Serkis (providing motion data for characters such as Gollum in *The Lord of the Rings: The Fellowship of the Ring*, Jackson 2001, *King Kong*, Jackson 2005, or Caesar in *Rise of the Planet of the Apes*, Wyatt 2011) lose even more autonomy, contributing merely digital information for animators and editors to work with later (see Balcerzak 2009; Carnicke 2012).

Even though authorship over characters is thus distributed among various people, art historian Erwin Panofsky famously stated that "[t]he character in a film
lives and dies with the actor" (Panofsky 1959, 29). In many films and TV shows,
embodied characters certainly seem somehow more "natural" than in other media, as if we were looking at them "directly" – just as we are looking at real people in film footage of family holidays or in documentaries. Actors' achievements
are then not immediately recognized as such, their results instead appearing as
immediate attributes (character traits) of the portrayed protagonists themselves.
Nevertheless, if we watch Russel Crowe play mathematician and Nobel Laureate
John Nash in his Oscar-awarded performance for *A Beautiful Mind* (Howard
2001), we cannot help but distinguish the represented character Nash in the film
from both the actual John Nash as well as from Crowe himself. Although questions of fictionalization will be discussed in more detail in chapter 10, it should
immediately be clear that, on the one hand, Crowe's character – to whose mind
the film simulates immediate access by means of perceptual overlays – cannot be
conflated with the historical person Nash (as represented, for instance, in Sylvia
Nasar's biography from 1998); both can only be similar to each other to some
degree, which is why many reviewers found that "A Beautiful Mind's John Nash
is nowhere near as complicated as the real one" (Suellentrop 2001, n.pag.). On
the other hand, when we see the film's Nash undergoing insulin shock therapy
as a treatment for his schizophrenia, his frightened eyes filled with tears, him
twitching, and his muscle spasming, we are imagining Nash (the film's protagonist) suffering without worrying about Crowe. The character thus remains a
clearly identifiable mimetic (intersubjective) construct situated between *both* actor
and historical person (or other Nash-representations in media texts claiming to
give access to the historical Nash).

Any assumed one-to-one correlation between characters and actors – and their
represented traits – can be even further complicated. From a transmedial perspective, narrative formats in which one actor embodies multiple characters are
surprisingly frequent (see Smith 1995, 17–39). Small theater companies often use
only one or a handful of actors to play a large cast of characters for pragmatic and
economic reasons. This is also an entirely commonplace representational practice for stand-up comedians and other one-person-performers, not necessarily
presenting any cognitive challenge or irritation for audiences at all. Film scholar
Murray Smith suggests (1995, 28) that the reason why we easily accept this sort of
break with established filmic actor-character-correlations is deeply rooted in oral
storytelling, in which narrators have always impersonated countless characters
mimetically as they were recounting their fates. The other way round – more
than one actor portraying the same character – is encountered less frequently, but
there are still countless examples. Experimental films such as Nagisa Oshima's
The Story of a Man Who Put His Will on Film (1970), Luis Buñuel's *That Obscure Object
of Desire* (1977), and Todd Haynes' *I'm not There* (2007) or plays like Caryl Church-
ill's *Light Shining in Buckinghamshire* (1976) have constructed narratives in which the
same character is played by more actors than one, looking noticeably different
from each other. The effects of these strategies cannot be generalized, but it is safe

to say that they are mostly directed toward the thematic (symbolic) level: Buñuel, for instance, wishes to stress that the "desirability" in the film's title is about the social category of "women" in general, rather than any individual one (see Riis 2013). This can only be the result of a symbolic interpretation if viewers first understand that both starring actresses (Carole Bouquet and Ángela Molina) are, in fact, intended as representations of the same continuous protagonist (Conchita) and start looking for reasons as to why the actor-character-relation is employed contrary to regular conventions. In the popular show *Doctor Who* (Newman et al. 1963–present), these reasons are not so much symbolic as symptomatic: When William Hartnell, the initial actor portraying the titular character, could no longer continue due to old age, the show resolved the problem presented by his replacement on the level of the storyworld (and thus "naturalized" it), not on the level of additional thematic meanings. As an alien "Time Lord," the show's protagonist is "regenerated" within new bodies between seasons, rendering all the 13 actors since 1963 as different incarnations of the same continuous consciousness frame. Accordingly, he (or rather *they*, as actress Jodie Whittaker was cast as the 13th Doctor in 2017), as well as supporting characters, make many references to the "previous" doctors and their experiences. Unlike many other transmedia characters played by multiple actors (such as James Bond), the Doctor remains the same character within the same canon (more on that in chapter 7), while the differences in appearance are integrated into the storyworld by a fantastic *diegetic* explanation. Another instance of this strategy occurs in Terry Gilliam's 2009 film *The Imaginarium of Doctor Parnassus*, where the death of starring actor Heath Ledger resulted in the casting of Johnny Depp, Jude Law, and Colin Farrell, who share the role with Ledger in the finished film. Here, too, the film's diegetic premise, which involves the titular character traveling through a shifting dream world, enabled a naturalization of the visible difference between the multiple actors. An entirely common duplicity of multiple actors playing the same character can be found in films and shows that portray characters over large spans of time. The show *This is Us* (Fogelman et al. 2016–2022), for instance, has many different actors playing the Pearson siblings as newborns, at the age of 3–4, age 8–10, age 15–17, and during the diegetic present of around age 40. The respective actors might still somehow "resemble" each other (who does not?), but audiences have to *learn* that they are intended as representations of the same, fictional protagonists on the level of the overall storyworld (the actors playing them within the diegetic present still seem to claim some priority within this assemblage of actors: When *This is Us* jumps ahead to the future in season 3s finale, 2019, the characters are *not* recast once again, but instead just made to look older through makeup). Again, there are obvious pragmatic reasons – connected to the mediality of real-life film – for the frequent multiplicity of child actors: It is just not feasible to record the same actors over the timespan of decades if the characters are not intended to age in "real-time," too, like the protagonists of the eight *Harry Potter* films or the Stark siblings in the eight seasons of *Game of Thrones*. Richard Linklater's film *Boyhood* (2014) was praised as a cinematic achievement for doing exactly that: The filmmaker followed the actor Ellar Coltrane (playing the character Mason Evans Jr.) over a period of 12 years, editing the footage together into one subsequent story of 165 minutes in which we can not only see the character, but also the actor aging over the same amount of time. We can appreciate this on the synthetic (and therefore media-specific) level, not the mimetic level of character comprehension. In a comic book, this would hardly deserve attention. *Boyhood* is thus just as much a documentary about the actor Coltrane as a fictional story about the character Mason, once again demonstrating that real-life fictional film and TV footage usually has at least a *double referentiality*. The pictures can be used to infer facts about the actors, props, and occurrences on the set – as if they were recording a theater stage – as well as about the fictional occurrences and characters represented by these means. The elusive third layer in between – the star persona – emerges to the degree that we *recognize* actors as celebrities from other roles or from public appearances.

Sometimes, actors pick up on earlier characters decades after their initial casting. In recent years, this has achieved great popularity in so-called "legacyquels" (a term popularized by journalist Matt Singer in a noteworthy article from 2015): *Tron Legacy* from 2011 by Joseph Kosinski (Jeff Bridges returning as Kevin Flynn from the 1982 *Tron* by Steven Lisberger), *Blade Runner 2049* from 2017 by Denis Villeneuve (Harrison Ford reprising his role as Rick Deckard from *Blade Runner*, Scott 1982), Ryan Coogler's *Creed* from 2015 (Sylvester Stallone as Rocky Balboa from *Rocky*, Avildsen 1976), Tim Miller's *Terminator: Dark Fate* from 2019 (Linda Hamilton as Sarah Connor from *Terminator*, Cameron 1984), the Netflix show *Cobra Kai* from 2018–present by Josh Heald and others (Ralph Macchio returning to his titular role in *The Karate Kid*, Avildsen 1984) (see Loock 2016). In the best of cases, these revivals provide a critical reflection on their source texts (and its respective ethos) as well as on the changed political circumstances (see Herbert 2020) – as we have discussed with recourse to the transmedial "legacyquel" of *Watchmen* in the previous chapter. In any case: In "real-life" media forms (in contrast to comic books, for instance), a corresponding amount of diegetic time has usually passed within the respective storyworlds as between their actual productions. Despite the fact that every aspect of films can now be digitally manipulated, actors are thus typically linked to their characters by the passing of real time – very differently from novel, comic book, or video game protagonists who can apparently resist aging for decades.

4.3 Introducing Representational Correspondence

Many irritations concerning actor-character-relationships can arise within transmedial franchises such as the MCU (Marvel Cinematic Universe) where a strong notion of continuity and canonicity is upheld across all media texts. A character is not only portrayed by a (specific) actor, but likewise represented within comic books, animated films, or video games which often try to portray the character *as played by a specific actor*. In Peter David's and Carlos Villa's *Black Widow Prelude* comic (2020), for instance, the titular heroine is clearly intended to resemble the actress Scarlett Johansson more so than in other Black Widow comics not connected to the MCU continuity. When the protagonists in the video game *Marvel's Avengers* (2020) did *not* resemble their established actors at all – the game company Crystal Dynamics did not buy the rights to use the actors' likenesses – many audience members expressed their disappointments and "deep-faked" the faces of Johansson, Mark Ruffalo, Robert Downey Jr., Chris Evans, and Chris Hemsworth into the game trailer (see Malone 2019 or Tassi 2020). If in film or TV, a character is recast with another actor (such as James Bond), this not only "becomes a challenge of both aesthetic and economic proportions" (Pomerance 2016, 172) but is also often considered a *reboot*: It restarts the franchise as another storyworld with the two "versions" of the character having no overarching fictional biography or any shared recollection (continuous consciousness frame) related to past events (see Chapter 7). A special case is the Netflix series *House of Cards* (Willimon et al. 2013–2018) which ran into troubles during the production of its concluding fifth season when its main actor Kevin Spacey was accused of sexual misconduct (creating the same sort of tension between actor and star persona as discussed before for Cosby or Depp). The *House of Cards* producers found themselves under huge pressure not to continue Spacey's contract for a show which mainly revolved around the seductive charisma of its corrupt protagonist Frank Underwood (played by Spacey). As they could not easily recast the main character for the story's conclusion after five years, the show resolved this tension somewhat clumsily by rewriting the concluding season's plot in such a way that Underwood had died in between seasons, focusing entirely on his wife Claire (played by Robin Wright) instead. Importantly, the show *did* reveal many new diegetic facts about her husband's final chapter – mainly by reports of other characters, without *showing* Spacey/Underwood in the diegetic present – as if the character had to be painfully disentangled from the actor and his "tarnished" persona.

If an actor appears in multiple roles within a franchise that makes strong claims to continuity and canonicity (and thus usually casts the same actors in a role only once), it causes irritations or questions. Actor Martin Starr, for instance, appearing as an unnamed computer scientist in *The Incredible Hulk* film (Leterrier 2008), returned years later as a nameless science teacher in *Spider-Man: Homecoming* (Watts 2017). It was not clear whether this was in fact meant to represent the same character (as a kind of "easter egg"), or whether the resemblance could be ignored. In Starr's case, the overall MCU producer Kevin Feige did make an "authorial announcement" in 2019 *declaring* the characters to be the same (see Outlaw 2019). The fact that he decided to do so – since audiences were confused or at least *curious* about this question – tells us more than the (certainly not very momentous) "decision" itself. Once again, we can see that characters must be analyzed on the level of discussions about media texts (including questions of authorship and alleged authorial intentions) as much as on the level of the texts themselves.

It is not possible to uphold a correlation between actors and characters, however, in shows or film series in which the same character *had* to be recast when the original actor died or left the production. One famous example is Richard Harris as Albus Dumbledore, who passed away from lymphoma and was then recast by Michael Gambon for *Harry Potter and the Chamber of Secrets* (Columbus 2002) (see again Pomerance 2016). Audiences simply had to "ignore" this recast. This introduces us to many fascinating problems of *representational correspondence*. This concept, introduced by philosopher Gregory Currie (2010, 58–64), asks which representational aspects in a given media text – for instance, what we can see in a film's pictures and hear in its sounds – we can "map" onto the fictional situation, a media text's storyworld: "[F]or a given representational work, only certain features of the representation serve to represent features of the things represented" (59). Thus, it is never *all* features of a representation that are relevant with respect to the diegetic situation, as Jan-Noël Thon expands on in his transmedial narratology (2016, 60): "[I]t makes sense to distinguish more systematically between presentational and representational aspects of a given narrative representation." It is easy to demonstrate that this difference can never be completely overcome, even in the photographic film image: Black-and-white films or flashbacks in sepia colors represent a "monochrome world" only in exceptional cases (for example, within *Pleasantville*, Ross 1998, or in the first three episodes of *WandaVision*, Schaeffer et al. 2020, audiences are introduced to media-reflective monochrome storyworlds which *are* intended to physical possess no colors at all).

Similar forms of "blocked" representational correspondence must be taken into account more often than we might think: Why does the fictional character Daario Naharis in *Game of Thrones* suddenly change his appearance "mysteriously"? In season three, he was played by the Brit Ed Skrein, but from season four onwards by the Dutchman Michiel Huisman, without any diegetic explanation being offered (while the exact cause of Skrein's exit from the show was never announced, it is clear that he was recast for *symptomatic* reasons, just like Harris as Dumbledore, see David 2021; other examples include the recasts of the titular hero in *Spartacus*, Raimi et al. 2010–2013, or of Reggie Mantle in *Riverdale*, Aguirre-Sacasa et al. 2017–present, after their respective first seasons). Valid conclusions – fictional truths – that Daario Naharis had "magic abilities" and could transform his appearance at will (just like the diegetically established "faceless men") would obviously not be accepted as intersubjectively plausible. The differences in representation in all these cases cannot be "mapped" onto the portrayed character but "remain" on the synthetic side of the character representation. The same is true for the auditory level: Many films and shows in a historical or "foreign" setting have all their characters speak modern English *representing* other languages for convenience and practicability. In *Game of Thrones*' Westeros, the regular language is known as the "common tongue." Everything that characters are reported to say in the original English books must hence be an "invisible translation." This can be no different from what we hear the actors say in the show. Other foreign languages, such as "Dothraki" or "High Valyrian" – less "common" to most characters – could likewise be translated, but the show's representational correspondence retains their "foreignness" by providing only subtitles for the respective exchanges. *Vikings* (Hirst et al. 2013–2020) makes this even more obvious. Characters are heard talking in (something intended to resemble) Old Norse, Old English, Old French, and Latin (all subtitled) only if overheard by other characters unfamiliar with these languages. The main protagonists from any scene will always be "switching" into modern English when we are *aligned* with their consciousness frames, stressing once again that there is a necessary representational gap between the medial representation (synthetic dimension) and the storyworld (mimetic dimension). Its auditory as well as visual aspects can only ever be in close correspondence but never entirely identical. As a communicative construct, we can neither see nor hear aspects of the storyworld itself, only have good reason to ignore or respect certain properties of the respective media aesthetics.

These *rules of the imagination* must always be related to specific medial, generic, and historical conventions. In a theater production in which the same actor plays various roles no one would assume that all the people portrayed by the actor are meant to "look like identical twins" within the storyworld. We would instead assume that their bodily features are instead "left open" to the imagination, while their patterns of speech, gestures, and movements represent only a *type* of appearance, with their exact visibility (or audibility, for that matter) remaining unclear. In different theatrical traditions, this "gap" between what we perceive and what it is supposed to represent (as an intersubjective communicative construct within the storyworld) can vary: Opera allows it to be "larger." Troublesome – and often blatantly racist – discussions of whether an actor of color "can" portray a northern European character (such as Hamlet or Hermione Jean Granger) are rarer for opera than for more "naturalistic" theater traditions (see Uno and Burns 2002; Milvy 2019). In film and TV shows, by contrast, where different rules of the imagination are established, we usually assume something akin to a one-to-one correlation between the bodily features of actors and the bodily features of characters. The fact remains, however, that representational correspondence always remains a convention: Drawing inferences from what we see and hear will always necessitate a "suspension of disbelief" to some degree.

Following the principle of minimal departure introduced before, we usually assume that fictional narratives imply worlds based on our "real" one as long as no reasons are given to assume a counterfactual, alternate history. Storyworlds set in the contemporary United States thus usually have a city called New York and a history entailing John F. Kennedy as a former president, even if neither of these elements is explicitly referenced. If Tom Cruise is playing a character such as Pete Mitchell (*Top Gun*, Scott 1986) or Ethan Hunt (in *Mission: Impossible*, De Palma 1996), and if they both look "just like" the actor, why is no one noticing their unmistakable similarity to Tom Cruise? Why do they pass as regular "everymen"? Apparently, there cannot be a famous actor called Tom Cruise in these worlds, then. Why does the secret agent James Bond give away his name "Bond, James Bond" openly to every bartender he encounters without worrying that this might "ring some bells"? The world(s) Bond operates in must hence be different from ours, at least to the extent that "James Bond" is *not* a media household name everybody recognizes. One could ask many more (perhaps silly) questions: Is there *another* prototypical secret agent who is known to everybody in the Bond storyworld(s)? Is there an actor named Sean Connery, and, if so, what is his most famous role? While many problems of representational correspondence are usually "left open" (asking them in earnest would be considered "silly," see Walton 1993, 174–183) they are brought back to our attention if explicitly addressed within reflexive (and often humorous) narratives that *do* highlight them. *Ocean's Twelve* (Sonderbergh 2004), for instance, exploits one of these apparent paradoxes. Julia Roberts portrays the fictional character of Tess Ocean, who "happens to look like" the well-known celebrity Julia Roberts in the fictional storyworld as well. The film's band of thieves aims to exploit this resemblance and have Tess impersonate the actress to gain access to an exclusive event. In this case, the epistemic incompleteness of the intersubjective character – whether they look *exactly* like the actor portraying them or not – is playfully resolved. This is rarely the case, however. When Peter Parker refers to the *Star Wars* movies in *Captain America: Civil War* (Russo and Russo 2016), audiences could wonder why he did not recognize the striking similarity of Nick Fury to Samuel L. Jackson (who portrays not only Fury but should be known to Peter from the *Star Wars* prequel trilogy in which he portrays Mace Windu, too). We could decide to solve such riddles either by assuming that these fictional storyworlds differ from ours in so far that the respective actors *do not exist* there or that they are somehow "replaced" by other actors with a different appearance (such as in the Arnold Schwarzenegger film *Last Action Hero*, McTiernan 1993, which shows a storyworld where the Schwarzenegger film *Terminator* exists as well, only that Schwarzenegger there is replaced by Sylvester Stallone); or we could assume that the characters are supposed to look only "something like" the actors that portray them (the same gender, age, body type) but not exactly so. Obviously, asking these questions would usually be "silly" again, to use the wording of philosopher Kendal Walton once more (1993, 174–183). No one would ask them "in earnest," neither screenwriters nor audiences, as both parties usually "ignore" these aspects charitably. Considering the exact likeness between characters and well-known actors is then usually *not* part of the rules of the imagination for movies and TV shows. One notable exception is formed by the Netflix mystery drama *Stranger Things* (Duffer et al. 2016–present): The series frequently references 1980s pop culture, in keeping with being set in that decade. Additionally, one of the starring roles is played by actress Winona Ryder, herself an 1980s movie icon. Talking about the fourth season of the series, showrunners Matt and Ross Duffer explicitly stated that *Stranger Things*' plot could not move beyond the year 1988, due to Winona Ryder's actual-world breakthrough in the film *Beetlejuice* (Burton), released that very year. The Duffers' reasoning addressed precisely the question that most similar media texts avoid: Since the show had established the existence of so many actual 1980s texts in its storyworld, the characters (and audience members) could not be expected to simply ignore the similarity between the (fictionalized) star of *Beetlejuice* and the strictly fictional Joyce Byers (see Huver 2022). In this regard, the show refuses to rely on the suspension of disbelief that is always, to some extent, necessary for the intersubjective construction of fictional worlds and characters, leaving these aspects undefined in most other cases. Which of them remain open and which do not, however, makes for an interesting point of comparison between works from different medial, generic, and historical traditions. Rules of the imagination concerning representational correspondence are far from stable and always subject to contested discourses, as all of these examples should show. They are thus an especially interesting object of analysis when they become problematic for political and ethical reasons.

4.4 Politics of Embodiment

When the role of the Marvel character Heimdall from Thor's pantheon of "Asgardians" was filled with Black actor Idris Elba in *Thor* (Branagh 2011), openly racist complaints from White supremacists were not only about the question of whether a Black actor "can" play an ostensibly White character, but whether *the character* of Heimdall can be Black (see Child 2010). As a "Norse god," they argued, this was not in line with the mythology, thus tacitly assuming a close representational correspondence between the appearances of actor and character. This debate not only ignores the fact that the MCU's "Asgardians" were not even intended to be the "actual" gods of myth (but instead an interdimensional species inspiring the myth within Marvel's storyworld as well). What is more, "faithfulness" to Nordic mythology or any other kind of "realism" was no claim the Marvel universe ever made, not to mention the obvious fact that "authenticity" should not be troublesome within a world of talking trees and space raccoons. Questions of ethnicity (or gender and other intersectional identity categories) in real-life media are thus always entangled between characters *and* actors in interesting and often complicated ways. In this final section of the chapter on embodiment, we would like to show how the portrayal of characters can never – and should never – be seen as something outside actual political implications and power relations in the "real world."

One important context that has to be kept in mind when we consider actor-character relations is the racist tradition of Blackface (see Gubar 1997; Strausbaugh 2006). In the late 1800s, US minstrel shows – but also similar practices in most countries in Europe with their histories of colonialism – had White actors put on pitch-black makeup to mimic people of African heritage. Such mocking caricatures of people of color were not only popular but also practical, since the latter were forbidden from stages, even as caricatures of themselves. Similar traditions existed for people from other "racialized" backgrounds that seem highly offensive today for these reasons. Respective performances nevertheless prevailed in film and TV for a long time. In 1954s *Apache* (Aldrich), Burt Lancaster played a "redfaced" Native American. Mickey Rooney portrayed a grotesquely "yellow-faced" caricature of a Japanese landlord in 1961s *Breakfast at Tiffany's* (Edwards), while Dan Aykroyd masked as a Black person in 1983s *Trading Places* (Landis) (in the last example, the Blackface was presented as a disguise even within the film's storyworld, opening up at least some possibilities for critical reflection in contrast to the two former examples). While most audiences today would agree that such *racialized* actor-character-relations are highly problematic, there are still many discussions surrounding cosplay where no mockery is intended – admiration for the portrayed character is one crucial source of motivation, after all (see Kukkii 2019). Cosplay is an increasingly popular fan practice in which people try to imitate their favorite characters by dressing up like them with self-fashioned costumes and props. Often, these are then presented at fan conventions where people change into warriors, superheroines, or pop stars for a day or two. As the general aim is to be as faithful as possible to a character's appearance, changing one's hair color or age with props or makeup is part of the performance – as might be painting your face green or blue if representing an alien species. In contrast to fantasy creatures, however, people of color do exist in our world, as do traditions of Blackface. It is for that reason that the French cosplayer Alice Livanart was disqualified from the 2019 EuroCosplay Championships for her impersonation of the character Pyke from the video game *League of Legends* (Riot Games 2009) due to "concerns regarding the costume" (see Plunkett 2019). As Pyke is a Black man, Livanart – a White woman – had changed her skin color with a prosthetic suit. A similar case went viral in 2014 already when a White German cosplayer uploaded a photo of herself posing as *The Walking Dead's* Black character Michonne at New York Comic Con (see Miller 2020, 65), or when a "White Katara" from *Avatar: The Last Airbender* (DiMartino et al. 2005–2008) was publicly performed (see Miller 2020, 71). All of these instances were immediately criticized as a continuation of Blackface. White people using skin color like a prop they can take on and off like a commodity continues to be problematic despite the best of intentions, when the same bodily distinctions serve as grounds for very real discrimination – or privileges – to this day. It also takes away some of the few "advantages" a PoC cosplayer could have in a still predominantly White filmmaking culture where actors and characters of color continue to be highly underrepresented (see Montpelier 2020). This leaves painfully little choices for a non-White audience to identify with – and to turn into. Play-acting a "Black Thor," in contrast (usually suspending the question of whether there was no representational correspondence between race of performer and character, or whether this was intended as another, alternate version of the character), seems quite unproblematic.

Another political issue especially salient in transmedial adaptations concerns the *Whitewashing* of characters when existing PoC protagonists are replaced by White versions, adding to the striking imbalance between White and "racialized" characters within international popular culture(s). Such contexts of "strategic [W]hiteness" (Projansky and Ono 1999, 149) have to be kept in mind when Jennifer Lawrence appears as Katniss Everdeen in the *Hunger Games* adaptations while the main characters were clearly described as non-White in the books ("straight black hair, olive skin," Collins 2008, 8; see also Stewart 2012 as well as Baker and Schak 2019). A different form of criticism concerns not the characters themselves but the franchises they belong to. When the White actor Justin Chatwin was cast as Son Goku in the US adaptation Dragon Ball *Evolution* (Wong 2009) and similar concerns about Whitewashing were brought up (see Frank 2017), some audience members immediately responded that Son Goku was not Japanese in the manga and anime series to begin with, but a member of the alien species "Saiyan." Nevertheless, Akira Toriyama's series was one of the first successful international "exports" of Japanese popular culture, so this form of cultural appropriation was strongly criticized. More contemporary US projects based on PoC culture and imagination pay attention to not only casting PoC actors in major roles but also hiring non-White directors or screenwriters and thus distributing at least *some* part of authorial control more evenly. *Black Panther* (2018) did not only cast Chadwick Boseman in the titular role (most of the other cast was Black as well, although Martin Freeman was included as a kind of "White figure of identification"); the film was also directed by Black director Ryan Coogler. *Shang-Chi and the Legends of the Ten Rings* (2021), in some contrast, was entrusted to director Destin Daniel Cretton who at least looked "non-White" to a hegemonic audience (he has a White father of Irish-Slovak descent and a Japanese American mother). Whether this is mere "tokenism" remains up for debate. From a transmedial perspective, it is especially interesting once again how different versions can comment upon each other. When Ben Kingsley was cast as the villain "The Mandarin" in *Iron Man 3* (Black 2013), it might seem like another case of Whitewashing at first glance: a British actor cast in the role of a "Chinese" character. In this movie, however, "The Mandarin" turns out to be a hired actor playing a stereotypical villain even within the storyworld, which can be read as a comment upon the fact that the original character in the comic books was little more than a racist, orientalist stereotype to begin with.

Returning to character representations, people of color portraying "originally" White characters – Black actor Idris Elba as Roland Deschain in *The Dark Tower* (Arcel 2017), for instance, or Chaka Cumberatch's famous cosplay performances as a Black Wonder Woman – must be judged very differently due to the actual sociopolitical and historical circumstances. Turning Roland or Wonder Woman Black *highlights* the usually "invisible" Whiteness of the originals. White people modifying their skin color due to a perceived "faithfulness to the character," by contrast, at the very least display a striking ignorance toward issues of actual (social) representation, putting their perceived interest in fictional characters over that in actual people, their emotions, and their disenfranchisement. Communication studies scholar Joan Miller concludingly points out that "Black cosplayers performing [W]hite characters – because of the history of Black oppression by [W]hites and the relative absence of Black characters in pop culture media – are doing something inherently different from [W]hite actors performing Black characters" (2020, 66). Turning a White character Black guides our attention toward the *unmarked* and thus *ideological* "invisible" race of the originals. The correspondence between representing and represented bodies, as we have seen, is hardly "natural" to begin with, and far from stable in different medial and generic contexts. As the rules of the imagination – the representational correspondences of embodiment – are mostly based on medial conventions anyways, we should always remain critical of them with respect to their actual sociopolitical contexts.

5 Cartoonish Characters in Comic Books and Animated Films

As we have discussed in the previous chapter, recordings of bodies and voices often function as nodal points or anchors for character traits, making up the intersubjective communicative construct that *is* the character within these media forms and formats. In comic books – including manga and graphic novels – and all kinds of animated film, however, characters are "assembled" from a variety of heterogeneous representational materials. Comics typically combine words and pictures (although "silent" comics without words exist as well), and their pictoriality itself is far from "stable" or uniform: Even within the same series (intended to represent a continuous storyworld), various artists with distinct drawing styles and techniques (pens, pencils, ink, in crayon or in paint, or generated by digital tools) are often employed interchangeably. "Western" animated feature films have by and large turned to digital animation, epitomized by the company Pixar, while popular animated shows such as *The Simpsons* (Brooks et al. 1989–present), *Family Guy* (MacFarlane et al. 1999–present), or *Rick & Morty* (Harmon et al. 2013–present) as well as Japanese anime in general retain hand-drawn aesthetics to this day (even if they, too, are largely produced digitally by now). Many other material aesthetics can be found, ranging from *South Park*'s (Parker et al. 1997–present) digital cutout animation to the *Fantastic Mr. Fox*'s (Anderson 2009) stop-motion. Sometimes these different styles are even combined with live recordings into "hybrid films." Already in *Mary Poppins* (Stevenson 1964), recorded embodied characters jumped into drawn images, while the animated characters in *Who Framed Roger Rabbit* (Zemeckis 1988), *Space Jam* (Pytka 1996), *The Sponge-Bob SquarePants Movie* (Hillenburg 2004), or *Space Jam: A New Legacy* (Lee 2021) are shown to share a world with their live-action counterparts. Animated films usually also employ voice actors to which most of the embodiment questions discussed in the chapter before apply as well. In original Japanese anime, voice actors are part of an elaborate star system that allows fans to follow "appearances" of their favorite voice actors, often cast in resembling roles, throughout stories and franchises (see Nozawa 2016). In American animated films, too, the casting of renowned actors and celebrities such as Robin Williams (as the genie in *Aladdin*, Clements and Musker 1992) or Angelina Jolie (as Tigress in *Kung Fu Panda*, Stevenson and Osborne 2008) are often prominently advertised. Mark Hamill is thus not only famous for his portrayal of Luke Skywalker in the *Star Wars* films,

DOI: 10.4324/9781003298793-8

but also for his vocal performance as the Joker in the *Batman: The Animated Series* (Radomski et al. 1992–1995) and many related video games. Actors are not always cast in correspondence with their actual age or gender, however. Prepubescent animated boys are often voiced by adult women, famous examples ranging from actress Mari Shimizu for *Astro Boy* (Bessho and Masaki 1963–1966) to Bart Simpson's portrayal by Nancy Cartwright.

A further distributed form of authorship that increasingly factors into animated characters can be found in motion capturing, although few actors are as famous – and as publicly visible – as Andy Serkis. As mentioned in the previous chapter, he not only provided the voice and the (digitally recorded) gestures and facial movements for Gollum in *The Lord of the Rings* trilogy (Jackson 2001; 2002; 2003) but also for Caesar (in the *Planet of the Apes* trilogy: Wyatt 2011; Reeves 2014; 2017) and for *King Kong* (Jackson 2005), among many others. Discussions on whether these recorded performances must be seen as a mere form of "digital make-up" (which would entitle the motion actors to "best performance" Oscar nominations, despite not being visible on screen at all) are likely to continue (see Askwith 2003; Carnicke 2012, 331). For some animated characters, the contributions of such motion actors can hardly be overstated. The narrative of *Happy Feet* (Miller 2006), for instance, revolves entirely around the "dancing career" of its penguin protagonist Mumble, whose tap-dance moves have been envisioned by and digitally recorded from dancer Savion Glover. As dancing is such a central part of the plot – and Mumble's gradual mastery thereof a most defining character trait – Glover might be as important to our character comprehension as the voices of E.G. Daily (baby Mumble) or Elijah Wood (teenage Mumble) (see Auslander 2008, 168). Due to digital effects, the barrier between "live-action" and animation has become blurred anyways: whereas *Avatar* (Cameron 2009) was still perceived as mostly "live-action," with only the alien CGI characters of the Na'vi notably integrated into the footage, Disney's *The Jungle Book* remake (Favreau 2016) features merely a few human actors (mostly Neel Sethi as Mowgli) among its cast of entirely animated animal characters – again, with prominent voice actors such as Ben Kingsley (Baghira) or Scarlett Johansson (Kaa). The new *The Lion King* (Favreau 2019) does without human characters and actors entirely (apart from voices), rendering it an animation film strictly speaking, even though it was marketed as a "virtual reality live-action film," to many observers' frustration (see Alexa 2020, as well as Manovich 2016 on the increasing coalescence of live-action and animation).

On the other end of the "realism spectrum," characters are even more "fragmented" and overtly "artificial" within comic books. Their body representations are distributed over the entire page, spread and split up between every single panel (see Klar 2013). Only the reading conventions of comics render these fragmented single images comprehensible as representations of the same individual within a space-time continuum. Prominent comic book theorists such as Ole Frahm (2000) proposed that, due to these material and medial conditions, comic books are an overt *parody* of the very idea that stable referents or identities (such as characters) even exist within graphic narratives. In practice, however, comics and manga are not only read every day for their stories, storyworlds, and characters, they often also function as foundations for rapidly expanding transmedia franchises and storyworlds such as *Attack on Titan* (which developed from a manga series into an anime show, a two-part live-action film, and many video games). In the American entertainment industry, too, it has become a commonplace practice to use (not so) independent comics as "tried and tested" source material for expensive TV shows (*The Walking Dead*, Darabont et al. 2010–2022, as the most prominent example, others being *The Umbrella Academy*, Blackman 2019–present, *The Boys*, Kripke et al. 2019–present, or *The Sandman*, Gaiman et al. 2022–present).

What all these drawn media forms share – to a greater or lesser degree – are characters that are not based on (photo)realistic, but *cartoonish* body representations. Artist Scott McCloud reinterpreted the term "cartoon" for a specific pictorial style that he described as "amplification through simplification" (1993, 30). Andrei Molotiu (2020, 153) defined cartooning – as a key term for comic studies – as a "graphic simplification of figurative shapes for purposes of communication, humor, and so on in comic strip and comic book rendering (as well as, of course, in gag cartoons, animation, and other fields of visual media)." Cartoons leave out a large number of details and exaggerate others. McCloud located comic book drawings on a scale ranging from photography to a completely simplified smiley face lacking any individual features. Media semiotician Stephan Packard (2017b) has expanded this concept into a nuanced instrument of comic book analysis that also proves useful for all kinds of animated films. Even CGI animated films such as *The Incredibles* (Bird 2004) or *Inside Out* (Docter 2015) *do* feature characters whose bodies are abstracted, simplified, and exaggerated, just like line drawings projected into 3D space. Character construction and reception may still not be *entirely* different from other media, however: "[T]he cognitive process by which we as reader-viewers identify an entity as a character is cross-medial and foundational," Frederick L. Aldama noted (2010, 319). To recognize something *as a character* still means to attribute human-like qualities, especially agency, intentionality, and a continuous consciousness frame to cartoonish body representations. However, there are many peculiarities and specificities for cartoonish characters due to their special "medial ontology": with regard to a primary threshold of "characterhood," with regard to questions of representational correspondence, as well as with regard to degrees of agency and complexity. The present chapter is thus going to look into some of the most prominent peculiarities of characters in comic books and animated films (as examples for cartoonish characters in other media forms as well).

5.1 Thresholds of Characterhood

Generally speaking, there has long been the misconception that comic book or cartoon characters are simple and "one-dimensional" by default. If Donald Trump is being insulted as acting "like a cartoon character" (see Jung and Wilde 2021), this is intended to capture the sense that cartoonish protagonists are incoherent, of short memory and little self-reflection. And while characters in comic books and animation *can* be as complex, conflicted, and multidimensional as in any other media form (in terms of their inner life as individuals as well as on a thematic level of ideas, ideologies, or worldviews), it is certainly true that stereotypes and simplifications play a highly significant role in many of these media forms. Goofy, for instance, has a rather small set of inner character traits, mostly limited to clumsy behavior and an innocent worldview that is always presented as likable (see Bertetti 2014). In writer E.M. Forster's influential terms (1927, 103), many comic and cartoonish characters could be characterized as "flat," rather than "round." While the latter are capable of surprising actions, lasting basic type changes, and psychological developments, flat characters are taken to possess a limited set of stable character traits that can often be summarized in a few words or sentences. To Donald Crafton (2012), this is aligned with two different acting traditions that cartoon characters can be modeled after. Animated protagonists can follow the tradition of "embodied acting" discussed in the chapter before. Many Pixar films – their cartoonish aesthetics notwithstanding – aspire to this direction, so that viewers are to forget, if only momentarily, the highly artificial state of heroes such as Woody from *Toy Story* (Lasseter 1995) or Mr. Incredible from *The Incredibles* (2004). On the other end of the spectrum, there is the tradition of "figurative acting," overexaggerated and schematic. While Crafton considers the latter more typical for animation, we should not forget that many other representational arts – where real performers *are* at the center – also aspire to "anti-illusionist" spectacle and physical performance (many silent films, music video clips, physical theater, circus shows). Psychological "roundness" (oriented toward embodied acting) vs. anti-illusionist "flatness" (oriented toward figurative acting) is thus not determined by media forms and formats but more so by individual genre traditions. The distinction is also not clear-cut. Forster himself remarked that both attributes can co-occupy the same character in different parts of a story (see Mikkonen 2017, 186). Some characters, however, gravitate toward one side of the spectrum, while others occupy a reverse position, even within one and the same series. In *BoJack Horseman* (Bob-Waksberg et al. 2014–2020), for instance, a side character like the anthropomorphic tree frog Charley Witherspoon is mostly defined by the *one* trait that he cannot properly function in his office environment due to his sticky fingers. His corresponding actantial role (see chapter 2) is then mostly limited to recurring comedy scenes in which he can't physically let go of things he touched. The show's main protagonist BoJack, by contrast, showcases a highly complex and contradictory psychology broaching issues of depression and alcoholism (his actantial roles throughout scenes and episodes are much more flexible as well). Such a difference in complexity is, at times, also signposted by a difference in the degree of "cartoonishness": In Jeff Smith's self-proclaimed "Cartoon Epic," *Bone* (1991–2004), the extremely simplistic drawing style of the three Bone cousins stands in stark contrast to other main characters' more detailed (albeit still cartoonish) representations. This difference is not only acknowledged on the level of the storyworld (with the Bones' big, round noses repeatedly being the subject of other characters' mockery), but it is also reflected in their interior lives. The Bones, while integral to the plot, remain almost completely unchanged throughout the comic's more than 1,300 pages, whereas other protagonists, such as princess Thorn, undergo significant inner and outer growth. That being said, it is true that many comic or animated characters do *not* seem to change all that much between episodes, or ever (see TV Tropes, "Status Quo Is God" for many fine distinctions and examples). Their physical appearance stays identical over large periods of time (Superman probably will be red-caped and spandexed forever). The same, however, could also be said about their personalities: we can read or watch their adventures in any order since they seem incapable of change, progress, or development. This, however, is rather a question of (different approaches to) seriality and continuity (something we will touch upon in detail in chapter 8) rather than of character complexity.

Even characters whose character traits are generally considered *unchanging* between episodes or iterations could still be distinguished as "round" *or* "flat," complex *or* simple. Charlie Brown, Snoopy, and the other characters of Charles M. Schultz's *Peanuts* (1950–2000), for instance, can certainly be described as con-tradictory, complex, and full of self-reflective thoughts (see Molotiu 2020). They are also barely conforming to stereotypes despite their limited, rather timeless "existence" within four-panel strips. With recourse to cognitive theory, we could rephrase Forster's earlier distinction differently: "Flat" characters are interpreted "top-down," with initial recourse to preexisting categories (that can then be mod-ified and contradicted), while "round" characters are interpreted "bottom-up," with narrative information contributing piece-by-piece to an intersubjective un-derstanding of their inner lives. The more "top-down" a character is constructed, the more they also represent a single (and often simple) social category on the the-matic level, such as a moral, social, or ethnic identity. Stereotypes in caricatures and editorial (one-panel) cartoons might be the "purest" form of this (see Dewey 2007, 10–20; Denson and Wilde 2022), never intended to assemble to any con-tradictory individual but rather to confirm (and to comment upon) a preexisting social category (often, these can or must also be criticized as offensive). Goofy, on the other hand, is hardly a stand-in for any existing social group or overall idea (on the thematic level); for him, the mimetic level in which he is intended as a (relatively "flat") individual remains foregrounded.

Notably, anything can *become* a character in comic books and animated films. "Real-live" films and TV shows, too, certainly feature countless non-human monsters, aliens, robots, and cyborgs – especially after digital effects allowed for the creation and seamless integration of all kinds of CGI entities. Yet in drawn forms of media (or those that are made to resemble drawings) we can neverthe-less find a far greater range of anthropomorphized animals and objects appear-ing as protagonists. Even an abstract geometrical shape may be sufficient as an "anchor" for character traits, provided that it engages in goal-oriented actions (whether these abstract shapes are intended to be interpreted as full-fledged hu-mans within the storyworld – and, accordingly, whether there is a huge "gap" between what we see and what this is intended to mean intersubjectively – is a question of representational correspondence that we will touch upon later). Ap-parently, there are few limits to what can become a character within these media forms: All that is needed in comic books, for instance, is a speech bubble or a thought balloon pointing to an object – any object – indicating that it has an intelligent inner live and intentionality, a command of language and thought, and finally agency and responsibility (see Mikkonen 2017, 174–200). In many animated films, characters are often recognizable just by their *movements* contrasting with still background images (see LaMarre 2009). Regular household objects can be turned into characters, such as *Fantasia*'s (Armstrong et al. 1940) "Magic Brooms," defying the will of their creator, the Sorcerer's Apprentice Mickey Mouse. Many cartoon films thus present a magical world in which anything can be (literally) "animated," possessing a life of its own. One of the most abstract reductions can be found in the Italian cartoon series *La Linea* (1971–1986) by Osvaldo Cavandoli, which features a nameless protagonist drawn in a single outline, walking on an infinite picture plane (he was also voiced by Carlo Bonomi, uttering gibberish occasionally resembling Italian or English). We can nevertheless infer countless character traits from his behavior, such as his strong temper, his spontaneity, and his impulsiveness. While this may seem one of the strongest reductions of the body schema imaginable, even more limited "catalysts" for characterhood are available in educational comics or public health information sheets. Here, objects and biological phenomena are frequently turned into minimal characters by applying a *face* to any object (see Wilde 2018a). While we have addressed the schema of a human *body* – or, at least, an anthropomorphic body configuration – as the primary nodal point of character construction in pictorial media forms before, this minimal condition can even be further reduced in favor of a mere *facial* scheme. Faces offer the richest sources of information to people about each other and can be regarded as our "primary identification organ." They also allow meaningful inferences about emotional dispositions and affective states and can thus generate strong affective reactions. Our innate human ability to "read" emotions can be activated particularly easily by line drawings and caricatures. Facial drawings, art historian Ernst Gombrich remarked, "will not be classed just as a face but will acquire a definite character and expression, will be endowed with life, with a presence" (1960, 288f). This is employed frequently within comics and animated films, resulting in astonishing protagonists. The "edutainment" children's series *Once Upon a Time... Life* (Barillé 1987), for instance, combined storylines about a fantastic journey into the human body with factual information about our inner working mechanisms. Every episode featured a different organ or system within the human body (like the brain, or the heart). Blood cells were turned into protagonists, while viruses and bacteria appeared as antagonists. Transforming biological phenomena into characters, the show invited its viewers to imagine them as subjective entities capable of self-initiated action, responsibility, and a continuous consciousness frame. A more recent example could be found in the manga (Shimizu 2015–2021) and anime (Takahashi 2018–2021) series *Cells at Work!* also featuring anthropomorphized cells of a human body as protagonists.

While the threshold of "characterhood" may thus be crossed incredibly easily within drawn media, upholding their continuous consciousness frame can be tedious from the side of production. Where literature needs to simply repeat a pronoun or invoke a proper name and where film can rely on technological means to record actors over extended periods of time, comic book and animation artists have to draw characters' bodies and faces continuously: within hundreds or thousands of printed panels, or up to 24 times per second in film (for seamless "full-animation," see Wells 1998). This is not only time-consuming but can easily become expensive. It also encourages character designs leaning toward easily repeatable shapes, patterns, and colors that can be recognized at a single glance – and reproduced with minimal effort. Often, the roles in animated film productions are distinguished between more experienced "keyframe" artists and "in-between" artists, the latter often outsourced to other studios (see the anime *Shirobako* [Mizushima 2014–2015] for an interesting self-reflection). Many works thus employ casts of characters that are all based on similar graphic base types, often distinguished only by a specific outline contour, certain props, or a recurring haircut: Scrooge McDuck is, on the level of his graphic representation, *exactly* a Donald Duck with whiskers and pinch glasses, while Daisy is a Donald with eyelashes and a bow. Such character designs, based on recognizable and repeatable iconographies, function very much like proper names in literature. For the manga and anime industry, character design has long surpassed issues of storytelling in relevance, as visually recognizable characters are considered the centerpiece of successful franchises (see Nozawa 2013). If characters are beloved by fans, they quickly gain a "life of their own" within fan manga, fan artworks, or cosplay (see Wilde 2019b) where they remain immediately recognizable by their iconography that can be mastered by amateurs in all kinds of material – something that is not as easily possible for characters based primarily on photographic pictures of actors. Some artists even reduce distinguishing features almost altogether. The nameless stick-figure protagonists of *XKCD* (Munroe 2005–present), one of the most popular webcomic series for decades, are almost entirely devoid of visible character traits. We cannot even be sure whether they *are* recurring characters from one episode to the next, except for an occasional prop that some of the matchstick people are carrying or wearing. According to medial conventions, this renders all "black hat persons" into representations of *the same character* – nicknamed "Black Hat" in online databases (see Explain XKCD 2022). Fans are nevertheless able to "gather" lasting inner character traits from his various appearances (being always judgmental and insulting, for instance) and attribute them to the same fictional entity. Although cartoonish representations of characters in comic books and animation can be incredibly simple, as this shows, this does not necessarily entail that the characters – their inner lives, their personalities – could not be as complex as those of canonical works of literature. Their pictorial representations, however, can be incredibly *vague*, lending special importance to media-specific questions of representational correspondence.

5.2 Representational Correspondence and the Physicality of Cartoonish Characters

In the chapter before, we discussed many instances in which it is quite hard – but nevertheless often necessary – to distinguish the perceivable aspects of a recorded performance attributed to an actor on the one hand from what they are intended to represent for the character on the other. Within the cartoonish imagery of comic books and animation, by contrast, it is never quite possible to overlook this fundamental distinction. In manga, for instance, characters are usually represented in black and white, while we assume that their world contains colors perceptible to its inhabitants just as ours does. And in fact, the cover illustrations and opening pages of manga often *do* feature colors, just as anime adaptations usually do. The "black-and-whiteness" is thus taken to be an aspect of the media form only, not the represented character. The representational correspondence is accepted as "blocked" with respect to the (lack of) coloration. The same "gap" must be negotiated for all aspects of cartoonization.

We can see this clearly if we look at autobiographical comics such as Riad Sattouf's *The Arab of the Future* (2014–2020) or Guy Delisle's travel comics (such as *Pyongyang*, 2005, or *Burma Chronicles*, 2008). Sattouf recounts the story of his upbringing in Middle Eastern countries (especially Syria), while Delisle documents journeys into places such as Myanmar, Israel, or North Korea. Both artists have been praised for their subjective, yet faithful and sincere representations of places and cultures foreign to most international readers (see Cooke 2012; Yassin-Kassab 2016). That these works – and many others – are accepted for their authenticity may be surprising to someone not acquainted with the media forms, as all the characters are strongly cartoonized. Heavily relying on caricature, their bodies and faces are reduced to mere outlines, bulbous noses, and pop-eyes. As there is little doubt about the comics' faithfulness to the artists' actual experiences, however, readers can be sure that the cartoonization is entirely on the side of the representation, not the represented characters. When Delisle's self-representation wonders "Aw Geez! If I looked a bit more Burmese, they would've let me through" (Delisle 2008, 34), it is clear that he does not mean the black outline without colors or internal features that we can see. These cartoonish characters are certainly intended to look like "regular," three-dimensional human beings within the represented storyworld, just as their personalities are complex and full of contradictions. On the level of the intersubjective construct, such characters are clearly people made of flesh and blood, but their specific visible appearances – to other characters within their diegetic environment – remain almost entirely *undefined*. At best, we can make diagrammatic (relational) claims, such as "has-a-larger-nose-than" or "is-bigger-than." We usually have no other, "unmediated" access to the corresponding storyworld, however. Depictions of cartoon protagonists are thus always inherently *vague*, leaving a lot of room for the individual imagination. The representational correspondence must be judged as extremely "loose." In comic books and animation, the pictorial style often does not even stay uniform or coherent throughout any one story. This does not mean, however, that the characters (and their appearances) change accordingly. Thon remarked rightfully that most readers of, say, Neil Gaiman's comic series *The Sandman* (Gaiman et al. 1989–1996)

> will understand that it would be pointless to ask why the outer appearance of the main character, Dream, has "changed so much," when what actually changes are the drawing styles of the various artists with whom Gaiman has collaborated over the course of the comics series.
>
> (Thon 2016, 90f.)

Morpheus, *The Sandman*'s supernatural protagonist, *does* possess shapeshifting powers and is perceived differently by different characters, but entirely human protagonists like Rose Walker also look strikingly disparate in interpretations of Mike Dringenberg (#10) or Marc Hempel (#65). In terms of storyworld properties, these differences are certainly "ignored" (not taken into account). In manga and anime, the stylistic device of *chibi* has characters "turning" into emoji-versions of themselves during moments of emotional duress. The changes in style indicate only inner, emotional changes, not outer, visible ones (see Wilde 2020b).

Does this mean, then, that we always have to "correct" our imagination toward "regular" human beings – as they could be represented by human actors? If we accept comics and animated films as autobiographical – and their claims to represent a reality much like ours as quite strong – this seems entirely plausible. But what about the fantastic worlds that we can encounter *only* through fiction? Do we have to "correct" them as well? Comic scholar Martin Schüwer (2008, 23/510) addressed this conundrum as the ultimate crucible of comic studies: Should one attribute the caricature-style of Charles M. Schultz' *Peanuts* solely to their representations and imagine that Charlie Brown and Snoopy "actually" look quite differently in the context of the narrated world? The assertion that they were "only drawn that way," but "actually" look like photographs of "real" people, does not seem to do justice to the drawing styles and their media forms of imagination. There is a systematic alternative to this assumption, of course: Fantastic worlds of comics, manga, or animation can not only break with physical laws (e.g., characters possessing superpowers) but could be taken to exhibit a special "visual ontology" that also *looks* entirely different from ours (see Lefèvre 2007). Intermedial transcriptions from comic books into animated films seem to support this idea: *The Peanuts Movie* film (Martino 2015) is a particularly good example of this. Even though its pictorial style, computer-rendered 3D graphics, is materially quite different from Schultz's drawings – the film contains colors instead of black and white pictures, the visible outlines have given way to simulated, shaded 3D bodies – they retain not only all the proportions and internal relations of bodies and faces but also implement "drawn" lines within facial representations that approximate or remediate the aesthetics of the original cartoons. A detachment of cartoon worlds from all demands of everyday reality is particularly prominent in Japanese manga and anime discourse: "Character design strives to give characters a sui generis reality, one that is irreducible to our kind of reality," anthropologist Shunsuke Nozawa summarized (2013, n.pag.). For anime shows such as *Made in Abyss* (Kojima 2017–present), set in a fantastic town cornering an nearly infinite abyss into the magical depths of the earth, fans would be entirely entitled to imagine the protagonists Riko and Reg looking *exactly* as they are represented – *chibi* heroes whose heads are almost the same sizes as the rest of their bodies, and their eyes about a quarter of their heads – only in a three-dimensional space instead of a two-dimensional one. The representational correspondence would accordingly be considered much "tighter" (more "literal").

We cannot generalize this, however, and have to decide case-by-case. Cartoon drawings can be intended as representations of "photorealistic" worlds (hiding "behind" their media forms of representations – on the plane of intersubjective communicative constructs), just as they can deliberately deny any claims of resembling "our" reality. On what grounds, then, can we distinguish between both? Once again, we can both look into surrounding discourses/paratexts as well as into the texts themselves. As for the latter, some comics and animated films provide *narrative reasons* to support a specific claim, for instance through tropes of disguise and masquerade. Their heroes can often become completely unrecognizable even for their diegetic environment by the slightest manipulation of their appearances, effortlessly slipping into the role of others without being exposed even by family members or close friends. This is by no means exclusive to Duckburg and other, more humoristic storyworlds: Think of Superman and his "disguise" as Clark Kent, which consists merely of a set of glasses. Even within the storyworld, abstract ("cartoonish") criteria for differentiation and identification must be assumed in these cases, which can be manipulated by the protagonists themselves. Mostly, however, the cartoonization remains unreliable, leaving ample room for the individual imagination.

5.3 Cartoonization as an Unreliable Narrative Mode

Intersubjectivity can also be traced along transcriptions into (a) other multimodal media or into (b) written discourses. Verbal claims – and disputes – about characters' appearances are frequent for anthropomorphic animal beings which we often encounter in comics and animated films. Indeed, one of the most discussed questions in comic book research in recent decades is whether the members of the Duck family are (special, human-like) *ducks* – or whether they are *people* just *represented* as ducks (see Packard 2017a). The Disney artist Don Rosa, for example, has always held a strong opinion on this:

> I have always known that Donald and Scrooge were human beings [drawn as Ducks]. I had written some plot where, to save his life in some predicament, Donald needed a feather... I guess he'd need to hunt down a pillow somewhere, because to have him simply pluck a feather off his tail would seem utterly bizarre to me!

> (Rosa 2014, 8)

The "funny animal" is indeed a standard character in comics and animation starting from the early 20th century (see Bliss 2017). With regard to such cartoon animals, we can never know for sure: "Are these humanized animals or animalized humans?" (LaMarre 2008, 82). Animation studies scholar Paul Wells (2009, 72) addresses this as "bestial ambivalence," i.e., the "strategic blurring of boundary between animal and human" (Alaniz 2020, 329). Goofy shares his storyworld with Pluto, who is intended to be an "actual" dog in contrast to his almost identical-looking master, who is "more anthropomorphic."

> Sometimes anthropomorphic characters speak, think, and act exactly like human beings; sometimes they display selective animal characteristics overlaid on primarily human behavior patterns, as in the species-based conflicts between predators like cats and wolves and their mouse or pig prey, all of whom come equipped with clothes, houses, and other trappings of middle-class domesticity.
>
> (Witek 2011, 30)

Packard, in one of the most foundational proposals of comic book theory, proclaimed a "semiotic third space" (see Packard 2017a; 2017b; Wilde 2020b) in which the "duckness" of Donald Duck would be located *if* we were to decide – perhaps agreeing with Don Rosa – that the Ducks were merely represented as Ducks, but are "actually" human beings. Since we can clearly *see* traits of a duck (feathers and a beak) that would be neither part of our reality (where only lines on paper exist) nor the storyworld (where there would be a *human* being), we must assume a *third domain* distinct from both, as neither reality *nor* fiction seems to have a place for these aspects. That does not mean that traits in the Third Space are redundant, or devoid of meaning: Art Spiegelman's celebrated graphic novel *Maus* (1980–1991) recounts the autobiographical story of his father Vladek, an Auschwitz survivor. Although the work is clearly intended and by now unanimously accepted as non-fictional (see Baroni 2021, as well as chapter 10), Spiegelman represents all Jewish people as mice and all Germans as cats. Nevertheless, it should be clear to every reader that these "disguises" are not to be taken "literally" but metaphorically. "[W]hat is represented here are not anthropomorphic animals but rather quite regular human beings whose affiliation with certain social groups is represented by more or less 'visible' but nevertheless exclusively metaphorical 'masks'" (Thon 2016, 93). Some of the mice also disguise themselves by putting on other animal masks, which cannot be seen through by any of the co-protagonists. The reason for this is, of course, that it is obviously not possible to tell whether someone actually "looks Jewish." The semiotic third space has a thematic meaning, indicating that these differences are merely *social projections* about *alleged* ethnic differences. The cartoon aesthetics are hence employed as a media-specific means of characterization, to comment on the character Vlad and his experiences within his social surroundings.

If the semiotic third space is taken seriously, however, the same ambiguity and unreliability in terms of representational correspondence can also be applied to any other narrative aspect. In many comic book or manga fight scenes, for instance, there is a huge discrepancy between the dialogue exchanged by the combatants on the one hand and the physical occurrences on the other: While the action could not take up more than a few seconds, even a fast speaker would need much longer to read all the speech bubbles aloud – maybe even minutes (see Thon 2017). Readers not familiar with this convention would criticize the medium's (or the genre's) artificiality, while it poses no problems for fans whatsoever. No internal (mimetic) explanation is needed, as the relationship between dialogue and action is *not* necessarily taken to correspond to the storyworld. The same could be said about other aspects of characters' behaviors. Visual (and audiovisual) exaggerations often serve to emphasize characters' inner states or emotions. When characters are shocked or surprised, for instance, their hats often jump into the air. Countless other visual shortcuts, often called "emanata" (see Cohn 2013, 34), exist to indicate characters' emotions. Some of them are specific to cultural origins (or media and genre traditions). In manga and anime, giant sweat drops stand for nervousness, protruding veins for anger, and a nosebleed for sexual arousal. But, as manga theorist Kentarō Takekuma has argued (1995), if we see a character with a giant teardrop in the corner of their eye, it doesn't necessarily mean that there is a *visible* phenomenon of that size – merely *that the character is crying*, or maybe not even that: it may merely be taken to represent (on the level of the storyworld) that the character *feels sad* (see Wilde 2020b). Emanata, too, do then not need to be taken "literally" (they would only be part of the semiotic third space). Fusanosuke Natsume, another pioneer of manga studies, discussed many manga conventions with reference to traditional Japanese theater forms such as Kabuki. A scene can, within the storyworld, take place in pitch-black darkness, while it is clearly visible to the audience (see Natsume 1997, 89). This points again to the fact that what we see – even on a theater stage – is still just a representation, not the represented situation, character, or world itself. The same is true for comic books and animation.

Emanata and other visual shortcuts can be derived from a sort of "pictogrammatic lexicon." That does not mean that the represented emotions are necessarily simple or repetitive. They can only be evaluated with regard to the narrative tropes and events themselves. Anime scholar Stevie Suan remarked that anime – as a recognizable media form, typically associated with Japan (although produced and received globally as well) – can be seen as a set of recognizable visual and narrative conventions "citing a system/database of conventionalized models in each iteration" (2017, 62). People unfamiliar with Japanese anime will often find the postures, facial expressions, internal monologues, or exaggerated expressions of emotions hilarious, awkward, or even embarrassing. Parodies – such as the Comedy Central clip "ANIME IN REAL LIFE!!!!" by Or Paz and Tom Trager (see Sugar Zaza 2015) – transcribe the style of action anime such as *Naruto* (Date 2002–2007), *Death Note* (Nakatani et al. 2003–2006), or *Attack on*

Titan (Kinoshita et al. 2013–2022) onto real (Israelian) actors shouting in "gibberish-Japanese" at each other. When people at a party start to fight over the last slice of Pizza (the rather negligible narrative probability disjunction being who does or does not eat it), every emotion and thought is absurdly exaggerated, and time appears hilariously stretched in freeze frames overlaid by dramatic interior monologue. What is playfully mocked here – some commentators do take this as an insult, while others enjoy the play with tropes – is anime's conventionality, its "database" of stock expressions that seems entirely removed from "real" experiences. But conventional means of representation do not need to correspond to the characters and their represented experiences. Once again, it is not necessary to take these aspects "literally." They are mere cues to the imagination, supposed to represent the affective, emotional "reality" of the characters – not a physical, external reality that we could "look at" (or "listen to") directly.

On the other hand, sometimes such generic expressions *do* seem to be taken "literally." Within the manga and anime *Dragon Ball* (Toriyama 1998–2004 and Tsuchiya et al. 1992–1994 respectively), the "nosebleed" of Master Muten-Rōshi – a conventional visual shortcut for sexual arousal – is instrumentalized by other protagonists at one point to turn around the tide of a battle. As the character Yamcha is fighting "See-Through the Invisible Man" (Suke-san) in the anime's 70th and the manga's 100th episode (vol. 9), one of the female protagonists' (Bulma's) breasts are exposed, causing Muten-Rōshi's nose to bleed. The blood then sprays onto the Invisible Man and thus reveals his position. It must hence be a part of the world's physical reality, not merely a conventionalized metaphor (in the edited English version of the anime, Krillin takes some tomato soup and dumps it on the invisible man). Crude gags like these play with audiences' familiarity with conventions. Many genres of comics and animated films are entirely based on a playful negotiation of representational correspondence. Within Warner Brothers or Tex Avery cartoons, for instance, the "laws" of physics are continuously broken for the benefit of some of the characters (see Limoges 2011). When cartoon characters walk through walls, it is often the wall that gives way. Cartoon figures are hit by anvils, run over by trains, and dismembered by hand grenades, but these maltreatments can disappear without a trace from one moment to the next. It is precisely this break with "natural" narrative expectations that makes such punch lines enjoyable and understandable. Cartoonishness can then also mean a special "worldness" that is subject to its distinct physical laws (see Rauscher 2018). We are not only dealing with a different mode of representation here, but with a represented world of a distinct ontology in which characters' *physical agency* – their ability to act, to withstand harm, and to manipulate their surroundings – is entirely different from "ours." In the real-life/animation hybrid film *Who Framed Roger Rabbit* (Zemeckis 1988), this cartoon world with its distinct physical laws (drawn characters) is *geographically juxtaposed* with the "realistic world" (filmed actors). The distinction is thus turned into a part of the overall storyworld itself: When anvils fall on heads "over there" – in the realm of cartoon characters – their inhabitants are merely physically distorted, seeing little stars and birds (which are also visible as part of the diegetic environment). To embodied characters such as Eddie

Valiant (played by Bob Hoskins), the same thing would mean death. Cartoonization is thus expanded from a *visual* mode into a uniquely *narrative* mode that "literalizes" visual metaphors. In summary, it would do cartoon aesthetics little justice to generalize a "natural" world that is "cleansed" from conventionality. Representational correspondence and the semiotic third space often remain undefined and unreliable, leaving equal room for the imagination of "literal" vs. "metaphorical" readings until reasons are provided in favor of one option or the other. To study characters in cartoonish media is then also to study the specific conventions that mediate between formal expressions on the one hand and characters and their assumed experiences on the other.

5.4 Degrees of Agency and Complexity

Everything that we perceive as characters must possess some degree of narrative and social agency: We assume that they are capable of self-initiated action, responsibility for these actions, and that they possess an inner life (a continuous consciousness frame). In comics and animation, however, we can find lots of character "doublets" or "triplets" that only act as one combined, hybrid actant together – although they must (or *should*) be considered as individual characters within their world. Examples include character groups such as Huey, Dewey, and Louie, the Beagle Boys, or *Tintin's* (Hergé 1929–1976) Thomson and Thompson (Dupont and Dupond in French) impossible to distinguish in most iterations. They are usually acting in unison, their goals and aims generally aligned (not in the new *Duck Tales* series from 2017, Youngberg, however, breaking with this tradition by assigning individual actantial roles to the triplets). Shenzi, Banzai, and Ed, the three hyenas who act as "henchmen" to *The Lion King's* (Allers and Minkoff 1994) antagonist Scar, *do* possess some small differences in character traits and visual/audio representation (Shenzi, voiced by Whoopi Goldberg, clearly appears as a leader, for example), but they also share most objectives and act in unison. We can hence interrelate groups of characters-as-actants (their role within the plot) with their visual representation. If we cannot distinguish and identify them by their design, the media texts often deny them individual narrative agency as well, even though we have to assume they must be individuals on the level of the storyworld. The narrative agency characters have within a story's plot (as actants) can thus be predetermined through their visual appearances.

Such a "prefiguration" of narrative agency can be found in various forms in different traditions of comics and animation. In some animated cartoon movies/ series that focus on anthropomorphic animals (such as *Tom & Jerry*, Ising et al. 1940–1967) or children, human adults are part of the storyworld, but only presented through their hands, legs, or from their hips up – their faces never shown. Their narrative agency is often equally limited to exposition or resolution and we never gain access to their subjective positions (much less their consciousness) within the story. In Disney comics, we can often identify protagonists at first glance, as they are afforded a more detailed character design than the background characters and nameless inhabitants of Duckburg who all seem to belong to the same species of human/dog creatures with black noses. Within Disney animated movies, the main protagonists mostly conform to identical body types (dynamic, tall, and, especially for women, incredibly thin) composed of similar basic geometric forms, while humorous secondary characters are often small, round, or irregular in their shape(s). Their role within the plot – as actants – can thus be anticipated from their first appearance. Manga and anime have different traditions: Here, the cartoonization of protagonists is often much stronger than that of background characters and antagonists which, perhaps surprisingly, are sometimes drawn with greater, even photorealistic detail. Within the Sci-Fi classic *Akira* (manga, Otomo 1982–1990, and anime movie, Otomo 1988), for instance, the heroes Kaneda and Tetsuo have strongly simplified cartoon faces (and eyes), while Colonel Shikishima is presented in more detail. In terms of representational correspondence, we could say that the main characters allow for a greater "gap-filling" by audiences than their environment, which is represented more intersubjectively and thus minimizes the range of the individual imagination (see McCloud 1993, 43). In anime, *movement* is often an attribute reserved for actants (characters at the center of the plot), while bystanders or observers (a "crowd of people") are presented in frozen still images (see LaMarre 2009). With recourse to the principle of minimal departure, we would still be right to assume that the people within these still images also have some inner life (that they are characters); as actants, however, they only function as a collective without interior differentiation.

The most interesting aspects of cartoonish characters' narrative agency, personality, and identity can probably be found in the fact that many social aspects of characterization can intentionally remain vague or "left open." In Lewis Trondheim's comics *Mister O* (2004) and *Mister I* (2007), the protagonists appear only as the simple letters I and O which mostly "conceal" their appearances and social identities. The animated show *Tear along the Dotted Line* (Foschini et al. 2021) intentionally hides the visual identity of the character Alice's toxic past boyfriend by showing him only as a silhouette. On the thematic level, this can be interpreted as him exemplifying countless male individuals who share the same patterns of behavior. If it will forever be disputed whether Donald is a duck or a human, many of his other aspects certainly remain undefined as well: How old is he, exactly, and what ethnicity does he represent? Anthropomorphic animals can thus be used as stand-ins for characters that are *undefined* in many respects (see LaMarre 2009). This cannot be generalized, however, since "funny animals" *were* often employed as mocking caricatures as well. Some of the most infamous examples are Disney's *Dumbo* (Sharpsteen 1941) and *The Jungle Book* (Reitherman 1967). The five crows in the former and King Louie in the latter were immediately recognized as offensive caricatures of people of color (mainly because of their stereotypical speech patterns and accents). In other cases, however, cartoon aesthetics are specifically employed to avoid social categorization – in a way unachievable by live-action film. A famous example can be found as early as in George Herriman's comic strip series *Krazy Kat* (1913–1944) which featured an anarchic love/hate triangle between the cat Krazy, the mouse Ignatz, and the dog Officer Pup. Kat is in love with Ignatz, and Pup with Krazy, while the cat's gender or sexuality is never revealed. Krazy has since been regarded in terms of their entirely fluid gender identity in comic book studies. While a literary text, at least by default, fixes and specifies the gender of its characters with each pronoun, cartoonish bodies can easily destabilize such gender roles, as well as other social categories. The rabbit-like character Nanachi from the anime and manga (Tsukushi 2012–present) *Made in Abyss*, for instance, has an unknown (or, rather, unspecified) gender despite the fact that they are voiced by female actresses in both Japanese (Shiori Izawa) and English (Brittney Karbowski). In fan discussions and polls, audiences like to imagine Nanachi's gender "in their mind" – with not only "girl" or "boy" as an option, but also "genderless" and "unspecified" (see Erens-Basement 2019; Lairucrem 2019). Similar discussions have evolved around the entirely human *Attack on Titan* character Hange Zoë, whose gender is (deliberately, as creator Hajime Isayama has clarified; see Romano 2021) never stated in the manga, while the anime and live-action adaptation opted for female pronouns and a corresponding (voice) actress. The conventions of the "visual language" of manga and anime thus contribute significantly to making characters unidentifiable on the level of nationality, ethnicity, and sometimes even gender. Following Elisabeth Nijdam, this

> [a]bsence of racial markers affords manga its adaptability to the representation of other ethnicities and geographic regions, while also offering an avenue through which individuals of marginalized demographics are able to empty their specific markers of racial and ethnic diversity, thus universalizing and perhaps normalizing their experience for all racial and ethnic groups.
>
> (2020, 42)

In "silent media" such as comic books or manga, we also cannot hear any voices to begin with, so the speech bubbles do not indicate whether we are to imagine them as male or female. *One-Punch Man*'s anti-hero Speed-o'-Sound Sonic was thought to be a woman in the original manga (ONE and Murata 2012–present) by some audience members due to their androgynous appearance. Casting their voice actor with a man (Yūki Kaji in Japanese and Erik S. Kimerer in English) in the anime (Matsui et al. 2015–2019) came as a surprise for many who took this as a disambiguation, even though Speed-o'-Sound Sonic's gender was never explicitly specified on the storyworld level (see Aka Steak and Iron 2015) Some fan wikis do still list *them* as bigender or gender-neutral (see Trans Characters 2018).

It certainly cannot be denied that many comic traditions (especially those aimed at a male audience) are embedded within a system of binary gender oppositions, so that bodies are exaggerated into caricatures of male vs. female appearances. American superhero comics mostly adhere to this tradition, as do many manga aimed at a male audience. *Sin City*, both the comics by Frank Miller (1999–2000) and the film adaptions (Miller and Rodriguez 2005; 2014), at the same time parodies and celebrates this hegemonic order in which male and female bodies are composed of entirely different sets of (rectangular vs. curvy) shapes. Some manga's pictorial conventions, by contrast, are ambiguous about protagonists' gender, as girls and "beautiful young boys" (*bishōnen*) can be composed of the same set of iconographic shorthands. The audience often has no immediate way of discerning a protagonist's sex or gender from their visual appearances as with Speed-o'-Sonic. Often, this is used for unconventional surprises, as many manga and anime stories aimed at a female audience (*shōjo*) feature cross-dressing and "gender-bending" prominently. Haruka Tenou, also known as Sailor Uranus from the third season of *Sailor Moon S* (Azuma et al. 1994–1995), is a well-known example of "misleading" the audience in terms of her categorization. When the character first appears, "he" is dressed in a male high school uniform, with short hair and a low, husky voice (which was, however, contributed by actress Megumi Ogata) (see Ishida 2019). This all works to conceal Haruka's female identity, which is only revealed when she transforms into Sailor Uranus: a magical warrior wearing a mini skirt and a tiara on her forehead. Intersubjective constructs based on cartoonish characters can thus remain much more open to interpretation and negotiation of social and narrative agency than any live-action film could ever hope for.

6 Interactive Characters in Video Games

So far, we have addressed several analytical approaches to characters in various media forms, always under the tacit assumption that our understandings of a given character arise from engagement with one or several media texts. However, these approaches are not entirely sufficient for a potential Transmedia Character Studies that aims to also deal with interactive media such as video games, in which audiences, or rather players, are no longer simply *presented* with characters and their traits. Rather, we are frequently invited to actively *participate* in the development of their properties and/or narrative trajectory – either by directly controlling them or by having our in-game decisions impact them indirectly. Thus, a character like Max Caulfield – the young, aspiring photographer at the center of Dontnod Entertainment's adventure game *Life is Strange* (2015) – is not only a fictional being that we can observe on our screen; she effectively constitutes an extension of the players, who can manipulate the complex simulated world of *Life is Strange* through her. In multiplayer contexts, characters acquire yet another dimension: The numerous characters that can be sent into battle in *League of Legends* (Riot Games 2009), or the entirely player-created characters of *World of Warcraft* (Blizzard Entertainment 2005) allow players to communicatively interact with each other, thus functioning as representations of other players. Characters, in this respect, are also called *avatars* (of actual players, see Klevjer 2006). Avatars in video games then serve at least three different functions for which Jonas Linderoth (2005) has coined the terms *roles* (their narrative or mimetic dimension), *tools* (their ludic dimension), and *props* (their social-communicative dimension, see also Gregersen 2019).

While this chapter will introduce analytical vocabulary to adequately describe these additional dimensions of interactive characters, it also accounts for the narrative non-linearity that many games permit: Whereas the external plot of a mainstream novel, film, or comic book will largely be intersubjectively stable (irrespective of certain interpretational options, ambiguities, and vaguenesses when it comes to characters' psyche, etc.), *Life is Strange* and similar games are designed around the players making choices that have a significant effect on how the plot develops going forward. Such choices frequently involve markedly different outcomes related to non-trivial narrative events for individual characters, to such an extent that we can regard two "Maxes," controlled by two different

DOI: 10.4324/9781003298793-9

players, as wholly incompatible on the level of their basic type. One player may decide to report one of Max's classmates brandishing a gun at school, making that classmate treat her with immense hostility for the remainder of the game, whereas another may keep quiet, thereby avoiding such antagonism and creating a differently configured sociality for the character.

Lastly, this chapter will look at games that do *not* offer a limited number of predetermined narrative paths of relevant narrative events, to begin with. Games such as *Minecraft* (Mojang 2011) or the *Crusader Kings* series (Paradox 2004; 2012; 2020) rely on emergent storytelling, i.e. narratives that are not entirely created by writers/designers but instead determined by game systems that respond to player input, creating random or semi-random situations that are still attributed narrative meaning by players. Rather than being "merely" non-linear, these media texts could be said to allow for an entirely different level of interactivity (see Bode and Dietrich 2013, 54) – one that is even more strongly present in role-playing communities within Massively Multiplayer Online Games MMOs or MMORPGs for the role playing subgenre, who use player characters in pre-designed settings to create spontaneous, collaborative stories.

6.1 Dimensions of Video Game Characters

Despite the numerous differences pointed out above between interactive and "static" characters, it is important to acknowledge, as Felix Schröter and Jan-Noël Thon (2014) have done, that all games that are in any significant way narrative or mimetic allow us to analyze their characters as fictional or fictionalized beings inhabiting a possible world. This even applies to many or most non-digital (traditional or modern) board or card games which more often than not do present a specific setting or characters-as-actants (see Booth 2021). While the once controversial question *to what degree* games are narrative to begin with will not be at the center of this chapter (see Aarseth 2012), we'd like to productively turn this concern around by pointing to the fact that once we do recognize characters within a game, we are not dealing solely with ludic, game-like structures anymore: We can interpret *Tetris* (z.B. Nintendo R&D1 1989) symbolically, perhaps (on the thematic level, Janet Murray found that it "is a perfect enactment of the lives of Americans in the 1900s," 1997, 144), but not mimetically, as there is no represented intentional being anywhere to be found. Other puzzle games such as *Dr. Mario* (Nintendo R&D1 1990), by contrast, feature similar ludic structures (players have to arrange emerging puzzle pieces under increasing time constraints), but they do so with a slight reference to a character representation, "Dr. Mario." We can hence imagine our successes and failures (in assembling puzzles made of pills and medicines) as the trials and feats of this "doctor" tasked with fighting deadly viruses, instead of merely our own (solving the very puzzles that we actually see on screen). For the actual gameplay, however, the character remains negligible, his traits mostly undefined. The "avatar" of any given game does not need to be a character at all then and can even be entirely non-mimetic (not part of the represented world) such as a mouse arrow in management and construction simulators like *Cities: Skylines* (Colossal Order 2015). In such cases, perhaps we can imagine an implied overarching actant like a government or an omnipotent being ruling over the world, but not a personalized continuous consciousness frame except our own.

By contrast, with regard to a game like Ubisoft Montréal's *Assassin's Creed II* (2009), we could look at its protagonist, Ezio Auditore da Firenze, and describe him as we would any character in the fictional world of a novel, film, or comic book: He is a Florentine nobleman living in the 15th and early 16th century who follows in his father's footsteps as a member of the secret order of the Assassins, eventually becoming the leader of the organization. On this level, we can apply the usual basic character type (with the categories of corporeality, sociality, and psyche) and other analytical tools introduced throughout this volume in order to map Ezio's development over the course of narrative events throughout the three *Assassin's Creed* games he stars in: from a privileged, mischievous teenager to an angry young man on a quest to avenge his father's death, to a responsible adult leading a political uprising against the Borgia family's control of Rome and the Vatican, all the way to an elderly man discovering the secrets of his ancestry in renaissance Constantinople. In our analysis, we would have to bear in mind that video games also involve some media-specific means of representing characters as fictional or fictionalized beings (see Schröter 2021, 155), such as interface elements (for example, the health bar representing whether Ezio is currently injured, or the map which shows us how familiar he is with his surroundings), haptic feedback on console controllers, or interactive sound.

However, many of these elements do not only contribute to the narrative dimension of the character but also give players relevant information for navigating the game as a mathematical simulation: Viewed through this lens, Ezio could be described as possessing a number of ludic abilities and attributes, as well as being connected to the game's overall goals, or its winning condition (see Schröter 2021, 159). Abilities would include things such as running, climbing, jumping, and performing a variety of combat maneuvers in a three-dimensional environment, whereas attributes refer to numerical values such as his health or the strength of his armor. Lastly, ludic goals include the specific objectives assigned to Ezio by the game, irrespective of their narrative justification. For example, in the final section of *Assassin's Creed II*, Ezio has a single, unchanging *narrative* goal: to prevent the current pope, Rodrigo Borgia, from opening a secret vault in the Sistine Chapel whose contents will grant him near-limitless power. However, this general narrative trajectory is expressed to the player through a series of much more specific goals that react dynamically to player input and change over the course of the level, from "Enter the Vatican" to "Kill Rodrigo Borgia." Of course, these are already "narrativized" versions of the actual ludic goals, which would be more adequately verbalized as "reach point X in the game world" and "bring the 'life points'-attribute of Rodrigo Borgia to zero." These goals regulate how other ludic elements of the game, such as target markers on the map, behave. However, not only are they not identical to the goals of Ezio as a fictional being (who, ultimately, decides to let Borgia live, regardless of his life points) – they can also differ greatly from the goals of the actual players. This is the case, for example, in so-called speedruns, in which one or several players attempt, often publicly, to finish a game or level as fast as possible, effectively adding a new goal to the game that is not present on the initial level of the simulation. Speedrunners also often use exploits, i.e., unintended elements of a game that permit skipping parts of it that would otherwise be necessary in order to reach the goal. Another, more radical divergence of game and player goals emerges within the aforementioned role-playing communities that will be discussed later on (see Bowman and Schrier 2018).

The connection between the ludic and the narrative properties of a game character can take on a variety of forms: The *Assassin's Creed* franchise typically connects changes in a character's ludic properties to specific narrative events that change the character's basic type. For example, players begin *Assassin's Creed: Brotherhood* (Ubisoft Montréal 2010), the second game in the series featuring Ezio, with a set of abilities and attributes that is much more limited than it was at the end of *Assassin's Creed II*. In fact, Ezio's ludic makeup at the beginning of both games is very similar, despite the immense narrative and ludic progression within the first game. From a design perspective, this choice can be easily justified by the need to accommodate players of *Brotherhood* who have not previously played an *Assassin's Creed* game, and who might therefore be overwhelmed by a large number of abilities to manage. Furthermore, "resetting" Ezio's ludic properties increases the potential for the players' sense of progress as they unlock new (or rather *old*) abilities. On the other hand, this kind of "reset" could potentially result in a notable discrepancy between the ludic and the narrative level of *Brotherhood*, which is, after all, intended as a direct, non-contradictory continuation of Ezio's life story. Within the logic of the storyworld, most players would probably not accept Ezio simply "forgetting" about all the acrobatic skills and combat moves he has learned over the course of *Assassin's Creed II*. In fact, this would constitute a significant change to his basic type (corporeality and/or psyche) and therefore necessitate an explanation – an explanation which *Brotherhood* provides by showing Ezio suffering a severe injury and loss of personal equipment early in the game. In other cases, the narrative and ludic dimensions of a character are much less strongly aligned: Many role-playing games, such as CD Projekt's *Witcher* series, as well as later titles in the *Assassin's Creed* franchise, feature a skill-tree system that allows players to unlock new or improved abilities for a character once that character has acquired enough "experience points" (another ludic attribute) by completing specific tasks in the game world. Notably, the kinds of activities through which experience is earned are completely independent of the new skills that can be acquired. This means that, in *The Witcher 3: Wild Hunt* (CD Projekt Red 2015), we might unlock an ability that improves the protagonist Geralt's marksmanship with a crossbow without ever having used the weapon before.

Schröter and Thon (2014, 50) note that, apart from being both fictional beings and game pieces, video game characters can also function as social stand-ins for actual players in multiplayer settings. This, too, applies to Ezio, who appears as a guest character in the fighting game *Soulcalibur V* (Project Soul 2012), in which players can select him as "their" character for two-player matches (local or online). In these situations, what players choose to do with, or rather *through* Ezio, might well be read by their opponents as a social act that has motivations and effects outside of the game's storyworld. A frequent example of such behavior in competitive 3D games is the practice of "teabagging": This term describes one player in a multiplayer environment making their character crouch repeatedly over the head of another character's corpse, to simulate placing one's scrotum on that corpse's face (see Myers 2017, 765). This is typically done to characters that the active player has just killed in-game and is partly motivated by the assumption that the other player will be aware of being teabagged. Brian Myers, in a qualitative study (2017), has identified a complex range of social meanings that players ascribe to the practice of teabagging, from expressions of dominance or humiliation of the defeated player to affirmations of mutual affection between participants. What all these meanings have in common is that they arise between actual players, with the characters' actions serving merely as mediators that fulfill no practical purpose in the narrative *or* ludic context of the game.

In other cases, the social dimension of game characters can also be in line with their narrative and/or ludic properties: In the multiplayer social deduction game *Among Us* (Innersloth 2018), each player takes on the (narrative) role of an astronaut aboard a spaceship or -station, which needs to be kept in working order. On the ludic level, this means that the characters can walk through the two-dimensional environment, work on numerous tasks in different locations, and report any dead bodies they find, with the goal of surviving and completing all their tasks. Some players, however, are randomly and secretly assigned the role of "impostor," whose goal is to kill all regular crew members. They also receive a largely different set of abilities, such as killing, moving through ventilation shafts, and sabotaging critical infrastructure. Verbal communication between players is limited to one specific situation: If any player (including an impostor) reports a dead body, all surviving players are invited to discuss their suspicions as to the impostor's identity via in-game chat or voice call, before voting which suspect to kick out of the airlock. Here, the social dimension of the game characters complements and directly interacts with their ludic properties and the narrative setup.

Rather than simply differentiating between these three different dimensions of game characters themselves, Schröter and Thon (2014, 51) apply similar categories to the levels of representational strategies and subjective player experience as well. The aforementioned skill trees can be said to represent a character mainly on the ludic level, whereas cutscenes – i.e., cinematic videos that show part of a game's story while temporarily suspending player interaction – are exclusively narrative representations of the same character. The same is true for the diary entries that *Life is Strange* creates as summaries of the events the player has just ludo-narratively actualized. However, it has also been noted that, with the advancement of video game engines, these categories become increasingly less clear-cut (see Schröter 2021, 63). While many modern first-person shooters permit players to control their character's field of vision during otherwise non-interactive segments, other games employ so-called "quick-time events" in which a specific sequence of keys or buttons must be pressed as fast as possible for a character to complete a specific action, such as fighting off a zombie that attacks in the middle of a cutscene in Telltale Games' *The Walking Dead* (Telltale Games 2012).

Importantly, the actual ludic makeup of a character is often not accurately reflected in how the game represents them, and/or the player's subjective experience of them. An interesting case in this regard is *Life is Strange 2* (Dontnod Entertainment 2018–2019): Like its predecessor, this game places great emphasis on the fact that the decisions players make in the role of teenager Sean Diaz affect the story's outcome, particularly through Sean's interactions with his younger brother, Daniel. Shortly before the release of the game's final episode in December 2019, the game's developers published an explanation of the ludic systems underlying the players' narrative agency. In their post, they noted that many players had made wrong assumptions about the ways in which their influence over Daniel worked:

> From what we've seen so far, Daniel's education is believed to rely on a "one-track" model [...] That is to say that you can, for example, only teach Daniel to either be "Good" or "Bad" and that only certain key decisions will affect his education by nudging him towards becoming either a good or an evil person. The truth, however, is that Daniel grows and learns from your example based on two separate values: Morality and Brotherhood.
>
> (Life is Strange Blog 2019, n.pag.)

What the developers are describing is a significant difference in how the characters of *Life is Strange 2* were represented, how players experienced them, and what the actual workings of the game engine were. While the ludic *representation* of the brothers' relationship to the players operates only via abilities, such as choosing among several dialogue options, many players' ludic *experience* of it was shaped by their knowledge of the first *Life is Strange* game's monocausal structure, leading them to certain assumptions about their ludic action's effect on the narrative. These assumptions were however proven wrong by the *actual* ludic makeup of Daniel as a character, which is based on two attributes that are never transparently represented to the players. Of course, authorial statements like the one quoted above can "rectify" such discrepancies and change the players' experience of subsequent playthroughs. Another type of change in player experience that is arguably much more frequent in video games affects the *narrative* representation and experience of a given game – or, more precisely, the possibility of a non-linear narrative that allows only one of many possible courses of events to be experienced per playthrough.

6.2 Narrative Non-Linearity

One of the possibilities afforded much more easily by video games than by non-digital media such as novels, films, or comic books is a dynamic reaction to player input. This obviously extends to the level of characters as well: Many video games, especially those in genres with a strong emphasis on the narrative dimension of gameplay, will give players the opportunity to modify characters not only on the ludic but also on the narrative level. Some of these choices modify the character before the game even starts:

> The Warden, protagonist in a typical high-fantasy role-playing game [*Dragon Age: Origins*, BioWare 2009] is, despite the rather tightly controlled branching narrative, not a person so much as an occupation, a vacancy to be filled by the player. Players are free to construct and/or choose not only the name, gender, sexuality, looks, race and skills of the Warden, but also their morals. But the game forces them to do the Warden's job. Is the Warden a character at all? Perhaps only in the sense of a player character, one that does not exist without the player, but also not without the game. The Warden is legion, possessed by millions of players.
>
> (Aarseth 2022, 275)

Instead of, or in addition to, distributing numerical attributes, games like *Dragon Age: Origins*, the *Mass Effect* trilogy (BioWare 2007; 2010; 2012) or the aforementioned *Life is Strange* give players the agency to make choices, often in the context of dialogue sequences involving both player and non-player characters, that will influence salient aspects of the games' story going forward. For example, in the *Mass Effect* series, players may recruit a number of Non-Playable Characters (NPCs) as members of their spaceship crew and call on their assistance in defeating the game's various antagonists. These crewmates have been described as "represent[ing] strong narrative points of view" and providing "a structure, a context, and a motivation for the player's journey through the game" (Bizzocchi and Tanenbaum 2012, 399), significantly shaping how the game's story is experienced. However, at several points in *Mass Effect* and its two direct sequels, the players' choices may result in the death of one or more crewmates, foreclosing their involvement in all subsequent events of the narrative. For players who manage to avoid these deaths, these characters will remain present and influence the outcome of later choices. In fact, players of *Mass Effect 2* may even choose to sacrifice the life of the player character, Commander Shepard, at the end of the story. The narrative structure of probability disjunctions described in chapter 2, chains of narrative events of which only one distinct outcome is ever realized, can thus be "literalized" in video games so that contradictory outcomes are equally achievable. While these disjunctions exist only within the mental models of producers and audiences in "predetermined" media such as novels, films, TV shows, or comics, they have a material substructure in a game's code that allows players to actualize these events. Such discrepancies between individual playthroughs pose a problem if we want to apply the analytical tools that have so far been presented in this introduction. Most of our concepts and approaches were explicitly intended for use in *intersubjectively stable* contexts, after all (see Aarseth 1997, 26).

As already suggested in the introduction to this chapter, doing justice to the non-linear nature of video games may involve approaching the protagonists of two different *Mass Effect* playthroughs not as a single character, *the* Commander Shepard in the narrow sense. Instead, it can be analytically useful to view them as two distinct versions of *a* Commander Shepard that share a significant amount of basic type traits (such as their second name, species, and social position as a member of the Systems Alliance N7 special forces program), while subsequently diverging in other respects (such as their first name, gender, pre-service history, and attitude toward individual characters and events in the game world). The subsequent chapter 7 is going into more detail on how different, partly contradictory "versions" of characters can be related to each other. For non-linear games like *Mass Effect*, it remains true, however, that, while there is a certain amount of player agency involved in the shaping of the game's story and character arcs, the broad narrative trajectory of the game is still clearly delineated by its writers and developers. Jim Bizzocchi and Theresa J. Tanenbaum have called such cases examples of "bounded agency" (2012, 401), in which developers offer a range of narrative possibilities for players to choose from, rather than letting them freely determine the development of the narrative. On the one hand, we cannot speak of a single, intersubjectively stable course of events that will necessarily be experienced by all players of such games. On the other, however, this does not mean that there is *no* intersubjectively stable foundation for the various versions of events and characters that a game potentially represents. Joleen Blom, drawing on a variety of scholars such as Brenda Laurel (2014) and Espen Aarseth (1997), characterizes the totality of all "paths" through a given game's narrative as the "possibility space" (Blom 2019, 147) of said game. Other than the question of which individual narrative possibility will be *actualized* by a specific player, the overall shape and scope of the possibility space is identical over all playthroughs (if the code itself was not modified through a practice called "modding," see Girina 2021). Non-linearity is also not an *exclusive* feature of games. During the 1980s, gamebooks such as the *Choose Your Own Adventure* (Bantam Books 1979–1998) or *Lone Wolf* (Dever et al. 1984–present) series became increasingly popular (see Costikyan 2007, 7–8). While these books offer varying degrees of rule complexity, their common basic principle is that readers, who are usually directly addressed by the text in second-person, can decide between multiple potential courses of events. The text body is typically divided into numbered sections, each of which ends with one or several options for where to continue reading. Section one of *Flight From the Dark* (Dever 1984), the first of the *Lone Wolf* books, offers readers perhaps the most archetypal choice of all:

> At the foot of the hill, the path splits into two directions, both leading into a large wood. [...]
> If you wish to take the right path into the wood, turn to 85.
> If you wish to follow the left track, turn to 275.
>
> (Dever and Chalk 2018, n.pag.)

Various experimental comics like *A Duck Has An Adventure* (Goodbrey 2012) or Marvel's *You Are Deadpool* (Ewing et al. 2018) have *remediated* this sort of non-linear narrative structure, and a range of notable films – most prominently the inter-active film *Bandersnatch* (Slade 2018) which is part of the *Black Mirror* anthology – have done the same, offering a variety of different storyworld/character versions that audiences can decide to actualize.

Of course, in games that procedurally generate parts or even the entirety of their world and/or narrative, the possibility space is infinitely larger, and the overlap between individual instantiations of characters and other elements may become so insignificant that the concept of character versions is no longer applicable. Such cases will be dealt with in the final section of this chapter. However, for games like *Mass Effect* or *Life is Strange*, which grant the player a specific amount of bounded agency, the possibility space can be a suitable site for the analysis of character, prompting us to ask, for example, questions about how the interaction of a character's stable and dynamic attributes shapes the players' relationship to them, or what ideological assumptions are naturalized by the presence or absence of specific choices. With regard to the latter issue, a minor controversy arose in 2012 around the then newly released **MMORPG** *Star Wars: The Old Republic* (henceforth *SWTOR;* BioWare Austin, 2011). Gam-ing news outlet *Kotaku* reported on how some of the in-game dialogue choices, which work similarly to the *Mass Effect* games, permitted players to brutally torture Vette, an enslaved female NPC who accompanied their character (see Fahey 2012). These options, if picked, are not entirely without consequence, since the game ludically assigns "dark side" points, which, when accumulated, can affect the player character's looks and available items. Until a 2015 update, further conversations with Vette would also be blocked if players treated her poorly. Nevertheless, the presence of this choice could be read in the vein of the "women in refrigerators" trope (see chapter 3): The violence potentially suffered by Vette is relevant only insofar as it affects the characterization of the player character (ludically quantified as "light side" or "dark side" points). Even before the 2015 update, she would readily begin a romance with her tormentor if the latter happened to be male and presented her with enough in-game gifts. A slightly different sort of controversy was presented by the public debate sur-rounding Rockstar Studios' open-world Western *Red Dead Redemption 2* (2018). Shortly after its release, prominent newspapers reported that some players had uploaded videos of themselves murdering suffragette NPCs in the game world, with the videos' titles and many comments expressing misogynistic sentiments (see Lyons 2018). Response articles were quick to point out that the game did, in fact, allow such violence against almost all non-player characters (children being the categorical exception), and that these actions were always connected with the ludo-narrative cost of criminalization (see Badham 2018). While this response does not mean that the game's stance toward women and/or violence is above criticism, it points to the importance of distinguishing the clearly de-lineated (and thus more transparently ideological) choices offered by games like *SWTOR*, *Mass Effect*, or *Life is Strange*, from the fuzzier and more emer-gent choice mechanics of open-world games, some of which will be explored at length below.

6.3 Game-Specific Forms of Representational Correspondence

Of course, the concept of the possibility space does not fully account for all types of narrative non-linearity that may occur in video games. Even within the constraints of a single possible course of events in games such as *Assassin's Creed II*, where players have no salient agency over the unfolding of the plot, they will frequently not experience that plot in strictly linear order: If a player character "dies" on the ludic level, i.e., if the variable representing their health is lowered to zero, many games will not treat this as the death of that character on the narrative level (see Juul 2005, 123). Instead, they employ automatic or manual "save points," to which a player character can be "reset" for a new attempt at successfully actualizing the intended course of events (a notable exception is formed by many so-called "roguelike" games such as *The Binding of Isaac*, McMillen and Himsl 2011, or *Sunless Sea*, Failbetter Games 2015, that are built around the mechanic of permanent character death, often involving the loss of some or all ludo-narrative progress made in the previous playthrough). For example, Ezio in *Assassin's Creed II* may face ludic death at the hands of enemy NPCs or from jumping/falling off a high building in the game world, both of which will lead to him being "revived" at a slightly earlier point in the game's diegetic timeline. Depending on a game's ludic difficulty and the skill of a given player, this mechanism potentially results in dozens of prematurely ended iterations of one and the same section of the game's plot. Grant Tavinor concludes from this that "the fictional worlds of videogames seem to present a *cluster* of fictional worlds in a single playing" (2009, 118), with each abortive attempt at successfully actualizing an event constituting a separate course of events that ends in the protagonist's death.

In such cases where a character "dies" only to be "reborn" without narrative explanation, it will be clear to most players that this was not an authorially intended course of events on the mimetic level, since it only causes a ludic fail-state. Thus, if a player were to stop playing *Assassin's Creed II* after having Ezio fall off a high ledge 15 minutes after the game's opening sequence, they could not reasonably claim to have "finished" or "beaten" the game. On the other hand, a player of *Mass Effect 2* who, like Bizzocchi and Tanenbaum in one of their playthroughs (see 2012), reaches the ending of the game's plot that sees Shepard sacrifice his or her life, they will have completely actualized one of the multiple courses of events intentionally scripted by the developers and reach a ludic win-state, as indicated by the end credits after the final cutscene. Said cutscene also shows other characters offering their views on Shepard's death, making clear that it is a consequential event within the storyworld, whereas Ezio's fall from a building will never be acknowledged intradiegetically: Ezio will only ever remember the successful actualization of an event once it has been achieved, rather than recounting a terrifying tale of perpetual death and resurrection to every character he meets. Thus, it seems more apt to treat repetitions and "endings" connected to ludic fail-states as cases of blocked representational correspondence, with a discrepancy not so much between multiple intended courses of events but between what is represented to the player and what is "actually happening" in the storyworld. Blocked representational correspondence also occurs in other areas of numerous video games (see Thon 2017). A prominent example is what is colloquially referred to as the "hammerspace," a hypothetical "pocket dimension" that would need to exist in order to explain the huge amount of items that characters in games like *The Elder Scrolls V: Skyrim* (Bethesda 2011) can ludically carry, while the means of storing and transporting them is never visually represented in a way that makes sense within the game's storyworld (see TV Tropes, "Hammerspace"). Another case would be the "quick-travel" ability that is also featured in *Skyrim*, as well as many other games with geographically large worlds, permitting players to skip the real-time representation of the player character walking somewhere and having them "teleport" there instead, without any intradiegetic explanation.

Some games *do* attempt to naturalize and narrativize such instances of potential friction between the synthetic and the mimetic level: Almost all *Assassin's Creed* games feature a present-day framing narrative in which characters can use a technological device, the so-called "Animus," in order to re-live digital simulations of their ancestor's memories that are stored in their DNA. This is acknowledged in multiple ways, including the game's loading sequences, which are supposed to resemble a digital environment slowly assembling itself, but also in the way that the player character's death is dealt with. Like any other unintended divergence from the intended course of events, such as the killing of friendly non-player characters, their death is framed as a "divergence from the genetically stored memories" that destroys the simulation, which then has to be re-loaded at the last save point. Similarly, titles like *Deathloop* (Arkane Lyon 2021) provide metaphysical explanations such as time-loops for their characters repeatedly coming back to life. Kojima Productions' *Death Stranding* (2019), by contrast, makes the weight and physical size of the items carried by its player character a central ludic element that is faithfully visualized and requires careful management from players. It also features no quick-travel system, ensuring a strong representational correspondence between the movement experienced by the player and player character, respectively.

A particularly striking example of the complexities of narrative non-linearity and representative correspondence in video games are so-called MMORPGs – Massively Multiplayer Online Role-Playing Games – in which hundreds, sometimes thousands of player characters share one persistent game world which allows them to interact with each other, and which therefore needs to appear largely the same to every single player (see Di Filippo 2017; Chen et al. 2018). Depending on the narrative focus of such games, the direct interaction of multiple player characters – each of whom may have chosen a different path through the game's narrative possibility space up to that point – can lead to friction regarding the coherence and/or representational correspondence of the world. Once again, *SWTOR* provides a good example: In yet another similarity to the *Mass Effect* games, some dialogue options offered to players in cutscenes visibly impact the fates of significant NPCs in the game world. Since many, if not most other players will at some point face the same choices but decide differently, it is common for a given player 1 to encounter another player character accompanied by an NPC who player 1 has just killed in a personal cutscene. Managing divergent narrative paths becomes even trickier when games are expanded upon in other, linear forms of media: In April 2021, *SWTOR* writer Caitlin Sullivan Kelly published a tie-in short story on the game's website. Three days after its original publication, the story had to be slightly edited after players had pointed out that one character that was originally mentioned in the story could not, according to the game's narrative as *they* had experienced it, be alive at this point in the timeline (see Sullivan 2021).

While the game's design attempts to draw attention away from such inconsistencies, for example by making the looks of NPC companions customizable or simply not mentioning player-specific events or characters in group-focused content, they are sometimes still glaringly obvious. When all players can potentially access a task that involves stopping an attack on a military outpost, this means that the attack will never *actually* end. Instead, the outpost will continue to be assailed by unending hordes of enemies for newly arriving player characters to battle (see Schröter and Thon 2014, 64). One way around this is the creation of so-called "instances," areas of the game world that are not shared between all players but rather created as individual "copies" specific to a single player or group. This means that, within the narrow confines of such an instance, actions will have consequences that are not contradicted by other players' versions of characters entering the picture. In other cases, such as those mentioned above, the game relies on its players' "charity" (their "suspension of disbelief") – reasonably so, if we consider that, as Schröter and Thon put it, "for most players [of MMORPGs] it is the social experience of online play that fundamentally affects the way characters are perceived, customized, and used as a means for communication with other players" (2014, 66). Furthermore, similar to procedurally generated elements, the social use of player characters in multiplayer contexts can also give rise to events that are entirely unscripted and test the limits of what we have so far termed *narrative* non-linearity.

6.4 Emergent Characters and Games as Performance

In dealing with games that offer a limited number of predetermined narrative trajectories, we have repeatedly alluded to forms of interactive narrative that are less constrained by developer-imposed limits, going beyond the strictly bounded agency afforded to players in games like *Mass Effect* or *The Witcher*. Henry Jenkins, in a broad but nevertheless useful definition, states that such "emergent narratives are not prestructured or preprogrammed, taking shape through the gameplay, yet they are not as unstructured, chaotic, and frustrating as life itself" (2004, n. pag.).

One of the most critically acclaimed recent examples featuring such a narrative structure is Paradox Development Studio's *Crusader Kings III* (2020), a historical grand strategy game set between the years 867 and 1453. Here, players take on the role of a medieval ruler with the goal of ensuring the survival of their dynasty through efficient management of diplomacy, warfare, and economy. Just like its predecessors in the *Crusader Kings* series, the game is based on a character-driven concept of feudal politics in which the interpersonal relations of individual rulers have a significant influence on political decision-making. Thus, the player character is represented, on the ludic level, as the aggregate of a large variety of numeric values which quantify traits like courage, piety, or attractiveness. These traits, in turn, determine the probability of success for many of the player's actions: If a Catholic player character wants to petition the pope for financial aid, their chances at succeeding will vary, depending on the value of their piety attribute. The complexity of these calculations is increased when players interact with other, non-player character rulers, who are ludically modeled in the same way: Differences and similarities in religion, culture, or specific attributes result in a separate attribute representing the positive or negative opinion other rulers hold of the player character, which again influences the outcome probabilities of interactions with these rulers, for example when negotiating a marriage. When the current player character dies, player control is transferred to their rightful heir, who, by way of a genetics and socialization system, may have inherited, through nature or nurture, some of their parent's traits on the ludic as well as the narrative level. The actual (collective) actant within the gameworld is thus the dynasty, the house lineage that a player controls. While there is a clear condition for losing – the player character dying without an heir in place – the game goal, i.e., the survival of the dynasty, can never be permanently ensured.

From this account of the game, we can already infer several salient differences from non-linear narratives of the kind discussed in the previous section. First, the degree of intersubjective stability across playthroughs is significantly lower for *Crusader Kings III* than for any of the games discussed so far. While the state of the game world at the start of a campaign will usually be deliberately modeled to resemble the historical geopolitical situation of the respective era, player input will immediately lead to probabilistic, rather than predetermined outcomes, so that even players who make the exact same inputs may be faced with entirely different results, and it becomes impossible to reproduce any specific ludo-narrative situation.

The second difference concerns the relationship between ludic and narrative attributes and events. When Jenkins describes "narratives [...] taking shape through the game play" (2004, n.pag.), this implies a primacy of the ludic dimension, which is on full display in *Crusader Kings III*. A mimetic situation nevertheless persists, as the gameworld never becomes an abstract one like that of *Tetris*: Players still observe and participate in represented situations located in time and space. While the game does feature direct verbal narration, either in the form of letters from NPCs or written first-person narration from the player character themselves, such snippets are almost always directly connected to a ludic event, such as when a potential spouse rejects the player character's marriage proposal, or a court spy reports having found compromising information on a rival nobleman. In both cases, explicit narration communicates the *result* of a ludic probability disjunction. This is in stark contrast to non-linear games working with cutscenes, in which scripted events may happen independently of the player's previous ludic input, such as when Ezio, at the end of *Assassin's Creed II*, lets Rodrigo Borgia live on the level of plot, even though players have previously reduced that character's ludic health attribute to zero. The difference persists in the other direction: Whereas cutscenes in a game-like *Mass Effect* may depict events that are relevant only on the level of plot but have no bearing on the ludic attributes of a character, unmotivated narration in *Crusader Kings III* will always translate directly and transparently to ludic attributes. For example, an upcoming feast might have to be paid for, and players will be confronted with the options of acquiring funds through a new tax or out of their own coffers. While the presentation of the choice is similar to the dialogue options in *Mass Effect*, here, each option will immediately adjust one or several ludic attributes: Not imposing a tax will cost money, i.e., decrease the value of the "wealth" attribute, whereas taxation will lower popular opinion of the ruler. This will, in turn, make other events, such as bankruptcy or a popular revolt, more or less likely. The concatenation of attribute adjustments and probability disjunctions is potentially, and quite literally, endless, as evidenced by the lack of any stable win-state in *Crusader Kings III*. This constitutes the third major distinction between non-linear and emergent narratives: Turning back to Joleen Blom, we could say that the possibility space marked out by the initial world state of any *Crusader Kings III* campaign will never narrow down to one ludo-narrative outcome that offers no further choices. We will rather see changes in the probability distributions of any and all future input's outcome(s).

Taken together, these three factors – the decreased intersubjective stability, the primacy of the ludic dimension, and the potentially infinite ludo-narrative continuation – provide valuable clues on how to adjust our analytic methodology for characters in the context of emergent narratives. Clearly, we can no longer rely on a set number of individual playthroughs to acquaint ourselves with the entirety of a game's possibility space. Nor can we focus on the explicitly narrative sections of the game to gain an initial understanding of a character's traits or dramatic function. Instead, our analysis must be based on the systems that generate new elements in the game world and determine the logic of their interactions. Ian Bogost (2007) has coined the term "procedural rhetoric" to describe how ideas can be expressed by such systems, in a "practice of persuading through processes in general and computational processes in particular" (3). This practice can take many forms but usually rests on the selective granting and denying of player agency and the relationship between player input and its results. In overtly political games, this may happen on purpose: *Watch Dogs: Legion* (Ubisoft Toronto 2020), an action-adventure game set in a near-future London, generates almost all of its non-player characters procedurally. Based on probabilities determined by their place of residence within the virtual cityscape, NPCs are assigned abilities, a number of biographical background traits that mainly serve narrative embellishment, and a daily schedule governing what they will be doing at any given time. Players can recruit any of these NPCs into their small group of dissidents, whose goal is to end the authoritarian reign of a private security company over the city. Once recruited, the former NPC will immediately become available as a player character, bringing all their procedurally generated attributes with them. This system, titled "Play as Anyone" by developer Ubisoft, encourages and sometimes even forces players to recruit a variety of NPCs to access all the skills needed in order to progress the game's central narrative goal. Thus, the player's ability to control any NPC, and the necessity of doing so to achieve the win-state supports the idea (on the thematic/symbolic level) that overthrowing an authoritarian government requires group effort, and that "[e]very Londoner has a reason to fight back" (Ubisoft Entertainment 2021, n.pag.), as the game's website states. Similarly, the *Crusader Kings* series has been noted for effectively communicating the unsentimental power politics of medieval Europe by simulating its characters in a way that often necessitates ruthless behavior in order to survive (see Lucat and Haahr 2015).

However, as Bogost acknowledges, other "commercial games may be less deliberate in their rhetoric, but [...] not necessarily free from ideological framing, [...] display[ing] complex procedural rhetorics with or without the conscious intention of the designers" (2007, 112). Such "rhetorics" may even play a salient part of character construction before the game even starts, when players are about to construct or modify their avatar alongside a line of possible choices. Nicolle Lamerichs (2022) refers to the case of Kassandra, a character in *Assassin's Creed: Odyssey* (Ubisoft Quebec 2018). While initially, players could choose to play Kassandra as a queer character (although with almost zero effect on the actual narrative and ludic progress of the game, see Hart 2020), a downloadable sequel forced players to engage in heterosexual relationships alone, considerably limiting the players' agency to define the character's identity. Other forms of procedural rhetorics concern the thematic focus of a game. A frequent symptomatic subtext of many games, for instance, is that of colonialism. As Jules Skotnes-Brown remarks, mainstream video games often do not only provide "orientalist representations of the other" on the narrative/mimetic level but also feature "rules [i.e., procedures] which normalize colonial conquest" (2019, 143). Two games that have recently been criticized for colonialist game systems are *No Man's Sky* (Hello Games 2016) and the wildly popular *Minecraft*. The former is a space exploration sandbox game, which sets a science fiction narrative with a small number of fixed characters in a procedurally generated world with a near-infinite number of possible planetary environments, creatures, and minor characters to encounter. Several critics have pointed out that the presence of ancient ruins on many of the game world's planets, together with the already-existing names for places and life forms that players will encounter, suggests a previous, indigenous presence on these planets (see Underwood 2016). Nevertheless, the game ludically rewards players for extracting any resources they find without any thought to ecological equilibrium, renaming what they encounter and claiming it as their "discovery" in an online database – in other words, for acting much like the European colonizers of Australia or the Americas. In the case of *Minecraft*, similar, albeit slightly more subtle, mechanisms have been documented: In a 2019 video, YouTuber

Dan Olson recounts how the emergent layout of one specific *Minecraft* world implicitly incentivized him to abduct and forcibly resettle "villager" NPCs who are marked by the game as racially other from the player character through their facial features (see Olson 2019). While neither of these games claims to offer any sort of commentary on colonialism, their procedural rhetoric can certainly be read as such. This is especially true in cases like *Minecraft*, which offers very little in the sense of explicit, scripted narrative, whereas *No Man's Sky* received a significant, linear story update after its initial release, which allowed for a slight re-framing of the ostensibly colonialist game systems as part of an elaborate simulation within the storyworld.

As the post-release addition of a linear story to *No Man's Sky* demonstrates, not all games take the implementation of an emergent narrative quite as far as *Crusader Kings III*. A number of recent third-person action-adventure games have become known for features that create emergent subplots, while their main storyline still follows a predetermined trajectory. In *Middle-Earth: Shadow of Mordor* (Monolith Productions 2014) and its sequel, *Shadow of War* (2017), players experience a largely linear plot set in J.R.R. Tolkien's fantasy storyworld, which is complemented by a so-called "nemesis system," a mechanic which tracks and reacts to the player character Talion's interactions with his orc opponents. Orcs who perform unusual feats, such as escaping from an encounter with Talion or even killing him, will rise in the ranks of the evil Sauron's army and may return later in the game, often referencing their previous interactions with the player character. Reversely, if an orc leader is killed by Talion, there is also a chance that they will "cheat death" and return with visible marks of their previous defeat. While these characters are created and made to behave according to a system of probability rules built into the game, which could theoretically generate new orcs and encounters forever, this "infinity" is embedded within a strictly finite plot. This is also the case for *Watch Dogs: Legion*. In such cases, the procedural rhetoric and the explicit, (non)linear narrative may convey contradictory messages, in what Clint Hocking has termed "ludo-narrative dissonance" (Hocking 2007, n.pag.). Video game critic and scholar Austin Walker argued that *Watch Dogs: Legion* gives rise to just such a dissonance: While the "Play as Anyone" system may communicate the insufficiency of individual resistance, the game mechanics do not simulate the kind of collective action needed to attain the lasting change that is achieved on the narrative level. As Walker puts it (2020, n.pag.), "even though the verbs of play are distributed among different characters, *Legion* is still a game about covert traversal, camera hacking, drone-based puzzle platforming, and the occasional overlong gunfight," rather than about community organizing and public demonstrations, or even riots.

While procedural rhetoric and ludo-narrative dissonance concern interactions between the ludic and narrative dimensions of games, another type of emergent narrative can arise on the social level of gameplay. This is the case in role-playing communities within MMORPGs (see Di Filippo 2017; Chen et al. 2018). "Role-playing" as a practice here refers not only to the game genre but to players actively "limiting [their] talk to entities and events of the fictitious game world and avoiding references to the physical world or their offline identities" (Williams et al. 2011, 173). This practice, which is only adhered to by a minority of players (see Taylor 2006), necessarily results in an increased emphasis on the player characters as narrative agents, rather than ludic constructs. Ironically, since most MMORPGs do not actually focus on immersive storytelling as much as on ludic player progression, role-playing often takes place apart from any of the pre-designed narrative content which restricts player agency and may sacrifice immersion and consistency in favor of ludic straightforwardness. The storyworlds of MMORPGs thus become "story settings" (Costikyan 2007, 9) that are taken as an adaptable common ground for the personal narratives of the players, which emerge not through gameplay in the sense of Jenkins, but through largely unscripted social interactions between multiple players by way of their characters (see Hammer 2018). Thus, role-playing can come to resemble an improvisational theater performance (see Hoover et al. 2018) in which each player types their character's utterances into the in-game chat, using emotes (i.e., character animations representing social gestures, such as waving, dancing, or clapping) to enhance their role-playing, sometimes working around the restrictions of the game engine by substituting non-existent emotes with text. In this framework, the specific virtual location that an role-play scene takes place in can be considered equivalent to a stage, whereas clothing and other in-game items serve as props. In accordance with this theatrical paradigm, role-playing has mainly been analyzed through the lens of sociology and cultural history, rather than as a specific narrative mode of video games (see Cole and Griffiths 2007; Chan 2010; Williams et al. 2011). An important analytical approach to role-playing in the video game medium could be the examination of how this practice is based on both the selective displacement of some game mechanics and the simultaneous introduction of additional narrative frames, premises that are not part of a game's "official" story but have been agreed upon by players for the purposes of their collaborative storytelling (see Chan 2010, 84). In many other respects, it can indeed be studied as one among several (mostly non-digital) forms of spontaneous role-playing, alongside the forms it genealogically evolved from: Tabletop role-playing games and live-action role-playing (LARP) (see Harviainen et al. 2018; Mochocki 2018). In the next chapter, we are going to take up the idea of character multiplicity, both within officially authorized texts and in playful audience/fan practices, for larger, transmedial contexts.

Section 3

Foundations of Transmedia Character Analysis

7 Transmedia Characters as Networks of Character Versions

All the approaches to the theory and analysis of characters discussed in earlier chapters were primarily concerned with individual texts or works. Whatever counts as such has been taken rather intuitively, so that we simply accepted many recurrent appearances of a given character within a *series* as a single "work" up to this point, from the five volumes of *A Song of Ice and Fire* (Martin 1996–2011) and the 193 *Walking Dead* comic books (Kirkman et al. 2003–2019), to the 62 episodes of *Breaking Bad* (Gilligan et al. 2008–2013) and episodes 1–9 of the 1977–2019 *Star Wars* films (e.g. Lucas 1977; Abrams 2019), to the 75 anime episodes of *Attack on Titan* (Kinoshita et al. 2013–2022): We "count" all the respective appearances of Daenerys Targaryen, Rick Grimes, Walter White, Luke Skywalker, or Zeke Jaeger as *one* continuous development, consisting of a series of narrative events, set within the same storyworld – even though they are "split up" into serialized segments. To Roberta Pearson (2019), these are all cases of transmedial "additionality," in which distinct media texts are not conceived in isolation, but in addition to each other, mostly with recourse to recognizable, *recurring* characters. Even in *serialized* form, these protagonists are thus characters in the narrowest sense of the word, as described by media studies scholar Shane Denson and American studies scholar Ruth Mayer: "In the course of their narrative development, series characters tend to acquire psychological depth, they are given complex biographies and branching genealogies, and they are primarily of interest because of their prehistories and potential future development" (2018, 67). The common-sense notion that characters' identity throughout a series is guaranteed through one or more authors who simply "created them that way," however, does not hold on closer inspection. While some author figures are generally treated as solely or primarily responsible for the works mentioned above – such as *Breaking Bad* showrunner Vince Gilligan, *Ice and Fire* writer George R.R. Martin, or *The Walking Dead* comic book creator Robert Kirkman –, authorship is usually distributed across numerous individuals, groups, and corporations. *Star Wars* would be an example of a franchise whose ownership was separated from the original creator George Lucas in 2012, so that the films 7–9 continued the stories of protagonists Han, Luke, and Leia in entirely different directions from what one could consider "originally intended." In fact, hundreds or even thousands of other authors had contributed to their fictional biographies in other media over the decades, albeit

DOI: 10.4324/9781003298793-11

to strongly varying degrees of public recognition (this will be discussed in more detail below, see Guynes and Hassler-Forest 2018). For many characters within transmedia character culture, there isn't even *any* overarching author to begin with. Empirical research by Mark Hibbett (2022) has shown that appearances of Dr. Doom, one of Marvel's most popular supervillains who, until recently, never had a series of his own, were credited to many hundreds of authors between 1961 and 1987, the majority of whom (59%) only used the character once for specific purposes within their respective projects.

Still, all of the cases mentioned above are instances of what media semiotician Paolo Bertetti called "characters based on a single course of events" (2014, 2350), meaning their multiple versions (at least the *authorized* ones) are intended – and mostly accepted – to "fit" within one continuous fictional biography. It is therefore not easily possible to tell stories about protagonists built on this paradigm without referencing a specific point in their plotlines relative to narrative events: Daenerys Targaryen before or after she hatched her three dragons, Walter White before or after he met and later challenged Gustavo Fring, Rick Grimes before or after he lost his hand, and so on. Characters based on a single course of events can still be – and often are – transmedial, their plots systematically dispensed across media. All of the references to *The Matrix*'s (Wachowski and Wachowski 1999) Neo in media as varied as comic books, animated films, and video games can be arranged into a continuous fictional timeline containing irreversible narrative events such as Neo's sudden blindness in *The Matrix Revolutions* (Wachowski and Wachowski 2003b). Even coherent characters' fictional biographies do contain many ellipses, however, so that transmedial expansions can take place in smaller or larger "gaps" without being specific about the exact temporal order. Adventures of Luke Skywalker generally do have to specify whether they take place before or after he learned that Darth Vader was his father at the end of *The Empire Strikes Back* (Kershner 1980), but some transmedial expansions (such as Marvel's two comic series *Doctor Aphra*, Gillen et al. 2016–2019, and *Star Wars*, Aaron et al. 2015–2019) are set *sometime* after the fourth but before the fifth *Star Wars* movie so that they cannot always be exactly related *to each other* in any temporal order.

In order to be accepted as "a single course of events," transmedial expansions are nevertheless bound to a certain degree of consistency with earlier texts. Or, as Pearson put it: "While a given storyworld can be presented through several different texts, these texts must respect the facts of the original text if they are to share its logical storyworld" (2018b, 149). Many or even most transmedia characters, however, especially if they are "around" for decades, do not exactly conform to the paradigm of continuity, even if their ownership is strictly governed by legal rights. First, even the characters mentioned above in fact *do* appear in more than one *version* – with strikingly contradicting fictional biographies: Rick Grimes, for instance, loses his hand in issue #28 of the *Walking Dead* comic books (Kirkman et al. 2003–2019), a major narrative event for the character that never occurred in the ABC TV show of the same name (Darabont et al. 2010–2022). Rick's son Carl, by contrast, dies in episode 9 of season 8 (2018) of the latter, while surviving the surprising death of his father in issue #193 of the comic books. For all accounts, both "Ricks" and "Carls" must hence be *different* fictional entities, different characters in heterogeneous storyworlds. The same is true for the book and TV versions of *Game of Thrones/A Song of Ice and Fire*: The TV show (Benioff et al. 2011–2019) might have positioned itself as a straightforward adaptation (a retelling) of *the same story* in its first season (although there were notable differences even back then which audiences might have been willing to "ignore"). As the series progressed and finally overtook the books with season six, some differences became so great that they could no longer be accounted for as the same characters. The TV version of Euron Greyjoy, for instance, resembles his book counterpart in name alone, while his backstory, his motivations, appearances, and actions were changed completely. In fan discourse, both "Eurons" are sharply distinguished accordingly (see Alt Shift X 2020). The superheroes of Marvel and DC are probably most prominent for dozens of reboots, retcons, and diverging transmedial iterations which no person in existence – neither creators nor readers – can claim to even *know* at this point (let alone have created or "planned" according to any overall intent) (see Friedenthal 2017; for DC also Brode 2022). For many transmedia characters, the overwhelming number of diverging works and character versions has led to the establishment of a "canon" of works or narrative elements that are accepted by creators and/or audiences as the "real story" to which future transmedial additions are generally expected to adhere. As we will see below, however, *canonicity* not only remains far from uncontested or stable, but there often is also more than one canon for any given character.

In addition, there are transmedia characters closer to protagonists of ancient myths in that no person or company controls their iterations or decides questions of identity/difference (canonicity) on legal grounds. The most prominent one might be Arthur Conan Doyle's Sherlock Holmes, whose ownership mostly went into the public domain and who has appeared in thousands of versions with countless intended or unintended contradictions (see Pearson 2015; Rosendo 2016). In contrast to characters based on a single course of events (the "paradigm of continuity," Jenkins 2009), Bertetti addresses those on the other side of the spectrum as "based on multiple courses of events" (Bertetti 2014, 2350). Jenkins (2009) coined the contrasting "paradigm of multiplicity." As our initial examples above show, consistency and continuity can only ever be upheld to a certain degree. This becomes evident even for characters intentionally built on continuity if we start taking fan fiction into account (see Coppa 2017). It seems clear, after all, that anyone can write, draw, or play-act a story in which a "Walter White" or a "Daenerys Targaryen" appears. As a transmedia character becomes more prominent, such a "life of their own" within fan communities is the rule, rather than the exception. However, within fan fiction, too, we can distinguish between *affirmational* forms which intend to adhere to accepted continuity and canonicity, and *transformational* forms which are engaged with the reimagination of characters in partly different identities (Stein and Busse 2012, 15–16; Scott 2019, 36; see also obsession_inc 2009 for a definition of the two terms).

The analysis of relations within such "character ecologies" (Blom 2019, 57), the "sphere[s] in which characters are constantly produced and reproduced [which] not only shapes [...] the nature of the character, but also shapes [...] their identity" (58), is the focus of this chapter and the next. Recurring appearances of characters were first investigated in scholarship on seriality (see Klein and Palmer 2016). As Denson and Mayer have argued (2018), contradictory versions can keep a character in transmedial circulation, for if a story is strictly linear and target-oriented, it is likely to end at some point and thus brings the character's circulation to an end, too. Both scholars point to the fact that Tarzan has been around for over a century precisely because his individual adventures showed less and less interest in continuity. Paradoxically, the character was thus made *compatible* with iterations that clashed with or even disregarded its literary origins, while another pulp hero created during the same period, "Whistlin' Dan Barry," is largely forgotten by now precisely because his story was concluded at some point. By contrast, "[r]egardless of whether we are watching a Frankenstein or Tarzan film or reading a Sherlock Holmes or a Fu Manchu story, there is no ulti- mate narrative, no finale, that can definitively conclude the series" (Denson and Mayer 2018, 69). Serial – and, even more so, transmedia – characters are hence "storytelling engines [that] keep on running, cranking out ever-new stories, even when their authors pass away or their production teams vary and change" (67). To account for the complexities within the transmedial circulation of fictional entities – contradictions as well as consistencies – we are first going to introduce the recent network model by media studies scholar Jan-Noël Thon (2019; 2022). It provides a clear vocabulary for decidable cases of continuity vs. multiplicity, as well as for the relations of entirely separate but *similar* characters such as Indiana Jones/Lara Croft. In chapter 8, we will then turn to characters for which these distinctions cannot be drawn easily, as well as to those to which the model does not seem to apply at all.

7.1 Contradictory Versions and Transmedia Character Networks

Contrary to the common-sense assumption in anthropology, cultural studies, or even everyday language (see Müller 1991; Wilde 2019b), Thon advocates first *not* to take "cultural icons" (Brooker 2013) or "second-level originals" (Margolin 1996, 116) such as "*the* James Bond" that exist "above" any particular media text as the starting point of any character analysis. Rather, its point of departure should always be *specific* texts featuring *specific* character versions. Although James Bond, for instance, has been discussed extensively as a "'free floating' signifier" (Bennett 2017, 8) or Batman in terms of "multiple but simultaneous variants; Batmen of many worlds, coexisting across alternate earths" (Brooker 2012, x), Thon points to the fact that *each* of these texts constructs a mostly consistent storyworld, featuring a local, world- and work-specific character called "Bond" or "Batman." Some of these *local* characters can then be constructed in such a way as to "coalesce" into a serialized "glocal transmedia character" if they are intended and accepted to be in continuity with each other. This happens only under certain conditions which we can find, typically, in straightforward series such as those mentioned above. These collections of texts then appear as one story "cut up" into various segments or dispersed across media. Creators intend them to be taken as representations of one fictional being presumed to exist in one coherent storyworld – and, ideally, audiences accept them as such. Within such a paradigm of continuity, two different textual relations are proposed as "redundancy" vs. "expansion" (Thon 2019, 188). The first can be found in straightforward adaptations promising a "retelling" of the same story, such as a book-to-film or a videogame-to-comic adaptation retaining all central narrative events. Doubtlessly, there will still be countless differences between these versions, but audiences are nevertheless intended to assume one identical storyworld "behind" two or more medial representations (on the level of an intersubjective communicative construct). Expansions, on the other hand, feature new elements (revolving around previously unrepresented segments of time or on other characters previously not in focus) which are still thought to exist within the same storyworld.

In addition to redundancies and expansions, however, Thon's model offers a third type of relations, in which two or more texts feature "character versions" which *cannot* be taken as a representation of the same individual within the same world. Reasons for such a discontinuity can be located on two different levels. Concerning external factors, it seems clear that someone needs the *authority* to declare multiple text-specific storyworlds and characters identical (see Wolf 2012, 271). Fan fictions will hence be considered "variations" from the outset (attributed to the respective creators and distinguished from the original), no matter their degree of faithfulness. Good examples are provided by many YouTube fan videos promising to "repair" a story they were unhappy with, such as a 40-minute video essay by Preston Jacobs trying to "fix" season seven of *Game of Thrones* (see Jacobs 2017). The commentator sets out to integrate his alternative proposal for the season's plot into the earlier (and later) continuity perfectly and even aspires to have the characters act *more* consistently with their earlier motivations than in the official texts. Such affirmational fan works can, once again, be distinguished from transformational ones which deliberately rewrite story arcs, storyworlds, or characters' identities. Affirmational works are typically associated with male fandom, whereas their counterpart has traditionally been considered more characteristic of predominantly female fan spaces (see Scott 2019, 25–50). In both cases, however, the resulting *versions* will not be confused with anything but distinguished renderings. "Secondary" works can even inspire *tertiary* ones if they become prominent enough in specific fan circles to spark further imaginations and rewrites (see Galbraith 2009, 163), as happened with the *Fifty Shades* (James 2011; 2012a; 2012b) trilogy (itself initially a fan fiction of the *Twilight* saga, see Moss 2017).

A legal rights holder, by contrast, can just *declare* two works as belonging to the same storyworld, which then necessitates a certain degree of consistency in terms of key narrative events. Even if there are no apparent contradictions, however, the degree of explicit continuity can vary. The earlier Marvel Netflix shows – *Jessica Jones* (Rosenberg et al. 2015–2019), *Daredevil* (Goddard et al. 2015–2019), *Luke Cage* (Coker et al. 2016–2018), *Iron Fist* (Buck et al. 2017–2018), and *The Defenders* (Petrie et al. 2017) – were all *said* to take place within the main Marvel Cinematic Universe, but actual links and references were limited to occasional mentions of "the Battle of New York" (meaning the ending of the first *Avengers* film, Whedon 2012). Otherwise, this declaration meant little to nothing since there were no further connections until Matt Murdock (Daredevil, played by Charlie Cox) reappeared in the film *Spider-Man: No Way Home* (and Kingpin, played by Vincent D'Onofrio, in the *Hawkeye* series) in 2021 (Watts), inciting countless discussions as to whether the earlier shows *do* count as MCU canon after all (see Grebey 2022). By contrast, the *Agents of Shield* TV show (Whedon et al. 2013–2020) intersected with the *Captain America: Civil War* (Russo and Russo 2016) film much more directly, changing its narrative direction in the middle of episode 17, "Turn, Turn, Turn," in "reaction" to the film's opening weekend. This illustrates a fact pointed out by Carlos Scolari, Paolo Bertetti, and Matthew Freeman (2014b, 7–12): Transmediality – understood here in a narrow sense as transmedial continuity and identity – has to be *built*, brick-by-brick, with recourse to techniques like "narrative expansions." Roberta Pearson likewise understands continuity in terms of specific *points of contact*, "the overlaps with previous texts that identify an addition as part of an established transfiction. Maximum points of contact lead to strong cohesion, while minimal points of contact lead to weak cohesion" (2018b, 149).

The other way round, however, contradictions between character versions may become too large to ignore when they concern relevant narrative events. Whether Albus Dumbledore extinguishes 12 street lamps at the beginning of *Harry Potter and the Philosopher's Stone* (Rowling 1997) or five, as in the novel's film adaptation (Columbus 2001), is of little importance, so audiences will be likely to disregard these inconsistencies as parts of the respective medial representations. If, by contrast, a relevant narrative event is altered – say the fact that Harley Quinn does not turn into a supervillain because she's been falling in love with the Joker but rather chooses to do so for her own sake as in the graphic novel *Harley Quinn: Breaking Glass* (Tamaki and Pugh 2020) – we must be in some kind of "alternate universe" in which we encounter a different version of the character. In many cases where continuity is not strictly managed, this will be a matter of interpretation for audiences. Whether or not the film adaptation of *The Lord of the Rings* (Jackson 2001; 2002; 2003) features *the same* characters as the books might thus be open to debate – cases could be made, and have been made for both positions with recourse to major thematic and diegetic differences (see LotR Fandom, "Tolkien vs. Jackson"). A view on *characters* reveals that these alterations may be of different importance for individual protagonists. Whereas the most relevant narrative events for both (book and film) versions of Frodo are generally retained, the story and actantial roles of Galadriel or Arwen have been altered significantly: Galadriel is "upgraded" into an extradiegetic narrating character in the film, while film-Arwen is granted the actantial roles of other (book) characters (such as rescuing the hobbits from the Nazgul and raising the river, merging the actantial role of Glorfindel and Elrond in the book).

Despite all room for debate, *some* character instances are clearly on the side of continuity, while others are undeniably on the side of multiplicity. For the former, the *WandaVision* (Schaeffer et al. 2021) TV show – set in the same transmedial storyworld as all other texts branded as the Marvel Cinematic Universe – makes for a good example once again, as the show necessitates familiarity with earlier events (especially the *Avengers: Endgame* film, Russo and Russo 2019). If we were *not* to assume that these are the same characters "carrying" memories from earlier moments, we would miss most of the first episodes' narrative suspense built around the mystery of how we can see Vision alive after he has been murdered in *Endgame*. Audiences can thus expect a narrative reason for his resurrection (which is in fact given in episode five). If we were to simply take the *WandaVision* characters as another set of "versions" (such as the comic books *not* set in the MCU, like Tom King's and Gabriel Walta's series *Vision*, 2018) the plot – and its narrative events – would disintegrate. On the other side of the divide, there are clear instances of character versions that *cannot* be taken to amount to the same individual. Examples would include so-called "Elseworlds" stories of DC Comics which reimagine Batman as a completely new individual. *Superman: Red Son* (Millar et al. 2003), for instance, depicts Batman as a Russian anarchist whose parents have been killed by the KGB, while *Batman & Dracula: Red Rain* (Moench and Jones 1991) presents a character version living his life as a vampire; *Batman: Dark Knight of the Round Table* (Layton and Giordano 1998–1999) even introduced readers to a "Bruce of Waynesmoor" at King Arthur's Camelot. Marvel has implemented similar character variations in their "What If…?" comics which were also introduced to a broader audience through the 2021 animated show of the same name. When characters appear in a different gender, race, or even species – as the many "Sherlock Holmeses" across media discussed before – we must also assume multiplicity, not continuity.

As of early 2021, the cinematic universes of Marvel/Disney and DC/Warner were modeled after these two paradigms so that every MCU text could be taken to coalesce into one overarching "hyper-narrative" (containing only compatible versions of its heroes that can be understood as single individuals), while the failed attempt at a DC Extended Universe has resulted in a variety of "Batmen" and "Jokers" existing entirely in parallel to each other. From 2021 on, however, the MCU increasingly adopted the multiplicity model of heterogeneous versions, especially in the TV show *Loki* (Waldron 2021–present), the film *Spider-Man: No Way Home*, and finally *Dr. Strange in the Multiverse of Madness* (Raimi 2022). Through the trope of a "multiverse" – more on that below – the MCU nevertheless aims to re-narrativize and naturalize its own multiplicity, so that characters can, in theory, travel between its heterogeneous storyworlds and character versions such as the three different "Spider-Men" played by Toby Maguire, Andrew Garfield, and Tom Holland can meet and interact with each other. In between these "poles," there might be indeterminacies which we will investigate in the subsequent chapter 8. In Thon's model, in any case, cases of *clear distinctions* generate *nodes* in a network of interrelated character versions (see especially Thon 2022). This is why his "local, work-specific characters" (that can coalesce into "glocal, transmedia characters" if they are *aligned* through continuity and canonicity) are interrelated not as one overarching transmedia character containing contradictory versions but through a loosely connected global *transmedia character network* of many versions by the same name (Thon 2019, 188).

7.2 Canonicity, Continuity Management, Authorship

Partly because of the heated debates that can arise in the face of a multiplicity of non-compatible character versions, many fan communities and/or corporate IP holders have established more or less rigid systems of canonicity management for their global storyworlds. Roy T. Cook defines canon in the context of transmedial storytelling as "a privileged subfiction that constitutes the real story regarding what is fictionally true [...], whereas non-canonical stories are 'imaginary' or are de-legitimized in some other sense" (Cook 2013, 272). The canon of the stealth video game series *Metal Gear* (1987–2018, e.g. Konami 1998), for example, currently consists of 11 games, which tell a linear story spanning several decades from 1964 to 2018 (see LoProto 2022). Other entries in the franchise, such as *Metal Gear Survive* (Konami Digital Entertainment 2018), are set in alternative dimensions or considered "unfaithful" (non-canonical) renderings of plotlines that are also represented in canonical games ("non-canonical" works often generate their own, competing continuity, however, so that canonicity is, in fact, a relative rather than an absolute term).

The question of what is or is not canon may be negotiated by textual or paratextual means. Since the late 1990s, canonicity debates frequently take place in online forums and fan-maintained wikis, some of which – like the *EverQuest 2 Wiki* – contain several hundred thousand entries. In a few cases, such databases are so comprehensive that creators themselves use them as reference works for the status quo of a given storyworld (Wookieepedia, "The Power and Relevance of Wookieepedia" documents this with regard to its own *Star Wars* fan wiki). Structurally, fan-created resources often mirror official systems of canonicity created by IP holders themselves: Before being bought up by Disney in 2012, Lucasfilm Ltd., the legal owner of the *Star Wars* franchise, maintained a database that attributed one of six hierarchical levels of canonicity to any character or event that ever appeared under the *Star Wars* brand. If new information (added on a certain level) contradicted established narrative elements on a lower one, these would be "overwritten" by the "more truthful" account of the new addition, potentially creating new, distinct character versions in the process. This hierarchy was also adhered to by *Wookieepedia,* the largest *Star Wars* fan encyclopedia. Besides such paratexts – both those authorized by an IP holder and those created by fans – the canonization of specific character versions and story elements can also take place within primary texts like the two-part comic *History of the DC Universe* by Marv Wolfman and George Pérez. Released in 1986, it covered all major events that formed part of the newly unified, canonical DC universe that had been established by *Crisis on Infinite Earths*' (Wolfman et al. 1985–1986) reorganization.

It is important to note that canonicity can be highly dynamic: As new additions are made to a given transmedial universe, what has so far been established as the "privileged subfiction" of that world may still be subject to change. Such alterations in the makeup of a narrative are referred to as *retconning*, a portmanteau term derived from "retroactive continuity." In the words of Andrew J. Friedenthal, retconning "involves the revisiting of past stories, told in previous installments of a long-form narrative, and adding a new piece of information to that older story" (2017, 6). In its subtler variety, this can take the form of a reinterpretation of (more or less) ambiguous elements of earlier texts. When, in reaction to audience protests, Arthur Conan Doyle revisited the character of Sherlock Holmes in a number of new stories, the detective's ostensible death from falling in 1893s "The Final Problem" (2022a) was "revealed" to be a cleverly constructed ruse in 1903s "The Adventure of the Empty House" (2022b). While certainly coming as a surprise to most readers, this new information did not directly contradict the earlier story, since its narrator, Dr. Watson, only infers Holmes' death from a number of footprints and other environmental clues. In other cases, the changes involved in a retcon are more explicit, necessitating an altered retelling (or, to put it with Friedenthal, 2017, a "reinscription") of events already presented in earlier works. This was the case with J.R.R. Tolkien's *The Hobbit* (1937), which was originally written with no plans for a sequel. When the first *The Lord of the Rings* book was released 17 years later, it contained a markedly altered summary of one of *The Hobbit*'s chapters: In the original narrative, the character Bilbo Baggins obtains a magical ring that grants him invisibility; in the new rendering, this was now "revealed" to be the One Ring of Power, the object that motivates the entire narrative of *The Lord of the Rings*. Inconsistencies between this new information and the older novel were framed as misrepresentations on the part of Bilbo. This retcon went so far that later editions of *The Hobbit* were revised from the original text to reflect this new course of events.

From these examples, we can see that all kinds of retcons resemble "multiverse" structures in that they potentially "*narrativize* [...] what was basically a marketing decision" (Rosenbaum 2014: n.pag, original emphasis), creating an intradiegetic explanation for the results of extradiegetic processes in media production. The result is always, in one form or another, the creation of a new, distinct storyworld populated by distinct character versions: One Bilbo Baggins finds "only" a magic ring, the other unwittingly pockets a weapon of mass destruction. Retcons and other changes to a given character/storyworld network's canonicity system are frequently controversial, especially in the case of widely received works with a large fan community, such as *Watchmen* (see below). While continuity management (in the form of retcons or extratextual measures) addresses an imaginary "ideal reader" who constructs their private imagination of the fictional world in exact accordance with the author's or IP holder's intention (see Jannidis 2004, 254), actual audiences might reject some aspects of a character that go against their own interpretation. Since the production of audiovisual media involves significant economic risks, IP holders have a strong interest in ensuring that audience members accept such changes and continue to invest money and time in a given storyworld. In this context, authorship once again holds considerable significance. As Pearson has observed, many transmedia characters and worlds are tied to the names of their original creators in the popular cultural consciousness (2018b, 152–154). In addition to the "textual author-function" (Freeman 2016, 33) – the people actually credited for writing, drawing, lettering, and inking a comic book, for instance – there is also a "market author-function" (33), all the entities *perceived* and *branded* as somehow responsible for the overall identity of characters, narratives, and storyworlds. In the case of Marvel comics, this includes writer and later publisher Stan Lee as the co-inventor of many characters and a kind of figurehead and "public face" for its creative output, as well as the company (image) itself that the former propagates ("Excelsior, true believers!") in distinction to their competitor DC Comics. For the transmedial Marvel Cinematic Universe, executive producer Kevin Feige has come to occupy such a privileged position, even being addressed as "our lord and savior Kevin Feige" half-jokingly in fan discourse (see Fuck DC 2017). We thus advocate once again for what John Thornton Caldwell (2008) called the "'institutional' (rather than personal or biographical) logic of authorship," viewing transmedia franchises as "an industrial – rather than merely artistic – practice" (201).

In order to reassure fans about the "authenticity" (i.e., canonicity) of new additions or changes to a global storyworld, paratexts often heavily publicize the involvement of such ostensible creators, or at least of "torchbearer" figures who can convincingly claim to be faithful to the "spirit" of the original author (see Wolf 2012, 273–276; Kunz 2019). Examples of this strategy to capitalize on the market author-function include all MCU films up until 2019s *Avengers: Endgame*, in which Stan Lee makes small appearances and is credited as executive producer, as well as the posthumously published parts of J.R.R. Tolkien's *Lord of the Rings* storyworld which were edited together from unfinished textual fragments by Tolkien's son Christopher. Of course, authority over characters or storyworlds is not necessarily inherited along traditional family lines. Dave Filoni, one of the writers and executives on the TV show *The Mandalorian* (Favreau 2019–present), repeatedly emphasized in interviews how strongly his creative process and vision were shaped by working directly with George Lucas, the creator of the *Star Wars* franchise, and asserted his desire to maintain the "authenticity" of future works in the *Star Wars* canon that will be created without Lucas' involvement (see Huver 2018). With these statements, Filoni positioned himself close to the center of what Mark Wolf has called the "circles of authorship" that can indicate canonicity for transmedial storyworlds. For Wolf,

> authorship [...] can be conceptualized as a series of concentric circles extending out from the world's originator (or originators), with each circle of delegated authority being further removed from the world's origination and involving diminishing authorial contributions. [...] Those works, [...] that

typically possess the highest degree of canonicity are those which come from the innermost circles of authorship, which surround the originator and main author of a world.

(2012, 269)

One example of extraordinarily strong adherence to this principle is the *Detective Conan* transmedia franchise (in the United States, Canada, and the United Kingdom, the franchise is also known under the title *Case Closed*), whose online fan encyclopedia meticulously tracks all differences between the original manga's (Aoyama 1994–present) more than 1,000 installments and their various transmedial adaptations and expansions since only elements directly referenced by manga creator Gosho Aoyama in his works and/or public statements are considered canonical and therefore constitute relevant clues to the series' numerous mysteries and criminal cases. In addition to legitimizing changes or additions to an established canon by invoking authorship, IP holders may also cater to multiple model readers instead of just one. For *Star Wars*, many transmedial expansions of the franchise after the 2012 sale to Disney could be regarded as examples of this strategy: Even though in 2014, most novels, comic books, and video games published before that point were declared non-canonical, characters (and other elements) from these works are frequently alluded to or directly depicted in later texts, with these iterations remaining largely consistent with their non-canonical versions in terms of their basic properties (see Kunz 2019). While such re-introduced characters, such as Grand Admiral Thrawn in the animated show *Star Wars Rebels* (Kinberg et al. 2014–2018) or the Dark Troopers in *The Mandalorian*, never require knowledge of non-canonical texts, their inclusion creates a sense of cohesion for audience members who were invested in the pre-2014 canon.

A similar effect can also be achieved through subjective representations: The 2016 remake of the 3D-platform video game *Ratchet & Clank* (Insomniac Games 2002) by Insomniac Games presents an altered version of the older game's plot while simultaneously functioning as an adaptation of the *Ratchet & Clank* animated film (Munroe) which was released in 2016 as well. Within the newer game, the inconsistencies between the remake and the original story were explained by a frame narrative in which Captain Qwark, one of the antagonists, tells *his* view of events to a fellow prisoner after the end of the main plot. This frame narrative is absent in the film which otherwise does not deviate from the video game remake in its story. This minimizes confusion for film audiences who are unfamiliar with the source material but simultaneously caters to long-time fans by reassuring them that the altered narrative is merely an unreliable, subjective retelling of the "actual events" occurring in the acclaimed first game.

7.3 Parodies, Transmedia Character Types, and Templates

If all versions of any given character contradicting an established canon can be said to form a kind of "network," then characters collectively addressed as

"Batman," "James Bond," or "Lara Croft" can be reconceptualized as distinct networks containing myriads of individual nodes. As we will see, however, the "borders" of these networks are far from clear-cut, and they can even overlap. The most common designator to identify characters as belonging to the same network are certainly proper names (all "Sherlock Holmeses"), but "Sherlock Hound" could also be considered a version of the famous detective and hence a node of the same network. It is thus more of a matter of interpretation and preference whether we want to address the characters of "gender bender" remake films like *What Women Want* (Meyers 2000) into *What Men Want* (Shankman 2019), of *Dirty Rotten Scoundrels* (Oz 1988) into *The Hustle* (Addison 2019), or from the 1995 novel (Hornby 2020) and the 2000 film (Frears) *High Fidelity* – where the main character's name had already been changed from Rob Fleming into Rob Gordon (the latter played by John Cusack) and the setting from London into Chicago – into the 2020 *High Fidelity* TV series (West and Kucserka) where the main character is now the female Robyn Brooks (played by Zoë Kravitz) as *different characters* or as *distinguished versions of the same character*. If we conceive of networks in terms of peripheral vs. more central areas, some iterations are closer or further removed from the most typical (or most well-known) version. As Paolo Bertetti put it: "[T]he reader will consider some occurrences to be more canonical, whereas others are more free and creative. […] The identity of characters is a fuzzy concept, and some of characters' occurrences [sic] are more typical than others" (2014, 2348). Audiences might also disagree about the center of a network, depending on their personal "first contact." The live-action film *Edge of Tomorrow* (Liman 2014) is a considerably altered American adaptation of the Japanese light novel *All You Need is Kill* (Sakurazaka 2004), which was adapted into a manga in 2014 as well. *Edge of Tomorrow*'s American protagonist Bill Cage (played by Tom Cruise) is then notably farther removed from the light novel's hero Keiji Kiriya than from the Keiji Kiriya of the manga version. As the latter aspires to be a straightforward retelling in terms of narrative events, both "Keijis" could be said to coalesce into a glocal transmedia character while Bill Cage is excluded as a distinct node. The latter certainly still shares many actantial roles with transmedial Keiji but has a completely altered backstory. His plotline also resolves entirely differently in the film: Cage is able to save his newfound lover Rita Vrataski, while Keiji's Rita Vrataski survives neither the light novel nor the manga.

E.L. James' *Shades of Grey* book series was initially published online as a fan fiction to the *Twilight* book/film series, with the protagonists Edward Cullen and Bella Swan being turned into Christian Grey and Anastasia Steele, respectively, to enable commercial publication. Here, the transparency of two characters' connectedness in a network also depends on legal considerations. Parodies pose even more complicated problems and show that character networks can also blend into each other: "Dark Helmet," a parody of Darth Vader in Mel Brooks' *Spaceballs* (1987) comedy, can only be appreciated for what he is if he is distinguished from the "more typical" versions of Darth Vader while still being clearly related to them *as a commentary*. In the same vein, Austin Powers could be considered a transmedia character network in its own right (appearing not only in three films, Roach 1997; 1999; 2002, but also in music videos by Madonna ["Beautiful Stranger"] and Beyoncé ["Work it Out"], and four video games, e.g. Rockstar Games 2000), rather than a far-removed node of James Bond. And while we would certainly regard Neo from the *Matrix* franchise as a network distinct from that formed by various medial representations of Jesus, there are enough significant similarities between them on the level of actantial structures to enable an argument for Neo as just one node of a larger "Jesus" network (see, for example, Stucky 2005). It is certainly not as important (and in many cases not even possible) to draw clear distinctions between different networks, rather than to acknowledge that differences *are* drawn – by creators, by actual audiences, and by the media texts themselves.

There are more intertextual relations between characters, however: Even characters who clearly belong to different character networks (or, in less technical language, who are entirely different characters by name) nevertheless bear similarities to each other. These similarities can be either on the level of actantial roles as discussed in chapter 2 (all anime characters conforming to the actantial role of *tsundere* are expected to appear hostile and angry at first only to later reveal their kind nature). They can also feature similar character traits that can eventually become medial prototypes. Thon addresses these as transmedia character *types*. His examples include

> "[b]eing a space marine" (in the transmedia universe of *Warhammer 40,000*, or some other, similar transmedia universe [...]); or "being an elf" (in the transmedia universe of *The lord of the rings* or some other, similar transmedia universe [...]); or "being a/the great detective" (as is the case for both Sherlock Holmes and Batman characters [...]); or "being an adventurous archeologist" (as is the case for both Indiana Jones and Lara Croft characters [...]).
> (2019, 184)

Bertetti refers to such types with reference to Greimas as characters' thematic roles ("for example, warrior, fisherman, father, barbarian," Bertetti 2014, 2348). On a sufficient level of abstraction, certainly, *all* superheroes resemble each other to some extent as one such *type*, but *Watchmen*'s (2014) Nite Owl is certainly closer to Batman than to, say, Superman (both the former wear animal masks, patrol their hometowns at night, and rely on technical gadgets instead of on superpowers). Nite Owl, in the original *Watchmen* comics by Alan Moore and Dave Gibbons, was in turn a variation of the older Blue Beetle character from Charlton Comics, which Moore intended to use as a new character version (alongside other Charlton heroes) if intellectual property rights had allowed it. Exactly like with Edward Cullen/Christian Grey, the renaming was mainly a legal procedure. Seen this way, it would be more appropriate to speak only of *one* transmedia character network instead of many, spanning all characters ever created. It is far from continuous, however, but rather segmented into "clusters" of recognizable variations. Interrelating characters in this way – as network connections of versions, types, and recurring actantial roles – means adopting the perspective of intertextuality by which *all texts* are connected to each other through narrative traditions that can be traced and pinpointed (see Allen 2011).

If it is not possible to distinguish precisely between nodes within the same character network on the one hand and different networks related to each other through thematic and actantial roles on the other, it is all the more important to note that *some* iterations of characters – which *are* accepted as variations of the same character – take more liberties than others with what has been established in earlier iterations. How does the network model account for the "most prototypical" character traits across heterogeneous worlds? If the network is not the *intersection* of commonalities but rather the *totality* of all conflicting and non-conflicting occurrences of a character, there are still *some* prototypical features that *all* "Batmen" – all local (work-specific) or glocal (transmedia) character versions globally recognizable as Batman – are expected to share. Thon addresses these with recourse to Pearson (2018a, 150) in terms of a "transmedia character template" which is the prototypical intersection or core of all network nodes. This cultural template contains the "physical, mental, and social characteristics" that "any work-specific character sharing the same name may or may not exhibit, but would initially be expected to exhibit" (Thon 2019, 150). For Batman, as William Uricchio and Roberta Pearson (1991) have elaborated, this template would include key components on five different levels (that entail but go far beyond our earlier basic character type):

- Established internal and external character traits such as wealth, physical prowess, deductive abilities and obsession
- An established backstory or fictional biography, as well as recurring events connected to an established actantial role (fighting criminals and supervillains)
- Relations to recurring side characters, good as well as bad, such as Robin, Commissioner Gordon, or the Joker
- An established narrative setting or environment, Gotham City
- His transmedial iconography through which he remains recognizable visually (mask, costume, logo) (Uricchio and Pearson 1991, 186–187)

Later, Pearson also added typical "speech patterns and dialogue" to this list (2018b, 150). This implicit template of recurring character traits, backstories, relations to other characters, settings, and iconographies is then merely a description of salient features proposed by the *most* prominent texts featuring a version of the character. Any given text will only retain some, but rarely all features: "[A] single addition cannot manifest all the potential character elements established in the myriad additions to the transfiction" (150). Any character template is then also not very "stable" in intersubjective terms: It will be somewhat different for each audience member depending on whether one considers the Batman from *Batman: The Animated Series* (Radomski et al. 1992–1995) as the most "typical" version of the character, the one from Christopher Nolan's film trilogy (2005; 2008; 2012), or the more light-hearted version from the 1960s live-action series

(Dozier 1966–1968). Since we cannot study this template in any one text, the only "site" where we encounter it is in discourses and discussions *about* specific versions which are deemed more or less "in character" than others by specific authors, fans, or critics. The template will also be constantly rewritten by every new text and it changes naturally over time: While the fact that Batman "does not use guns" and "does not kill" features prominently in a large number of stories, so much so that it can be considered essential for his template nowadays, it was not introduced in his earliest comic book adventures (now considered non-canonical, i.e., being a different version/character node) where he frequently *did* use a "Bat-Gun." Even a contemporary canonical text like the DC crossover *Infinite Crisis* (Johns et al. 2005–2006) can still break with this – Batman uses a special gun here (loaded with a "Radion bullet") attempting to kill the cosmic supervillain Darkseid. Such a breach of conventions will then mark a huge (psychic) narrative event for the character, signposting the *extraordinary* circumstances in which the whole universe was at stake. The negotiation of creative freedom vs. tradition is necessarily highly political. The new *Ghostbusters* film of 2016 by Paul Feig met a right-wing, misogynistic backlash against the creators' decision to recast its male protagonists as female. The issue, "one of the most polarizing in recent memory" according to one reviewer (Parker 2016, n.pag.), was not at all whether the new film modified the original characters (as did the *Slimer! and The Real Ghostbusters*, Medjuck 1986–1991, animated series and its related comic books, e.g., Carnell et al. 1989–1992, or the 2009 *Ghostbusters: The Video Game* by Terminal Reality, continuing their earlier stories). The new Ghostbusters of 2016 were clearly new fictional individuals in a new universe, leaving the earlier character nodes entirely "untouched" (the original actors Bill Murray, Dan Aykroyd, and others even appeared in cameo roles as different characters). At stake were the most prototypical traits of *all* character versions within their network, which, according to the more toxic participants in fandom, should be fixed as male, not female – even, and maybe especially, in contradicting reboots of the franchise. The terms transmedia character network, transmedia character type, and transmedia template thus provide a clear heuristic to analyze such phenomena and account for the complexity of character ecologies in historical as well as in transmedial terms.

7.4 Multiverses and Asymmetrical Hierarchies

So far, this chapter has mainly dealt with cases in which multiple versions of a character are distributed over multiple local or glocal storyworlds. In some medial, generic, and cultural traditions, however, contradicting character versions are *re-integrated* into an overarching "multiverse" (see Kukkonen 2010). This has an especially rich history in superhero comics, where DC introduced the idea of "parallel universes" as early as 1953: In *Wonder Woman* Vol. 1, #59 (Kanigher and Peter), the titular heroine is transported to a "mirror earth" where she meets a character named Tara Terruna whose name is stated to mean "Wonder Woman" in that reality's native language and who is an almost exact double of Wonder Woman herself, from costume iconography to actantial roles. Such individual instances of ontological multiplicity were eventually formalized in the *Flash* story "Flash of Two Worlds" (*The Flash* Vol. 1, #123, Fox and Infantino 1961), which introduced the concept of an "Earth-Two," one of several named, parallel story-worlds within the overall "multiverse" of all superhero stories published by DC. Many of these sub-worlds featured local and glocal versions of iconic characters like Superman or the Flash which differed in individual aspects of their character template and basic character type. Originally, of course, the differences and incompatibilities between the multiple Supermen and Flashes were partly a by-product of the unwieldy number of published storylines, partly the result of conscious editorial changes made to explore new narrative possibilities, or simply to increase a character's marketability. Over time, however, DC invited its readers to view the plurality of character versions as an ontological feature of the overarching universe in which all DC stories took place. Using Eder's model of characters, we could say that readers were asked to interpret Golden Age and Silver Age Flash on the level of different *fictional beings* rather than (or at least in addition to) understanding the inconsistencies between them as *symptoms* of specific publishing practices. The first culmination of this practice occurred in the 1985–1986 cross-over comic *Crisis on Infinite Earths*, which provided a collective origin story for the DC multiverse while simultaneously attempting to reduce the plurality of (g)local character versions to a more manageable number (see Friedenthal 2017, 71–92).

Ultimately, the *Crisis* crossover ends with the merging of the hitherto parallel universes into a single, uniform reality, giving both readers and creators, for the first time, an unambiguous idea of the narrative state of affairs in the newly unified DC universe. Twenty years later, in the crossover *Infinite Crisis*, the multiverse was reinstated again, so that earlier contradicting versions did exist separately again (and characters could travel from one storyworld to another). According to author Grant Morrison's concept of "hypertime" proposed in the subsequent crossover *Final Crisis* (Morrison et al. 2008–2009), every story ever written was in fact canon, even things that explicitly contradicted each other – but every story takes place in its discrete storyworld. Since the 2020/2021 crossover event *Dark Nights: Death Metal* (e.g., Snyder and Capullo), the heroes and villains of DC even remembered all non-canonical appearances of themselves (or, rather, of different character nodes of themselves). The earlier comic multiverse was now said to be part of an even larger "omniverse" containing even DC's many animated films and TV series as well as its various live-action "multiverses" (see Schedeen 2021). Ironically perhaps, this concept does nothing but explicate and codify how transmedial meaning-making in complex franchises works anyways, but it reintegrates this into a narrative (mimetic) dimension. We could address these strategies as acts of continuity management to keep distinctions between character versions (network nodes) clear and unambiguous. More recently, this approach has also been taken up in film and TV. Again, some of the most prominent examples are superhero media such as the DC TV crossover also titled *Crisis on Infinite Earths* (2019), which involves five shows that form part of the glocal "Arrowverse" storyworld in a loose adaptation of the eponymous comics, ultimately setting up a new status quo for their worlds and characters. *Spider-Man: No Way Home*

(2021) was certainly the most ambitious attempt to date to "re-canonize" earlier existing storyworlds (the Spider-Man trilogy starring Toby Maguire and the two films starring Andrew Garfield) within the larger MCU multiverse. Notably, the *Star Trek* franchise used this strategy a little bit earlier to tie its 2009 "soft reboot" of the film series into established continuity. In the 2009 film (Abrams), a young version of Captain James T. Kirk, played by Chris Pine instead of original actor William Shatner, encounters both a similarly recast Mr. Spock (Zachary Quinto) and the "original" version of that character, still played by Leonard Nimoy, who explains to Kirk that he comes from a different point in time in a parallel universe. Once again, while the existence of these multiple Spocks and Kirks could be seen exclusively as a symptom of economic and narrative decisions made during production, the film itself proposes to its audience a reading on the level of the storyworld and its fictional beings. In other words, the "multiverse" trope allows to re-conceptualize characters that would usually be deemed non-compatible nodes in a global character network: by including the network itself in the ontological structure of a local or (more often) glocal storyworld, these texts can now be viewed as expansions of each other.

Whereas multiverse structures usually serve to explain inconsistencies by splitting a global storyworld into explicitly demarcated sub-worlds (see Wolf 2012), other media texts attempt to do the opposite: They incorporate versions of different characters that are usually conceptualized as inhabiting separate storyworlds into a single, non-contradictory (g)local narrative. This would be the case for the *Kingdom Hearts* videogame series, which develops a multiverse comprised of established Disney animated films (alongside Square Enix' *Final Fantasy* games) that characters can travel and visit. While this was only legally possible through the collaboration of IP holders Disney and Square Enix, older characters that are in the public domain can be re-integrated much easier. One recent example of this is the TV series *Penny Dreadful* (Logan et al. 2014–2016), in which several figures from works of 19th-century English literature, including Count Dracula, Victor Frankenstein, and Dr. Henry Jekyll, join forces to battle supernatural threats. Alan Moore's and Kevin O'Neill's comic series *The League of Extraordinary Gentlemen* (1999–2019) and its film adaptation (Norrington 2003) likewise "unite" 19th-century pulp heroes from distinct worlds into one superhero team sharing the same diegetic space. The comic series *Kill Shakespeare* (Del Col et al. 2010–2017) presents a world in which major characters from across Shakespeare's plays, such as Hamlet, Richard III, Macbeth, or Juliet Capulet are at war over who will rule the "realm" they all inhabit; the series even playfully points to the fictionality of all its characters by featuring a mysterious wizard named "William Shakespeare" who is revered as a god by some of the characters, while being the target of assassination attempts by others. These works differ from the Marvel/DC multiverses described before in two key respects: First, they do not specify any ontological relationship between their character versions and the "originals." (The term "original" may be somewhat misleading here since even Shakespeare himself frequently adapted his plays from older sources. However, the character portrayals in *Kill Shakespeare* clearly only refer back to the Shakespearean iterations, or nodes.) While we may be able to point out numerous continuities and inconsistencies between the Dr. Jekyll from Robert L. Stevenson's 1886 novella (2022) and the one from the 2015 show (Higson), we are not given any explicit instructions on how to read them in relation to each other. Second, these media texts only incorporate characters who are already in the public domain, making it possible to have them appear next to each other without any third party's legal approval or financial involvement.

However, even characters whose copyright *is* privately owned may still appear in shared storyworlds, as they do in Disney's *Wreck-It Ralph* (Moore 2012). In this animated feature film, numerous video game villains (Bowser from the *Super Mario* games, 1985–2021, one of the ghosts from *Pac-Man*, Namco 1980, and various combatants from the *Street Fighter* series, 1987–2020) meet in a self-help group to cope with the challenges of being "the bad guy" in their respective storyworlds. In contrast to the cases described above, this scenario still acknowledges that the characters involved originally appeared in separate storyworlds. However, rather than constructing an elaborate multiverse ontology or simply presenting its shared storyworld without comment, *Wreck-It Ralph* posits its own world as superordinate to the individual games it references: For the Bowser depicted in the film, *Super Mario* is a fictional game in which he only *plays* the villain. With Karin Kukkonen, we could describe this process as creating "a doubling of ontological layers, one holding the fictional character (the storyworld) and one holding the character reflecting about fiction" (2009, 506), creating a metareferential effect. Such metareferences can have a number of functions (see Wolf 2009, 64–71): While they almost inevitably draw our attention to characters as artifacts by highlighting the process of their construction, they can also allow characters to critically engage with the narratives they are a part of. In the case of *Wreck-It Ralph*, their metafictional knowledge allows the members of the self-help group to critically comment on the actantial role of the "villain" that they have been assigned in their original storyworlds. Marvel did the same more explicitly in its 2021 series *Loki* in which the protagonist has to learn, accept, and ultimately resist the notion that "all Lokis" (variants in different alternate timelines) will always follow a predictable pattern of behavior. Just like in the earlier (non-MCU) animated film *Spider-Man: Into the Spider-Verse* (Persichetti et al. 2018), the multiverse structure has already become a stable narrative trope in *Loki*, so that the presented alternate storyworlds and characters have not even been existing before. They were specifically "invented" within and for their respective media texts. This nicely demonstrates how a narrative technique specifically developed to manage existing complexities and continuity problems can evolve into an autonomous trope ready for its application in individual media texts where these problems did not even occur. As we have discussed in chapter 2, this trope, too, can now traverse different medial and generic contexts; for example, a "multiverse" can also be found as a decisive plot device in the (entirely self-reliant) independent film *Everything Everywhere All at Once* (Kwan and Scheinert 2022) or the horror comic book series *Gideon Falls* (Lemire and Sorrentino 2018–2022). Another particularly good example is the animated show *Rick and Morty* (Harmon et al. 2013–present) which pushes the narrative and humorous limits of having an infinite number of alternative versions of its two protagonists clash with each other to dizzying heights.

Whereas all our examples so far were instances in which contradictory or ontologically separate characters (or character versions) were made compatible within a single storyworld, the opposite can also occur: Some character networks have brought forth two or more versions of a character that constitute "competing," mutually incompatible expansions to a shared point of origin. Frank Miller's widely acclaimed comic series *The Dark Knight Returns* (1986), for example, is set in a world in which Batman, after the death of his sidekick Jason Todd (a.k.a. Robin), has retired from crime-fighting for ten years. This scenario can be considered an expansion of the diegetic status quo of the regular, ongoing *Batman* comic series at the time, in which Jason Todd was very much alive. However, while that series *did* indeed go on to depict Todd's death in the 1988 story *A Death in the Family* (Starlin and Aparo 1988–1989), it subsequently did not show Batman retiring and instead introduced the character of Tim Drake who replaced Jason Todd as the bearer of the moniker "Robin." While both *The Dark Knight Returns* and the *Batman* issues featuring Tim Drake are intended as expansions of the same story, their respective "Batmen" cannot be regarded as the same character (even if we were to disregard the dramatic differences in each text's portrayal of Gotham City and its other inhabitants). Both "timelines" are thus presented as *branching* from a joint point of divergence. Although only the regular series was canonical for the main DC universe at the time, the *Dark Knight* universe established its own canon with sequels like *The Dark Knight Strikes Again* (Miller 2001–2002), *The Dark Knight III: The Master Race* (Miller et al. 2015–2017), and *Dark Knight Returns: The Golden Child* (Miller and Grampá 2020).

While multiverse structures like that of *Star Trek* or *Crisis on Infinite Earths* assure their audience that all included versions of a given character are "equally valid," cases of competing expansions can still lead to fervent fan discussions on which course of events to accept as "true" (i.e., more canonical). One such controversy occurred around the 2019 release of HBO's *Watchmen* TV series (Lindelof et al. 2019), a continuation of the 1986–1987 comic book of the same name. In the TV show, the journal kept by a character from the comic – the vigilante Rorschach – becomes the manifesto of a fictive White supremacist militia. While a vocal group of fans denounced this continuation as unfaithful to what they perceived as Rorschach's heroic portrayal in the source material, others pointed to explicit comments by the comic's creators, Alan Moore and Dave Gibbons, who had stated their own view on the character as authoritarian and morally questionable (see chapter 1). In the same year, DC Comics released the final issues of their *Doomsday Clock* comic (Johns and Frank 2018–2020) which also functions as a direct continuation of *Watchmen*. In this storyworld, however, Rorschach's journal was widely published and thereby exposed the villain from the original comic. Another character, the powerful Dr. Manhattan, migrated into the regular DC Universe in *Doomsday Clock*, changing the fictional timeline of the established storyworld and thus "narrativizing" another reboot. Dr. Manhattan's powers were later absorbed by another villain ("The Batman Who Laughs") in the 2020 cross-over event *Dark Knights: Metal* (e.g., Snyder and Capullo 2020–2021), rendering this whole fictional history – including *Watchmen* – canonical and even essential for following the complicated, convoluted plot.

More to the point, *both* alternative, branching expansions of *Watchmen* were criticized for not involving the original writer, Alan Moore, in their creations (see Polo 2019). While Moore had long distanced himself from all adaptations and expansions of his work made by other creators, the original artist Gibbons *did* contribute character designs to the TV series, thereby rendering it the "more legitimate" expansion in the eyes of some audience members and critics. Ultimately, both authorship itself and the (alleged) intentions of a character's original creators were considered relevant in determining which of the two competing "futures" of the *Watchmen* characters should be regarded as the "correct," (i.e., more canonical) representation of events. This implies a rather complex relationship between different types of authorship and their respective effects on how continuity is being understood by audiences. As we have seen, the circulation of characters within and between different storyworlds and media texts is subject to complex negotiations involving both audiences and creators. For some characters within specific narrative traditions, however, questions of continuity and canonicity seem less important than for the examples discussed here. This creates the necessity for different analytical tools where the network model of distinguished nodes does not apply. In the next chapter, we will look at how these latter cases can be productively approached.

8 Serial, Pre-narrative, and Meta-narrative Characters and Figures

In the previous chapter, we have distinguished text-specific, local as well as serial, "glocal" characters (both based on a single course of events, the paradigm of continuity) from "global" transmedia character networks dispersed across multiple courses of events (the paradigm of multiplicity). We have also discussed many strategies to manage continuity and canonicity to uphold these distinctions in increasingly complex character franchises. While the terminology is in no way consistent throughout literature (see Wilde 2019b), most approaches to fictional characters distinguish both paradigms in *some* ways. We have presented Jan-Noël Thon's (2019; 2022) network model as it reveals most clearly the transmedial relations between coherent character versions intended to coalesce into a single "glocal" transmedia character and those which do not. The model is built on the assumption that on the level of any given narrative text (novels, films, TV shows, comic books, and narrative video games) a protagonist would always be a character in the narrow sense of the word, while their "ability to extract themselves fully from the diegetic construct of a narrative world" (Denson and Mayer 2018, 69) only describes the relations *between* different character instances as nodes within extensive character networks. Shane Denson and Ruth Mayer introduced another prominent term for the theory and analysis of characters, however, that is the *serial figure*. Whereas characters in the narrow sense of the word grow and develop a more or less linear biography, "figures" are thought of as flat and unchanging: "They undergo a 'virtual beginning' with each new staging" (67).

At first, a lack of narrative progress does not seem to necessitate any *continuity distinction*, so one might wonder why a new term is indeed needed. The present chapter is first going to address two different *modes of seriality* that can easily be described *within* the network model, as both amount primarily to differences in the range of individual story arcs and the consequentiality of narrative events. However, as we will see, a competing model of transmedial seriality systematically dissolves our ability to decide about identity vs. difference of local, text-specific character versions in general. In some or even many cases of transmedia character circulation, questions about canonicity and continuity are of little concern for either creators or audiences, generating a systematic temporal and ontological indeterminacy (more on this below) to which the network model no longer applies properly. For some anthropomorphic fictional beings whose

DOI: 10.4324/9781003298793-12

most prominent representations circulate *outside* of narrative contexts to begin with, the term "character" might even be misleading as they seem to "exist" prior to and beyond any storyworld context. Examples include protagonists from political cartoons such as Uncle Sam, "virtual idols" such as Hatsune Miku, political icons such as Pepe the Frog, or product placement figures such as Hello Kitty. They can appear across fictional contexts without any irritations on the side of audiences precisely because they did not carry any expectations of storyworld consistency from the outset. For such entities, Denson's and Mayer's alternative term of a pre-narrative "figure" – instead of a "character" – is more appropriate to highlight their many differences from the strategies of transmedial continuity and canonicity discussed in chapter 7.

8.1 Transmedial Seriality and the Oneiric Climate

One of the most important distinctions in TV studies is that of a "series" vs. a "serial," two different paradigms or modes for serialized narratives (see Oltean 1993; Creeber 2004; Kelleter 2017). A series is intended as a continued plot – basically *one* story – split into smaller segments that have to be watched in the intended order to make sense of the narrative events. Forms of "serial television," by contrast, can be watched in any order as there is no overarching narrative progress between episodes and every installment is set back to a recurring baseline situation. *The Simpsons* (Brooks et al. 1989–present) are a prominent example of this, as Homer, Marge, and their family seem to have no lasting memory concerned with occurrences in earlier episodes: Their continuous conscious frames do not seem to transcend each individual episode. The same is true for many or most "ritualized" TV shows before the advent of "complex TV" from the 1990s onwards (with shows such as *Twin Peaks*, Frost et al. 1990–2017, *The Sopranos*, Chase et al. 1999–2007, *Lost*, Abrams et al. 2004–2010, or *Heroes*, Kring et al. 2006–2010, and later *Breaking Bad*, Gilligan et al. 2008–2013, or *House of Cards*, Fincher et al. 2013–2018, which propagated the very idea that TV was able to tell ongoing narratives like serialized novels, see Mittell 2015). The original *Star Trek* series running from 1966–1969 (Roddenberry) was very different in that regard from the contemporary *Star Trek: Discovery* (Fuller et al. 2017–present) or *Star Trek: Picard* (Goldsman et al. 2020–present) as each episode of the original contained a closed narrative segment which does not seem to interact with other episodes in terms of continuity or temporality. Even more pronounced forms of the discontinuous serial paradigm can be found in comic strips, where characters such as Charlie Brown (Schultz 1950–2000), Garfield (Davis 1978–present), or Nancy (Bushmiller et al. 1938–present) seem trapped in "temporal loops" of three or four panels that keep the central setting, as well as defining character traits, unchanged for decades without any progress or memory across episodes. Naturally, there are also countless mixed forms situated between both extremes. *The X-Files* show (Carter et al. 1993–2002), for instance, usually presented audiences with individual, unrelated mystery cases in each installment – the "monster of the week," a recurring narrative structure with stable actantial roles for the two main protagonists Agent Mulder and Agent Scully – that could be watched in any order, except for the occasional "legacy episode" which *did* contribute to an ongoing, overall narrative resolved in a later film, *The X-Files* (Bowman 1998). The show is thus seen as "an interplay between the demands of episodic and serial storytelling" (Mittell 2006, 33).

In the network model of transmedia characters introduced before, the difference between a series and a serial is mostly a matter of dramaturgy, not of storyworlds or character nodes: Despite any lack of overall temporality, "looped serials" such as *Star Trek*, *The Peanuts*, or *The Simpsons* do allow for the imagination that all of their installments take place in the same fictional world. All of their characters' appearances throughout episodes or strips are, in fact, usually not distinguished as different "character versions" by audiences. However, this often requires a considerable amount of charity from audiences willing to ignore contradictions between episodes that, technically, could not take place in the same storyworld. On *The Simpsons*, for instance, many episodes close on irreversible changes for the family or their hometown of Springfield, only to be "reset" in the next episodes' beginning. In "We're on the Road to D'ohwhere" (Se17E11, 2006), for instance, Marge is sent to prison and Homer decides to disappear with Bart, leaving Lisa to fend for Maggie and herself. The episode ends with Lisa's statement that she is going to look for work in the morning. The next episode, however, starts just as always; the family has never dissolved. This technique is referred to as the narrative trope "Snap Back" by *TV Tropes*, as audiences are expected (and accustomed) to ignore the fact that all occurrences introducing lasting changes to the status quo can and must simply be ignored. An even more "troublesome" example (requiring considerably more charity) could be found in *South Park* (Parker et al. 1997–present) where, mostly in the earlier seasons, Kenny dies every episode only to be alive again in the next (referred to as "Negative Continuity" by *TV Tropes* when "not only does nothing ever change, it doesn't even require an explanation In-Universe, the world just resets at the end of every episode," TV Tropes, "Status Quo Is God," n.pag.). Within the network model, every *South Park* episode should clearly take place in its own continuity/storyworld, rendering the characters throughout the whole series a network of contradicting nodes – otherwise, audiences would be required and willing to simply "ignore" major narrative events. There is an alternative to both options, however.

In his 1962 essay, "The Myth of Superman" (1972 in English), semiotician Umberto Eco traced a similar concern for superhero comics of the time. At the beginning of every *Superman* story, both the storyworld of Metropolis and the characters inhabiting it reflect the same status quo that also marked the start of all preceding adventures, with the events of those earlier episodes going entirely unacknowledged. These stories thus make readers "lose [...] the notion of temporal progression" (18). In this way, Superman conforms strongly to the paradigm of the serial, in which individual installments' plots do not causally or temporally interact with each other in any salient fashion. There are crucial differences to the media texts under discussion before, however: While *The Simpsons* or *South Park* occasionally deploy unexplained "resets" of events that *have* been depicted, the *Superman* comics mentioned by Eco mostly *suspend* any significant events in the lives of their main characters. Using the terms introduced before, we could say that these comics do not depict any major alterations to a protagonist's basic type: Superman's secret identity is never revealed to the public, and his alter-ego Clark Kent never gets seriously romantically involved with Lois Lane (except for explicitly marked "what if"-scenarios whose consequences are not explored in future installments; see 18). This suspension – rather than resetting – of narrative progress is *also* present in the earlier examples, such as Bart Simpson's perpetual attendance of Springfield Elementary School. The result of both, however, is what Eco addressed as an "oneiric climate [...], where what has happened before and what has happened after appears extremely hazy" (17). As has been stated in the introduction to this chapter, such a *dreamlike* narrative logic does not automatically answer the question of whether we are dealing with singular, continuous consciousness frames – "characters" in the narrow sense proposed by Thon or by Denson and Mayer – or with multiple nodes in a network of non-compatible character iterations. Rather, it creates a deliberate *ambiguity*, since *no* statements are being made on the relationship between the different installments. To Will Brooker, this is the level of "myth" on which characters like Batman are not bound to any canon or to "the strict sense of what counts and what happened, what is 'true' and what isn't" (Brooker 2012, 154). The oneiric climate can thus be deliberately upheld as a strategy of transmedial production and reception.

Some media texts explicitly lean into this ambiguity, as Christoph Ernst (2012) has proposed with regard to the 1960s US TV series *The Fugitive* (Martin 1963–1967), a show that shares its structural makeup with more recent texts such as the animated show *Phineas and Ferb* (Povenmire and Marsh 2007–2015) or the comedy show *How I Met Your Mother* (Bays et al. 2005–2014). These serials all feature a broad, overarching plot objective that is stated in every episode's introduction but is neither advanced nor reached by the protagonist(s) during the episodes. Instead, every self-contained story features an iteration of a rather limited set of narrative elements: Richard Kimble, the titular fugitive in Ernst's example, who has been wrongfully accused of murder, will spend each episode resolving a social conflict in a new location before being driven from said location by the pursuing police. Similarly, the eponymous stepbrothers in *Phineas and Ferb* will, again and again, pass the time during summer vacation by engaging in a large-scale project that their older sister Candace aims to thwart. However, whenever Candace convinces their mother to look in on the boys, a secondary plotline surrounding their pet platypus has caused all traces of the project to vanish, leaving the brothers untouched by blame. What also remains untouched in this recurring actantial set-up is the progression toward the event anticipated by the show's opening song: the end of summer vacation and the boys' eventual return to school, which is dealt with only in the very last episode of the final season, after 221 episodic installments (far more than the "104 days of summer vacation" referred to in the title sequence). Similarly, none of Richard Kimble's adventures further his quest to track down the actual killer of his wife and clear his own name, which is accomplished entirely in the final two episodes of the show.

In both these examples, the central event that the protagonists ostensibly work toward (consciously or unconsciously), and which could be described as an alteration of their sociality, cannot take place without the narrative as a whole being immediately brought to a close. Thus, while Phineas, Ferb, and Richard Kimble do act as unified characters in that they constantly anticipate actual narrative progress, their repetitive and causally unconnected actions from episode to episode correspond more to the definition of Denson's and Mayer's *figure*. Of course, this, too, works across a spectrum: While *The Fugitive* or *Phineas and Ferb* completely "reset" their narrative trajectory at the end of each installment, shows like *How I Met Your Mother* or *The Walking Dead* also feature an iterative plot structure, but will occasionally show noteworthy, irreversible events that alter the status quo for all following iterations. In *The Walking Dead* (both the comic, Kirkman et al. 2003–2019, and the TV show, Darabont et al. 2010–2022), Rick Grimes' group of survivors repeatedly finds an ostensibly safe haven from the hordes of zombies that threaten them, only to be driven away from it again by internal dispute or external danger. While these conflicts are structurally (and actantially) repetitive, they frequently entail fundamental changes to individual characters, such as the death of Rick's best friend Shane Walsh.

8.2 Historical, Industrial, and Commercial Considerations to Seriality

Far from being a one-time decision, the negotiation of different modes of seriality (for storyworlds as well as for characters) is an ongoing process that is also tied up with historical conditions of production and reception. Two examples of this would be changes to the distribution of scripted TV shows and superhero comic books in the United States (see Proctor 2018). From the late 1930s through the 1960s, superhero comic books were primarily sold at newsstands and drug stores to a mass audience of both children and adults (see Gabilliet 2010; Woo 2018). The heterogeneous reading and buying habits of such a broad audience that could not be guaranteed to pick up every single issue of a given title, together with the equally heterogeneous and uncertain stocking policies of non-specialized retailers that could hinder the regular availability of specific titles would have made an emphasis on continuity commercially risky. Thus, Superman's oneiric climate as described by Eco could be considered, in part, a reaction to this specific set of market relations. By contrast, today's superhero comic books are primarily marketed and sold through several thousand specialty stores across the US, which are "principally oriented toward a relatively restricted, subcultural audience of fans and collectors" (Woo 2018, 32). Digital distribution through apps like ComiXology equally caters to a base of fans who, in principle, are able to get any new or dated issue they wish to buy. Such a more homogeneous readership can be expected to proactively ensure they follow their favorite series, which is enabled by a preorder system on the distributor level and many stores' policy of offering a subscription service to their customers. Recent works such as the one-shot *DC Universe: Rebirth* #1 (Johns et al. 2016), which explicitly takes up many past plot elements and characters that had gone "unremembered" under the publisher's previous *New 52* branding, can be understood as a reaction to this change in audience and economic structure.

The context in which TV series are watched has also changed significantly in the last 30 years: As Jason Mittell (2015) points out, the emergence of the DVD led to the wide availability of TV series and serials on home media, to be watched independently from the scheduling of linear TV stations. This new reception context enabled "binge-watching" (a practice that has become only more commonplace with the advent of streaming services, see Jenner 2018) and deeper audience engagement with the material, which could now easily be watched completely and in the intended order. According to Mittell (2015, 36–41), this was one of the decisive factors contributing to the popularization of highly continuity-oriented, narratively complex shows like *The Wire* (Simon et al. 2002–2008), *Lost* or *Breaking Bad* in the 2000s. An increasing orientation toward continuity can, however, also be traced over multiple seasons of long-running TV shows of the time: When the British science fiction serial *Doctor Who* (Newman et al. 1963–present) was relaunched in 2005 after a 16-year absence from TV, the show's continuation initially retained much of the original run's loose temporal structure, adding only small allusions during each season that would hint at core elements of the respective season finale (such as the recurring slogan "Big Bad Wolf" in season one). However, with the position of executive producer being passed from Russell T. Davies to Steven Moffat in 2010, the number of continuity-relevant events and elements increased markedly, best exemplified by the character of River Song. Originally created by Moffat for a two-part story in 2008, the character had frequent appearances between 2010 and 2015. In these stories, her relationship with the show's titular character is strongly shaped by the fact that they can both travel through time and therefore experience their encounters in subjectively different orders. This narrative device effectively forecloses an oneiric structure because the difference in what River and the Doctor remember of each other is salient enough to necessitate explicit acknowledgment of numerous past events from these characters' lives.

Once seriality stretches beyond the confines of a single series or serial – i.e., into the realm of transmediality – the ambiguity that characterizes the oneiric climate becomes especially hard to maintain. This is because, as the examples in chapter 7 have already shown, sprawling transmedia storyworlds tend to produce contradictions of varying salience. The way in which these contradictions are dealt with often resolves the question of whether we are supposed to read these texts as a series or a network. Comic book publishers DC and Marvel currently both frame their storyworld(s) as a multiverse, disambiguating their characters toward the paradigm of multiplicity (a multiplicity, however, that is often naturalized and narrativized again through the overarching multiverse trope). Lucasfilm, the IP holder for the *Star Wars* franchise, chose to explain the various contradictions in that storyworld in terms of representational correspondence (see chapter 4 before): If two texts contain opposing statements on a character, event, or any other narrative element, one of these texts will simply be considered an "incorrect" representation of what "actually" happened – in other words, it will be rendered non-canonical and unreliable, thereby *enforcing* a paradigm of continuity. In transmedial franchises and character environments that do not explicitly regulate canonicity in this way, the networks' size and complexity can give rise to a number of different, sometimes contradictory systems of relationships between individual nodes. Especially interesting for a potential Transmedia Character Studies are then those fictional beings for which canonicity and continuity were never a salient part of the rules of imagination to begin with – but which nevertheless cannot avoid coming back to them all the same, with different strategies.

8.3 Creative Engagement with the Oneiric Climate

Questions of continuity and canonicity are usually discussed with respect to franchises in which such matters are extensively regulated, and contested, often for decades. In order to get a better understanding of the inner workings of the oneiric climate that arises where such a management is less strictly governed, it is helpful to look at characters such as Disney's Duck family of Donald, Scrooge, and the nephews Huey, Dewey, and Louie. Even though, or especially because continuity management has never been an important part of their circulation, they make for an excellent case study to investigate how the oneiric climate can be, and often is approached from very different directions within a single character network. Donald Duck first originated in the pre-WWII "golden age" of American animation when a duck in a sailor suit appeared in the 1934 (Jackson) humoristic short movie *The Wise Little Hen* (see Freeman 2017). He was introduced as a mere supporting character living a merry life on a boat, but then quickly reappeared as a companion to other Disney protagonists such as Mickey Mouse in subsequent animated shorts (for instance in *Orphan's Benefit*, Gillet, from the same year). Soon afterward and in overlaps, comic book artists such as Ted Osborne, Tony Strobl, or Al Taliaferro developed Donald as the main protagonist of their own comic strips. Additional side characters like his three nephews or the setting of Duckburg were gradually introduced, although Donald still appeared together with Mickey and Goofy. Importantly, Donald was also featured in short gag comic strips without any overarching narratives or continuity concerns. Only Carl Barks, who would become the "most canonical" American Donald author from 1942 on, started to write and draw longer adventures for the Duck family and also established a clear separation from Mickey Mouse who never appeared in his stories (see Bryan 2021).

Donald and Mickey could soon be said to exist in their own storyworlds – although this was never made explicit and, especially in the Italian Disney tradition, they *did* continue to meet up for (increasingly rare) crossovers. The oneiric climate operating at Disney comics never necessitated any kind of "multiverse" explanation, however: Mickey could also be said to just live in a different district of Donald's Duckburg, or in a neighboring town that was sometimes referred to as "Mouseton" (in the Disney Comics 1990–1991 comic book series *Mickey*

Mouse Adventures, for instance). However, it is quite typical for Disney's narrative traditions that such issues were never conclusively resolved. For Donald's adventures, too, many things remained contradictory or undecided: Over the decades, the comics' various authors from many countries – William Van Horn, Floyd Gottfredson, Vicar, Daan Jippes, Flemming Andersen – rarely took note of each others' works. All their "Donalds" could nevertheless coexist with each other in the oneiric climate, precisely because continuity and canonicity were never explicitly managed by rights holder Disney or their work-for-hire artists and licensees around the world. The oneiric climate and the "Snap Back" mechanism described earlier were also operating *within* each series between issues. In the comics of Barks (and many others), for instance, Donald is shown working lots of different jobs which never last to the next issue, no matter how exceptional he is at them.

In some cases, however, various people – creators as well as fans – *did* take stances to resolve the oneiric climate's ambiguity in one way or the other. Such is the case for the fan-turned-creator Don Rosa, who revitalized the Duck family in the United States from the 1980s on by building his entire career explicitly – and exclusively – on the Duck stories of Carl Barks. Equally interesting is the fact that in Italy, separated by an ocean from the United States, an entirely different Disney tradition of Donald Duck comics emerged that is still alive today, whereas Donald has mostly survived as a mascot and in animated film in the United States. While the "Barks-Rosa Universe" is clearly distinguished from the "Italian Duck Universe" even in fan discourse (see Scrooge McDuck Wiki, "Barks-Rosa Universe"), both iterations generally remain compatible with each other, allowing us to imagine them both to be the adventures of the same Duck family – except for specific characters which *do* necessitate a distinction. Grandma Duck, for instance, is referred to as Scrooge McDuck's sister in the Italian tradition while having no blood relation to him at all in the Barks-Rosa Universe (young Scrooge *Mc*Duck was a Scottish immigrant, after all).

Looking at three newer iterations of the Duck family proves highly interesting, as they all adopted different strategies to dissolve, ignore, or rework the oneiric climate – both across different iterations and within their respective serialities themselves. These strategies are fascinating for a potential Transmedia Character Studies, precisely because continuity and canonicity are the exception, not the rule. Don Rosa started to situate his entire work in relation to the Duck stories of Barks, treating them as continuity in a way they were never intended to. He had Donald and his family returning to places of earlier adventures where side characters *remembered* their prior encounters (Lah Deedah in the mythical land of "Tralla La" in Rosa's "Return to Xanadu," 1990, reappearing from Barks' 1956 "The Lost Crown of Genghis Khan," Barks 2017): "Mister Scrooge! You have returned" "Yeah, yeah, I remember you" (Rosa 2015, 64). Rosa also tasked himself with addressing specific "continuity errors" generated by the oneiric climate *within* Barks' works decades earlier. All of Barks' stories could not only be read in any order, but they frequently also caused contradictions that – much like with *The Simpsons* or *South Park* later – could not easily be imagined with recourse to the same storyworld. In Barks' 1951s "A Christmas for Shacktown" (2012a), for instance, the episode ended with Scrooge McDuck's money bin disappearing into an inaccessible underground cavern for good. Merely intended as a humoristic resolution within this individual story, Scrooge reappeared as the main protagonist of his own new series soon after (1952s "Only a Poor Old Man," 2012b). There, naturally, he was still (or: again) presented as the world's richest man as if the closing event of "A Christmas for Shacktown" had never occurred. The oneiric climate allowed audiences to charitably ignore the disappearance of the money bin. Rosa, however, decided on an opposite solution, adding a "missing link" within his 1990 story "Gyro's First Invention" which explained what had happened during the "few months" in which Scrooge lived with his nephews until they excavated his riches and restored his status as the richest man alive. Such a "gap filling" was continued almost obsessively in Rosa's 12-issue masterpiece *The Life and Times of Scrooge McDuck* (1992–1994) in which he constructed an extensive "origin story" of Scrooge that connected each and every little piece of background information on Scrooge (in Barks' work) into one continuous narrative overlaid onto actual 19th/20th-century history. Again, Rosa had to resolve many inconsistencies and contradictions, some of which did not only concern inconsequential endings, but Scrooge's most central character traits.

One of Rosa's biggest problems was presented in Barks' 1949 story "Voodoo Hoodoo" (2011) which revealed that Scrooge had ruthlessly stolen land from indigenous people in "Africa" when he was younger – a premise that started a plot in which Donald was haunted by a vengeful Zombie as he resembled Scrooge in his younger days. Quite obviously, Barks' individual works were never intended to amount to the same, continuous story and characterization: In 1949, he had used Scrooge only a couple of times since his introduction two years earlier. To all accounts, Barks had no idea that Scrooge would become such a popular figure as to reappear as a major character in Duckburg. The oneiric climate allowed inconsistent punchlines and plot necessities of individual story information to be ignored by readers. To Rosa, however, "Voodoo Hoodoo" entirely contradicted Scrooge's characterization as a grumpy, yet honest businessman, morally distinguished from villains like Flintheart Glomgold. To resolve this apparent contradiction, Rosa retold the entire occurrence as a decisive *turning point* in Scrooge's career in which his protagonist shortly succumbed to evildoing (taking "shortcuts" to riches). The resulting chapter "The Empire-Builder from Calisota" from 1992 presents a major narrative (psychic) event for young Scrooge in which he has to decide between good vs. evil for the rest of his career, to be haunted by this "one mistake" for the rest of his life.

The 1996 Italian comic reboot of Donald Duck as the "Duck Avenger" Paperinik (*Paperinik New Adventures*, Sisti et al. 1996–2001) took a different road, reimagining Donald Duck in an entirely different actantial role as an American-style superhero accompanied by a completely new cast of side characters of intergalactic and time-traveling heroes and villains (see Packard 2019). The 56 issues of *PKNA*, as well as their continuation in the sequel series *PK2*, deviated strongly from the tone and style of earlier stories and presented complicated topics for a more mature readership. A range of new artists and writers developed multi-issue story arcs that could not be read in any order, as Donald became gradually involved in an interplanetary war against a species of space parasites, the Evronian Empire. Contrary to Rosa, who obsessively built connections to earlier stories (initially not intended to be connected), the *Paperinik* series mostly ignored all earlier occurrences and sidelined established characters and settings like Scrooge, the nephews, or the money bin in favor of new ones, such as the Artificial Intelligence Uno inhabiting the iconic Ducklair Tower which would become Donald's new residence. Interestingly, although the Duck Avenger stories mostly dissolved the oneiric climate within their own series, they nevertheless allowed readers to imagine a tacit connection to all earlier (Italian) Disney comics. Donald's superhero identity of Paperinik was invented by Italian artist Guido Martina in 1969 as a playful reference to the Italian pulp character Diabolik (in "Paperinik il diabolico vendicatore," Martina and Carpi 1969). The new artists of the 1996 series did build on that backstory – Donald *was* Paperinik already. Donald also *moved into* the Ducklair Tower from his regular, established home. The complete absence of Donald's nephews was then explained with a brief aside that they went on a "super-important long term junior woodchucks world operation": "We just returned from the arctic! Now we're on our way to Africa" (Sisti et al. 2017, 33). Just like with Marvel's "What If…" stories discussed in chapter 7, which connected seamlessly with the main Marvel continuity in order to then "branch off," the *Paperinik* authors, too, allowed for the imagination that this was a possible future of the "actual" Donald readers grew up with. The 2002 videogame *PK: Out of the Shadows* (Ubisoft Montréal) was then an adaptation of the Duck Avenger story and Donald's fight against the Evronian Empire, with the one difference being that, in the game, the earlier Italian Disney stories were *not* an existing backdrop to Donald's later space adventures.

A third approach can be found in the new *DuckTales* animated series from 2017 (Youngberg), which did establish entirely new versions of Donald and the nephews – it is thus a proper reboot with its own, distinct continuity (sometimes referred to as the "Disney Afternooniverse" or the "2017 Continuum" in fan discourse, see Scrooge McDuck Wiki, "2017 Continuum"). Hence, the animated show did cut all "oneiric" connections to Barks, Rosa, or their Italian counterparts entirely – Donald and his nephews meet Scrooge *for the first time* in season 1's pilot. The show also reimagines Huey, Dewey, and Louie with distinct personalities and features, dissolving their collective actantial identity (just like with the Beagle Boys). The episodes also tackle – and resolve – many issues that were never addressed in earlier instances. The nephew's mother Della Duck, for instance, was only ever mentioned in a short Sunday strip by Al Taliaferro from 1937 as a reason why the children were to live with their uncle. Even Don Rosa had her appear only shortly in flashbacks to Donald's youth (now Donald's sister instead of his cousin) until she was reintroduced as a major character in the second season of 2017s *DuckTales*. Knowledge about the earlier absence of any "narrative facts" around these issues certainly increases the pleasure of watching how *DuckTales* addresses them (and, perhaps as importantly, so does some familiarity with the many settings, characters, and tropes that are reimagined from Don Rosa as well as from the earlier *DuckTales* show of 1986, Magon et al., which, in turn, was strongly influenced by Barks). Nevertheless, these are *new versions* of Donald, Scrooge, and the nephews which are best addressed as individual character nodes within a network as established in chapter 7. We also find these same glocal transmedia characters within the IDW comic book series *DuckTales*, also published from 2017 on. What all of these examples are intended to show, however, is that there are various narrative strategies to deal with the oneiric climate "below" the network model, when inconsistencies are readily ignored since no overall claims of continuity and canonicity are part of the established narrative tradition from the outset.

8.4 Pre-narrative and Meta-narrative Figures

For some characters, the oneiric climate is "ingrained" into their medial identity even stronger than in Donald Duck's case. They are then almost entirely devoid of overarching claims to continuity and consistency – because they did not originate in narrative media representing a non-contradictory storyworld, to begin with (see Wilde 2019a; Wilde and Denson 2022). This is what we would finally like to address as "pre-narrative figures," since their proper names and their iconographies are not derived from or connected to any specific narrative in which they first appeared. Examples include protagonists of "modern myths" like Santa Claus, pictorial symbols such as Uncle Sam, or product placement figures such as Hello Kitty, which all seem to exist in the cultural imaginary without any (specific) story about them.

Santa Claus at first seems mostly consistent in his many depictions across media. He is always thought of as some kind of magical being living at the North Pole where he is tasked with a specific job (a recurring actantial role): delivering presents to children around the world with the support of a range of side characters such as elves and his nine reindeers (of which Rudolph is the main protagonist of his own story, first published in the 1939 department store takeaway booklet "Rudolph the Red-Nosed Reindeer" by Robert L. May, see May and Caparo 2014). At first glance, Santa's identity seems non-contradictory throughout media. He could easily be imagined to exist in a single, transmedia storyworld. His origins, however, cannot be traced to any story or a media text representing a *specific* cause of events – or even one single, memorable narrative event (in contrast perhaps to Rudolph in May's booklet story, who is mocked and excluded by the other reindeers until he heroically saves Christmas). There certainly are a range of specific works decisive for Santa's proliferation: Clement Clarke Moore's poem "A Visit from St. Nicholas" (aka "The Night Before Christmas") from 1837, in which the author reimagined the legend of Saint Nicholas by introducing the sleigh pulled by eight reindeers and the protagonist entering houses via chimneys. Even in the poem, however, this is not represented as a singular event but as one which happens regularly. No additional backstory, motivation, or resolution is provided. This also holds true for Santa's subsequent appearances throughout popular culture when his iconic look was first defined by cartoonist Thomas Nast and later solidified in 1931 by the Coca-Cola Company "employing" the figure as a mascot. The point here is that for pre-narrative figures such as Santa Claus, our "original" imagination consists of little more than a transmedia character *template* as discussed in chapter 7, some vague notions about "physical, mental, and social characteristics […] that any work-specific character sharing the same name may or may not exhibit" (Thon 2019, 184). In this example, Santa's template includes his appearance (red suit, white beard, etc.), some personality dispositions (good-humored, friendly, plump, living withdrawn from civilization), as well as a recurring, "eternal" job he is tasked with every Christmas. There is not, however, a specific original story (a series of narrative events) serving as a benchmark for whether a new representation must be thought of as identical or derivative. At his core then, Santa is merely a figure born out of the oneiric climate, not a character that emerged from a specific narrative. To be clear, countless versions of Santa Claus within individual narrative texts do exist: Different Santa Claus characters appear, for instance, in Tim Burton's animated film *The Nightmare Before Christmas* (1993), Bill Willingham's and Mark Buckingham's comic book series *Fables* (2002–present), or the films *Bad Santa* (Zwigoff 2003, in which the protagonist is played by Billy Bob Thornton), *The Christmas Chronicles* (Kaytis 2018, played by Kurt Russell), or *Fatman* (2020, played by Mel Gibson). In all these narrative texts, the figure is transformed into an individual character version that can and must be distinguished from all other "Santa network nodes." One of the main reasons that this is not easily possible for the foundational, pre-narrative figure is that most representations of Santa circulate on single, isolated images providing little to no narrative context.

We have even fewer narrative contexts for the figure of Uncle Sam, the anthropomorphic personification of the United States or, more precisely, of the US government (see Wilde and Denson 2022). Again, there are many actual characters of that name in narrative media texts to which the network model of distinguished nodes applies well: Comic artist Will Eisner imagined an Uncle Sam as a generic superhero in Quality Comics' (later DC) *National Comics* #1 (Eisner and Berg 1940) which would later be integrated with DC's superhero multiverse; another version appeared in the two-issue Vertigo comic *US—Uncle Sam* (1997) by Steve Darnall and Alex Ross, and yet another futuristic one in the ongoing Image series *Undiscovered Country* (Soule et al. 2019–present) by Scott Snyder and Charles Soule. In all these works, a fictional being bearing the name and iconography is presented as a contextualized diegetic character distinguished from other "network nodes" through mutually closed textual worlds (*Undiscovered Country* multiplies his identity once again, as there seem to exist many different versions of Sam even within Snyder's and Soule's storyworld). As a pre-narrative figure, he emerged in the 1830s already, when political cartoons developed rapidly due to new printing technologies, especially lithography (see Ketchum 1959), which made the production and reproduction of pictorial materials much cheaper and easier. His name refers to the actual Samuel Wilson who worked as a contractor for the American military in the War of 1812. Sam Wilson and his brother butchered and packed cattle and produced the casks in which they dealt salt for the troops stationed at the city of Troy in Northern New York. Each of the large casks and packages was marked with the letters "U.S." Since the acronym for "United States" was not in wide circulation yet, people referred to "Uncle Sam providing for the troops" (see Fischer 2005, 230). His depictions were not cast in a single mold, however, as each artist (probably none of whom had met Samuel Wilson) created their own version or used local models for individual appearances. Once his appearance was memorable enough to be recognized by a general audience, mostly once again owed to cartoonist Thomas Nast who codified his iconic looks after the Civil War (a slender body, whiskers, beard, and stars and stripes for pants), he was depicted in various versions of different age, gender, or social status by other cartoonists such as Joseph Keppler, Fred Opper, or Homer Davenport. He appeared as Shakespeare's Oberon, as Samson, Santa Claus, and Quixote, as Moses, Wotan, and Hercules – as well as in countless other roles and functions fitting the individual depicted context (see Ketchum 1959, 133). By the 1890s he was impersonated at festivals, parades, and fairs, and he was long a standard fixture of the circus. A few years later he even made an appearance in George M. Cohan's Broadway musical show "Little Johnny Jones" (1903). Like other pictorial symbols (such as flags or logos), pre-narrative figures such as Uncle Sam seem to possess a range of relatively stable, symbolic/thematic meanings (the United States Government, Freedom, Hope – different ones for artists from other countries) but without any consistent storyworld context to which these are attached.

This is also true for our third example of pre-narrative figures, the international icon Hello Kitty. Kitty was invented in 1974 by the designer Yūko Shimizu for the Japanese Sanrio Group to appear exclusively on material products such as handbags, school cases, T-shirts, mobile phone tags, towels, and countless other products (see Belson and Bremner 2004; Yano 2016). In 2013, media studies scholars Corinna Peil and Herbert Schwab (2013) listed over 60,000 Kitty products worldwide. In Japanese studies, such pre-narrative figures are referred to as "kyara" or "charas," a simplified and more fundamental phenomenon than a "character." *Kyara* are not derived from (or "filtered by") narrative media or represented worlds to begin with (see Wilde 2019a). Instead, they seem to address their audiences directly and personally. Sanrio is transparent with regard to its marketing strategy to create a communication culture among its consumers with Kitty products. The "Hello" can therefore be taken as a prompt: The purchase of Kitty products should not be understood as a one-off material appropriation, but instead serve as an invitation for consumers to greet and gift each other through their products. Myriads of regionalized Kitty products ("gotōchi kitty") presented the feline in ever-changing site-specific roles, settings, and contexts without any irritation from audiences (see Toratani 2013). We can see from this that pre-narrative figures can also attain meta-narrative or transfictional qualities: Within the network model, most Kitty representations would amount to individual, distinguished character versions/nodes as her countless appearances are strongly contradictory. In one illustration, she is presented as a samurai warrior, and in the next as Mt. Fuji. Since Kitty mostly circulates as a figure outside of narrative contexts, however, her proper name and her iconography are only linked to a template of vague traits (cuteness and friendliness) without any demands for consistency. The oneiric climate, which dissolves the demand to sort out questions of continuity and canonicity, is the *foundation* of Kitty's circulation on material products and other non-narrative media.

Pre-narrative figures (as well as the many related company mascots we will look at in the subsequent chapter) are thus specifically designed to be appropriated by their consumers without any distinction between original and "fan fiction." They lean into a long history of "characters" in an entirely different sense: Mere *types* of individuals, "stock characters," as they are used in political cartoons to mock a whole group of people embodied in one person (the "businessman," the "conservative") or as they were performed in the theatrical tradition of the Commedia dell'arte (Il Capitano, a braggart and a swaggerer, or Il Dottore, a decadent old man). Even in ancient Greece, Theophrastus' (371–287 b.c.) compiled a moral treatise on "characters" in 30 revealing lists of distinguishing actions and behaviors (the Flatterer, the Boaster, the Vain Man, etc.) (see Garber 2020, 321–348). Any individual could be recognized to be *like* one of those types. In the Commedia dell'arte, the cast of stock characters was well known to its audiences and has been performed for centuries over and over again in ever new (and entirely discontinuous) situations. Modern pre-narrative figures like Kitty, by contrast, are characterized by the fact that they can be invented *ad hoc* by companies and are mostly based on pictorial media without any intention to exemplify actual persons. They are not primarily symbols for the character traits they exemplify but motivated and distinguished mostly by an attractive visual design to sell products or to gain a "life of their own" for customers and fans.

Other medial traditions likewise emphasize the meta-narrative quality of their protagonists to appear in contradictory roles like an actual movie star does. For the protagonists of many animated film genres, such as the *Looney Tunes* cartoons (Harman et al. 1930–1969), the prerequisite of world-coherency is difficult to maintain – in many cases even outright counter-intuitive (see Feyersinger 2017, 79–101). Jenkins conceded that a "modern" transmedia character ("who carries with him or her the timeline and the world depicted on the 'mother ship,' the primary work which anchors the franchise," Jenkins 2009, n.pag.) should be clearly distinguished from protagonists of earlier animated cartoons, such as Felix the Cat ("a character who is extracted from any specific narrative context," n.pag.). Watching cartoons in which such protagonists are placed within different roles, worlds, and identities in between almost every episode – maintaining their *gradual* identity only by iconography and certain character dispositions, not by any coherent contextualization – does not require any "sharing or not of a common fictional universe" (Bertetti 2014b, 2358) as a criterion for identity or difference. The Walt Disney studios are also well known for using "stars" such as Mickey, Donald, or Goofy transfictionally, just like actors: as if they, too, could take on any character roles in highly contingent and contradictory contexts. William Uricchio and Roberta Pearson likewise observed that

> Bugs Bunny and Mickey Mouse [...] function as actors/celebrities rather than as characters. Bugs Bunny can appear in an opera, a Western, a Sherwood Forest adventure, a science fiction film, or even, as "himself" at the Academy Awards. In each case, he plays a role within the narrative as well as constantly remaining Bugs Bunny, in a similar fashion to such flesh and blood counterparts as Groucho Marx.
>
> (1991, 185)

Many video game characters whose narrative dimension is much less emphasized than their ludic one (see chapter 6) operate in the same way. The countless appearances of Nintendo's Super Mario, for instance, might allude to a range of different canons in some of his most prominent games (of at least a "Kong canon," a "Super canon," and a "Paper Mario canon," see cardboard boxer 2014). In many other Nintendo games, however, Mario is also "employed" as a doctor, a painter, a racer, a martial artist, a professional baseball, soccer, tennis, and basketball player, among many other "occupations" (see Adams 2019). While all of these might be conceptualized as a non-contradictory array of astonishing hobbies or additional incomes, it is hard to imagine why King Koopa is engaging in friendly racing games with him in the *Mario Kart* series when they are otherwise trying to kill each other. More consistently, perhaps, Nintendo is using Mario like a fictional celebrity play-acting all these roles, which makes him, again, more of a meta-narrative figure. Bugs Bunny, Felix the Cat, Mario, and many other such figures seem to stay "themselves" no matter which diegetic "role" they are placed in – just like Harrison Ford or Scarlett Johansson. Within these medial contexts, the "actual" character seems to exist on the plane of a decontextualized, trans-fictional, trans-world, meta-narrative entity (as a mere template), which is why Denson's and Mayer's term figure seems more appropriate.

To summarize these last two chapters, the network model that approaches transmedia characters as distinguished versions or nodes is a powerful analytical tool for the description of characters in contexts where canonicity and continuity are strongly expected, managed, and negotiated between creators and audiences. We have seen, however, that this is neither "natural" nor necessary for fictional and fictionalized characters, but merely the result of specific medial practices and traditions. The oneiric climate, the willingness of audiences to suspend questions of coherence and identity, is equally important to explain the prominence and longevity of characters circulating in our media ecologies for decades. New iterations can always approach oneiric ambiguities with various strategies to weaken or strengthen earlier expectations of consistency. "Retcons" aim to overlay continuity where there has not been any before, while reboots may generate a distinct sub-world in which canonicity is suddenly of great importance. On the other end of the spectrum, characters may be entirely disentangled from narratives to such a degree that Denson and Mayer's term of a transmedia figure might be more appropriate: There is then no original story as a series of narrative events in a specific media text that can serve as a benchmark for identity vs. difference. Some pre-narrative figures are even meta-narrative or transfictional to the core, as they can appear in strongly contradictory settings, roles, and worlds from one depiction to the next without any irritations from audiences. For transmedia figures, the template of prototypical character traits is not merely the intersection of commonalities between different character versions. The figure *is* the template, or more precisely: The figure is only thought of as a set of prototypical appearances, traits, and dispositions that may otherwise display striking contradictions. Meta-narrative figures are thus like performers or actors, able to adopt any fictional role across storyworlds and contexts. As a result, pre- and meta-narrative transmedia figures are especially well suited to be employed by companies, authorities, and other institutions as mascots in actual contexts where audiences are to imagine interactions with them directly – instead of being fundamentally separated in different (actual vs. fictional) worlds. This is what we will look at in the following chapter 9.

Section 4

Characters and Non-Fiction

9 Fictional Characters and Figures (Imagined to Exist) in Actual Contexts

This chapter is investigating some of the conceptual tensions between characters and aspects of media that are generally considered non-fictional (i.e., inherently related to *our* world) as well as non-narrative (i.e., not representing stories or series of narrative events at all). For a potential Transmedia Character Studies, this is highly relevant in two different ways. First, even characters derived from narrative media and stories often play a much more significant role in merchandise products, at least in commercial terms. "As Superman tee shirts circulate more widely than Superman comic books, the latter might be lubricating the exchange with the meaning embodied in the former, as opposed to the reverse," media historian Ian Gordon found (2016, 327). Images of characters, their costumes, or their logos have become recognizable brands that people identify with by wearing them on clothes, quite similar to wearing a shirt of their favorite rock band or one with an iconic brand logo. Fans consume and purchase merchandise as a form of self-expression or affiliation to a certain group or fan culture. Looking at these material objects, we might analyze which pieces of a character's identity (their transmedia template, see chapter 7) are reinforced while others are deemphasized. Products of Spider-Man, for instance, will most probably show him in established poses and scenes – swinging from skyscrapers with his webs – and rarely in dialogue with other characters. Aspects of his physical mobility and agility are thus highlighted on shirts, while other character traits salient for his template – his sense of playfulness or the mantra (ethos) "with great power comes great responsibility" – are usually neglected in this context.

Some character products clearly refer to specific instances or versions (nodes) of a transmedia character network and, with that, to specific media texts. A new Batman film release will be accompanied by merchandise showing images of *that* specific actor portraying the most recent character version (Christian Bale, Ben Affleck, or Robert Pattinson). Other products, by contrast, only evoke an overarching, generic notion of a "second-level-original" (Margolin 1996, 116), "*the* Batman," addressed as a transmedia *figure* in the preceding chapter. It cannot be linked back to any specific story or media text (especially if only the logo is present). In any case, iconic *visuals* (recognizable colors, expressions, gestures, poses, outfits) are the main aspects representing a character's identity in non-narrative

DOI: 10.4324/9781003298793-14

media contexts. For this, a high level of visual consistency is required. Japanese studies scholar Marc Steinberg has pointed out that the "anime system" – a transmedial network of interrelated media products propelled by characters – essentially developed out of the standardization of character images across narrative and non-narrative media alike. "[T]he same character, in the same drawing style and in the same poses, now inhabited manga, and anime alike – not to mention the other media forms to which the character image migrated" (Steinberg 2012, 109). It comes as no surprise then that a character's visual identity is often adopted by the material objects themselves. Most Spider-Man products have in common the main colors of red and blue, for instance, so that even the material "backgrounds" on which the image will be applied (the plastic of a frisbee, the fabric of a satchel or a sports bag, the porcelain of a coffee cup) will be blue. Investigating which images, poses, gestures, and colors are used to reference characters in non-narrative media products can thus be a way to reveal which parts of the overarching intersubjective construct (the character template) are most salient within specific cultural and commercial contexts.

Secondly, and maybe even more importantly, it is no exaggeration that we are surrounded by characters (or rather *figures*, in the terms proposed in the chapter before) connected to no narrative contexts whatsoever (see Wilde 2018b, 2019a). "Pre-narrative" or "non-narrative" characters or figures seem to share the common trait of existing in absence of any "mandated" narratives, official stories, or fictional worlds surrounding them. One might immediately think about mascots, also discussed as "spokes-characters" (Garretson and Niedrich 2004), "brand characters" (Hosany et al. 2013), or "brand mascots" (Cayla 2013) in research literature. The Haribo Goldbear, for instance, is internationally recognizable without any narrative information about the "storyworld" he is supposed to exist in: are there other bears like him, what country did he grow up in, are there humans existing in it as well? Although he is represented as responsible for self-initiated activities – in 2019 and 2022 roadshows, actors in Goldbear full-body suits were interacting with visitors in cities all over Germany (see Haribo 2022) – we know close to nothing about his motivations, feelings, aims, or about any kind of backstory. Even the Goldbear's gender is left ambiguous in almost all advertisements, with the sole exception of several German TV spots aired throughout the 1980s and early 1990s, which featured a male voice actor in the role (see Haribo Deutschland 2022). For such mascots, it is clear that their intended *symptomatic* meaning – representing the actual Haribo company, the brand, as well as their main product – is strongly foregrounded (see Hosany et al. 2013, 51) while mimetic aspects, especially their inner life, remain underemphasized (in research on mascots, however, there are ongoing discussions about which character traits – which *are* on the mimetic level, after all – make mascots and, by proxy, brands and products, likable and relatable, see Garretson and Niedrich 2004, 33). Mascots' symbolic, political meanings may seem negligible at first glance, yet these, too, can become contested sites and symptoms of heated cultural negotiations. In January 2022, for instance, Fox News host Tucker Carlson was apparently outraged by a redesign of the M&M mascots and published a series of aggravated rants after the company decided that the (female-coded) green M&M traded her knee-high boots for comfy trainers, while the (likewise female) brown M&M had shortened the height of her heels in an attempt to make both "less sexy" (or, perhaps, less sexist). "M&M's will not be satisfied until every last cartoon character is deeply unappealing and totally androgynous. Until the moment you wouldn't want to have a drink with any one of them. That's the goal," Carlson complained on live TV (quoted after Di Placido 2022, n.pag.). Naturally, social media made fun of the fact that he apparently liked to entertain romantic/erotic fantasies with vaguely anthropomorphic cartoon characters, but there's much more at stake here. Once again, it is about an ostensibly "natural," "normal" depiction of "female" characters/figures, which seems an especially thorny issue when there are almost no other traits involved than their more or less stereotypical visual depiction.

In contrast to company or product logos, mascots are attributed communicative agency by creators and audiences alike. Hence, they are often used as fictional mouthpieces of and for actual institutions (see Garretson Folse et al. 2012; Wilde 2021). Mascots can thus be addressed as *media of communication*, but it is once again the immaterial communicative construct that serves such a function: Audiences presuppose that *there is* one entity or, maybe, a group of entities – the Goldbears – acting as fictional stand-ins, not merely a series of unrelated "images of yellow bears." One might also consider communicational mascots like the (discontinued) German Railway (DB)'s Max Maulwurf or Paris RATP's Serge the Rabbit used for official announcements and instructions (see Nozawa 2013); "fictional celebrities" like Hatsune Miku, a Japanese transmedial franchise consisting entirely of the figure circulating in "official" live performances, fan artworks, and fan videos (see Leavitt et al. 2016); or figures invented for digital stickers like Line's Cony or Brown the Bear. Further examples are fictional beings marketed only as toys, such as Mattel's Barbie doll (albeit Barbie has by now become a "proper" transmedial character in her own right, starring in movies, video games, etc.); and, finally, "pure" product placement figures such as Sanrio's Hello Kitty or Thomas Goletz' Diddl Maus which circulate on clothes, coffee mugs, and office supplies. A feature that most of these non-narrative character/figure representations share is that audiences are encouraged to imagine these beings within the actual spacetime settings in which the representational materials (images and signs, statues and costumes, toys and interfaces) are located. They are designed to "overlay" the actual environment in which they are represented as a kind of interface between real spaces and audiences' imagination. For this to become more evident, we are first going to look at "working characters/figures" on signage and other informational media in public spaces that *do* present a storyworld – or, at least, a represented situation distinct from actual observers. Then, we are going to explore how characters or figures can be represented and interpreted without any such represented context, instead looking at observers "directly" like a pictorial dummy. Third, this chapter will address how mascots are used in theme parks and public events where an audience seems to be able to interact with them directly. In all these cases, character/figure representations are strategically employed to bridge the gap between fiction and real-life settings – at least in some imaginary frame of play that includes actual audiences as much as the (often) cartoonish protagonists. The final section of this chapter concludes with some critical remarks on the rhetorical functions of these character/figure images in contexts where they serve as a "blackbox" or a "mask" hiding the actual agency of institutions, corporations, platforms, or celebrities.

9.1 Working Characters and Figures on Street Signs Presenting Diegetic Situations

Does the emergency exit sign invented by Ōta Yukio in 1979 represent a story-world in which a single, largely unspecified character is just about to make a run for a door? Our most intuitive answer would probably be: No, exit signs just communicate ("tell") observers where the next respective emergency exit is actually located. Philosopher Neil McDonell's exemplary statement on this difference is that "[t]he picture of a man on a restroom sign does not refer to any particular man but to all men" (McDonell 1983, 85). Pictograms thus only exemplify concepts. They represent *classes of objects* falling under certain categories (see Kjørup 2004). The signs posted on many trains and trams prohibiting the consumption of food and beverages show only exemplary items, but these stand for other objects in the same, more abstract category ("food"). Pictographic no-smoking signs showing cigarettes are thus also meant to prohibit pipes, e-cigarettes, etc., i.e., "smoking" in general. Of course, the exemplifying function of pictograms is itself subject to interpretational conventions and, potentially, disputes. This is demonstrated very clearly by the case of bathroom pictograms, which caused widespread confusion upon their introduction at the 1967 World's Fair in Montreal (see Buterman 2013, 434–435). To many attendants, the meaning of what McDonell labels the "picture of a man" was, in fact, so general as to potentially refer to any human being.

By making pictogrammatic representations of people more specific and adding features that indicate a subjective inner life, by contrast, they can be turned into something akin to fictional characters or figures. Especially in Japan, nameless "working characters" (*hataraku kyara*) can be found on signs in public spaces on almost every street corner (see Wilde 2018a, 2018b). They feature the most improbable combinations of anthropomorphized flowerpots, TV sets, household appliances, ashtrays, cars, or even molecules, which draw attention to rules in the immediate environment (see Harrison and Harrison 2011; Tokyo Files, "Funny Japanese Street Signs"). Sometimes, they even employ actual transmedia characters such as Osamu Tezuka's Astro Boy, derived from narrative media like manga and anime within official forms of communication (see Thaler 2004). Different from mere official written statements, these representations evoke *personal* lifeworld experiences, ways of seeing things and acting, deeply entrenched within specific situations. In other words, even in these entirely functional cases, character representations act as gateways into narrative meaning-making. They enable audiences to frame their real-world environments differently by imagining the perspective of others or by imagining themselves from the perspective of others, even if these others are anthropomorphic objects.

On a sign from the German Railway (DB) that can be found on many railway stations since spring 2017 a speech bubble reads: "In my day, this was unheard of! Back then everyone still threw their garbage in the trash can." This text is attributed to an anthropomorphic train, commenting with a visibly shocked facial expression on a scene taking place in front of it: a filthy station in which a (juvenile?) culprit carelessly hurls a beverage cup onto the ground. By turning the train into a character/figure, the company not only communicates that it does not wish any loitering. It rather invites audiences to imagine a specific situation from the perspective of a "characterized" train who is shown to have feelings, experiences – or rather: a full-fledged past as indicated by the phrase "in my day" – and (negative) emotional reactions toward what is going on. The abstract rule can thus be inferred from a specific represented situation (in which it is not followed).

It is worth repeating some of the foundations of a potential Transmedia Character Studies introduced in chapter 1, as they still apply to minimal figures on signage in public places or official leaflets (see Christian 2017, 436–453). Worlds filled with characters or anthropomorphic figures are always worlds *for someone* experiencing them "from within." Each and every consciousness has, as philosopher John Searle has put it, a "first-person ontology" (Searle 1992, 20). They carry, by necessity, a certain point of view, a worldview. Audiences comprehending characters/figures thus always perform a kind of imaginative "recentering," to use another term by Mary-Laure Ryan (1991b, 18): We *mentally relocate* to the fictional situation that the characters/figures inhabit. All the objects, entities, and events within a storyworld – or even a represented situation involving a character/figure – are then not only related in temporal, spatial, and sometimes causal terms but also within subjective experiences. Characters/figures are able to perceive this situation as well, build mental models about it, and act according to their own beliefs and desires. Characters/figures in pictorial representations do not "stick out" from their represented environment(s) because they seem "lifelike," exactly. On the contrary, the impression of aliveness is rather the consequence of the fact that their implied consciousness frame is ontologically (and representationally) distinguished from its surroundings (see Hilmer 2009). The represented beings often have to draw inferences about the diegetic situation themselves, and they can potentially be mistaken when doing so. "Carrying" their own subjective consciousness frames with them, characters multiply the represented situation once again into distinguished *modal versions*: states of the world they desire or fear, long for, or try to avoid, and states of the world they remember (correctly or falsely).

A storyworld – and, as such, any represented situation – has been defined as a *possible world* before, in the sense that it is imaginable from our perspective. If part of this imagination, however, includes characters or figures, then, *to them*, the represented state of affairs is not merely possible, but actual: It has "real" consequences for them and all other represented participants. According to philosopher Gregory Currie, "[n]arratives represent things as existing, and circumstances as being so" (Currie 2010, 7). At the same time, *different* states of affairs become possible (imaginable). By introducing characters/figures, and thus subjectivities, into a representation, a distinction is drawn between the actual and the possible *within the realm of the possible*. Narrative actuality – what is sometimes called the "basic-fact domain" of a storyworld situation (Margolin 2007, 71) – is that which is *not up to the characters/figures* to change at will. To them, it remains a "brute fact." Integrating characters/figures into official communication thus means encouraging audiences to imagine a subjective perspective within a specific represented context. All of this, however, can be reconstructed intersubjectively, since the respective images will be understood largely in the same way by audiences, at least as far as the represented situation is concerned.

9.2 Characters and Figures without any Diegetic Context

A systematic semiotic alternative to the representation of characters/figures within specific situations and worlds (distinct from ours) consists of the *dummy*. A dummy simulates characters or figures in the actual context of their placement. A common example can be found in pictorial "stand-ins" for construction site workers who are intended to substitute for actual supervisory personnel (see Figure 9.1). They trigger imaginations about themselves, or more precisely: about the local material of their representation. Art historian Rudolf Arnheim (1980) went so far as to suggest that a carved wooden bird does not merely *represent* a bird (as would be the case in a painting), but that it *embodies* a bird because we imagine it to exist "here and now." It is intended as a prompt to modify the actual situational context within the imagination. Not only three-dimensional objects but also some images function in the same way. James Montgomery Flagg's famous war recruitment poster of Uncle Sam from 1917 – "I want you for U. S. Army" –

Figure 9.1 "Characterized" construction site barriers as stand-ins for official personnel, pictures taken by Lukas R.A. Wilde in Ueno, Tokyo (Japan), September 2015 and Ise, Mie (Japan), February 2017.

shows Sam pointing his finger directly at the viewer as if the personification of the US government was addressing each and every observer individually "right then and there," and not from any fictional storyworld situation (the background of the poster was indeed left empty, as if it was merely the actual, material paper on which the figure was really printed). For many other "cut-out" figures on blank spaces (walls as well as signages), too, the boundary of the picture is indeed the very outline of the figure. The background *is* the actual ground of the material sign. This is a central semiotic aspect of street art as well: "Unlike paintings, which can be received independently of the place of their hanging or presentation, graffiti 'live' from the communication and commentary with the place of their application" (Weixler 2020, 63; translation ours). Many representations of "cartoon beings," aliens, or spaceships affixed in public spaces need not, or should not, be interpreted as offering selective glimpses into distinct situations and storyworlds. Site-specific graffiti instead lend themselves to being interpreted as representations of beings and objects that climb or fly over the actual walls on which they are affixed.

A toy doll, too, can not only be used to imagine a baby (somewhere). Usually, we imagine the doll itself *as a baby* (see Walton 1993, 117). This modification can then even involve audiences themselves: "Children are almost invariably characters in their games of make-believe; the imaginings they engage in are partly about themselves" (209). Many dummies also look directly at observers, who thus can become part of an imaginary interaction themselves. Anthropologist Shunsuke Nozawa described everyday Japanese working characters, anthropomorphic figure displays in public spaces, in similar ways, as special semiotic interfaces: "[Characters/figures] constitute an interface of objects and spaces that relays signs between other semiotic actants – between pedestrians and a construction site, between smokers and the city, between commuters and the subway station" (Nozawa 2013, n.pag.). Walton (1993, 117) described this principle of *reflexive imagination* quite extensively for statues and monuments. Some monuments are intended to be understood as fictional people that are nevertheless located in the actual spaces surrounding them. Attention is thus once again drawn back to the actual situational context.

We use emoji or digital stickers in much the same way. On February 6, 2009, the California-based Unicode Consortium defined a first set of 674 emoji for global use in telecommunication software. One year later, this emoji set was made available to software developers worldwide (see Evans 2017; Giannoulis and Wilde 2020a). All in all, there are now 3,304 emoji (including the so-called "skin tone modifiers" for faces and other emoji). So far, no emoji has ever been removed from the set. The admission procedures for new candidates are relatively complex and involve a range of political negotiations (see Berard 2018). This is demonstrated, for example, by the prolonged efforts to integrate a hijab emoji for Muslim women ("woman with headscarf", U+1F9D5), which finally succeeded in 2017. Gender-neutral emoji have only existed since 2019. The cartoon-like manga aesthetic of emoji serves, in any case, above all to depict affect and emotions, which is diametrically opposed to the rational ethos of earlier pictographic scripts (see Danesi 2017; Wilde 2020a). Crucially, emoji are usually interpreted not as pictures of individual characters but rather as exemplifications of emotions of the *actual* sender of a message (although given that emoji tend to show what one could describe as extremely hyperbolic reactions, this exemplification must not be confused with a quantitatively faithful depiction of the sender's actual emotional state; the representational correspondence between what is shown and what it is intended to signify can once again be quite loose, see chapter 5). The communicational context is thus never "left" in favor of any fictional storyworld situation. A further technical development is provided with digital stickers which are offered on various messaging services such as WhatsApp, Line, Telegram, or Signal. One set may, for example, consist of Marvel superheroes, a second of the protagonists of the French *Blacksad* comics series, a third of cartoon versions of William Shakespeare, and so on. Most digital stickers, however, are not based on existing characters but rather on pre-narrative figures without any stories connected to them. Either way, their everyday use in digital communication always points back to the actual communicational context in which they are intended to address receivers directly by exemplifying emotions and affects of the actual sender. Emoji and digital stickers thus function just like avatars in video games (see chapter 6), representing mostly the users "behind" them.

Especially in Japan (as well as South Korea), there are entire "character goods" industries continuously developing non-narrative figures such as Hello Kitty for private imaginations and uses. Kitty was invented by Sanrio designer Yūko Shimizu back in 1974 and subsequently appeared on tens of thousands of products such as handbags, satchels, T-shirts, cell phone charms, towels, and countless other products (see McVeigh 2000; Yano 2016). The "Kitty world" sold through such items is not the storyworld of any narrative representation, however. Kitty products can rather be described as deliberately blurring the boundaries between representation and everyday life, as audiences establish imaginative spheres within their actual world through the consumption and circulating of Sanrio products. One can wake up in a Kitty bedroom, eat breakfast in a kitchen full of Kitty, work at a Kitty desk with a Kitty computer, and ride a Kitty scooter. Kitty is thus intended as an "imaginary friend" that mostly exists within the individual imagination and not as an overall intersubjective construct. Her audiences can establish their own imaginative relationships with her by assuming a part of the authorship over their own character version(s). This is precisely where the secret of Kitty's success is seen to stem from: Fans are "animated [...] to ascribe meaning to her, [but] also have more opportunities to do so due to the lack of attachment to a story" (Peil and Schwab 2013, 348, our translation). As media anthropologist Mizuko Ito has pointed out in many essays, it is precisely the instrumentalization of play and imagination which constitutes a special feature of such franchises, "mobilizing the imagination in everyday play" (Ito 2008, 397). Such character/figure products are "explicitly designed to allow for user-level reshuffling and reenactment" (404). Although the characters or figures thusly created are ("only") located in private worlds of the imagination, these are still their authorized and intended uses. They indicate an invitation to imaginative participation. This can be connected to recent theories of the increasing "gami-fication" (Deterding 2016, 101) of public spheres. Augmented reality games like *Ingress* (Niantic 2013) or *Pokémon GO* (Niantic 2016) likewise include the actual situational environment within their gameworlds, creating a kind of reflex-ive, technology-driven interface between real spaces and the imagination (see Hjorth 2017).

Far from everything about these character/figure interactions is purely sub-jective, however. The aesthetics of cute ("kawaii") imagery, for instance, may be understood as a "generic cue," activating communicative expectations that are familiar and internalized from media forms such as manga, anime, or car-toon films (see Occhi 2012, 127). Lisbeth Klastrup and Susanna Tosca have de-scribed this as a certain "ethos" of transmedial storyworlds, as we have discussed in chapter 1: "How does the good and the bad behave, and what behaviour can be accepted as 'in character' or rejected as 'out of character' in that world. Thus ethos is the form of knowledge required in order to know how to behave in the world" (Klastrup and Tosca 2004, n.pag.). For pre-narrative characters or fig-ures, this is an entirely decontextualized ethos, no longer bound to any one sto-ryworld, but nevertheless conveying a generic "world-view." Conflicts, dissent, or "sensitive" subjects are often not envisioned within these frameworks, and neither is criticism of social power relations. The aesthetics of character or figure representations thus provide probabilities and patterns of how persons in specific environments (coded in ethnic, social, or gender-related norms) can behave suc-cessfully, of what is considered a violation of norms, or more generally: which distribution of social agency is to be expected.

9.3 Interacting with Mascots

Mascots make a fascinating case for the study of transmedia characters. In addi-tion to the two domains discussed in the previous sections – characters or figures placed within pictorial diegetic settings, as well as outside of such settings on pictures "looking directly" at audiences – mascots are often also employed in real-life performances with actors in full-body suits or costumes. One example can be found in Germany's Europa-Park, featuring 18 "countries" modeled after actual European counterparts on 950,000 m² (the following analysis was first published in Wilde 2021). After entering the main gate of the park, visitors imme-diately encounter a huge plastic sculpture of a mouse, welcoming approximately 5.6 million people annually to the venue. A giant book in front of the sculpture poses as a mixture of a fairy tale book and a diary, seemingly signed by the char-acter/figure behind it: "At the dawn of my life, July 12th 1975, I had a dream […]. My dream [was] to realize one Europe without frontiers […]. Leave reality behind and come into my world! Welcome to Europa-Park," signed: "Ed Euro-maus." This story is in fact not too far from reality, as Europa-Park was indeed opened on that day. Ed and Edda (Ed's female counterpart), however, emerged only from a public voting contest for the park's 40th anniversary (July 2015) in which a general internet audience decided against other options. The mascots

were created by MackMedia, a sub-company of Europa-Park's co-owner Jürgen Mack, proudly presenting Ed Euromaus on its website as a "transmedially
distributed" (MackMedia 2019, n.pag.) franchise that consists of nothing but the
mascot. Ed and Edda could be analyzed with many of the tools of a potential
Transmedia Character Studies presented in chapters 7 and 8. The earlier, original mascots of the park (1975–2015) were a couple of unnamed cartoon mice
simply referred to as "the Euromice." They were presented in iconic 2D drawings
with black outlines and flat colors. Ed and Edda could then be understood as a
kind of "reboot," generating a distinct node in a transmedia character network.
Their obvious resemblance to Mickey Mouse, the mascot of the park's biggest
competitor Disneyland Paris, could be seen as an intertextual reference through
an almost identical character type ("friendly, anthropomorphic cartoon mouse").
In some important respects, however, such mascots far transcend characters derived from narrative media.

Ed and Edda are playfully (re)presented to possess agency themselves, that is,
on the same ontological plane their audiences find themselves in. They interact
with visitors of the park on a daily basis, although it is clear to everyone that it
is actually a paid employee, or rather the company, that is "really" behind Ed
and Edda. The mice, however, address potential visitors even on the park's official website as if they were founders, owners, personnel, and janitors combined:
"Hello friends! I'm Ed Euromaus and I'd like to welcome you to the official website of Europa-Park! Europa-Park is my home, along with my friends […] we're
always excited to welcome you to the park"! (Europa-Park 2019, n.pag.). Once
inside the park, visitors can encounter Ed in various representational media at
almost every corner (much more often than Edda, it should be noted). He can not
only be seen on material presents and gifts that one can buy in the shops, ranging from clothes and office supplies to giant stuffed toys. One also encounters
Ed on all sorts of pictorial representations on instruction signs or entry points,
often dressed in local attires of the respective countries, or in thematic clothes
appropriate to the various thrill rides (compare this to the meta-narrative, or
transfictional aspect of figures discussed in the previous chapter). There are also
countless 3D models placed around the streets and squares in the park as if Ed
was standing right "then and there" where the representational material is located. In fact, it is more than likely that visitors will stop and pose for photographs "together with him," and not only children will interact with these figure
representations in playful ways (see Figure 9.2).

Another medium of representation is performances by actors in full-body suits
on stages and in parades. Ed is presented to have a regular schedule like any
other employee of the park: The website mentions that he has very busy days,
starting with visits to the Park Hotels at 7:45 am where he meets up with guests
for breakfast, circling the tables of the restaurants. When the park opens at 9:00
am, Ed will be at the entrance to wave and smile. From 11:00 am on, he then
parades through the park to take photographs with visitors. During all of this, the
"world" he is represented to exist in – in which Ed is *not* a mere mascot that every
employee with the respective suit can impersonate, but an actual celebrity – is

Figure 9.2 A theme park visitor interacting with a representation of Ed Euromaus, picture taken by Lukas R.A. Wilde in Europa-Park, Rust (Germany), September
2019, used with permission of the guest.

in no way different from the one visitors find themselves in. On the internet and
on social media platforms, there are official accounts as well as fan pages "by"
and about Ed and Edda (see euromaus_euromausi_travel) where people share
their stories about these encounters (It is also becoming increasingly common for
production companies to stage such fictitious accounts for characters of narrative media texts like BBC's *Sherlock*, too; see Gauthier 2019). Ed sometimes even
leaves the premises of the park for visits to local hospitals in Baden-Württemberg,
organized by Jürgen Mack's wife Mauritia who sometimes functions as a kind
of manager for their most famous spokesperson and ambassador (see Ortenau
Klinikum 2019). Even the statues in the streets of the park are not merely playful
forms of decoration; sometimes useful functions are attributed to them. Some
plastic versions of Ed, for instance, present him holding a meter that indicates
the minimum height of visitors allowed inside the thrill rides. People regularly
interact with these mascot representations (posing for pictures, shaking hands
with them) as if Ed was, in fact, providing a useful service here.

Ed and Edda are obviously not really present where their representational
material is located (full-body suits, pictures, toys). Neither, however, is that material identical to the fictional celebrities it represents. After all, there is only

one Ed and one Edda, not as many as there are employees that impersonate them. Yet in terms of make-believe, the visitors are intended and encouraged to imagine themselves as part of the same world that (one) Ed and (one) Edda inhabit. This world is, not accidentally, exactly the same as "our" world with one major difference: Within this domain, Ed and Edda are not merely mascots but actual intentional beings to which we attribute autonomy and personal agency. We, as visitors, exist there as well, as do all our performative interactions with Europa-Park's mascots. We hence have to account for various reflexive aspects which turn the local environment – and, possibly, even the spectators, ourselves – into part of what is to be imagined. Like pictorial "dummies" for construction workers on road signs, working characters/figures and mascots are intended to trigger narrative imaginations about themselves: If Ed and Edda look directly at audiences, it is not thought of as some kind of breach of the "fourth wall." The observers are meant to be a part of these "imaginary encounters" from the outset. The participants in such a performance – "regular" people as well as company representatives – are at the same time co-authors, props (representational material), and objects (represented entities) of representation. There is an interesting rhetoric behind the "imaginary agency" of such mascots, however. Regardless of how we wish to analyze mascots, a fact that should not be overlooked is that they are constructed, performed, and maintained in such a way as to mediate, filter, or mask the responsibility and agency of the actual institutional, corporate, or personal actors.

9.4 The Blackboxing and Masking of Distributed Agency

For Europa-Park, this "black-boxing" or "masking" has specific economic–political implications related (not only) to issues of sponsorship. The Silver Star rollercoaster, for instance, is co-financed and advertised by car manufacturer Mercedes Benz ("enlisting" Ed as a Mercedes race car driver in their advertisement for the ride). Somewhat more troubling is the Blue Fire Megacoaster, sponsored by the Russian energy company Gazprom. The company contributed a "Gazprom World of Experience" building at the entrance of the ride that advertises the company's endeavors. It also financed a huge conference center within the park that can be used by the company and other business enterprises. Gazprom also regularly publishes pictures of its employees posing together with Ed Euromaus on its website. The company was repeatedly criticized for its close ties to the Russian government. Other institutions sponsored by Gazprom – such as the German soccer club FC Schalke 04 – felt the need to publicly justify their involvement with the gas manufacturer several times even before the spring of 2022. After Russia started its war campaign against Ukraine, Europa-Park finally announced it would end its cooperation with Gazprom (see Spiegel 2022). Gazprom's activities in Europa-Park before 2022 were not limited to financial support and the subsequent possibilities to advertise the company on-site. Most of the rides also construct immersive, representational spaces. The queues are thus turned into imaginary experiences as well. If we would like to visit the wooden Wodam Timbercoaster, for instance, the waiting line leads through a recreation of Nordic mythology (from Midgard to Asgard) by means of plastic models, moving projections, special effects (fire, fog, spray water), haptic interactions, and even a soundtrack. The fact that the representational aspects of even such theme park rides can become a "site" of political and ideological battles has been demonstrated by the controversies and petitions surrounding the renaming and redesign of Disney's log flume rollercoaster "Splash Mountain" (versions of it exist in Disneyland Anaheim, Florida, and Tokyo). It was based on the 1946 film *Song of the South* (directed by Harve Foster and Wilfred Jackson), a particularly notorious example not only of troubling portrayals of Black people, the reinforcement of racist stereotypes, and a dangerously glorified picture of slavery but also of White appropriation of Black folk stories (see Sperb 2012). These aspects might seem far removed from a theme park ride, but many critics have proven that it is far from innocent, especially in its use of uncredited printed quotes taken from the film's Black character Uncle Remus, as well as due to its uses of songs and queue music based on openly racist minstrel shows (see Bellissimo and McDermott 2022). Despite many protests within reactionary Disney fandom, the ride is now planned to reopen in 2024 as "Tiana's Bayou Adventure," based on the 2009 animated film *The Princess and the Frog* (directed by John Musker and Ron Clements),

In the case of Europe-Park's Blue Fire Megacoaster, the design of the ride and the waiting lines are an imaginary space dedicated entirely to the "wondrous adventure" of natural gas production. Created by the international company P&P Projects and built by one of the Mack brothers' sub-firms, MACK Rides, it advertises the "romantic" period of early gas producers, educating its visitors about their importance. The ride's tagline is "Discover Pure Energy." Although the fictionalized gas producer inviting to its "labs" and "warehouse facilities" is labeled "International Institute for Energy Research," it seems hardly a coincidence that the imaginary experience could be seen as nothing but an advertisement for Gazprom once again. All the written signage within the Blue Fire Megacoaster site presenting information on the ride (and how to use it), however, is signed by "Ed Euromaus" who appears as the sole "fictional actant" behind – or at least put in charge by – the entangled relations between all the actually responsible human and corporate entities: Europa-Park, MackMedia and MACK Rides, Roland, Jürgen, and Mauritia Mack, P&P Projects, Gazprom, and maybe even the Russian government. Mascots such as Ed and Edda facilitate a rhetorical redistribution of agency, creating "virtual actants" which, in turn, mask the actual human and corporate actants and their surrounding materialities.

The same could be said for many "minimal characters" implemented through Intelligent Virtual Assistants (IVAs) such as Siri, Alexa, and other interfaces that are given a proper name and a voice to resemble interaction with actual human beings (see Blom 2022). What users are actually interacting with, of course, is an entangled network of hardware, software, global telecommunication structures, and algorithms employed for commercial reasons. Adding a proper name, a human voice, or even an anthropomorphic picture to these "black boxes" is not merely a surface feature. On the contrary, it is a central rhetoric to generate an imaginary "unity" that hides its complexity behind the appearance of personalized agency. Even though IVAs are far removed from prototypical narrative characters, they nevertheless incorporate similar stereotypes as other medial character representations. As Yolande Strengers and Jenny Kennedy (2020) have illustrated, old-fashioned gender "ideals" of the home, its role for women and a "good wife," are embedded in today's smart home technologies. Strenger and Kennedy trace how the character of Rosie the Robot, a protagonist from the 1960s cartoon series *The Jetsons* (Hanna and Barbera 1962–1963) associated with a stereotypical dutiful and submissive 1950s housewife, served as inspiration for actual, consumer-ready robots of today. Many new ("smart") devices such as robot vacuums, smart laundry machines, and all manners of kitchen appliances are intended to lessen what is traditionally thought of as work for women:

> While gendering technology has already existed, technologies that have humanlike personalities, and the ability to speak back and respond to our needs, [are] unique to the present. If we don't act swiftly and boldly, we may set ourselves up for a feminized future that takes society back to the "good old days" when women's place was to act in the service of all others.
>
> (Strengers and Kennedy 2020, 228)

The relation between characters and interface design through new technology is perfectly reflected in the 2013 Sci-Fi film *Her* (Jonze) in which Theodore Twombly (played by Joaquin Phoenix) falls in love with his AI operating system SAMANTHA (voiced by Scarlett Johansson). Within the film's storyworld, the AI is in fact represented as a disembodied character developing genuine feelings, emotions, and certainly personal agency for her actions. Another example of recent AI characters is Joi (portrayed by Ana de Armas) in *Blade Runner 2049* (Villeneuve 2017), a purely holographic AI girlfriend that exhibits true affection for her companion K (himself a kind of robot, played by Ryan Gosling), or Ada, a female android capable of intelligent human interaction, in the graphic novel *Alex + Ada* (Luna and Vaughn 2013–2015). While we can approach narrative representations of SAMANTHA, Joi, or Ada with all the analytical tools presented within this volume, a potential Transmedia Character Studies should also highlight a clear distinction of fictional characters from "interface figures" implemented in actual IVAs, despite or even *because* tech companies employ some of the same techniques as film directors or comic book authors: the inclusion of attractive, often highly gendered voices and appearances, for instance. As tech users, we are to overlook the actual algorithms, technologies, and economic structures behind these devices in order to imagine – just like with mascots – a human-like person on the other side of the screen that we are communicating with directly.

The development of personalized "interface characters/figures" through IVAs is certainly just in its infancy. Not only artificial intelligence is developing rapidly, but also new forms of hardware such as love dolls and sex robots that likewise impersonate people (often female) on a haptic and material level (see Schiller and McMahon 2019). Tech companies are also employing sophisticated semiotic strategies to enhance our "make-believe" attitude toward their products. The Japanese company Vinclu, for instance, released the personal assistant Azuma Hikari for their smart device Gatebox in 2018 (see Lamerichs 2019). In contrast to Siri or Alexa, whose outer appearance can only be constructed within the individual imagination, Azuma Hikari is accompanied by official, anime-inspired artworks of her body, her face, and an iconic outfit. What is more, the interface was marketed as a "virtual wife" (*waifu*) that users can even "marry" in a frame of play by submitting a registration form on the official website. "Interestingly," fan studies scholar Nicolle Lamerichs observed,

> not only are intimacy and affect emphasized by Gatebox, but also the idea that the character is not one entity, but multiple [...]. Because she is a dimension-travelling entity, not unlike the famous Doctor in *Doctor Who*, she can exist in multiple places at the same time and be in countless individual emotional relationships with all her users and fans.
>
> (2019, 107)

Virtual reality, artificial intelligence, and other new forms of technology are developing character representations in entirely new directions, as Lamerichs and Blom have been tracing for many years. Characters/figures can "learn" facts about their audiences from databases and algorithms, and their "stories" can be crowdsourced and multiplied. The representational correspondence between their different versions – and the resulting contradictions – can then be naturalized or narrativized once again by intellectual property rights holders, as with the claim that Azuma Hikari is a "dimension-traveling entity" (explaining the contradictions between "your" version and "mine"). In theory, this is nothing new, as we have discussed in chapter 6 on video games already. Kai Mikkonen likewise notes that

> [V]ideo game characters and AI-driven robots, androids, and toys, can similarly adapt to user decisions and player performance, and this interaction may subsequently result in considerable differences in their behavior and personality for the same game, toy, or device. Like video game avatars, Hikari is at once a fictional and ludic object with specific functions.
>
> (Mikkonen 2022, 178)

There are many other ways in which game studies (see chapter 6) might help us to understand the functions of pre-narrative characters or figures as well. For instance, character/figure representations are also employed as "stand-ins" for celebrities or bands in recent decades, just like an avatar in video games would serve as a representation of (or a "digital mask" for) the actual player. One might think of the "virtual" music group Gorillaz (formed in 1998), represented by drawn alter egos of the actual music producers Damon Albarn and Jamie Hewlett:

> In 2005, the British rock band "Gorillaz" played a concert at the MTV Europe Music Awards in Lisbon. To a viewer at the back of the big hall, their performance might, due to the distance, have seemed at first sight like any other rock show: the band members sang or played their instruments in front of the large audience, displaying some of the inevitable rock poses and walking around the stage or interacting with their fans. However, Gorillaz is a virtual band, made up of cartoon characters. They do not exist in a physical form. This concert thus marked a significant point both in music history and in the history of visual media: it is said to be the "world's first 3D hologram performance".
>
> (Hofer 2011, 232)

In German entries on Wikipedia, the characters/figures are identified as a "comic book band" or a band of "comic book characters" (see Wikipedia, "Gorillaz"), even though authoritative comics on or about the Gorillaz do not even exist. The fictional protagonists can be seen mainly on artworks (such as CD covers), in animated music video clips or projections during live concerts. They all feature specific cartoon/comics aesthetics connected to a generic ethos of playfulness, artificiality, and inconsequentiality (see chapter 5) – Hewlett is also known as co-creator of the comic book series *Tank Girl* (Martin and Hewlett 2002 [1988]).

Since 2017, the South Korean music group BTS has taken this to the next level. Together with the Line Friends Corporation which has developed a range of pre-narrative figures like Brown, a bear, or Cony, a white bunny, for digital stickers of their messenger app, the seven-member music group created a complete "avatar ensemble" of the fictionalized cartoon group "BT21." Each of the seven avatars is based on a simple, iconic design, allegedly created by the represented band members themselves (an eighth fictional member, the rocket-shaped robot VAN, is intended to collectively represent the band's fans and audiences). Their traits can often be summarized in a few keywords, and they are supplied with short, fictional backstories and settings (in their YouTube series "BT21 Universe," for instance) that belong to the figures, not the actual BTS band members. Still, even as the fictionalized "BT21" figures are explicitly gender-neutral in contrast to BTS, the mutual relationship between both groups is continuously foregrounded. The figures were not only personally created after hand drawings of each music artist, but they are also intended to "hold each [actual] member's personality and soul" (BT21 2017, n.pag.). The "BT21" member Koya, for example, is defined by their traits of "multi-talented" and "brilliant" (BT21, "About," n.pag.), referring to the BTS member Namjoon, who is known to possess an IQ of 148. Another way to think about such "cartoon avatars," perhaps, is to consider them as even more elaborate versions of star personas (see chapter 4), further disentangled even from the bodies of the actual band members into completely controlled (and strongly fictionalized) pre-narrative figures, "masking" even the appearances of the stars. While it is clear that such new and emerging character/figure phenomena cannot be sufficiently analyzed from the perspective of narrative texts alone, character theories derived from video games might not be the only possible approach to their conceptualization. From the perspective of a potential Transmedia Character Studies, pre-narrative and meta-narrative mascots, "working characters/figures," or emoji and sticker figures could provide an equally interesting starting point to investigate and compare the affordances of private make-believe and imagination-based appropriation. A complimentary, certainly more established approach (at least within narratology, literature and film studies) would be to turn to existing theories of the gradual fictionalization of actually existing people which has been an important topic of text analysis for many decades. This is going to be the focus of the following, final chapter.

10 Fictionalized and Non-Fictional Characters

In the previous chapter, we have looked at fictional characters (or pre-narrative figures) in actual, "real-world" contexts, or more precisely: character/figure representations that facilitate a kind of reflexivity intended to include the actual context as well as audiences into "what is to be imagined." The present chapter about a potential Transmedia Character Studies is turning this perspective around, discussing the many instances in which actual people (historical figures, politicians, celebrities, and so on) appear as fictionalized protagonists in films, TV shows, or comic books. The terms "fiction" and "fictional" have been used rather intuitively throughout this volume so far, referring to protagonists who "do not really exist," or more precisely: they exist only as communicative constructs, represented by media texts and artifacts, as well as within the individual imagination, and finally in discussions and discourses surrounding and co-constructing a public, intersubjective form of imagination. While the English language offers a range of adjectives denoting that a protagonist has been "made up" for narrative or artistic purposes, the terms "fictional," "fictive," and "fictitious" are often used synonymously and not at all consistently throughout literature (see Rajewsky 2020). One useful terminological suggestion proposed by literary scholar Frank Zipfel (2014) and many others would be to apply "fictive" to represented events, characters, or entities that are invented (and thus possess "fictiveness"), while reserving "fictional" for media texts themselves (novels, films, comic books, video games, and so on). *Fictional* artifacts then highlight that they do not make an overall "truth claim" to a faithful representation of unmediated reality, usually by way of labels outside the narrative text itself (i.e., in the paratext). A book, for instance, can signpost its fictionality through the label "a novel," while non-fictional films, by contrast, are often advertised the other way around as "documentaries." We have been addressing transmedia characters as "fictional" up to this point; as a technical term, it would be more appropriate to speak of *fictive* characters instead, as these are usually thought of as entities represented within a work or a storyworld. However, since transmedia characters can appear across texts and storyworlds – as a transmedia character network or as a meta-narrative figure – it still makes sense to speak of *fictional characters* throughout (such as "the Batman") when their appearance denotes the overall fictionality of all stories they appear in. In the present chapter, we then suggest using "fictive" in a quite narrow sense

DOI: 10.4324/9781003298793-15

for materially non-existing, protagonists of media texts (as well as for materially non-existing objects, places, or events), while "fictional" will be reserved for the texts and artifacts themselves.

We will see, however, that even these basic distinctions can become quite complicated for fictionalized protagonists based on actual persons "converted into fiction" (Ronen 1994, 76). Importantly, an untruthful account – labeled as non-fictional but turning out to be false, whether intentionally, out of neglect, or because of "honest mistakes" – is not the same as a fiction and will never quite become one (see Martínez and Scheffel 2003; Fludernik and Packard 2021). If we, as audiences, follow the adventures of Borat, knowing that this is a fictive character played by Sacha Baron Cohen, we are aware of the character's fictiveness (see MacLeod 2011). "Borat Sagdiyev" is a reporter from Kazakhstan who left his wife Oksana in order to produce a documentary about "the US and A," the "Greatest Country in the World." This fictional protagonist is mainly produced by its author Cohen who has very few biographical details in common with his creation. Borat's fictive journeys are intended to reveal many cultural stereotypes and misconceptions about American culture and society as well as about the imagined "Kazakhstan" his character comes from. The many people Cohen interacts with as Borat, however, often have no reason to assume that they are part of a hoax. To them, Cohen's performance will never be a fiction but a deliberate deception (indeed subject to many lawsuits), just as their documented personalities are not at all fictive to the audiences. The overall film *Borat: Cultural Learnings of America for Make Benefit Glorious Nation of Kazakhstan* (Charles 2006) is as much a documentary about Cohen's elaborate ploy as it is a fictional character representation of the fictive protagonist Borat (operating in a "fictional bubble more than a distinct fictional universe," MacLeod 2011, 115) for the knowing audience. If "fooled" politicians (such as Alan Keyes and Bob Barr) were revealed to be actors or participants in this game (just like Cohen) as well, merely playing their ignorance about the character/actor distinction, the audience would certainly likewise be disappointed.

10.1 Minimal Departure and Counterfactional Histories

It is important to note at the outset that even entirely fictional characters – like James Bond, Lara Croft, or Wonder Woman – can hardly be said to exist in a *storyworld* that is entirely "non-existent" or fictive. After all, the planet Earth as well as real cities like New York serving as the backdrop for many stories of fictive characters is clearly part of "our" world. This is, in fact, a necessary consequence of one of the first rules of imagination we have discussed, the principle of minimal departure. All elements of our regular world knowledge are usually "imported" into characters' worlds and stories if not explicitly "outruled" or "overwritten" by the texts themselves. Fictiveness is thus always a *gradual* aspect of any represented world, while fictionality is often seen as *categorical*. On a global textual level, a story is either presented as invented or truthful. The *Broken Earth* book series (e.g., Jemisin 2015), the cartoon show *Avatar: The Last Airbender* (DiMartino et al. 2005–2008), the manga *One Piece* (Oda 1997–present), or the TV show *The Witcher* (Hissrich 2019–present), all take place in completely fictive worlds (or even entirely fictive universes, since all their locations are not even necessarily within our solar system). Basically, all respective entities are invented for the purposes of the stories they appear in. The continents, the people inhabiting them, and their entire histories seem to have no relation to "our" world at all. Minimal departure, however, is still a necessary mechanism for many aspects of narrative meaning-making, as we presuppose that *Avatar*'s four nations, for instance, are still populated by humans with more or less the same attributes as protagonists in more "realistic" settings (they age, they can die, they have internal organs). We also have no reason to assume that gravity works differently in these worlds (at least until magic is introduced). What is "imported" in these cases are thus generals (humans, the laws of physics, "commonsensical" moral values, and so on), not specifics. Other fantastic storyworlds at least imply some relation to "our" world and its history. The 2008–2010 *Hunger Games* books (e.g., Collins 2008) and films (e.g., Ross 2012) are set in a North America which seems to have deviated from our timeline at some point in the near future; the 1965–1985 *Dune* Sci-Fi novels (e.g., Herbert 2010) and films (e.g., the 2021 reboot by Denis Villeneuve) repeatedly mention a planet called "Terra" and reference prominent historical figures, nations, and events (although the latter are set in a far more distant future of about 20,000 years, in contrast to *Hunger Games*' three centuries). *The Lord of the Rings*' Middle-Earth was intended to be a kind of backstory to "our" world by writer Tolkien, set in an imaginary period of the Earth's past with the end of the "Third Age" about 6,000 years ago when magic was about to leave our world permanently. The *Battlestar Galactica* remake show (Moore and Eick 2004–2009) first appears to be set far in the future, but in the show's conclusion it turns out to be Earth's (fictional) prehistoric backstory. Often, this implied relationship amounts to little, however. *Star Wars* famously opens with the words "A long time ago in a galaxy far, far away...," hinting at *some* spatio-temporal relation to contemporary Earth that ends up never being specified. In other Sci-Fi works like the many *Star Trek* shows and films, the *Terminator* franchise, or the *Years and Years* TV show (Davies et al. 2019), a truly *continuous* historical relation to our actual history is of far greater importance, as is the exact trajectory of how its fictive people got from "now to then." A typology of fictional stories, worlds, and characters could then be charted in terms of *accessibility relations* (the relative "distance" or accessibility of the fictive from the perspective of the real) by addressing both in terms of aligned vs. deviating narrative events (see Ryan 1991a). Are only individual entities (such as characters) added to a world that otherwise claims to be set in the same universe with the same history? Or are the locations – and thereby the characters – more "distant," so that parts or all of their worlds' histories are notably altered?

In some cases, these "deviations" are precisely marked. *The Man in the High Castle* (Spotnitz et al. 2015–2019), a show loosely based on a 1962 novel of the same name by Philip K. Dick (1992), presents a counterfactual history in which

Nazi Germany and the Japanese Empire have won the Second World War and conquered North America. There is no reason to believe that, in this "parallel universe," the even more distant past – the American Civil War, let us say – should not be exactly the same as presented in our history books. The show *Bridgerton* (Van Dusen et al. 2020–present) reimagines 19th-century London in an alternate universe that "deviated" from ours when a White king fell in love with a Black woman (Queen Charlotte) and ended slavery much earlier than in reality. According to this particular storyworld, Queen Charlotte's ascension also led to racial integration throughout society (so that the show conveniently never has to address racism directly, presenting few openly racist characters). In Brian K. Vaughan's and Tony Harris' comic book series *Ex Machina* (2004–2010), the fictive addition of one single person with superpowers (protagonist Mitchell Hundred, the "Great Machine") interfered with the actual events of 9/11, as Hundred prevented the destruction of the second Twin Tower (but not of the first one). In many cases, however, these "points of deviation" are not clearly marked. Shows, films, or novels featuring a fictive president of the United States – such as Bill Pullman as President Thomas J. Whitmore in the film *Independence Day: Resurgence* (Emmerich 2016) or Michel Gill as President Garrett Walker in the show *House of Cards* (Fincher et al. 2013–2018) – can be expected to retain a John F. Kennedy as a *former* president. Sometime in between his assassination and the election of his most recent successors, many fictive characters must have entered the storyworld, replacing our actual historical figures. Often, then, there is a functional zone of indeterminacy within any storyworld between where minimal departure still applies and where it does not. The same holds true for places and locations: While most adventures of Marvel superheroes are set in (a) New York City – a clearly fictionalized New York which features the "Stark Tower" prominently in its skyline – DC's heroes protect entirely fictive cities such as Gotham City or Metropolis. Where *exactly* these are meant to be located within the real geography of the United States remains programmatically open.

Characters are especially interesting in that regard where celebrities are concerned. DC Comics has often used entirely fictive presidents of the United States (Lex Luthor held the office once in the "President Lex Luthor" comic book storyline, 2000–2001), while Marvel comics frequently prefers to use real (fictionalized) ones or to hide the identity of the respective office holder by showing them from behind or shrouded in shadows (see CBR Staff 2017). They thus allow audiences to imagine actual politicians such as George W. Bush to be part of the story without making this explicit. Spider-Man did meet "Barack Obama" (obviously a fictionalized version) in a detached, special story ("Spidey Meets the President!," a backup feature in *The Amazing Spider-Man*, Vol. 1: #583, Waid and Kitson 2009), but it should have no effect on further continuity. The same holds true for the famous black issue #36 of *Spider-Man*, Vol. 2 by J. Michael Straczynski and John Romita Jr. (2001), which takes place directly after 9/11 and presents Marvel's heroes and some villains supporting firemen and police officers in the cleanup of the destroyed World Trade Center. The issue is clearly marked on page one as an "interruption" of the regular continuity (see Leaver 2012), thus relegating it to a kind of distinct sub-storyworld that has no strong connections to the later canon.

The respective use of fictiveness, as a form of *gradual* fictionalization, can thus be subject to media and genre traditions, as well as to properties of individual works or franchises. Media texts can then not only be analyzed with regard to which elements are fictive and which are imported through minimal departure but also with respect to how clearly (nor not) deviations are marked, traced, or narratively justified through counterfactual histories. The more "global" the adventures of any given protagonist are (or become), the clearer deviations will be highlighted. Entirely ordinary "slice-of-life stories" about high school romances or daily struggles such as the comic book *Laura Dean Keeps Breaking Up with Me* (Tamaki 2019), the film series *To All the Boys I've Loved Before* (Johnson 2018; Filmognari 2020; 2021), or the film *Tick, Tick … Boom!* (Miranda 2021) usually give no reason to assume that the storyworld (entailing its complete history) has been altered for specific purposes – a question that usually does not even come up until highlighted as in a fantasy or Sci-Fi story. *Shōnen* manga and anime series like *One Piece* (Oda 1997–present), *Made in Abyss* (Tsukushi 2021–present), or *One-Punch Man* (ONE and Murata 2012–present), by contrast, are regularly set within entirely fictive storyworlds. *Demon Slayer* (Gotouge 2016–2020) yet again provides one of many examples for a strongly fictionalized historical era, the Japanese taishō period from 1912 to 1926. Other historical fictions such as the *Babylon Berlin* TV show (Arndt et al. 2017–present), set in Weimar Republic Berlin, or the manga (Kōno 2007–2009) and anime (Katabuchi 2016) *In this Corner of the World*, set in 1930–1940 Hiroshima and Kure, make strong claims that *only* the characters and their specific adventures are fictive, while the setting remains entirely unmodified (i.e., "authentic"). It thus makes sense to distinguish between *character and event authenticity* on the one hand (the events depicted actually took place in reality) versus *type authenticity* on the other (the characters and their stories are fictive, but their traits are representative of the period, social positions, and regions depicted, see Pandel 2006).

If Barack Obama exists, however, while *The Amazing Spider-Man* #583 cover that shows him alongside the titular protagonist is fictional, what does this mean for the "Obama" we encounter within the comic? How about John F. Kennedy shaking hands with the fictive Forrest Gump through special effects? How do we understand fictionalized versions of actually existing people? One way to answer this question would be to not acknowledge it as a problem at all: After all, any author or artist can give one of his fictive creations a name (or iconography) referring to any real person. As long as the work as a whole is clearly recognizable as fiction, no confusion should arise among the audiences as to the fictive status of such protagonists. This "inclusion" of people from the real world into fiction can serve numerous functions: On the one hand, our entire background and world knowledge about the actual person can be "imported" for the character via minimal departure. When we meet a "George W. Bush" in the *Captain America Annual* #2001 (Jurgens et al. 2001), discussing the "Superhuman Registration Act" with Tony Stark and others, readers can assume that this fictionalized character likewise declared a "War on Terror" which saw the United States Army invade Iraq like in our world. Fictionalizing actual people can thus be a rather efficient way to communicate implied narrative information. On the other hand, it should be clear that the corresponding fictionalized character, as an intersubjective communicative construct, can often be understood as a *commentary* on the real person with whom they share a name or likeness, rather than only a faithful depiction of their actual behavior. This is especially evident for political cartoons showing real-life politicians in situations that, taken literally, are surely not meant to have happened, but they serve as commentary on ones that did occur (see Declercq 2019). As Janis L. Edwards noted in a monograph about political cartoons commenting on the 1988 US-presidential campaigns, real situations and events are presented "as something that they are not in order to arrive at a new definition of what they are" (1997, 128; see El Refaie 2009, 175). Of course, such commentary by way of fictionalization has often been met with legal action from those who considered themselves unjustly depicted. Hence, many fictional media texts now include a disclaimer denying any intended relation between fictive characters and real-life persons, even (or perhaps especially) if parallels between the two are obviously present (see Davis 1988).

10.2 The Napoleon Problem: A Typology of Fictionalizations

Fictionalizations of existing people have been discussed extensively in literary studies, philosophy, and narratology. They are epitomized by the "Napoleon problem" that poses many complex ontological questions of cross-identification and possible worlds within theories of fictionality (see Crittenden 1991, 129–157; Ronen 1994, 48–61; Zipfel 2001, 90–103). Napoleon really existed, yet protagonists bearing his name appear in historical fictions such as Tolstoy's 1869 novel *War and Peace* (2020), the Russian film and TV mini-series *Vasilisa* (Sivers 2014), or alternate reality comic books like Bryan Talbot's *Grandville* (2009–2017). Napoleon is not only "the most portrayed/referenced real life person to be captured on film" (IMDB 2018, n.pag.), "he" can also be included in any artwork or political cartoon with incredible ease by evoking a commonly recognizable iconography (perhaps as easily as by including the famous hand-in-waistcoat gesture owed to several historical portraits made by Napoleon's contemporary artist, Jacques-Louis David). If the worlds and situations represented by these works and media texts are fictive, however, how can a non-fictive protagonist appear within them? Thomas G. Pavel (1986; see also Parsons 1980) distinguished between three different relations that objects and entities within fictional narratives can have toward unmediated reality. If we apply this to characters, these are the following: *Natively fictive characters* "born" entirely within fiction. This applies to most transmedia characters discussed in the present volume up to this point. However, it is important to note that this does not mean that these characters cannot still exemplify traits shared by actual people (social representation) or even "symbolize" real people in the thematic dimension. Yet, in the mimetic dimension, a natively fictional character exists only within the storyworld that a text generates (or that many texts generate, if they "coalesce" into a glocal, transmedia character, see chapter 7).

Immigrant characters, by contrast, are "migrated," metaphorically speaking, from the real world into fiction without any modifications. What actually happens, of course, is that authors create fictive protagonists which are nonetheless "protected" from any fictional modifications, so that minimal departure applies to all their traits and biographical details. Interestingly, this means that they cannot interact with natively fictive characters in any way, as this would contradict our real-world knowledge about them. Thus, immigrant characters are often only observed or discussed "from afar" by natively fictive characters, such as in Emil Ferris' graphic novel *My Favourite Thing is Monsters* (2017), in which two characters in 1968 Chicago watch a TV broadcast of (a) Martin Luther King Jr.'s "I Have a Dream" speech while discussing his recent death. Here, the real Martin Luther King has "moved into" the fictional text as a fictive version without any alterations to his biography. By contrast, the Barack Obama shaking hands with Spider-Man cannot quite be a true immigrant in that sense, as this encounter contradicts reality in which no such superhero exists. In cases of overt fictionalization, Pavel's third category applies: *surrogate characters*, or "fictional [or, rather, fictive] counterparts of real objects in those fictional texts that substantially modify their descriptions" (Pavel 1986, 29). We find such a Napoleon in the strongly fictionalized account of *Grandville*, for example, where France has won the Napoleonic Wars and invaded Britain, aside from the fact that Talbot's world features steam-powered road vehicles and "automaton" robots – and that this "Napoleon" is actually an anthropomorphic animal.

In contrast to such blatantly fictionalized examples, a more subtle "surrogate Obama" can be found in the show *Mr. Robot* (Esmail et al. 2015–present). In the second season's opening, the then-president can actually be seen and heard (in "real life" pictures and sound) on an intradiegetic TV broadcast where he accuses the fictive organization "F Society" of having engaged in some cyberattack. In reality, that footage was created through digital visual effects and lip manipulation, since the actual former president did not participate in the production of the show. Even if he did, however, play-acting his fictionalized counterpart like the actual Queen Elizabeth, who participated in the production of the "James Bond and the Queen London 2012 Performance" where her surrogate character meets James Bond and parachutes out of an airplane, the representation would still fall in the exact same category of surrogate character. Both examples would merely be using different medial means of representation, digital effects vs. actual people fictionalizing themselves. The *character* Obama is depicted as believing in the existence of "F Society," after all, something that the "real" Obama most certainly does not. His counterpart must therefore be a modified, fictive surrogate of the real person, no matter how the media text was actually created. The characters "Seth Rogen" and "Jay Baruchel" in the film *This is the End* (Rogen and Goldberg 2013) are dragged into the biblical apocalypse within their story. They are clearly not the actual Rogen and Baruchel, even though the actors embodied their own fictional surrogates. In the Kennedy and Forrest Gump case, the modifications are more subtle, almost unrecognizable. The handshake could hardly have been a remarkable event to the former president, he would probably not even remember the encounter a week later. The rest of his life, therefore, can be expected to remain unmodified (and he can therefore largely be considered an otherwise immigrant character).

Importantly, minimal departure – the relationship between fact and fiction – always works *asymmetrically*. Stephan Packard (2019) illustrates this with respect to a fictional children's book about a young George Washington who cut down his father's cherry tree but did not try to avoid punishment by lying about it. If we are aware of the fact that the real George Washington crossed the Delaware river on December 25, 1776, in a moment of strategic and political importance to the American Revolutionary War, then we would be likely to assume that the "surrogate" child protagonist will eventually grow up to cross the Delaware on that very day, too, even if it is not mentioned in the children's book. We can then measure some of his character traits (exhibited by the fictionalized surrogate character, such as honesty and truthfulness), against his later actions (which also happened in reality). Fiction thus serves as a means to comment on, explain, and make sense of reality. The opposite would not be the case, however: If we go on to read about Washington's deeds in a historiographical account, we would *not* assume that the same person had already excelled in his truthfulness as a boy, even though we have read that story before. Narrative information is thus always imported in one direction only, while everything we identify as fictionalization remains contained to the storyworld that a specific text generates.

These categoric distinctions, however, are always drawn from the perspective of an audience member already *knowing* whether a specific "narrated fact" is fictive or not – whether a given narrative representation constitutes a deviation from unmediated reality, or not. In many or most cases, however, our knowledge about this reality is entirely based on media texts as well, and many things will remain unknown to us. Often, we have to rely on educated guesses and intuitions as to whether a specific narrative event entailing a surrogate character is fictionalized or not if we are not to continuously fact check through Wikipedia everything we read or watch. This is why conventions, rules of the imagination, are once again of special importance to guide our understanding of the fictional/non-fictional distinction. Packard hence coined the term *inventability* (see 2018) to denote the specific kind of knowledge shared between creators and audiences about the often implicit, sometimes explicit, negotiations of the borders of fictionality and factuality. Some aspects of any given story will always appear more "inventable" than others (see Jung and Wilde 2021). The *TV Tropes* entry "Aluminum Christmas Trees," for instance, documents countless elements of fictional texts that audiences are likely to consider fictive, even though they actually existed in real life. The trope's name is derived from the 1965 *Peanuts* TV special *A Charlie Brown Christmas* (Melendez), in which Lucy instructs Charlie Brown to buy an aluminum Christmas tree painted pink. What might seem like a bizarre element of the cartoon storyworld was actually a popular item in the United States from 1958 until about the mid-1960s, and you can still buy them today.

Often, the assumed inventability of characters, places, or events will also be subject to their respective salience in (other) media texts. In the Netflix show *The Crown* (Morgan et al. 2016–present) about Queen Elizabeth, for instance, the abdication speech of King Edward VIII. (played by Alex Jennings) on public radio can be expected to follow the actual, historical one word-by-word (although with some abridgments), while the design of the room he broadcasts the speech in and his private dialogue leading up to the broadcast can be fictionalized without any expectations to the contrary. In fact, the exact same speech can be heard in the film *The King's Speech* (Hooper 2010, where another version of King Edward VIII. is played by Guy Pearce), while many other details differ significantly. Even before audiences decide to "fact check," they probably attribute a much higher inventability to the broadcasting room's interior design than to the content of the speech, simply because the actual facts concerning the latter are easily publicly available while they would be much harder to evaluate for the former.

The conventions of inventability will also be different for various media forms and genres. Disney artist Don Rosa, for instance, did not only use the fictive Duckburg as a setting for his stories about Donald, Scrooge, and the nephews. Building on his predecessor Carl Barks, he also sent the Ducks on many treasure hunts around the world involving actual historical facts and real places which were accurately researched as a "backdrop" to his stories. Scrooge accordingly has met such personalities as Wyatt Earp, Theodore Roosevelt, and P.T. Barnum in his youth (Rosa 1992–1994), at least in the form of strongly fictionalized surrogate characters with dog noses. Readers familiar with Rosa's comics and his creative process, however, will know that many or most historical facts presented are well-researched and can be trusted to deviate from history only in specific instances (mostly in historical figures' encounters with young Scrooge). Often in comics, the degree of cartoonization can already hint at the degree of fictionalization or the fictivity of any given entity: Rosa's backgrounds are often presented in almost naturalistic detail drawn from actual photographs in correct perspectives – such as the building of the Finnish Literature Society, which really exists in Helsinki (shown in the story "The Quest for Kalevala," Rosa 2004). By contrast, the museum's director is presented as a strongly cartoonized dog, indicating that he is not supposed to serve as a stand-in for the institution's actual director but as an entirely (natively) fictive protagonist (see Packard 2017a). The negotiation of inventability – what readers *assume* the artist wants to mark as fictionalized, and, more importantly, to what degree and in which respect – can hence become exceedingly complicated. It nevertheless remains one of the most important tasks of a potential Transmedia Character Studies focusing on fictionalized protagonists to reconstruct which *claims* to reality a text makes by situating the respective cues within the specific traditions of its media form and genre. In the following section, we are going to take a closer look at the many representations of Donald Trump within recent media texts in a culture utterly obsessed with the 45th president of the United States after his unexpected election win in 2016.

10.3 Fiction, Fact, Fictionalization, and the Problem of Inventability

Even *natively fictive characters* can be used as a commentary on real-life politicians such as Donald Trump. Frank Miller's and Rafael Grampá's comic book *Dark Knight Returns: The Golden Child* (2020), for instance, shows the supervillains Joker and Darkseid teaming up to install a corrupt politician as mayor of Gotham City. Their "puppet" is never identified by name, but he bears an undeniable likeness to Donald Trump and even displays his typical speech patterns ("It's going to be beautiful! You're gonna love it! … I'm talking streets so safe you can let your kids go play and not even think about 'em!", Miller and Grampá 2020, 38). The mayor is employed by the villains to generate a media spectacle, occupying the citizens of Gotham with protests in favor of and opposition against him while they themselves strive to plunge the world into chaos. The – not entirely subtle – commentary Miller and Grampá seem to make is that contemporary media are so obsessed with Trump (and the ratings his screen presence promises) that they do not even consider the damage they are doing by fixating on his every word. No additional aspects of Donald Trump and his biography are transferred or, in fact, necessary to bring this point across. The mayor then remains a natively fictive character in all respects.

By contrast, documentary films such as *Fahrenheit 11/9* by Michael Moore (2018) claim to comment directly on Donald Trump without any fictionalizations. Moore compares the Trump campaign and the 2016 election with Adolf Hitler's rise to power. In his closing plea, the director leaves no doubt that he considers the danger represented by the then-president is real and existential: "We'd comfort ourselves that the Constitution would save us, that elections would save us; the special prosecutor would save us; impeachment would save us." Everything that the film presents as factual about Trump must therefore conform to all other medial representations we accept as non-fictional. While the concluding part of this chapter will reflect more about such non-fictional media texts, we can already point to the fact that there is a spectrum of gradually fictionalized Trump appearances across media between these two extremes – natively fictional characters merely symbolizing Trump on the one hand and non-fictional representations held accountable for their complete faithfulness to reality on the other.

First, let us consider *Our Cartoon President* (Colbert et al. 2018–2020), a satirical animated TV show based on Stephen Colbert's recurring sketches in *The Late Show with Stephen Colbert* (Colbert et al. 2015–present). The series stands in the tradition of workplace comedy shows or animated sitcoms, featuring cartoon versions of Donald Trump's family, his administration, and members of Congress going about their daily routines. Each episode references (actual) political events, such as the 2020 Democratic Primaries, in a strongly fictionalized manner for satirical comedy. The term "Cartoon President" in the title refers not only to the medial aesthetics of the show – Donald Trump is presented as an oversimplified, drawn caricature voiced by Jeff Bergman – but also to the overall genre of the comedy sketches. The President, as well as other members of the administration, is turned into "flat" cartoon characters without any interior complexity or lasting memory. The show thus strongly deviates from reality, turning Trump into a surrogate character clearly held separate from most pieces of real-life information we have about him. The same is true for other protagonists: Jeff Sessions, United States Attorney General from 2017 to 2018, has been altered into a diminutive, drunk grandfather, while Goldman Sachs' Steven Mnuchin suggests putting smallpox on pennies. Despite all these deviations from reality, the relation to the actual politicians can never be overlooked, as the producers' intentions were probably to ridicule the 45th President and make fun of his inconsistent political decisions – precisely by creating surrogate characters functioning as exaggerated placeholders for their counterparts. The show received mixed critical responses, many reviewers arguing that the satirical approach was actually humanizing ("our") Trump by making him appear more likable and harmless (see Meslow 2018). Within the frame of cartoon films as a generic *mode of storytelling* (see chapter 5), nothing that happens within the episodes is of lasting consequence, after all.

Yet, as has been discussed earlier in chapter 5, cartoonization does *not necessarily* imply a correlation between cartoonish aesthetics (simplified drawings) and cartoonish characters as flat stereotypes within a storyworld. An interesting contrast to *Our Cartoon President* can be found in James Sturm's celebrated graphic novel *Off Season* (2019), which recounts the 2016 election from the personal perspective of a young working-class couple, Mark and Lisa, and their two small children living in New England. It is a story about crises and tragedies, as Mark's and Lisa's marriage is about to collapse, Mark's mother falls sick with cancer, and he can hardly find employment as a construction worker anymore. Overshadowing these personal events, Mark is devastated about Bernie Sanders' loss in the primaries while Lisa works tirelessly as an activist for the Hilary Clinton campaign. Both are deeply shocked when they learn the results of the election ("I fell asleep putting the kids to bed and didn't find out till this morning … I hope you're all right. Call me back, okay?", Sturm 2019, 77–78). Making matters worse, Mark's father suddenly puts on a MAGA/Trump cap during a family reunion at Mark's parents. While Lisa stares in disbelief, his father "jokes obliviously. 'Does it go with the apron? Chuckle'," as the narrator recounts (188). While *Off Season* is a fictional work, too – Mark's fictive life is not that of the author, Sturm – the graphic novel promises *type authenticity* and presents no indications that this "Trump" is fictionalized in any way. It instead offers a sincere account of the emotional reality lots of people must have felt during that period – in "our" world as much as in Mark's and Lisa's, as well as with regard to actual political issues such as toxic masculinity in Trump's America. This can come as a surprise to some readers, as the book's protagonists are not even represented as humans. What we can see in the book are anthropomorphic dogs and other canines driving in cars and going about their business. In one isolated panel, Sturm even draws the TV screen when Mark watches the first Presidential debate between Trump and Clinton.

Trump, too, is represented as a dog in a suit (albeit with his recognizable mop of hair) while uttering actual historical statements such as "The Justices that I'm going to appoint will be pro-life" (48). What initially looks like a strong fictional-ization is located just on the level of the representation, not of what is represented (see again Baroni 2021). The fact that all the protagonists within *Off Season* are actually thought of as humans within the storyworld – merely *represented as dogs* –– is even made explicit in one scene where Mark plays the "Hungry Giant game" with his children. He pretends to be a monster that they have to run away from. His exclamation "Mmm Human Food Mmmm!" (19) refers to his children not as canines, but as regular human beings. To make this fact even more pronounced, an intradiegetic discussion about theater stage performances reminds the reader that "Using animals as human stand-ins is as old as storytelling… as an actor it's liberating to wear the mask" (52). Just like in Art Spiegelman's *Maus* (1980–1991) discussed earlier, the animal appearances of Sturm's protagonists are such masks, too, delegating the "dog traits" of his protagonists to the semiotic third space introduced in chapter 5: They are neither part of the representational material (lines on paper) nor of the represented storyworld situations in which Trump re-mains entirely unmodified and thus an immigrant character, not a surrogate one. One has to be familiar with the respective conventions of comic books, however, to appreciate this subtle play with fictionality.

Sometimes, the cues as to which aspects of a character are fictionalized and which ones are "imported" from reality in a straightforward manner can be dif-ficult to decipher. Such a play with *inventability* is at the center of another real-life show about Trump, CBS' *The Good Fight* (King et al. 2017–present, the following developed together with Berenike Jung in Jung and Wilde 2021). The show fo-cuses on the mainly African-American law firm Reddick, Boseman & Lockhart and an extensive cast of protagonists with their daily routines and various cases. One of its main characters, however, remains always in the background of the show's storyworld. The very first episode opens with Trump's words from the TV screen, uttered only a month earlier at the (actual) inauguration ceremony of January 20, 2017. Just like *Off Season*, *The Good Fight* positioned itself as en-tertainment *and* political commentary on the cultural processing of the Trump presidency, his administration, and actual political events. *The Good Fight* is "the only TV show that reflects what life under Trump feels like for many of us who abhor him," *The New York Times* found (Goldberg 2019, n.pag). It still is clearly a fictional show, albeit one which heavily references factual events and people. As fictive entities, characters such as Diane Lockhart (played by Christine Baranski) cannot interact with the Donald Trump of "our" world. The President is only visible on TV screens showing actual footage, mostly untouched by fictionalizing modifications. Trump's mediated presence is growing more and more palpable throughout the narrative, however, as the show progresses. The series does come very close to turning their version of the members of the White House into fully fictionalized surrogate objects in season three. In "The One with the Celebrity Divorce" (Se3E06), a mysterious female client contacts the firm's divorce law-yer Luca Quinn (played by Cush Jumbo). The client is looking for counsel with regard to a postnuptial agreement and a hypothetical annulment of marriage. Various clues suggest that this potential client could in fact be "Melania Trump." When the mysterious woman finally agrees to meet up with Luca, the show deliberately leaves to the viewer's imagination whether the woman is, within the storyworld, the "real" Melania or an imposter who only wants to retrieve a certain incriminating tape from the firm. The audience actually gets to watch an on-screen appearance of a woman in a dimly lit room, but her face always remains in the dark. The line between fact and fiction remains clear, however, as no one would assume that this is really the President's wife participating in the show (and even if she were, it would be clear that she is fictionalizing herself and not actually declaring a divorce within a fictional TV show).

More interesting than such (touched upon) fictionalizations of people surrounding the Trump presidency are the more implicit dimensions of inventability where we – as audiences – cannot be sure whether aspects of what we see are altered from reality or not. Beginning with the opening sequence, TV inserts of and about the President permeate the episodes, creating a background layer of constant noise. But from season two onwards, when Diane experiments with microdosing hallucinogenic drugs, these news snippets become stranger and stranger, and they appear exclusively in relation to Trump's representation in the media. "Day 422" (Se2E3, three episodes into the microdosing endeavor) presents a tired, exhausted Diane watching TV. Again, she finds Trump on every channel. In between news snippets that are as real in our world as in Diane's, however, a report claims that the President has adopted a "pot-bellied pig named Petey" who is supposed to live in the White House from now on. Diane watches without expressing emotions, but at the very end of the episode, she asks her colleague Adrian whether he has heard that particular piece of information. Adrian just laughs and changes the subject – leaving viewers again without final confirmation as to the level of veracity or reality of this news report on the President. Diane's drug-induced hallucinations and the resulting narrative unreliability pass on to the viewers of *The Good Fight* the question of which reports on Trump – or which alleged tweets and utterances by Trump – are part of both Diane's and our realities, and which are imaginations in her world and satirical fiction in ours. In some cases, the lines are clear; in others, they are not. The "Trump" living with a "pot-bellied pig named Petey" must clearly be fictive, while the one calling the press the "enemy of the people" is *not* an invented one. But what about a news report according to which "President Trump tweeted Mr. Nasrallah [the *actual* Secretary General of the Lebanese Hisbollah] looks like a stupid, fat Santa in a turban," to which "German chancellor Merkel" responded that "the comment by the American President [was] 'unhelpful'" (Se2E5)? A viewer might wonder if they had just missed the latest verbal missile, and the really shocking fact lies in how many outrageous claims we have to double check before we can discard them. Since Trump's mediated behavior seemed to contradict many established political and public routines, we cannot be sure without conducting our own Google search. The inventability of Trump's medial articulations is thus alarmingly hard to assess. Living with the "Trump Shock," the show seems to indicate, means "not knowing what [is] crazy and what [is] not" (Se2E13), since "what starts out as satire becomes the real deal these days" (Se3E4).

A final text we would like to turn to – in order to indicate how productive the play with inventability and fictionalization can become – is the comic book *The Unquotable Trump* by R. Sikoryak (2017), featuring a gallery of 48 discontinuous artworks that each present the President in different storyworlds, genres, and settings. Most of the illustrations are based on famous (actually existing) comic book covers, such as the *X-Men*, *Sin City*, or *Wonder Woman*. While Sikoryak's drawings are thus blatantly fictional, turning "Trump" into (natively fictional) comic book supervillains fought by heroes such as "Hombres Fantasticos" (parodies of the Fantastic Four) or the "Black Voter" (i.e., the Black Panther), the satirical relevance of Sikoryak's work lies in the fact that *all* the textual utterances attributed to the natively fictional Trumps are *actual quotes* by the real President of the United States. A cover titled "PAWN" – a pun on Spawn, a 1990s comic book hero fighting demons and other monsters – presents Trump as a hellish nightmare monster shouting "I am not ranting and raving. I love this. I'm having a GOOD TIME doing it" – words uttered by Trump himself during his first solo news conference on February 16, 2017, when he accused reporters of ignoring a poll showing him with a 55% approval rating at odds with most other surveys. In another cover, Trump walks away from a horribly murdered Aquaman, mumbling "I am to a large extent an environmentalist. I believe in it, but it's OUT OF CONTROL." These are the words the President said on the morning he signed two executive actions (January 24, 2017) to advance the controversial Keystone XL and Dakota Access pipelines, strongly opposed by environmentalists. Incoherent, and often also sexist and racist utterances such as these seem to fit perfectly in the imagined mouth of a generic supervillain, so that each page is primarily a biting commentary on Trump's rhetoric which *should* belong in the realm of fiction, but has somehow pervaded reality.

The examples discussed here are obviously far from the only fictionalizations of Trump. In fact, as *The New York Times* found in 2018, "Who, at this point, does not have a Donald Trump? 'Saturday Night Live' does, and Comedy Central does, and talk shows do, and Johnny Depp does. There are more Trump-branded spoofs, parodies and sendups than there are Trump-branded hotels" (Poniewozik 2018, n.pag.). Fictionalized Trumps can then be seen as a genuine transmedia character network of distinct nodes (see chapter 7), just like entirely fictional characters can be regarded under such a perspective. We could then analyze the transmedia character template – the shared features all or most fictionalized character versions can be expected to share – of fictionalized Trumps, Obamas, Napoleons, or any other for their ideological implications. Even the strongly fictionalized protagonist of the film *Abraham Lincoln: Vampire Hunter* (Bekmambetov 2012) (played by Benjamin Walker) does contribute to our "image" of the actual historical person. Surrogate Lincoln's war against the undead is connected to his hatred of slavery in the film's plot after all (the vampires there feed off the blood of slaves), reinforcing that particular trait of his which audiences are likely to consider non-fictional. If actors participate in their own fictionalization such as Rogen and Baruchel in *This is the End*, they also deliberately contribute to our understanding of their star personas. The film starts with their surrogates playing video games and smoking weed, for instance, certainly inviting the notion that the actors, too, are at least open to that sort of lifestyle. "Michael Cera's" excessive use of cocaine and his many sexist remarks (the character is likewise played by Cera himself), by contrast, are probably intended as a humorous, self-confident parody of the idea that celebrities like him are all despicable behind their personas (see Colangelo 2013). Many other aspects of all these self-fictionalizations – the fact that Rogen was "traumatized and bullied as a kid for my 'man-tits,'" as the character reports – are deliberately within the indeterminate zone of inventability where audiences cannot be quite sure whether this was intended as a fictional or non-fictional piece of information. Taken together, the negotiations between fact and fiction – as well as the shared knowledge between artists and readers about how to distinguish between both, and by which codes and conventions – can be an important site to analyze the political meaning attributed to characters. This should not be underestimated for purely fictional works, too, which are not only connected to reality on a symbolic or symptomatic level. In the mimetic dimension of any storyworld, there are various aspects connecting it to "our" world, *imported* (or only slightly modified) to comment upon lifeworld experiences as faithful representations of type authenticity. If any celebrity, however, can be considered a transmedia character network once they generate enough media attention to appear as, say, a surrogate in *The Simpsons* (Brooks et al. 1989–present) or *South Park* (Parker et al. 1997–present), what does this then tell us about the potentials and limits of a Transmedia Character Studies with regard to actual people and entirely non-fictional media texts?

10.4 A Non-fictional Character Theory?

Non-fictional media texts entail vast arrays of forms and formats, ranging from documentary, journalism, film essays, and educational videos to museum exhibitions, scientific films, institutional, industrial or propaganda videos, to name just a few (see Gifreu-Castells et al. 2016). Even if we must refrain from going into detail about all these formats or even only some of them, we do want to come back to the concluding question of whether we are, in fact, not dealing with character representations in all these texts and contexts. As we have outlined in our introduction, "characters" are usually defined as *fictional* entities represented in media texts and thus sharply distinguished from actual persons. This conceptual as well as terminological divide takes a stance against notions of panfictionalism, the idea that there is no essential difference between fact and fiction as both are constructed in similar ways (see Ryan 1997; Zipfel 2020). Panfictionalist positions can be found in various variations, although the term itself is usually applied as a criticism. Poststructuralist philosopher Jean Baudrillard (1983), for instance, famously declared the concept of a contemporary "murder of the real," according to which fact and fiction have become interchangeable, and, consequently, it is essentially pointless to differentiate between the two. Often, such claims are connected to an alleged "postmodern condition" of contemporary societies (see Lyotard 1993). Jean-Marie Schaeffer, however, remarked that

> even if it may be true that fictional narrative as a socially recognized prac-
> tice is not an interculturally universal fact, all human communities seem to
> distinguish between actions and discourses that are meant to be taken "se-
> riously" and others whose status is different: they are recognized as "playful
> pretense" or as "make-believe." (2013, n.pag.)

If we, too, defend the assumption that the difference between fact and fiction is an important and relevant one, not only from an academic perspective but especially for actual audiences, it is nevertheless uncontroversial that the fiction-ality of any given text is not a feature of what is represented but rather subject to the pragmatics of communication. John Searle (1975, 327) illustrated that "ut-terance acts in fiction are indistinguishable from the utterance acts of [every day, non-fictional] discourse." Henrik Skov Nielsen, James Phelan, and Richard Walsh recently (2015, 66) expanded on a similar view, stating that "fictionality is an interpretive assumption about a sender's communicative act," and that "no formal technique or other textual feature is in itself a necessary and sufficient ground for identifying fictive [fictional] discourse." In autobiographical media texts, this becomes especially apparent. Phillippe Lejeune (1989) coined the term *autobiographical pact* for the agreement established between writers and readers of such texts (see Missinne 2019). The former can claim – and the latter can accept – that there is some sort of identity between the writer (as identified, for instance, on a book cover), the narrator within the work (the "telling I"), and the repre-sented character (the "experiencing I"), usually by a shared proper name. When Robert Macfarlane includes an "I" in his monumental essayistic reflections on the relationship between nature and culture in *Underland* (2019, 17) – "I was so drawn to mountains as a young man that I was, at times, ready to die for love of them" – readers expect the referenced "young man" not only to be the same character as the older one, the homodiegetic narrator reflecting upon his youth in these very words. Both are also intended to coalesce into readers' understanding of Macfarlane himself, the writer of *Underland*, who actually did embark on all the journeys recounted in its 13 chapters (see, for instance, Ackermann 2019). The cartoonish character "Sarah Glidden" in the "travel memoir" comic *How to Understand Israel in 60 Days or Less* (2010) is understood as the same individual who also narrates her story in caption boxes approximating her interior thoughts ("This isn't how I had imagined a kibbutz to look at all," 20). She is also presented to correspond to the comic book artist Glidden depicted in a photograph in the book's dedications (4) who wrote all the texts and painted all the watercolor pic-tures. The lettering, i.e., the actual handwriting within the book, is attributed to Clem Robins, which does hardly undermine *60 Days or Less*' autobiographical claims (see Mazowita 2022).

Acceptance of the autobiographical pact and, by extension, of the non-fictionality of protagonists created that way is then clearly a matter of continuously negotiated trust and often contested agreement, as all three levels of creator, narrator, and character can and must be strongly distinguished from each other in principle. It is thus perhaps more appropriate to speak of a mere "autobiographical promise" (McLennan 2013, 113). What is more, actual agency in the creation of any media text is usually much more dispersed than a narrow notion of authorship suggests: In pictorial media, we often find countless other individuals and artists responsible for a comic book (e.g., different artists, letterers, colorists in Harvey Pekar's autobiographical comic memoirs, see Pekar et al. 2003) or for a film or TV show (literally hundreds of thousands of people involved in any production, even in works generally considered autobiographical such as Marjane Satrapi's film *Persepolis*, 2007, the screenplay written and directed together with Vincent Paronnaud, or Agnès Varda's *The Beaches of Agnès*, 2008). Even literary autobiographies are often transparently co-created by ghostwriters – such as Tony Schwartz, Donald Trump's hired writer for his autobiography *The Art of the Deal*, 1987, or Maryann Vollers, the co-creator of Hillary Clinton's *Living History*, 2003 – but authorized by the celebrity or politician in question appearing as narrator and main character. As such, both are intended to feed back into the creator's persona as a kind of "cultural *legend* created by texts" (Branigan 1992, 87; original emphasis), participating in the negotiation of how a general public should understand and remember (aspects of) their personalities and of their lives.

For non-autobiographical works, too, we have already discussed many character representations retaining all relevant descriptions from their real counterparts (as immigrant entities). In purely analytical terms, an entirely non-fictional text could then perhaps be seen as one in which the "immigrant" state applies to all characters, their represented actions, and behaviors. In narratology it is in fact quite uncontroversial by now that there are non-fictional as well as fictional narratives, the former likewise entailing protagonists that are constructed in similar ways as fictional or modified ones (see Cohn 1999; Fludernik and Ryan 2020). From this perspective, we must follow Thon (2019, 178) in his suggestion that the term "character" should likewise not be linked to fictionality at all since any such assessment remains independent from the semiotic construction of protagonists within such works. Characters are then first and foremost *represented entities*, whether they are invented or intended to correspond to reality. James Phelan has recently (2022) also updated his foundational model of characters spread across a mimetic, a thematic, and a synthetic dimension, stressing that "the approach works, with appropriate modifications, for nonfictional as well as for fictional narrative" (256). This might seem surprising at first because characters and persons certainly possess quite a different ontology. Fictive characters exist *only* as intersubjective communicative constructs, while actual persons have a material existence beyond any media text. But the "actual person" that we might encounter on the street is not identical to their truthful representation in non-fictional media texts: to the contrary, we can only assess a non-fictional character representation as truthful if the represented entity *does* conform to other empirical evidence available about the human being in question.

From the perspective of a potential Transmedia Character Studies, this has many interesting consequences (see Gambarato 2018; Karlsen 2019). Transmediality has been investigated in all the previous chapters (especially in 7 and 8) as a complex semiotic strategy facilitating the *rhetoric* that a represented character retains an existence beyond the actual media text in which they are constructed:

> This performance of transmediality thus is seen to depend upon a series of active feats of universalization, which construct the overarching transmedial entity even as they construe its severability from the intermedial moments of contact and reference among the concrete media productions that launch them.
>
> (Packard 2015, 62)

Transmediality thus insinuates that a range of character representations in a variety of media texts or media forms with different affordances and constraints can or should, in fact, represent an identical entity; transmediality enables the coalescence of local, work-specific character representations into glocal, transmedia characters. Individual authorship often gets suspended in the process, since a transmedia character then seems independent and dissolved from any one authority producing and distributing the texts in question. All of this is mostly rhetoric that audiences are invited to accept, "playing along" by ignoring differences and inconsistencies between media representations intended to "add up" to the same fictive individual. Glocal transmedia characters thus often break up into networks of distinguished nodes or versions that are not taken to be identical by either creators or audiences.

For actual persons – or, more specifically, for non-fictional character representations – transmediality is always already established and presupposed. "[J]ournalists have been producing transmedia storytelling for years, even before the arrival of the World Wide Web," Carlos A. Scolari, Paolo Bertetti, and Matthew Freeman (2014b, 4) observed. As soon as any text claims to faithfully represent actual people, we assume and expect that all other non-fictional representations of the same person must, to a certain degree, be consistent with each other, regardless of their authors or their media forms. Otherwise, one or the other text must be discarded as untruthful, not as merely another character version as we would allow for fictive protagonists. "[T]ransmedia storytelling," Renira Rampazzo Gambarato (2019, 90) suggests, also "characterizes contemporary journalism, which constructs a narrative that creates various entry points dispersed across multiple media platforms and involves different audience segments" (see also Tellería 2016; Gambarto and Alzamora 2018). Everything that the documentary *Fahrenheit 11/9* by Michael Moore (2018) presents as factual about Donald Trump must thus conform to any other medial representation we accept as non-fictional, such as the journalistic reportages *Devil's Bargain: Steve Bannon, Donald Trump, and the Storming of the Presidency* by Joshua Green (2017), *Fire and Fury: Inside the Trump White House* by Michael Wolff (2018), or *Trumpocracy: The Corruption of the American Republic* by David Frum (2018). It is important to note that even non-fictional character representations such as these cannot give unmediated access to reality, but only to intersubjective communicative constructs (a variety of local Trump characters). Ideally, these should all confirm each other mutually, and they should also be confirmed by empirical evidence outside of these texts which reporters or "eyewitnesses" can attest to when the majority of audience members will never make their personal acquaintance with, say, the former President. Fiction, by contrast, is "a pragmatic instruction lifting the constraints of cross-checking and isomorphism on the framework of a communication" (Caïra 2011, 79, as quoted in Baroni 2021, 91). The authorship function of non-fictional character representation is then also a different one when directors such as Michael Moore present themselves only as *messengers* or *mediators*, never as the actual creators of the facts presented – even though they certainly *did* create the media texts which propose these questions in the first place. Importantly, however, the suspension of authorial agency as well as the necessity for transmedial consistency of non-fictional character representations applies only to the "basic-fact domain" of referential meaning: the non-fictional storyworld of interconnected situations and events – allegedly our one, intersubjectively shared world. In terms of evaluation, however, as well as in attribution of actantial roles and thematic meanings, non-fictional character representations can be, and usually are, strongly contrasting to each other. "[T]he fact that discourse in general, and narrative discourse in particular, are constructions does not by itself disqualify ontological realism or the distinction between fact and fiction" (Schaeffer 2013, n.pag.)

Searching for Sugar Man (2012), a Swedish-British documentary film written and directed by Malik Bendjelloul, provides a particularly illuminating example of a non-fictional character representation. It also demonstrates how the construction of actual people in media texts is not necessarily any different on the synthetic level than that of fictive protagonists. In discourses and controversies, however, slightly other concerns are brought up. The documentary won awards at almost every festival in which it was entered, creating a huge media buzz and winning the Academy Award for Best Documentary in 2013 (see Mail and Guardian 2013). Bendjelloul reconstructs the life and career of the half Mexican-American, half Native American musician Sixto Rodriguez. He primarily builds on interviews with two South-African music fans, Stephen "Sugar" Segerman and Craig Bartholomew Strydom, who had engaged in a search for clues and traces about Sixto Rodriguez on their own in the late 1990s. Sixto Rodriguez's two released folk albums – from 1970 and 1971 – were and still are of major popularity in South Africa, with a whole generation of music lovers growing up with his songs. Apparently, Sixto Rodriguez was considered as a pop star along the lines of Bob Dylan, Neil Young, or Leonard Cohen, although little to nothing was known about the artist who was rumored to be long dead. In the documentary, Sixto Rodriguez thus remains entirely absent at first. We only hear accounts of his life through verbal narration, taken from interviews with Segerman and other people in the music industry who had worked with the artist or tried to find out about his identity for years. Segerman came across a number of quite spectacular, albeit contradictory urban myths:

> And then we found out that he had committed suicide. He set himself alight on stage and burnt to death in front of the audience. It was the most incredible thing. It wasn't just a suicide. It was probably the most grotesque suicide in rock history.

Opening with these recounts, the audiences of Bendjelloul's film can imagine a spectacular narrative event – a live suicide on stage – surrounding the film's elusive protagonist. The South African newspaper *Mail & Guardian* (2013, n.pag.) recounts other "alternate character versions" of Sixto Rodriguez as well: "[S]ome said he had joined a leftwing terrorist group and had gone into hiding. He was also said to have died of a drug overdose, gone to prison or blown his head off in a fit of existential despair."

It turns out, however, that Sixto Rodriguez' decade-spanning success and fame in South Africa had remained entirely unknown to the artist himself until Segerman did indeed locate him alive and rather well in 1997. Rodriguez continues to live in Detroit, although in relative poverty in a house he bought for 50 Dollars, making ends meet through construction work and demolition jobs. While all of this might seem hard to believe for a non-fictional story, *Searching for Sugar Man* goes on to become even more of a "fairytale" from that point on. After Sixto Rodriguez was contacted by Segerman, audiences learn, he went on his first South African tour, playing a range of stadium concerts in front of many thousands of fans. At this point in the documentary, Bendjelloul interviews the real Sixto Rodrigues in front of the camera, who appears as the homodiegetic narrator of his own, non-fictional life story. From the perspective of a potential Transmedia Character Studies, many things are of note here. First, Bendjelloul's film is certainly about the striking contrast between Rodriguez' persona in South Africa – considered a celebrity superstar alongside Bob Dylan – when, in reality, he is just a regular working-class guy making ends meet with lots of difficulties. He was not even aware he *had* some sort of public persona in another country. The continuous tension between both aspects of the artist is emphasized by a range of semiotic means giving access to different parts of his mediated and his mostly unmediated life (verbal accounts, still photographs and historical video footage, even animated reenactments), all "adding up" to a coherent "character model" in the minds of audiences, a model just like we would expect from any fictional media text. We even have to revise our model several times when we learn that various rumors turn out *not* to be true. The non-fictionality of the overall narrative facts has not been questioned by other sources – the almost incredible premise of the film that "Rodriguez could have remained ignorant of the fact that he was a superstar in South Africa, while we [in South Africa] remained ignorant of his continued survival" (Mail and Guardian 2013, n.pag.). – *Searching for Sugar Man* has still been criticized for the ways in which the film constructs a specific, highly selective understanding of its protagonist, endowed with a likewise problematic actantial role (see, for instance, Watson 2013).

Sixto Rodriguez – the "person behind the persona," as Bendjelloul seems to suggest – is portrayed as a working-class hero neglected by his own society, mainly due to racist ignorance in his home country. "Everybody knew 'Rodriguez,' that's a Spanish name, a Latin name. Latin music was not happening then," Clarence Avant, former owner of the artist's record label comments. "[T]he story of the slight Latino demolition worker carrying a fridge down the stairs on his back is an important one for people to hear," Jonathan Hyslop (2013, n.pag.) wrote in the *Journal of South African and American Studies*. Being a country of a multitude of social tensions, plenty of politically radical documentaries get made in the United States. But they seldom win Oscars as did *Searching for Sugar Man*. Not stopping there, however, Bendjelloul indicates strongly that Sixto Rodriguez's music was a central catalyst for the South-African anti-apartheid struggle, and this is what occasioned some criticism toward the film. According to the selection and arrangement of narrative facts presented, Sixto Rodriguez could only become famous in South Africa since people there were allegedly ignorant of – and not subject to – the systemic racism in the United States where a half-Mexican, half-Native American poet was an unthinkable "actantial role." The artist is also presented as a central actant in the abolition of apartheid, his songs instrumental in inspiring protest and dissent according to the film. In all the scenes showing South-African protests and rallies, the crowds consist almost entirely of White people, as do most of Bendjelloul's interview partners, downplaying that "this was of course, overwhelmingly a Black revolt driven by racial oppression" (Hyslop 2013, n.pag.). In short, the plot presented by the documentary caters mostly to a *White*, South-African nostalgia, unduly misrepresenting Sixto Rodriguez as well as its target audience as central actants in the abolition of apartheid while "there was nothing inherently politically progressive about the Rodriguez cult" (n.pag.). Bendjelloul also entirely neglects the fact that the singer was a recovering alcoholic: According to sources outside the film text, many seemed to remember his South African concert in Carnival City far less benevolently due to the artist's drinking on stage when he also made sexist remarks (see Titlestad 2013). *Searching for Sugar Man* is thus a film "in which all critical voices, partners, wives, or mothers are unaccountably absent" (n.pag.). Summing up all these points of concern, we could say that while none of the narrative information presented on Sixto Rodriguez was untruthful, their selection and arrangement, the "simplistic portrayal of the anti-apartheid struggle and it [sic!] disingenuous evasion of racial politics" (Hyslop 2013, n.pag.), as well as the resulting represented *character* of Sixto Rodriguez, remains manipulative or at the very least highly selective.

In other words, while the film's story is about the difference between Sixto Rodriguez as a persona and an actual person, audiences' understanding of the "real person" is guided like that of any other character. The non-fictionality of the central plot, as well as the fact that Sixto Rodriguez co-authored its presentation through his own words in interviews, feeds back into yet another, revised "public image" of the singer (as a neglected working-class hero) for a larger, international audience at major film festivals. Put differently once again, the non-fictional character presented as the actual person becomes a *revised persona*. The basic "narrative facts" about his life remain undisputed (although hardly balanced). As an actually existing person, audiences can also expect (and easily verify) trans-medial access to the *same* Rodriguez through other media channels. The music streaming platform Spotify, for instance, does in fact feature his two albums "Cold Fact" and "Coming from Reality." As such, the film's protagonist appears as something entirely different from any (fictional) character. His characterization, however – by a specific arrangement of (flattering) character traits and by the assignment of a specific actantial role within the documentary's simplistic anti-apartheid story – remains open to criticism. To audiences watching only *Searching for Sugar Man*, the character "Sixto Rodriguez" remains an intersubjective communicative construct – composed of character traits and actantial roles – like any other protagonist in fictional media texts.

To summarize some key findings of this concluding chapter, then: At a certain level of recognition and visibility, celebrities and other people of public interest seem to accommodate or even facilitate a transmedia character network: They appear in fictional stories as unmodified immigrant characters or as fictionalized surrogates across a whole spectrum ranging from counterfactual histories to biting satires and caricatures. The individual nodes (character versions) of such a network can thus be differentiated from each other based on the mutually exclusive storyworlds they inhabit, just as with fictive protagonists. Connecting and interrelating any network of fictive transmedia characters is the continuously contested *template* of presupposed, typical traits each character version is expected to share. By contrast, in the case of characters based on fictionalizations of real people, the "actual human being" from whom we distinguish all fictionalized representations seems to occupy the place of such a template. However, since we mostly do not know celebrities personally but rather only through media representations, this center can also be examined as an intersubjective communicative construct, which we have already come to know as an intentionally produced star persona. In contrast to fictional transmedia character representations, all media texts claiming and upholding non-fictionality must, in principle, be free of contradictions with all other texts that are likewise recognized as truthful. This does by no means entail that actual persons should also be considered mere "textual constructs" – the panfictionalist fallacy. The difference between fact and fiction should in no way be underestimated, and, for the most part, it also plays a central role for audiences. A character as represented by a non-fictional text, however, can only be consistent with other non-fictional character representations of the same person – as well as with empirical facts from outside media texts – if they are first differentiated from reality as well as from other media texts. We can then judge them as consistent or inconsistent, truthful or deceiving. Characters are thus not necessarily fictive. The concepts, models, and tools presented in this volume apply to fictional as well as to non-fictional character representations. Interestingly, the *transmediality* of non-fictional character representations (which often has to be painfully established and upheld for fictive characters) is always presupposed and expected in non-fictional texts: As soon as we recognize a representation as non-fictional, we expect that the same character (not just a similar one) can also be represented by other media texts and that the author function is strongly suspended toward a mere "messenger" or "mediator." The demand for consistency – if a non-fictional media text should not be considered untruthful – concerns only the "basic fact domain" of represented events, however, not the symbolic and thematic dimension or the actantial role of a given non-fictional character representation. For fictional as well as for non-fictional character representations, these remain highly selective and can also stand in strong contradiction to each other. Our knowledge about real persons is thus continuously transformed into and negotiated by intersubjective communicative constructs – alongside, against, or independently of the respective celebrities themselves, always able to co-create their personas through autobiographical texts or media self-presentations. A potential Transmedia Character Studies could thus provide many tools not only for the analysis of fictional narratives but also of celebrity culture and political discourse in mediated societies.

Perspectives and Reflections
Transmedia Character Studies?

This volume has presented ten different approaches on how to theorize and analyze characters across media within one coherent framework presented in our introduction. Where does this leave a potential Transmedia Character Studies as an interdisciplinary field of research? Much could be said about the roads *not* taken, as our scope of examples – mostly limited to comparably recent anglophone and Japanese media texts – was as limited as the highly selective questions we investigated. Instead of a summary or a definite set of conclusions, we would like to offer some final perspectives on further lines of inquiry as well as some reflections. We would also like to close with some thoughts that are perhaps most controversial but that also seem to connect the investigations within this volume most consistently. One of our perhaps most surprising claims – in the previous chapter 10 – was to *not* subsume characters under fictionality, as non-fictional media texts construct their "protagonists" in exactly the same way – as actants in represented courses of events, selectively charged with thematic (symbolic and symptomatic) meaning. The "truth claims" of such character representations can only be evaluated if they are consistent with other media texts accepted as non-fictional, as well as with empirical facts and sources from outside narrative media texts. As intersubjective communicative constructs, characters thus easily traverse fictional *and* non-fictional contexts. They have also long left the domains of verbal accounts, literature, or drama from where their theory and analysis initially originated. Anthropomorphic protagonists are not only spreading within various new and emerging narrative media forms like films, TV shows, comic books, or video games but also across them, linking heterogeneous media texts into transmedia franchises and character networks while blurring the institutional roles of artists vs. audiences in continuous cycles of fan production and reappropriation. For a potential Transmedia Character Studies, this opens up some final considerations.

First, as much as we have put the agency of actual social actors, the struggles over interpretation, appropriation, recognition, canonization, and discursivation of characters, at the center of all our considerations, there are some words to be said about *characters' agency* as well (see Lamerichs 2021). It is certainly uncontroversial that a literary text has a specific structure that *affords* some interpretations over others, potentially even against the intentions of actual creators – although

DOI: 10.4324/9781003298793-16

their stated or inferred intentions will usually contribute significantly to any interpretation. In the same way, every transmedia character as such (every "character network") can be seen as a specific structure of affordances for interpretation, circulation, and reappropriation. This structure, or matrix, is composed of their complex hybrid ontology, their epistemic incompleteness, an internal network governed by canonicity and continuity negotiation, as well as by blurred (but far from arbitrary) boundaries to other characters ("character networks") in intertextual parodies, homages, or pastiches. Yet, an uncanny impression of personal intentionality, agency, and distinctness will prevail as a central aspect of their semiotic affordances – and this aspect keeps being exploited by industrial and institutional actors to generate nodes of *artificial agency* (see Wilde 2021). We have seen this not only concerning interface and IVA design but also for considerably older phenomena like corporate mascots.

Another way to think about transmedia characters, then, would be to consider them as immaterial, *virtual actants* (see Nozawa 2013). We use "virtual" here in the sense of Gilles Deleuze and Félix Guattari:

> The virtual is not opposed to the real but to the actual. Indeed, the virtual must be defined as strictly part of the real object – as though the object had one part of itself in the virtual into which it is plunged as though into an objective [material] dimension.
>
> (Deleuze and Guattari 1994 [1968], 208)

Just like the rules of a chess game or the laws in a courtroom have a *real* existence even if they are not enacted/embodied/materialized in concrete moves or rulings, transmedia characters have a virtual presence in society and culture that we can pinpoint and trace. Our ten approaches to transmedia characters could certainly be seen as broadly narratological, at least insofar as we tried to highlight the *limits* of comprehending an anthropomorphic being as belonging to a (specific) course of events situated within a (specific) possible world. Perhaps transmedia characters can only be experienced as social resistance to, agreement with, or a playful (re)appropriation of such virtual actants in different settings, worlds, ages, genders, or ethnicities – not only when canonicity and continuity are managed and/or contested, often against the authority of actual intellectual property rights holders, but especially when their intersubjective core is composed of little more than a potential for shared or contradicting affects and emotions.

Second, if what we argue for characters' *epistemic* incompleteness is correct (see our introduction), a methodology emerges that we have tried putting to the test throughout this volume: The intersubjective communicative construct that *is* the character can only be observed where it is contested, negotiated, or otherwise challenged. This assumption is built on the foundational media theoretical paradigm of transparency vs. opacity – or immediacy vs. hypermediacy (see Bolter and Grusin 2000). Accordingly, mediality only becomes observable when it is not functioning "smoothly," when it is disrupted or contested. For transmedia characters – those elusive communicative constructs or virtual actants oscillating between media texts, media forms, and media discourses to which we are contributing with every scholarly article and analysis as well – this assumption might call for a methodology of *recursive triangulation*. Granted, our academic thoughts and observations might be of little impact on the wider character ecologies and their cultural domains. Popular discussions and controversies, emotional debates, and passionate posts from influential social media accounts, on the other hand, should be taken seriously – as "silly" or "cringe-worthy" as many of these public emotional outbursts might often seem in hindsight. Accordingly, pop-culture news pages like *Slate*, *Vulture*, or *IGN*, as well as collaborative databases and forums like *TV Tropes* or *Quora* have provided rich points of departure for reflections again and again throughout these pages, and we can only hope that our resulting discussions prove the usefulness of such an approach.

The very distinction between "transparent" immediacy vs. "constructed" hypermediacy of characters, after all, has often proven to be an effect of character politicization: the constant negotiation of what is considered "normal" and "natural" (and thus a transparent representation) vs. "political" (and thus a mere media construct) in any given media text (see Sina 2016). In other words, hegemoniality and othering are perhaps the most powerful "fuels" behind any impression of transparency vs. opacity (or immediacy vs. hypermediacy) surrounding transmedia character representation. As "silly" and inconsequential as Tucker Carlson's angry rants about the moderate redesign of the M&M promotional figures might seem, moments like these are exactly where ideological stakes become especially visible and accessible to researchers of cultural negotiations. As these discussions are seemingly about nothing, they are about everything – they are about what should remain unquestioned! Social, political, and ideological implications can precisely be traced where *some* aspects of mediality and media representations are discussed as "political," while others remain unquestioned for decades, across media forms, or traversing different genres. Studying transmedia characters not only means analyzing political hierarchies of social agency critically but also reframing mediality – impressions of transparent immediacy vs. opaque hypermediacy – as a highly political tension between hegemoniality and othering vs. subversion and criticism.

Third, characters have also proven to be independent, at least to a certain degree, from narrative media and the domains of narratology. One of the most prominent areas where characters – or at least deliberately designed *character impressions* – play an increasingly important role is material commodities like shirts, cups, or office supplies, as well as street signs, information leaflets, and (often AI-driven) apps and interfaces (see Gauthier 2019). Characters on surfaces of products and signage or within digital interfaces may or may not be distinguished from "actual" characters (embedded in narrative media texts and attributed to coherent storyworlds). We have done so with recourse to the specific term pre- or meta-narrative *figure*, as opposed to *character*, while still trying to locate such "transmedia figures" *within* a transmedia character theory as an essentialized template of prototypical character traits and dispositions. Most importantly, however, even for pre- and meta-narrative transmedia figures on products and interfaces, many of the same questions and concerns reemerge that we would direct toward protagonists within narratives as well: discussions about their corporeality, their ethos and worldview, their social agency, and their representation of actual groups of people. As we have seen, even corporate mascots or the interfaces of Siri and Alexa can become a "site" of important political, social, and ideological character debates.

Theoretical and analytical approaches to character phenomena (even if merely considered as "figures") are relatively scarce with respect to these evolving and emerging *non-narrative* media forms. Perhaps this is because most character theories are still deeply rooted in narratology (transmedia or otherwise), in questions surrounding stories, storyworlds, and comparably *stable* intersubjective constructs. Media studies, by contrast, have admittedly moved far beyond concerns of semiotics, representation, and even human-to-human communication in recent years and developed a pronounced interest in science and technology studies and interface studies (see, for instance, Hookway 2014 or Hadler and Haupt 2016) where characters *could* be a prominent topic for reflection. To date, however, little character theory can be found within these lines of inquiry, perhaps because characters also appear too entangled in narrative theory, semiotics, and other "representationalist" views that are perceived as somewhat outdated for these concerns. From both perspectives, then, pre- and meta-narrative transmedia characters or figures seem to fall somewhere outside established disciplinary boundaries, which could provide further reasons for a distinct field of inquiry.

Finally, however, there is still much to be learned from the long-established and continuously developing theoretical and analytical perspectives on characters and we have certainly barely touched the surface of the rich methodologies derived from literature studies, film studies, and television studies, as well as from semiotics or phenomenology. Rapidly developing newer fields like fan studies, game studies, or transmedia narratology contribute considerably to our understanding of these emerging phenomena not only through their distinct vocabularies but especially since they are embedded in transmedia contexts from the outset and thus especially well equipped to mediate between existing theories. Furthermore, as characters are identical neither with their medial nor with their (private) mental representations but rather constituted in a perpetually contested zone of social intersubjectivity and incomplete epistemology, it should have become clear that intersectional perspectives from gender studies, postcolonial studies, or disability studies are as indispensable to their theory and analysis as fine-grained views on their legal, economic, and political propagation – and temporal differences and specificities from historical investigations matter just as much as cultural and regional ones from fields like American Studies or Japanese Studies.

Primary Sources, Media Texts

Novels and Other Primary Books

Atwood, Margaret. 1985. *The Handmaid's Tale*. Toronto: McClelland and Stewart.

Bantam Books. 1979–1998. *Choose Your Own Adventure* Series. New York: Bantam Books, 184 vol.

Brown, Jeffrey. 2012. *Darth Vader and Son*. San Francisco, CA: Chronicle Books.

Brown, Jeffrey. 2013. *Vader's Little Princess*. San Francisco, CA: Chronicle Books.

Brown, Jeffrey. 2014. *Goodnight Darth Vader*. San Francisco, CA: Chronicle Books.

Clinton, Hillary, and Maryann, Vollers. 2003. *Living History*. New York: Simon & Schuster.

Collins, Suzanne. 2008. *The Hunger Games*. New York: Scholastic Press.

Corey, James S.A. 2011. *Leviathan Wakes*. London: Orbit Books.

Dever, Joe. 1984. *Flight from the Dark*. New York: Berkley/Pacer.

Dever, Joe, Ben Dever, and Vincent Lazzari. 1984–present. *Lone Wolf* series. New York: Berkley/Pacer, 31 vol.

Dick, Philip K. 1992 [1962]. *The Man in the High Castle*. New York: Vintage Books.

Doyle, Arthur C. 2022a [1893]. "The Final Problem." In *The Memoirs of Sherlock Holmes: Short Stories*. Project Gutenberg, April 27. https://gutenberg.org/ebooks/834.

Doyle, Arthur C. 2022b [1903]. "The Adventure of the Empty House." In *The Return of Sherlock Holmes*. Project Gutenberg, April 27. https://gutenberg.org/ebooks/108.

Frum, David. 2018. *Trumpocracy: The Corruption of the American Republic*. New York: Harper.

Gaiman, Neil. 2001. *American Gods*. London: Headline.

Green, Joshua. 2017. *Devil's Bargain: Steve Bannon, Donald Trump, and the Storming of the Presidency*. New York: Penguin Press.

Hammett, Dashiell. 2003 [1929]. *Red Harvest*. London: Orion.

Herbert, Frank. 2010 [1965]. *Dune*. New York: Ace.

Hornby, Nick. 2020 [1995]. *High Fidelity*. Riverhead Trade Paperback/Hulu Tie-in Edition. New York: Riverhead Books.

Ishiguro, Kazuo. 1989. *The Remains of the Day*. London: Faber and Faber.

James, E.L. 2011. *Fifty Shades of Grey*. New York: Vintage Books.

James, E.L. 2012a. *Fifty Shades Darker*. New York: Vintage Books.

James, E.L. 2012b. *Fifty Shades Freed*. New York: Vintage Books.

Jemisin, N.K. 2015. *The Fifth Season*. New York: Orbit.

Jordan, Robert. 1990. *The Eye of the World*. New York: Tor Books.

King, Stephen. 1982. *The Dark Tower: The Gunslinger*. New Hampshire: Grant.

Lippincott, David. 1999. *Mr. Dalloway*. Louisville: Sarabande Books.

Macfarlane, Robert. 2019. *Underland*. New York: W. W. Norton & Company.

Martin, George R.R. 1986. *Tuf Voyaging*. Wake Forest: Baen Books.

Martin, George R.R. 1996–2011. *A Song of Ice and Fire* series. New York: Bantam, 5 vol.

Martin, George R.R. 2018. *Fire & Blood*. London: Harper Voyager.

May, Robert L., and Antonio Javier Caparo. 2014 [1939]. *Rudolph the Red-Nosed Reindeer*. New York: Little Simon.

Mitchell, David. 2010. *The Thousand Autumns of Jacob de Zoet*. London: Sceptre.

Mitchell, David. 2014. *The Bone Clocks*. London: Sceptre.

Mitchell, David. 2015. *Slade House*. London: Sceptre.

Mitchell, David. 2020. *Utopia Avenue*. London: Sceptre.

Nasar, Sylvia. 1998. *A Beautiful Mind: The Life of Mathematical Genius and Novel Laureate John Nash*. New York: Simon & Schuster.

Naslund, Sena J. 1999. *Ahab's Wife*. New York: William Morrow.

Nimoy, Leonard. 1975. *I Am Not Spock*. Berkeley: Celestial Arts.

Rowling, J. K. 1997. *Harry Potter and the Philosopher's Stone*. London: Bloomsbury.

Ruff, Matt. 2016. *Lovecraft Country*. New York: HarperCollins.

Sakurazaka, Hiroshi [桜坂洋]. 2004. *All You Need Is Kill*. Tokyo: Shueisha.

Stevenson, Robert L. 2022 [1886]. *Strange Case of Dr Jekyll and Mr Hyde*. New York: W. W. Norton & Company.

Takami, Koushon [高見広春]. 1999. *Battle Royale [Batoru Rowaiaru]*. Tokyo: Ohta Publishing.

Tolkien, J.R.R. 1937. *The Hobbit*. London: George Allen & Unwin.

Tolkien, J.R.R. 1954. *The Fellowship of the Ring*. London: George Allen & Unwin.

Tolstoy, Leo. 2020 [1869]. *War and Peace [Voyna i mir]*. Newburyport: Open Road Media.

Trump, Donald J., and Tony Schwartz. 1987. *The Art of the Deal*. New York: Random House.

Valente, Catherynne M. 2017. *The Refrigerator Monologues*. New York: Simon & Schuster Books for Young Readers.

Wolff, Michael. 2018. *Fire and Fury: Inside the Trump White House*. New York: Henry Holt and Company.

Films

Abrams, J.J., director. 2009. *Star Trek*. Paramount Pictures. 2 hrs., 7.

Abrams, J.J., director. 2015. *Star Wars: The Force Awakens*. Walt Disney Studios Motion Pictures. 2 hrs., 18.

Abrams, J.J., director. 2019. *Star Wars: The Rise of Skywalker*. Walt Disney Studios Motion Pictures. 2 hrs., 22.

Adamson, Andrew, director. 2005. *The Chronicles of Narnia: The Lion, the Witch and the Wardrobe*. Buena Vista Pictures. 2 hrs., 23.

Adamson, Andrew, director. 2008. *The Chronicles of Narnia: Prince Caspian*. Walt Disney Studios Motion Pictures. 2 hrs., 30.

Addison, Chris, director. 2019. *The Hustle*. Universal Pictures. 1 hr., 34.

Aja, Alexandre, director. 2021. *Oxygen*. Netflix. 1 hr., 41.

Aldrich, Robert, director. 1954. *Apache*. United Artists. 1 hr., 27.

Allers, Roger, and Rob Minkoff, directors. 1994. *The Lion King*. Buena Vista Pictures. 1 hr., 28.

Anderson, Wes, director. 2020. *Fantastic Mr. Fox*. 20th Century Fox. 1 hr., 27.

Apted, Michael, director. 2010. *The Chronicles of Narnia: The Voyage of the Dawn Treader*. 20th Century Fox. 1 hr., 53.

Arcel, Nikolaj, director. 2017. *The Dark Tower*. Sony Pictures Releasing. 1 hr., 35.

Armstrong, Samuel, James Algar, et al., directors. 1940. *Fantasia*. RKO Radio Pictures. 2 hrs., 6.

Avildsen, John G., director. 1976. *Rocky*. United Artists. 1 hr., 59.

Avildsen, John G., director. 1984. *The Karate Kid*. Columbia Pictures. 2 hrs., 7.

Bekmambetov, Timur, director. 2012. *Abraham Lincoln: Vampire Hunter*. 20th Century Fox. 1 hr., 45.

Bendjelloul, Malik, director. 2012. *Searching for Sugar Man*. NonStop Entertainment, StudioCanal. 1 hr., 26.

Bird, Brad, director. 2004. *The Incredibles*. Buena Vista Pictures Distribution. 1 hr., 55.

Black, Shane, director. 2013. *Iron Man 3*. Walt Disney Studios Motion Pictures. 2 hrs., 11.

Bowman, Rob, director. 1988. *The X-Files*. 20th Century Fox. 2 hrs., 2.

Branagh, Kenneth, director. 2011. *Thor*. Paramount Pictures. 1 hr., 54.

Branagh, Kenneth, director. 2017. *Murder in the Orient Express*. 20th Century Fox. 1 hr., 54.

Brooks, Mel, director. 1987. *Spaceballs*. MGM/UA Communications Co. 1 hr., 36.

Buck Chris, and Jennifer Lee, directors. 2013. *Frozen*. Walt Disney Studios Motion Pictures. 1 hr., 42.

Buck Chris, and Jennifer Lee, directors. 2019. *Frozen 2*. Walt Disney Studios Motion Pictures. 1 hr., 43.

Buñuel, Luis, director. 1977. *That Obscure Object of Desire*. GEF-CCFC. 1 hr., 42.

Burton, Tim, director. 1988. *Beetlejuice*. Warner Bros. 1 hr., 32.

Burton, Tim, director. 1989. *Batman*. Warner Bros. 2 hrs., 6.

Burton, Tim, director. 1992. *Batman Returns*. Warner Bros. 2 hrs., 6.

Burton, Tim, director. 1993. *The Nightmare before Christmas*. Buena Vista Pictures Distribution. 1 hr., 16.

Cameron, James, director. 1984. *Terminator*. Orion Pictures. 1 hr., 47.

Cameron, James, director. 1986. *Aliens*. 20th Century Fox. 2 hrs., 17.

Cameron, James, director. 2009. *Avatar*. 20th Century Fox. 2 hrs., 42.

Campbell, Martin, director. 1995. *GoldenEye*. United International Pictures. 2 hrs., 10.

Campbell, Martin, director. 2006. *Casino Royale*. Sony Pictures Releasing. 2 hrs., 24.

Caro, Niki, director. 2020. *Mulan*. Walt Disney Studios Motion Pictures. 1 hr., 55.

Charles, Larry, director. 2006. *Borat! Cultural Learnings of America for Make Benefit Glorious Nation of Kazakhstan*. 20th Century Fox. 1 hr., 24.

Chbosky, Stephen, director. 2012. *The Perks of Being a Wallflower*. Summit Entertainment. 1 hr., 43.

Clements, Ron, and John Musker, directors.1989. *The Little Mermaid*. Buena Vista Pictures. 1 hr., 23.

Clements, Ron, and John Musker, directors. 1992. *Aladdin*. Buena Vista Pictures. 1 hr., 30.

Clements, Ron, and John Musker, directors. 1997. *Hercules*. Buena Vista Pictures. 1 hr., 33.

Coen, Joel, director. 1998. *The Big Lebowsky*. Gramercy Pictures. 1 hr., 57.

Columbus, Chris, director. 2001. *Harry Potter and the Philosopher's Stone*. Warner Bros. Pictures. 2 hrs., 32.

Columbus, Chris, director. 2002. *Harry Potter and the Chamber of Secrets*. Warner Bros. Pictures. 2 hrs., 41.

Comar, Jean-Christophe "Pitof," director. 2004. *Catwoman*. Warner Bros. Pictures. 1 hr., 44.

Coogler, Ryan, director. 2015. *Creed*. Warner Bros. Pictures. 2 hrs., 13.

Coogler, Ryan, director. 2018. *Black Panther*. Walt Disney Studios Motion Pictures. 2 hrs., 14.

Cook, Barry, and Tony Bancroft, directors. 1998. *Mulan*. Buena Vista Pictures. 1 hr., 27.

Cretton, Destin D., director. 2021. *Shang-Chi and the Legend of the Ten Rings*. Walt Disney Studios Motion Pictures. 2 hrs., 12.

Davis, Andrew, director. 1993. *The Fugitive*. Warner Bros. 2 hrs., 10.

Demme, Jonathan, director. 1991. *The Silence of the Lambs*. Orion Pictures. 1 hr., 58.

De Palma, Brian, director. 1996. *Mission: Impossible*. Paramount Pictures. 1 hr., 50.

Docter, Pete, director. 2015. *Inside Out*. Walt Disney Studios Motion Pictures. 1 hr., 35.

Docter, Pete, director. 2020. *Soul*. Walt Disney Studios Motion Pictures. 1 hr., 41.

Edwards, Blake, director. 1961. *Breakfast at Tiffany's*. Paramount Pictures. 1 hr., 54.

Emmerich, Roland, director. 2016. *Independence Day: Resurgence*. 20th Century Fox. 2 hrs.

Favreau, Jon, director. 2010. *Iron Man 2*. Paramount Pictures. 2 hrs., 5.

Favreau, Jon, director. 2016. *The Jungle Book*. Walt Disney Studios Motion Pictures. 1 hr., 45.

Favreau, Jon, director. 2019. *The Lion King*. Walt Disney Studios Motion Pictures. 1 hr., 58.

Feig, Paul, director. 2016. *Ghostbusters*. Sony Pictures Releasing. 1 hr., 56.

Filmognari, Michael, director. 2020. *To All the Boys: P.S. I Still Love You*. Netflix. 1 hr., 42.

Filmognari, Michael, director. 2021. *To All the Boys: Always and Forever*. Netflix.1 hr., 55.

Fincher, David, director. 1999. *Fight Club*. 20th Century Fox. 2 hrs., 19.

Fincher, David, director. 2014. *Gone Girl*. Century Fox. 2 hrs., 29.

Fleischer, Ruben, director. 2018. *Venom*. Sony Pictures. 1 hr., 52.

Foster, Harve, and Wilfred, Jackson, director. 1946. *Song of the South*. Walt Disney Productions. 1 hr., 34.

Fukunaga, Cary J., director. 2021. *No Time to Die*. Universal Pictures, 2 hrs., 43.

Frears, Stephen, director. 2010. *High Fidelity*. Buena Vista Pictures, 1 hr., 53.

Gabriel, Mike, and Eric Goldberg, directors. 1995. *Pocahontas*. Buena Vista Pictures. 1 hr., 21.

Geronimi, Gale, director. 1959. *Sleeping Beauty*. Buena Vista. 1 hr., 15.

Geronimi, Gale, Hamilton Luske, and Wolfgang Reitherman, directors. 1961. *101 Dalmatians*. Buena Vista. 1 hr., 19.

Gillespie, Craig, director. 2021. *Cruella*. Walt Disney Studios Motion Pictures. 2 hrs., 4.

Gillet, Burt, director. 1934. *Orphan's Benefit*. United Artists. 9 mins.

Gilliam, Terry, director. 2009. *The Imaginarium of Doctor Parnassus*. Lionsgate. 2 hrs., 3.

Glen, John, director. 1981. *For Your Eyes Only*. United Artists. 2 hrs., 7.

Hand, David, director. 1937. *Snow White and the Seven Dwarfs*. RKO Radio Pictures. 1 hr., 23.

Hardwicke, Catherine, director. 2008. *Twilight*. Summit Entertainment. 2 hrs., 1.

Haynes, Todd, director. 2007. *I'm not There*. Endgame Entertainment. 2 hrs., 15.

Hill, Walter, director. 1996. *Last Man Standing*. New Line Cinema. 1 hr., 41.

Hillenberg, Stephen, director. 2004. *The SpongeBob SquarePants Movie*. Paramount Pictures. 1 hr., 27.

Hitchcock, Alfred, director. 1959. *North by Northwest*. Metro-Goldwyn-Mayer. 2 hrs., 16.

Hooper, Tom, director. 2010. *The King's Speech*. Paramount Pictures. 1 hr., 59.

Howard, Ron, director. 2001. *A Beautiful Mind*. Universal Pictures. 2 hrs., 15.

Iñárritu, Alejandro G., director. 2014. *Birdman or (The Unexpected Virtue of Ignorance)*. Fox Searchlight Pictures. 1 hr., 59.

Jackson, Peter, director. 2001. *Lord of the Rings: The Fellowship of the Ring*. New Line Cinema. 2 hrs., 58.

Jackson, Peter, director. 2002. *Lord of the Rings: The Two Towers.* New Line Cinema. 2 hrs., 59.

Jackson, Peter, director. 2003. *Lord of the Rings: The Return of the King.* New Line Cinema. 2 hrs., 41.

Jackson, Peter, director. 2005. *King Kong.* Universal Pictures. 3 hrs., 8.

Jackson, Wilfred, director. 1934. *The Wise Little Hen.* United Artists. 7 mins.

Johnson, Mark S., director. 2003. *Daredevil.* 20th Century Fox. 1 hr., 43.

Johnson, Rian, director. 2017. *The Last Jedi.* Walt Disney Studios Motion Pictures. 2 hrs., 32.

Johnson, Rian, director. 2019. *Knives Out.* Lionsgate, MRC. 2 hrs., 10.

Johnson, Susan, director. 2018. *To all the Boys I've Loved Before.* Netflix. 1 hr., 33.

Jones, Duncan, director. 2011. *Source Code.* Summit Entertainment. 1 hr., 33.

Jonze, Spike, director. 2013. *Her.* Warner Bros. Pictures. 2 hrs., 6.

Kasdan, Jake, director. 2017. *Jumanji: Welcome to the Jungle.* Sony Pictures Releasing. 1 hr., 59.

Katabuchi, Sunao [片渕須直], director. 2016. *In This Corner of the World [Kono sekai no katasumi ni].* Tokyo Theatres. 2 hrs., 9.

Kaytis, Clay, director. 2018. *The Christmas Chronicles.* Netflix. 1 hr., 43.

Kershner, Irvin, director. 1980. *The Empire Strikes Back.* 20th Century Fox. 2 hrs., 4.

Knight, Steven, director. 2013. *Locke.* Lionsgate. 1 hr., 25.

Kosinski, Joseph, director. 2011. *Tron Legacy.* Walt Disney Studios Motion Pictures. 2 hrs., 5.

Kubrick, Stanley, director. 1968. *2001: A Space Odyssey.* Metro-Goldwyn-Mayer. 2 hrs., 22.

Kurosawa, Akira [黒澤明], director. 1950. *Rashomon.* Daiei Film. 1 hr., 28.

Kurosawa, Akira [黒澤明], director. 1961. *Yojimbo.* Toho. 1 hr., 50.

Kwan, Daniel, and Daniel, Scheinert, directors. 2022. *Everything Everywhere All at Once.* A24. 2 hrs., 20.

Landis, John, director. 1983. *Trading Places.* Paramount Pictures. 1 hr., 56.

Lasseter, John, director. 1995. *Toy Story.* Buena Vista Pictures Distribution. 1 hr., 21.

Lawrence, Francis, director. 2007. *I Am Legend.* Warner Bros. Pictures. 1 hr., 41.

Lee, Malcolm D., director. 2021. *Space Jam: A New Legacy.* Warner Bros. Pictures. 1 hr., 55.

Leone, Sergio, director. 1964. *A Fistful of Dollars.* Unidis. 1 hr., 39.

Leterrier, Louis, director. 2008. *The Incredible Hulk.* Universal Pictures. 1 hr., 52.

Liman, Doug, director. 2014. *Edge of Tomorrow.* Warner Bros. Pictures. 1 hr., 53.

Lin, Justin, director. 2013. *Fast & Furious 6.* Universal Pictures. 2 hrs., 10.

Linklater, Richard, director. 2014. *Boyhood.* Universal Pictures. 2 hrs., 45.

Lisberger, Steven, director. 1982. *Tron.* Buena Vista Distribution. 1 hr., 36.

Lucas, George, director. 1977. *Star Wars: A New Hope.* 20th Century Fox. 2 hrs., 1.

Luske, Hamilton, Wilfred Jackson, and Clyde Geronimi, directors. 1950. *Cinderella.* RKO Radio Pictures 1 hr., 14.

MacLane, Angus, director. 2022. *Lightyear.* Walt Disney Studios Motion Pictures. 1 hr., 45.

Martino, Steve, director. 2015. *The Peanuts Movie.* 20th Century Fox. 1 hr., 28.

McTiernan, John, director. 1993. *Last Action Hero.* Columbia Pictures. 2 hrs., 11.

Meirelles, Fernando, and Kátia Lund, directors. 2002. *City of God.* Globo Filmes, Miramax Films. 2 hrs., 10.

Melendez, Bill, director. 1965. A *Charlie Brown Christmas.* CBS. 25 mins.

Mendes, Sam, director. 2015. *James Bond 007: Spectre.* Sony Pictures Releasing. 2 hrs., 28.

Mendes, Sam, director. 2019. *1917*. Universal Pictures. 1 hr., 59.

Meyers, Nancy, director. 2000. *What Women Want*. Paramount Pictures. 2 hrs., 7.

Miller, Frank, and Robert, Rodriguez, directors. 2005. *Sin City*. Miramax Films. 2 hrs., 4.

Miller, Frank, and Robert, Rodriguez, directors. 2014. *Sin City: A Dame to Kill for*. The Weinstein Company. 1 hr., 42.

Miller, George, director. 2006. *Happy Feet*. Warner Bros. Pictures. 1 hr., 48.

Miller, Tim, director. 2019. *Terminator: Dark Fate*. Buena Vista International. 2 hrs., 8.

Miranda, Lin-Manuel, director. 2021. *Tick, Tick … Boom!* Netflix. 2 hrs., 1.

Moore, Michael, director. 2018. *Fahrenheit 11/9*. Briarcliff Entertainment. 2 hrs.

Moore, Rich, director. 2012. *Wreck-It Ralph*. Walt Disney Studios Motion Pictures. 1 hr., 41.

Munroe, Kevin, director. 2016. *Ratchet & Clank*. Focus Features. 1 hr., 34.

Musker, John, and Ron Clements, directors. 2009. *The Princess and the Frog*. Walt Disney Pictures. 1 hr., 37.

Nolan, Christopher, director. 2005. *Batman Begins*. Warner Bros. Pictures. 2 hrs., 20.

Nolan, Christopher, director. 2008. *The Dark Knight*. Warner Bros. Pictures. 2 hrs., 32.

Nolan, Christopher, director. 2012. *The Dark Knight Rises*. Warner Bros. Pictures. 2 hrs., 45.

Norrington, Stephen, director. 1998. *Blade*. New Line Cinema. 2 hrs.

Norrington, Stephen, director. 2003. *The League of Extraordinary Gentlemen*. 20th Century Fox. 1 hr., 50.

Oshima, Nagisa [大島渚], director. 1970. *The Story of a Man Who Put his Will on Film [Tokyo Sensō Sengo Hiwa]*. Art Theatre Guild, Sozosha. 1 hr., 34.

Otomo, Katsuhiro [大友克洋], director. 1988. *Akira*. Toho. 2 hrs., 4.

Oz, Frank, director. 1988. *Dirty Rotten Scoundrels*. Orion Pictures. 1 hr., 50.

Parry, Madeleine, and John Olb, directors. 2018. *Hannah Gadsby: Nanette*. Netflix. 1 hr., 9.

Persichetti, Bob, Peter Ramsey, and Rodney Rothman, directors. 2018. *Spider-Man: Into the Spider-Verse*. Sony Pictures Releasing. 1 hr., 57.

Pytka, Joe, director. 1996. *Space Jam*. Warner Bros. 1 hr., 28.

Raimi, Sam, director. 1992. *Army of Darkness*. Universal Pictures. 1 hr., 21.

Raimi, Sam, director. 2022. *Doctor Strange in the Multiverse of Madness*. Walt Disney Studios Motion Pictures. 2 hrs., 6.

Ramis, Harold, director. 1993. *Groundhog Day*. Columbia Pictures. 1 hr., 41.

Ratner, Brett, director. 2014. *Hercules*. Paramount Pictures. 1 hr., 38.

Refn, Nicholas W., director. 2011. *Drive*. Film District. 1 hr. 40.

Reggio, Godfrey, director. 1982. *Koyaanisqatsi*. Island Alive, New Cinema. 1 hr., 26.

Reeves, Matt, director. 2014. *Dawn of the Planet of the Apes*. 20th Century Fox. 2 hrs., 10.

Reeves, Matt, director. 2017. *War for the Planet of the Apes*. 20th Century Fox. 2 hrs., 20.

Reitherman, Wolfgang, director. 1967. *The Jungle Book*. Buena Vista Distribution. 1 hr., 18.

Reitherman, Wolfgang, director. 1973. *Robin Hood*. Buena Vista Distribution. 1 hr., 23.

Ritchie, Guy, director. 2009. *Sherlock Holmes*. Warner Bros. Pictures. 2 hrs., 9.

Roach, Jay, director. 1997. *Austin Powers: International Man of Mystery*. New Line Cinema. 1 hr., 35.

Roach, Jay, director. 1999. *Austin Powers: The Spy Who Shagged Me*. New Line Cinema. 1 hr., 31.

Roach, Jay, director. 2002. *Austin Powers in Goldmember*. New Line Cinema. 1 hr., 35.

Rogen, Seth, and Evan Goldberg, directors. 2013. *This is The End*. Sony Pictures Releasing. 1 hr., 47.

Romero, George A., director. 1978. *Dawn of the Dead*. United Film Distribution Company. 2 hrs., 6.

Ross, Gary, director. 1998. *Pleasantville*. New Line Cinema. 2 hrs., 4.

Ross, Gary, director. 2012. *The Hunger Games*. Lionsgate. 2 hrs., 22.

Russo, Anthony, and Joe Russo, directors. 2016. *Captain America: Civil War*. Walt Disney Studios Motion Pictures. 2 hrs., 27.

Russo, Anthony, and Joe Russo, directors. 2019. *Avengers: Endgame*. Walt Disney Studios Motion Pictures. 3 hrs., 1.

Safdie, Benny, and Josh Safdie, directors. 2019. *Uncut Gems*. Netflix. 2 hrs., 14.

Sandberg, David F., director. 2019. *Shazam!* Warner Bros. Pictures. 2 hrs., 12.

Satrapi, Marjane, and Vincent Paronnaud, directors. 2007. *Persepolis*. Diaphana Distribution. 1 hr., 36.

Scanlon, Dan, director. 2020. *Onward*. Walt Disney Studios Motion Pictures. 1 hr., 42.

Scott, Ridley, director. 1982. *Blade Runner*. Warner Bros. 1 hr., 57.

Scott, Ridley, director. 2021. *The Last Duel*. 20th Century Studios. 2 hrs., 33.

Scott, Tony, director. 1986. *Top Gun*. Paramount Pictures. 1 hr., 50.

Scorsese, Martin, director. 2013. *The Wolf of Wall Street*. Paramount Pictures. 3 hrs.

Serkis, Andy, director. 2021. *Venom: Let There Be Carnage*. Sony Pictures. 1 hr., 37.

Shankman, Adam, director. 2019. *What Men Want*. Paramount Pictures. 1 hr., 57.

Sharpsteen, Ben, director. 1941. *Dumbo*. RKO Radio Pictures. 1 hr., 4.

Shortland, Cate, director. 2021. *Black Widow*. Walt Disney Studios Motion Pictures. 2 hrs., 14.

Siegel, Don, director. 1971. *Dirty Harry*. Warner Bros. 1 hr., 42.

Singer, Bryan, director. 1996. *The Usual Suspects*. Gramercy Pictures. 1 hr., 46.

Sivers, Anton, director. 2014. *Vasilisa*. Russian World Studios. 1 hr., 40.

Slade, David, director. 2018. *Black Mirror: Bandersnatch*. Netflix. 1 hr., 30 on average.

Snyder, Zack, director. 2007. *300*. Warner Bros. Pictures. 1 hr., 56.

Sonderbergh, Steven, director. 2004. *Ocean's Twelve*. Warner Bros. Pictures. 2 hrs., 5.

Sonderbergh, Steven, director. 2011. *Contagion*. Warner Bros. Pictures. 1 hr. 46.

Stallone, Sylvester, director. 2010. *The Expendables*. Lionsgate. 1 hr., 43.

Stevenson, John, and Mark Osborne, directors. 2008. *Kung Fu Panda*. DreamWorks Animation, Paramount Pictures. 1 hr., 32.

Stevenson, Robert, director. 1964. *Mary Poppins*. Buena Vista Distribution Company, Inc. 2 hrs., 19.

Strauss-Schulson, Todd, director. 2019. *Isn't It Romantic*. Warner Bros. Pictures. 1 hr., 29.

Stromberg, Robert, director. 2014. *Maleficent*. Walt Disney Studios Motion Pictures. 1 hr., 37.

Tamahori, Lee, director. 2002. *James Bond 007: Die Another Day*. 20th Century Fox. 2 hrs., 13.

Tarantino, Quentin, director. 1994. *Pulp Fiction*. Miramax Films. 2 hrs., 34.

Tarantino, Quentin, director. 2015. *The Hateful Eight*. The Weinstein Company. 2 hrs., 48.

Trousdale, Gary, and Kirk Wise, directors. 1991. *Beauty and the Beast*. Buena Vista Pictures. 1 hr., 24.

Twohy, David, director. 2000. *Pitch Black*. USA Films. 1 hr., 44.

Varda, Agnès, director. 2008. *The Beaches of Agnès*. Les Films du Losange, The Cinema Guild. 1 hr., 50.

Villeneuve, Denis, director. 2017. *Blade Runner 2049*. Sony Pictures Releasing. 2 hrs., 43.

Villeneuve, Denis, director. 2021. *Dune*. Warner Bros. Pictures. 2 hrs., 33.

Wachowski, Lana, and Lilly Wachowski, directors. 1999. *The Matrix*. Warner Bros. 2 hrs., 16.

Wachowski, Lana, and Lilly Wachowski, directors. 2003a. *The Matrix Reloaded*. Warner Bros. Pictures. 2 hrs., 18.

Wachowski, Lana, and Lilly Wachowski, directors. 2003b. *The Matrix Revolutions*. Warner Bros. Pictures. 2 hrs., 9.

Wachowski, Lana, Lilly Wachowski, and Tom Tykwer, directors. 2012. *Cloud Atlas*. Warner Bros. 2 hrs., 52.

Warhol, Andy, director. 1964. *Sleep*. 5 hrs., 21.

Watts, Jon, director. 2017. *Spider-Man: Homecoming*. Sony Pictures Releasing. 2 hrs., 13.

Watts, Jon, director. 2021. *Spider-Man: No Way Home*. Sony Pictures Releasing. 2 hrs., 28.

Weir, Andy, director. 1998. *The Truman Show*. Paramount Pictures. 1 hr., 43.

Whedon, Joss, director. 2005. *Serenity*. Universal Pictures. 1 hr., 59.

Whedon, Joss, director. 2012. *The Avengers*. Walt Disney Studios Motion Pictures. 2 hrs., 23.

Whedon, Joss, director. 2015. *Avengers: Age of Ultron*. Walt Disney Studios Motion Pictures. 2 hrs., 21.

Wiseman, Len, director. 2003. *Underworld*. Screen Gems. 2 hrs., 1.

Wong, James, director. 2009. *Dragon Ball Evolution*. 20th Century Fox. 1 hr., 25.

Wright, Joe, director. 2012. *Anna Karenina*. Universal Pictures. 2 hrs., 10.

Wyatt, Rupert, director. 2011. *Rise of the Planet of the Apes*. 20th Century Fox. 1 hr., 45.

Yan, Cathy, director. 2020 *Birds of Prey: The Emancipation of Harley Quinn*. Warner Bros. Pictures. 1 hr., 49.

Young, Terrence, director. 1965. *James Bond 007: Thunderball*. United Artists. 2 hrs., 10.

Zemeckis, Robert, director. 1988. *Who Framed Roger Rabbit*. Buena Vista Pictures Distribution. 1 hr., 44.

Zwigoff, Terry, director. 2003. *Bad Santa*. Columbia TriStar Film Distributors International. 1 hr., 31.

TV Shows

Abrams, J.J., and Damon Lindelof, et al., producers. 2004–2010. *Lost*. Buena Vista Television, Disney–ABC Domestic Television. 121 episodes.

Aguirre-Sacasa, Roberto, and Jon Goldwater, et al., producers. 2017–present. *Riverdale*. Warner Bros. Television Distribution. 113 episodes.

Aniston, Jennifer, and Reese Witherspoon, et al., producers. 2019–present. *The Morning Show*. Apple Inc. 20 episodes.

Arndt, Stefan, Uwe Schott, and Michael Polle, producers. 2017–present. *Babylon Berlin*. Sky 1, Das Erste. 28 episodes.

Azuma, Iriya [東伊里弥] et al., producers. 1992–1997. *Sailor Moon* [*Bishōjo senshi Sērā Mūn*]. Cartoon Network [TV Asahi]. 200 episodes.

Azuma, Iriya [東伊里弥] et al., producers. 1994–1995. *Sailor Moon S* [*Bishōjo Senshi Sērā Mūn Sūpā*]. Cartoon Network [TV Asahi]. 38 episodes.

Ball, Alan, Gregg Fienberg, et al., producers. 2008–2014. *True Blood*. Warner Bros. Domestic Television. 80 episodes.

Barbera, Joseph, William Hanna, and Freddy Monnickendam, producers. 1981–1989. *The Smurfs* [*Les Schtroumpfs*]. Taft Broadcasting, Television Program Enterprises, SEPP International S.A. 258 episodes.

Barillé, Albert, creator. 1987. *Once Upon a Time... Life* [*Il était une fois... la vie*]. Canal+. 26 episodes.

Bays, Carter, Craig Thomas, et al., producers. 2005–2014. *How I Met Your Mother*. 20th Television. 208 episodes.

Benioff, David, D.B. Weiss, et al., producers. 2011–2019. *Game of Thrones*. Warner Bros. Television. 73 episodes.

Bessho, Koji [別所孝治], and Mori Masaki [真崎守], producers. 1963–1966. *Astro Boy* [*Tetsuwan Atomu*]. Nine Network [Fuji TV]. 193 episodes.

Bob-Waksberg, Raphael, et al., producers. 2014–2020. *BoJack Horseman*. Netflix. 77 episodes.

Berlanti, Greg, et al., producers. 2016–2022. *Legends of Tomorrow*. Warner Bros. Television. 110 episodes.

Berlanti, Greg, J.P. Finn, et al., producers. 2014–present. *The Flash*. Warner Bros. Television. 167 episodes.

Blichfeld, Katja, and Ben Sinclair, creators. 2012–2020. *High Maintenance*. Vimeo, HBO. 53 episodes.

Brooks, James L., et al., producers. 1989–present. *The Simpsons*. 20th Television. 726 episodes.

Buck, Scott, et al., producers. 2017–2018. *Iron Fist*. Netflix. 23 episodes.

Cappiello, Katie, et al., producers. 2020–present. *Grand Army*. Netflix. 9 episodes.

Carsey, Marcy, et al., producers. 1984–1992. *The Cosby Show*. 201 episodes.

Carter, Chris, et al., producers. 1993–2002. *The X-Files*. 20th Television. 218 episodes.

Carver, Jeremy, et al., producers. 2019–present. *Doom Patrol*. Warner Bros. Television. 34 episodes.

Cavandoli, Osvaldo, creator. 1971–1986. *La Linea*. RAI. 90 episodes.

Chase, David, et al., producers. 1999–2007. *The Sopranos*. Warner Bros. Television Distribution. 86 episodes.

Clement, Jemaine, et al., producers. 2019–present. *What We Do in The Shadows*. 20th Television, Disney Media Distribution. 30 episodes.

Coker, Cheo H., et al., producers. 2016–2018. *Luke Cage*. Netflix. 26 episodes.

Colbert, Stephen, Chris Licht, and R.J. Fried, producers. 2018–2020. *Our Cartoon President*. CBS Media Ventures. 46 episodes.

Colbert, Stephen, Jon Stewart, et al., producers. 2015–present. *The Late Show with Stephen Colbert*. CBS Media Ventures. 1278 episodes.

Condal, Ryan, et al., producers. 2022. *House of the Dragon*. HBO. 10 episodes.

Darabont, Frank, et al., producers. 2010–2022. *The Walking Dead*. 20th Television, Disney–ABC Domestic Television. 169 episodes.

Date, Hayato, director. 2002–2007. *Naruto*. TV Tokyo. 220 episodes.

Davies, Michael, Jen K. Patton and Brandon Monk, producers. 2011–2022. *The Talking Dead*. AMC Networks. 221 episodes.

Davies, Russell T., et al., producers. 2019. *Years and Years*. Studio Canal. 6 episodes.

Dibb, Mike, producer. 1972. *Ways of Seeing*. BBC Two. 4 episodes.

DiMartino, Michael D., Bryan Konietzko, and Aaron Ehasz, producers. 2005–2008 *Avatar: The Last Airbender*. MTV Networks. 61 episodes.

Dong-hyuk, Hwang [황동혁], creator. 2021–present. *Squid Game* [*Ojing-eo Geim*]. Netflix. 9 episodes.

Dozier, William, producer. 1966–1968. *Batman*. 20th Television. 120 episodes.

Duffer, Matt, et al., producers. 2016–present. *Stranger Things*. 34 episodes.

Erickson, Dan, et al., producers. 2022–present. *Severance*. Apple Inc. 9 episodes.

Esmail, Sam, et al., producers. 2015–2019. *Mr. Robot*. NBCUniversal Television. 45 episodes.

Favreau. Jon, et al., producers. 2019–present. *The Mandalorian*. Disney Platform Distribution. 16 episodes.

Fergus, Mark, et al., producers. 2015–2022. *The Expanse*. Legendary Television. 62 episodes.

Fincher, David, et al., producers. 2013–2018. *House of Cards*. Sony Pictures Television. 73 episodes.

Fogelman, Dan, et al., producers. 2016–2022. *This is Us*. 106 episodes.

Foschini, Michele, et al., producers. 2021. *Tear Along the Dotted Line [Strappare lungo i bordi]*. Netflix. 6 episodes.

Frost, Mark, David Lynch, and Sabrina S. Sutherland, producers. 1990–2017. *Twin Peaks*. CBS Television Distribution, Showtime Networks. 48 episodes.

Fujio, Akifumi [藤尾明史], et al., producers 2019–present. *Demon Slayer: Kimetsu no Yaiba*. Adult Swim [Fuji TV]. 44 episodes.

Fuller, Bryan, et al., producers, 2017–2021. *American Gods*. Lionsgate Television, Fremantle. 26 episodes.

Fuller, Bryan, et al., producers. 2017–present. *Star Trek: Discovery*. CBS, CBS All Access, Paramount+. 55 episodes.

Gaiman, Neil, et al., producers. 2022–present. *The Sandman*. 10 episodes.

Gilligan, Vince, Mark Johnson, and Michelle MacLaren, producers. 2008–2013. *Breaking Bad*. Sony Pictures Television. 62 episodes.

Gilligan, Vince, et al., producers. 2015–2022. *Better Call Saul*. Sony Pictures Television. 55 episodes.

Goddard, Drew, et al., producers. 2015–2019. *Daredevil*. Netflix. 39 episodes.

Goldsman, Akiva, et al., producers. 2020–present. *Star Trek: Picard*. CBS All Access, Paramount+. 20 episodes.

Gomez, Selena, et al., producers. 2017–2020. *13 Reasons Why*. Netflix. 49 episodes.

Gough, Alfred, et al., producers 2001–2011. *Smallville*. Warner Bros. Domestic Television. 217 episodes.

Green, Misha, et al., producers. 2020–present. *Lovecraft Country*. Warner Bros. Television. 10 episodes.

Hanna, William, and Joseph Barbera, producers. 1962–1963. *The Jetsons* (Season 1). Screen Gems. 24 episodes.

Harman, Hugh, et al., producers. 1930–1969. *Looney Tunes*. Warner Bros., The Vitaphone Corporation, Vitagraph Company of America, Turner Entertainment Co.

Harmon, Dan, Justin Roiland, et al., producers. 2013–present. *Rick and Morty*. Warner Bros. Television. 51 episodes.

Heald, Josh, Jon Hurwitz, et al., producers. 2018–present. *Cobra Kai*. Netflix. 40 episodes.

Higson, Charlie, creator. 2015. *Jekyll and Hyde*. ITV. 10 episodes.

Hirst, Michael, et al., producers. 2013–2020. MGM Television. 89 episodes.

Hissrich, Lauren S., et al., producers. 2019–present. *The Witcher*. Netflix. 16 episodes.

Ising, Rudolf, et al., producers. 1940–1967. *Tom & Jerry*. Metro-Goldwyn-Mayer. 161 episodes.

Jenkins, David, et al., producers. 2022–present. *Our Flag Means Death*. Warner Bros. Discovery Global Streaming & Interactive Entertainment. 10 episodes.

Judkins, Rafe, et al., producers. 2021–present. *The Wheel of Time*. Sony Pictures Television. 8 episodes.

Khan, Nahnatchka, et al., producers. 2015–2020. *Fresh Off the Boat*. 20th Television. 116 episodes.

Kinberg, Simon, Dave Filoni, and Greg Weisman, producers. 2014–2018. *Star Wars Rebels*. Disney–ABC Domestic Television. 75 episodes.

King, Robert, et al., producers. 2017–present. *The Good Fight*. Paramount Global Distribution Group. 50 episodes.

Kinoshita, Tetsuya [木下哲哉], et al., producers. 2013–2022. *Attack on Titan* [*Shingeki no Kyojin*]. Adult Swim [MBS, NHK G]. 87 episodes.

Kojima, Masayuki [小島正幸], director. 2017–present. *Made in Abyss*. Adult Swim [AT-X et al.]. 13 episodes.

Kring, Tim, et al., producers. 2006–2010. *Heroes*. NBCUniversal Television Distribution. 77 episodes.

Kripke, Eric, et al., producers. 2005–2020. *Supernatural*. Warner Bros. Television, Amazon Studios. 327 episodes.

Kripke, Eric, et al., producers. 2019–present. *The Boys*. Sony Pictures Television, Amazon Studios. 16 episodes.

Lindelof, Damon, et al., producers. 2019. *Watchmen*. Warner Bros. Television. 9 episodes.

Logan. John, et al., producers. 2014–2016. *Penny Dreadful*. Showtime. 27 episodes.

Lyonne Natasha, et al., producers. 2019–present. *Russian Doll*. Netflix. 15 episodes.

MacFarlane, Seth, et al., producers. 1999–present. *Family Guy*. 20th Television. 389 episodes.

Magon, Jymn, et al., producers. 1987–1990. *DuckTales*. Buena Vista Television. 100 episodes.

Martin, Quinn, producer. 1963–1967. *The Fugitive*. ABC Films. 120 episodes.

Matsui, Chinatsu [松井千夏], et al., producers. 2015–2019. *One-Punch Man* [*Wanpanman*]. Adult Swim [TV Tokyo]. 24 episodes.

Matsutani, Hiroaki [松谷浩明], et al., producers. 2020–present. *Jujutsu Kaisen*. Crunchyroll [JNN]. 24 episodes.

Matsuya, Yuuichirou [松家雄一郎], Atsushi Sugita [杉田敦], and Hisanori Kunisaki [国崎久徳], producers. 2002–2005. *Ghost in the Shell: Stand Alone Complex* [*Kōkaku kidōtai Sutando Arōn Konpurekkusu*]. SBS One, Adult Swim [Production I.G.]. 52 episodes.

Medjuck, Joe, producer. 1986–1991. *Slimer! and The Real Ghostbusters*. Coca-Cola Telecommunications, Columbia Pictures Television Distribution. 140 episodes.

Miller, Bruce, et al., producers. 2017–present. *The Handmaid's Tale*. MGM Television. 46 episodes.

Mizushima, Tsutomu [水島努], director. 2014–2015. *Shirobako*. Sentai Filmworks [Tokyo MX]. 24 episodes

Moore, Ronald D., and David Eick, producers. 2004–2009. *Battlestar Galactica*. NBC Universal Television Distribution. 76 episodes.

Morgan, Peter, et al., producers. 2016–present. *The Crown*. Netflix. 40 episodes.

Nakatani, Toshio [中谷敏夫], Manabu Tamura [田村学], and Masao Maruyama [丸山正雄], producers. 2006–2007. *Death Note*. ABC2 [Nippon TV]. 37 episodes.

Newman, Sydney, C.E. Webber, and Donald Wilson, creators. 1963–present. *Doctor Who*. BBC Studios. 870 episodes.

Noxon, Marti, et al., producers. 2015–2018. *UnREAL*. Lifetime, Hulu. 38 episodes.

Nunn, Laurie, Jamie Campbell, and Ben Taylor, et al., producers. 2019–present. *Sex Education*. Netflix. 24 episodes.

Oliver, John, et al., producers. 2014–present. *Last Week Tonight with John Oliver*. 255 episodes.

Parker, Trey, et al., producers. 1997–present. *South Park*. Paramount Global. 317 episodes.

Petrie, Douglas, et al., producers. 2017. *The Defenders*. Netflix. 8 episodes.

Povenmire, Dan, and Jeff Marsh, producers. 2007–2015. *Phineas and Ferb*. Disney–ABC Domestic Television. 129 episodes.

Radomski, Eric, et al., producers. 1992–1995. *Batman: The Animated Series*. Warner Bros. Television Distribution. 85 episodes.

Raimi, Sam, et al., producers. 2010–2013. *Spartacus* Starz Media. 39 episodes.

Rhimes, Shonda, et al., producers. 2005–present. *Grey's Anatomy*. Buena Vista Television, Disney–ABC Domestic Television. 397 episodes.

Roddenberry, Gene, producer. 1966–1969 *Star Trek*. CBS Paramount Television. 79 episodes.

Roddenberry, Gene, et al., producers. 1987–1994. *Star Trek: The Next Generation*. Paramount Domestic Television. 178 episodes.

Rosenberg, Melissa, et al., producers. 2015–2019. *Jessica Jones*. Netflix. 39 episodes.

Ruggiero, Diane, et al., producers. 2004–2019. *Veronica Mars*. Warner Bros. Television, Hulu Originals. 72 episodes.

Schaeffer, Jac, et al., producers. 2021. *WandaVision*. Disney Platform Distribution. 9 episodes.

Schur, Michael, et al., producers. 2016–2020. *The Good Place*. NBCUniversal Television. 53 episodes.

Shore, David, et al., producers. 2004–2012. *House*. NBCUniversal Television. 177 episodes.

Siega, Marcos, et al., producers. 2018–present. *You*. Warner Bros. Television. 30 episodes.

Simon, David, Robert F. Colesberry, and Nina K. Noble, producers. 2002–2008. *The Wire*. Warner Bros. Television, HBO Enterprises. 60 episodes.

Spotnitz, Frank, et al., producers. 2015–2019. *The Man in the High Castle*. Amazon Studios. 40 episodes.

Straczynski, J. Michael, producer. 1993–1998. *Babylon 5*. Warner Bros. 110 episodes.

Suckle, Richard, et al., producers. 2015–2018. *12 Monkeys*. NBCUniversal Television. 47 episodes.

Surnow, Joel, et al., producers. 2001–2010. *24*. 20th Television. 192 episodes.

Suwa, Michihiko [諏訪道彦], et al., producers. 1996–present. *Detective Conan* [*Meitantei Konan*]. Adult Swim [NNS]. 1.052 episodes.

Takahashi, Yūma [高橋祐馬], producer. 2018–2021. *Cells at Work!* [*Hataraku Saibō*]. Animax Asia [David Production]. 21 episodes.

Terrace, Dana, and Wade Wisinski, producers. 2020–present. *The Owl House*. Disney Channel. 40 episodes.

Tsuchiya, Tokizō [土屋登喜蔵], et al., producers. 1992–1994 [1986–1989]. *Dragon Ball*. Cartoon Network [Fuji TV]. 153 episodes.

Tudyk, Alan, Philip-Jon Haarsma, and Nathan Fillion, producers. 2015–2017. *Con Man*. Vimeo, Comic-Con HQ. 25 episodes.

Van Dusen, Chris, et al., producers. 2020–present. *Bridgerton*. Netflix. 16 episodes.

Vaughan, Brian K., et al., producers. 2021. *Y: The Last Man*. Disney–ABC Domestic Television. 10 episodes.

Waldron, Michael, et al., producers. 2021–present. *Loki*. Disney Platform Distribution. 6 episodes.

Waller-Bridge, Phoebe, et al., producers. 2016–2019. *Fleabag*. 12 episodes.

West, Veronica, and Sarah Kucserka, producers. 2020. *High Fidelity*. Midnight Radio, Hulu. 10 episodes.

Whedon, Joss, and Tim Minear, producers. 2002. *Firefly*. 20th Television. 14 episodes.

Whedon, Joss, et al., producers. 2013–2020. *Agents of Shields*. Walt Disney Television. 136 episodes.

Willimon, Beau, et al., producers. 2013–2018. Netflix. 73 episodes.

Wolf, Dick, Joseph Stern, et al., producers. 1990–2010. *Law & Order*. NBC Universal Syndication Studios. 456 episodes.

Yodo, Akiko [淀明子], et al., producers. 2016–2018. *March Comes In like a Lion* [*Sangatsu no Raion*]. Aniplex of America [NHK G]. 44 episodes.

Youngberg, Matt, producer. 2017–2021. *DuckTales*. Disney XD, Disney Channel. 69 episodes.

Youssef, Ramy, et al., producers. 2019–present. *Ramy*. Hulu. 20 episodes

Zuiker, Anthony E., et al., producers. 2000–2015. *CSI: Crime Scene Investigation*. King World Productions, CBS Television. 337 episodes.

Comics and Manga

Aaron, Jason (wri), Kieron Gillen (wri), et al. (wri), John Cassaday (art), Salvador Larroca (art), et al. (art). 2015–2019. *Star Wars*. Marvel Comics. 75 issues.

Akutami, Gege [芥見下々] (wri/art). 2018–present. *Jujutsu Kaisen*. Shueisha. 19 volumes.

Aoyama, Gosho [青山剛昌] (wri/art). 1994–present. *Detective Conan* [*Meitantei Konan*]. VIZ Media [Shogakukan]. 101 volumes.

Arakawa, Hiromu [荒川弘] (wri/art). 2001–2010. *Fullmetal Alchemist* [*Hagane no renkinjutsushi*]. Viz Media [Enix, Square Enix]. 27 volumes.

Aso, Haro [麻生羽呂] (wri/art). 2010–2016. *Alice in Borderland* [*Imawa no kuni no arisu*]. VIZ Media [Shogakukan]. 18 volumes.

Azzarello, Brian (wri), and Richard Corben (art). 2002. *Cage*, Vol. 2. Marvel Comics. 5 issues.

Baker, Dave (wri), Nicole Goux and Ellie (art). 2021. *Everyone Is Tulip*. Dark Horse Books.

Barks, Carl (wri/art). 2011 [1949]. "Voodoo Hoodoo" In *The Complete Carl Barks Disney Library*. Fantagraphics. Volume 7.

Barks, Carl (wri/art). 2012a [1951]. "A Christmas for Shacktown" In *The Complete Carl Barks Disney Library*. Fantagraphics. Volume 11.

Barks, Carl (wri/art). 2012b [1952]. "Only A Poor Old Man" In *The Complete Carl Barks Disney Library*. Fantagraphics. Volume 12.

Barks, Carl (wri/art). 2017 [1965]. "The Lost Crown of Genghis Khan" In *The Complete Carl Barks Disney Library*. Fantagraphics. Volumes 16.

Baron, Mike, et al. (wri), Klaus Janson, et al. (art). 1987–2018. *Punisher*, Vol 2. Marvel Comics. 115 issues.

Buckley, Tim (wri/art). 2002–present. *Ctrl+Alt+Del*. https://cad-comic.com/.

Bushmiller, Ernie, Al Plastino, et al. (wri/art). 1938–present. *Nancy*. United Feature Syndicate, United Media, Andrews McMeel Syndication.

Carnell, John, et al. (wri), Anthony Williams, et al. (art). 1989–1992. *The Real Ghostbusters*. Marvel Comics. 193 issues.

Culliford, Pierre "Peyo" (wri/art). 1963–1992. *The Smurfs* [*Les Schtroumpfs*]. Random House [Cartoon Creation, Lombard, Dupuis]. 16 volumes.

Darnall, Steve, and Alex Ross (wri), and Alex Ross (art). 1997. *U.S.—Uncle Sam*. Vertigo. 2 issues.

David, Peter (wri), and Carlos Villa (art). 2020. *Black Widow Prelude*. Marvel Comics. 2 issues.

Davis, Jim (wri/art). 1978–present. *Garfield*. United Feature Syndicate, Universal Press Syndicate, Universal Uclick, Andrews McMeel Syndication.

Del Col, Anthony, and Conor McCreery (wri), Andy Belanger, et al. (art). 2010–2017. *Kill Shakespeare*. IDW Publishing. 21 issues.

Delisle, Guy (wri/art). 2005 [2004]. *Pyongyang: A Journey in North Korea* [*Pyongyang*]. Drawn & Quarterly [L'Association].

Delisle, Guy (wri/art). 2008 [2007]. *Burma Chronicles* [*Chroniques Birmanes*]. Drawn & Quarterly [Delcourt].

DenBleyker, Rob, Dave McElfatrick, and Kris Wilson (wri/art). 2005–present. *Cyanide and Happiness*. https://explosm.net/.

Disney Comics, et al. (wri/art). 1990–1991. *Mickey Mouse Adventures*. Timonium: Gemstone Publishing.

Eisner, Will (wri), and Dave Berg (art). 1940. *National Comics*, issue. #1. Quality Comics.

Ennis, Garth (wri), Darick Robertson, et al. (art). 2006–2012. WildStorm, Dynamite Entertainment. 72 issues.

Ewing, Al (wri), Salvador Espin, and Paco Diaz (art). 2018. *You Are Deadpool*, Vol. 1. 5 issues.

Ferris, Emil (wri/art). 2017. *My Favourite Thing is Monsters*. Fantagraphics.

Fox, Gardner (wri), and Carmine Infantino (art). 1961. *The Flash*. DC Comics. Vol. 1: issue #123.

Gaiman, Neil (wri), et al. (art). 1989–1996). *The Sandman*. DC Comics. 75 issues.

Gillen, Keiron (wri), Simon Spurrier (wri), and Kev Walker (art). 2016–2019. *Doktor Aphra*. New York: Marvel Comics. 7 issues.

Glidden, Sarah (wri/art). 2010. *How to Understand Israel in 60 Days or Less*. Drawn and Quarterly.

Goodbrey, Daniel M. (wri/art). 2012. *A Duck Has An Adventure*. http://e-merl.com/stuff/duck.html.

Gotouge, Koyoharu [吾峠　呼世晴] (wri/art). 2016–2020. *Demon Slayer: Kimetsu no Yaiba*. Viz Media [Shūeisha]. 23 volumes.

Hanazawa, Kengo [花沢健吾] (wri/art). 2009–2017. *I Am a Hero* [*Ai amu a hīrō*]. Viz Media [Shogakukan]. 22 volumes.

Hergé (Remi, Georges) (wri/art). 1929–1976. *The Adventures of Tintin* [*Les Aventures de Tintin*]. Hachette Book Group [Casterman]. 42 volumes.

Herrima, George (wri/art). 1913–1944. *Krazy Kat*. King Features Syndicate.

Holkins, Jerry (wri/art). 1998–present. *Penny Arcade*. https://www.penny-arcade.com/.

Isin, Nisio [西尾維新] (wri), and Oh! great [大暮維人] (art). 2018–present. *Bakemonogatari*. Vertical [Kodansha]. 17 volumes.

Jemisin, N.K. (wri), and Jamal Campbell (art). 2021–present. *Far Sector*: Vol. #1: *The Far Sector*. Marvel Comics.

Johns, Geoff (wri), and Gary Frank (art). 2018–2020. *Doomsday Clock*. DC Comics. 12 issues.

Johns, Geoff (wri), and Phi Jemenez, et al. (art). 2005–2006. *Infinite Crisis*. DC Comics. 7 issues.

Jurgens, Dan (wri), and Lee Moder, et al. (art). 2001. *Captain America Annual*, issue #2001. Marcel Comics.

Kanigher, Robert (wri), and Harry G. Peter (art). 1953. *Wonder Woman*, Vol. 1: issue #59. DC Comics.

King, Tom (wri), and Gabriel Walta (art). 2018. *Vision*. Marvel Comics.

Kirkman, Robert (wri), Tony Moore, and Charlie Adlard (art). 2003–2019. *The Walking Dead*. Image Comics. 193 issues.

Kishimoto, Masashi [岸本斉史] (wri/art). 1999–2014. *Naruto*. Viz Media [Shūeisha]. 72 volumes.

Kōno, Fumiyo [こうの史代] (wri/art). 2007–2009. *In This Corner of the World* [*Kono sekai no katasumi ni*]. Seven Seas Entertainment [Futabasha]. 3 volumes.

Kupperberg, Paul (wri), Steve Lightle, et al. (art). 1987–1995. *Doom Patrol*, Vol. 2. DC Comics. 87 issues.

Layton, Bob (wri), and Dick Giordano (art). 1998–1999. *Batman: Dark Knight of the Round Table*. DC Comics. 2 issues.

Lee, Stan (wri), and Don Heck (art). 1964. *Avengers*, Vol. 1: issue #10. Marvel Comics.

Lee, Stan (wri), and Bill Everett (art). 1964. *Daredevil*, Vol. 1: issue #1. Marvel Comics.

Lee, Stan (wri), and Jack Kirby (art). 1965. *Journey into Mystery Annual*, Vol. 1: issue. #1. Marvel Comics.

Luna, Jonathan, Sarah Vaughn (wri), and Jonathan Luna (art). 2013–2015. *Alex + Ada*. Image Comics. 15 issues.

Martin, Alan C. (wri), and Jamie Hewlett (art). 2002 [1988]. *Tank Girl 1*. Titan Books.

Martina, Guido (wri), and Giovan Battista Carpi (art). 1969. "Paperinik il diabolico vendicatore." *Topolino*. issue *705*. Mondadori.

Marz, Ron (wri), Steve Carr, et al. (art). 1994. *Green Lantern*, Vol. 3: issue #54. DC Comics.

Millar, Mark (wri), and Bryan Hitch (art). 2002–2004. *The Ultimates*. Marvel Comics. 13 issues.

Miller, Frank (wri/art). 1986. *The Dark Knight Returns*. DC Comics. 4 issues.

Miller, Frank (wri/art). 1998. *300*. Dark Horse Comics. 3 issues.

Miller, Frank (wri/art). 1999–2000. *Sin City: Hell and Back*. Maverick. 9 issues.

Miller, Frank (wri/art). 2002–2003. *Batman: The Dark Knight Strikes Again*. DC Comics. 3 issues.

Miller, Frank, and Brian Azzarello (wri), Frank Miller, et al. (art). 2015–2017. *The Dark Knight III: The Master Race*. DC Comics. 9 issues.

Moore, Alan (wri), and Dave Gibbons (art). 2014 [1986/87]. *Watchmen: International Edition*. DC Comics.

Miller, Frank (wri), and Rafael Grampá (art). 2020 [2019]. *The Dark Knight Returns: The Golden Child: Collected Edition*. DC Comics.

Miller, Frank (wri), Dave Johnson, et al. (art). 2003. *Superman: Red Son*. DC Comics. 3 issues.

Moench, Doug (wri), and Kelley Jones (art). 1991. *Batman & Dracula: Red Rain*. DC Comics.

Miller, Frank (wri), and David Mazzucchelli (art). 1988 [1987]. *Batman: Year One*. Marvel Comics.

Moore, Alan (wri), and Kevin O'Neill (art). 1999–2019. *The League of Extraordinary Gentlemen*. Wildstorm, DC Comics, Top Shelf Productions, Knockabout Comics. 6 volumes.

Morrison, Grant (wri), and Frank Quitely (art). 2004. *WE3*. Vertigo. 3 issues.

Morrison, Grant (wri), and J.G. Jones, et al. (art). 2008–2009. *Final Crisis*. DC Comics. 7 issues.

Munroe, Randall (wri/art). 2005–present. *XKCD*. https://xkcd.com/.

Oda, Eiichiro [尾田栄一郎] (wri/art). 1997–present. *One Piece*. Viz Media [Shueisha]. 102 volumes.

Ohba, Tsugumi [大場つぐみ] (wri), and Takeshi Obata [小畑健] (art) 2003–2006. *Death Note*. Madman Entertainment [Shueisha]. 12 volumes.

ONE (wri), and Yusuke Murata [村田雄介] (art). 2012–present. *One-Punch Man [Wanpan-man]*. VIZ Media [Shueisha]. 25 volumes.

Otomo, Katsuhiro [大友克洋] (wri/art). 1982–1990. *Akira*. Madman Entertainment [Kodansha]. 6 volumes.

Pekar, Harvey (wri), and Harvey Pekar, et al. (art). 2003. *American Splendor: The Life and Times of Harvey Pekar*. Ballantine Books.

Rosa, Don (wri/art). 1992–1994. *The Life and Times of Scrooge McDuck*. Egmont Publishing. 12 issues.

Rosa, Don (wri/art). 2004. "The Quest for Kalevala." In *Uncle Scrooge*: issue #334. Dell Comics.

Rosa, Don (wri/art). 2015. *Uncle Scrooge and Donald: Treasure Under Glass. The Don Rosa Library*, volume 3. Fantagraphics.

Rose, Joel (wri), and Langdon Foss (art). 2012. *Get Jiro!* DC Comics.

Sadamoto, Yoshiyuki [貞本義行] (wri/art). 1994–2013. *Neon Genesis Evangelion [Shin Seiki Evangelion]*. VIZ Media [Kadokawa Shoten]. 12 volumes.

Sattouf, Riad (wri/art). 2014–2020. *The Arab of the Future [L'Arabe du Futur]*. Metropolitan Books [Allary Éditions]. 5 volumes.

Schultz, Mark (wri/art). 1950–2000. *Peanuts*. United Feature Syndicate

Shimizu, Akana [清水茜] (wri/art). 2015–2021. *Cells at Work! [Hataraku saibō]*. Kodansha USA [Kodansha]. 6 volumes.

Sikoryak, R. (wri/art). 2017. *The Unquotable Trump*. Drawn and Quarterly.

Sisti, Alessandro, Francesco Artibani, et al. (wri), and Claudio Sciarrone, et al. (art). 1996–2001. *Paperinik New Adventures*. Disney Italy. 56 issues.

Sisti, Alessandro, Ezio Sisti, et al. (wri), and Alberto Lavoradori (art). 2017. *Duck Avenger: New Adventures*, issue #1. IDW Publishing.

Smith, Jeff (wri/art). 1991–2004. *Bone*. Cartoon Books, Image Comics. 55 issues.

Snyder, Scott (wri), and Greg Capullo (art). 2020–2021. *Dark Nights: Death Metal*. DC Comics. 7 issues.

Sorachi, Hideaki [空知英秋] (wri/art). 2003–2019. *Gintama*. Viz Media [Shueisha]. 77 volumes.

Soule, Charles, and Scott Snyder (wri), Daniele Orlandini, et al. (art). 2019–present. *Undiscovered Country*. Image Comics. 20 issues.

Sousanis, Nick (wri/art). 2015. *Unflattening*. Cambridge, MA: Harvard University Press.

Spiegelman, Art (wri/art). 1980–1991. *Maus*. Pantheon Books.

Starlin, Jim (wri), and Jim Aparo (art). 1988–1989. *Batman*, Vol. 1: issues #426–429. *A Death in the Family*. DC Comics.

Straczynski, J. Michael (wri), and John Romita Jr. (art). *Amazing Spider-Man*, Vol. 2: issue #36. Marvel Comics.

Sturm, James (wri/art). 2019. *Off Season*. Drawn and Quarterly.

Talbot, Bryan (wri/art). 2009–2017. *Grandville*. Jonathan Cape. 5 issues.

Tamaki, Mariko (wri/art). *Laura Dean Keeps Breaking Up with Me*. First Second.

Tamaki, Mariko (wri), and Steve Pugh (art). 2020. *Harley Quinn: Breaking Glass*. DC Comics.

Takeuchi, Naoko [武内直子] (wri/art). 1991–1997. *Sailor Moon [Bishōjo senshi Sērā Mūn]*. Kodansha Comics [Kodansha]. 18 volumes.

Takeuchi, Ryōsuke [竹内良輔] (wri), and Takeshi Obata [小畑健] (art). 2014. *All You Need Is Kill*. Weekly Shonen Jump [Shueisha]. 2 volumes.

Toriyama, Akira [鳥山明] (wri/art). 1984–1995. *Dragon Ball*. Viz Media [Shūeisha]. 42 volumes.

Trondheim, Lewis (wri/art). 2004 [2002]. *Mister O.* Delcourt.

Trondheim, Lewis (wri/art). 2007 [2005]. *Mister I.* Delcourt.

Tsukushi, Akihito [つくしあきひと] (wri/art). 2012–present. *Made in Abyss.* Bamboo Comics [Takeshobo]. 11 volumes.

Vaughan, Brian K. (wri), and Pia Guerra, et al. (art). 2002–2008. *Y: The Last Man.* Vertigo. 60 issues.

Vaughan, Brian K. (wri), and Tony Harris (art). 2004–2010. *Ex Machina.* DC Comics, Wildstorm. 50 issues.

Vaughan, Brian K. (wri), and Niko Henrichon (art). 2006. *Pride of Baghdad.* Vertigo.

Vaughan, Brian K. (wri), and Fiona Staples (art). 2012–present. *Saga.* Image Comics. 57 issues.

Venditti, Robert, and Van Jensen (wri), Scott Hanna and Neil Edwards (art). 2014. *Green Lantern Corps Annual,* Vol. 2: issue #2. DC Comics.

Waid, Mark (wri), and Barry Kitson (art). 2009. *The Amazing Spider-Man,* Vol. 1: issue #583. Marvel Comics.

Watterson, Bill (wri/art). 1985–1995. *Calvin & Hobbes.* Universal Press Syndicate.

Watterson, Bill (wri/art). N.d. [1985]. "Calvin and Hobbes by Bill Watterson for November 22, 1985." *GoComics.* https://www.gocomics.com/calvinandhobbes/1985/11/22/.

Willingham, Bill (wri), and Mark Buckingham, et al. (art). 2002–present. *Fables.* Vertigo, DC Black Label. 162 issues.

Wolfman, Marv, et al. (wri), and George Pérez (art). 1985–1986. *Crisis on Infinite Earths.* DC Comics. 12 issues.

Wolfman, Marv (wri), and George Pérez (art). 1986. *History of the DC Universe.* DC Comics. 2 issues.

Zdarsky, Chip (wri), Eddy Barrows, et al. (art). *Batman: Urban Legends,* Vol. 1: issue #6. DC Comics.

Video Games

Arkane Lyon. *Deathloop.* PC/PlayStation 5. 2021.

Bethesda. *The Elder Scrolls V: Skyrim.* PC/PlayStation 3/Xbox 360. 2011.

BioWare. *Mass Effect.* PC/PlayStation 3/Xbox 360. 2007.

BioWare. *Dragon Age: Origins.* Xbox 360. 2009.

BioWare. *Mass Effect 2.* PC/PlayStation 3/Xbox 360. 2010.

BioWare. *Mass Effect 3.* PC/PlayStation 3/Xbox 360/Wii U. 2012.

BioWare Austin. *Star Wars: The Old Republic.* PC. 2011.

Blizzard Entertainment. *World of Warcraft.* PC/Mac. 2005.

Bungie. *Halo 3: ODST.* Xbox 360. 2009.

Capcom. *Resident Evil.* PlayStation. 1996.

CD Projekt Red. *The Witcher 3: Wild Hunt.* Windows/PlayStation 4/Xbox One. 2015

Colossal Order. *Cities: Skylines.* PC/Mac/Linux. 2015

Crystal Dynamics. *Marvel's Avengers.* PC/PlayStation 4/Xbox One. 2020.

Dimensional Ink Games. *DC Universe Online.* PC. 2011.

Dontnod Entertainment. *Life Is Strange.* PC. 2015.

Dontnod Entertainment. *Life Is Strange 2.* PC. 2018–2019.

Epic Games. *Fortnite: Battle Royale.* PC/Mac. 2018.

Failbetter Games. *Sunless Sea.* PC/Mac/Linux. 2015.

Hello Games. *No Man's Sky.* PC/PlayStation 4/Xbox One. 2016.

Innersloth. *Among Us.* Android/iOS/PC. 2018.

Insomniac Games. *Ratchet & Clank*. PlayStation 2. 2012.

Insomniac Games. *Ratchet & Clank*. PlayStation 4. 2016.

JetDogs. *The 12 Labours of Hercules*. Nintendo Switch. 2019.

Klei Entertainment. *Don't Starve*. PC/Mac/Linux. 2013

Kojima Productions. *P.T.* PlayStation 4. 2014.

Kojima Productions. *Death* Stranding. PlayStation 4. 2019

Konami. *Metal Gear Solid*. PlayStation. 1998.

Konami Digital Entertainment. *Metal Gear Survive*. PC/PlayStation 4 /Xbox One. 2018

McMillen, Edmund, and Florian Himsl. *The Binding of Isaac*. PC/Mac/Linux. 2011.

Mojang. *Minecraft*. PC/Mac/Linux. 2011.

Monolith Productions. *Middle-Earth: Shadow of Mordor*. PC/ PlayStation 3/PlayStation 4/ Xbox 360/Xbox One. 2014.

Monolith Productions. *Middle-Earth: Shadow of War*. PC/PlayStation 4/Xbox One. 2017.

Nadeo. *TrackMania*. PC. 2020.

Namco. *Pac-Man*. Arcade. 1980.

Niantic. *Ingress*. Android/iOS. 2013.

Niantic. *Pokémon Go*. Android/iOS/iPadOS. 2016.

Nintendo EAD. *The Legend of Zelda: Majora's Mask*, Nintendo 64. 2000.

Nintendo R&D1. *Tetris*. Game Boy. 1989.

Nintendo R&D1. *Dr. Mario*. NES/Game Boy. 1990.

Paradox Development Studio. *Crusader Kings*. PC/Mac. 2004.

Paradox Development Studio. *Crusader Kings II*. PC/Mac. 2012.

Paradox Development Studio. *Crusader Kings III*. PC/Mac. 2020.

Polyphony Digital. *Gran Turismo* 5. PlayStation 3. 2010.

Project Soul. *Soulcalibur V.* PlayStation 3/Xbox 360. 2012.

Remedy Entertainment. *Alan Wake*. PC/Xbox 360. 2010.

Riot Games. *League of Legends*. PC. 2009.

Rockstar Games. *Austin Powers: Oh, Behave!*. Game Boy. 2000.

Rockstar Studios. *Red Dead Redemption 2*. PlayStation 4/Xbox One. 2018.

Rocksteady Studios. *Batman: Arkham Knight*. PC/PlayStation 4/Xbox One. 2015.

Square. *Final Fantasy VII*. PlayStation. 1997.

Superhot Team. *Superhot*. PC/Mac/Linux. 2016.

Telltale Games. *The Walking Dead*. PC/Mac/PlayStation 3/Xbox 360/iOS. 2012

Terminal Reality. *Ghostbusters: The Video Game*. PC/PlayStation 3/Xbox 360. 2009.

Traveller's Tales. *Lego Star Wars: The Video Game*. PC/Mac/PlayStation 2/Xbox 360. 2005.

Ubi Soft Montréal. *PK: Out of the Shadows*. GameCube/PlayStation 2. 2002.

Ubisoft Montréal. *Assassin's Creed II*. PlayStation 3/Xbox 360. 2009

Ubisoft Montréal. *Assassin's Creed: Brotherhood*. PlayStation 3/Xbox 360. 2010

Ubisoft Quebec. *Assassin's Creed: Odyssey*. PC/PlayStation 4/Xbox One. 2018.

Ubisoft Toronto. *Watch Dogs: Legion*. PC/PlayStation 4/Xbox One. 2020.

Valve. *Half Life*. PC/Mac/Linux. 1998.

Valve. *Portal*. PC/Mac/Linux. 2007.

Secondary Sources, Paratexts

Aarseth, Espen J. 1997. *Cybertext: Perspectives on Ergodic Literature*. Baltimore: Johns Hopkins University Press.

Aarseth, Espen J. 2012. "A Narrative Theory of Games." In *FDG '12: Proceedings of the International Conference on the Foundations of Digital Games*, edited by Magy Seif El-Nasr, 129–133. New York: Association for Computing Machinery. https://dl.acm.org/doi/10.1145/2282338.2282365.

Aarseth, Espen J. 2022. "Characters without Signifiers." *Narrative: The Journal of the International Society for the Study of Narrative*, no. 30 (2): 269–278.

Aarseth, Espen J., and Joleen Blom, eds. 2022. *Narrative: The Journal of the International Society for the Study of Narrative*, no. 30 (2), Special issue on *Characters*.

Abdullaeva, Nelli. 2021. "The Bechdel Test and Gender Equality in the Film Industry: The Issues of an Oversimplified Analysis in Assessing the Representation of Women in Cinema." *Blog ABV Gender- und Diversitykompetenz FU Berlin*, December 13. https://blogs.fu-berlin.de/abv-gender-diversity/2021/12/13/the-bechdel-test-and-gender-equality-in-the-film-industry/.

Ackermann, Diane. 2019. "An Interview with Robert Macfarlane." *Conjunctions*, no. 73 (Fall/November): 63–77.

Adams, Robert N. 2019. "Mario Officially Holds 7 Jobs, Nintendo Says." *TechRaptor,* January 03. https://techraptor.net/gaming/news/mario-officially-holds-7-jobs-nintendo-says.

Ahmed, Sara. 2010. *The Promise of Happiness*. Durham: Duke University Press.

Aka Steak, and Iron. 2015. "Why Is Speed o' Sound Sonic Drawn as a Woman but Is Apparently a Man?" *Reddit,* October 28. https://www.reddit.com/r/OnePunchMan/comments/3ql4hi/why_is_speed_o_sound_sonic_drawn_as_a_woman_but/.

Alaniz, José. 2014. *Death, Disability, and the Superhero: The Silver Age and Beyond*. Jackson: University Press of Mississippi.

Alaniz, José. 2020. "Animals in Graphic Narrative." In *The Oxford Handbook of Comic Studies*, edited by Frederick L. Aldama, 326–334. Oxford: Oxford University Press.

AlanMooreVids. 2007. "Alan Moore Talks – 02 – Watchmen." *YouTube*, October 15. https://www.youtube.com/watch?v=qKebCtCTbCA.

Aldama, Frederick L. 2010. "Characters in Comic Books." In *Characters in Fictional Worlds: Understanding Imaginary Beings in Literature, Film, and Other Media*, edited by Jens Eder, Fotis Jannidis and Ralf Schneider, 318–328. Berlin: de Gruyter.

Alexa, Laurén. 2020. "Live-Action v Animation: The Debate Surrounding 'The Lion King.'" *Animation World Network*, January 09. https://www.awn.com/news/live-action-v-animation-debate-surrounding-lion-king.

Allen, Graham. 2011. *Intertextuality*. 2nd ed. London: Routledge.

Allen, Joseph. 2022. "'Lightyear' Features a Same-Sex Kiss, but Who Exactly Is Doing the Kissing?." *Distractify*, June 21. https://www.distractify.com/p/who-kisses-in-lightyear.

Alt Shift X. 2012–present. *YouTube*. https://www.youtube.com/channel/UCveZqq GewoyPiacooywP5Ig.

Alt Shift X. 2020. "Euron Greyjoy's Apocalypse in the Game of Thrones Books". *YouTube*, March 14. https://www.youtube.com/watch?v=sbX_ak0N1EI.

American Film Institute. 2008. "Alfred Hitchcock on Mastering Cinematic Tension." *YouTube*, December 13. https://www.youtube.com/watch?v=DPFsuc_M_3E.

Anderson, Benedict R. 1983. *Imagined Communities: Reflections on the Origins and Spread of Nationalism*. London: Verso.

Ang, Ien. 1982. *Watching Dallas: Soap Opera and the Melodramatic Imagination*. Amsterdam: Amsterdam University Press.

Aristotle. 2018 [335 b.c.]. *Poetics. The James Hutton Translation: Ancient Contexts, Interpretations*. Edited and with a revised translation by Michelle Zerba and David Gorman. London: W.W. Norton.

Arnheim, Rudolf. 1980. "Das Rotkehlchen Und Der Heilige." In *Zur Psychologie Der Kunst*, 243–260. Frankfurt a.M.: Ullstein.

Askwith, Ivan. 2003. "Gollum: Dissed by the Oscars?" *Salon*, February 18. https://www.salon.com/2003/02/18/gollum/.

Auslander, Philip. 2008. *Liveness: Performance in a Mediatized Culture*. London: Routledge.

Avery-Natale, Edward. 2013. "An Analysis of Embodiment among Six Superheroes in DC Comics." *Social Thought and Research*, no. 32: 71–106. http://hdl.handle.net/1808/12434.

Azuma, Hiroki. 2009. *Otaku: Japan's Database Animals*. Translated by Jonathan E. Abel and Shion Kono. Minneapolis: University of Minnesota Press.

Backe, Hans-Joachim. 2022. "Centaurs and Horsemen: Composite Avatars and the Epistemology of the Playable Figure." *Narrative: The Journal of the International Society for the Study of Narrative*, no. 30 (2): 241–249.

Bacon, Henry. 2019. "Being Typical and being Individual." In *Screening Characters: Theories of Character in Film, Television, and Interactive Media*, edited by Johannes Riis and Aaron Taylor, 77–92. New York: Routledge.

Bacon, Thomas. 2021. "Star Wars: High Republic's Trans Non-Binary Jedi Twins Take the Spotlight." *ScreenRant*, April 1. https://screenrant.com/star-wars-high-republic-ceret-tenec-non-binary/.

Badham, Van. 2018. "Red Dead Redemption 2: Calls to Ban Violence against Women in Games are too Simplistic." *The Guardian*, November 08. https://www.theguardian.com/games/2018/nov/08/red-dead-redemption-2-calls-to-ban-violence-against-women-in-games-are-too-simplistic.

Baker, David, and Elena Schak. 2019. "The Hunger Games: Transmedia, Gender and Possibility." *Continuum*, no. 33 (2): 201–215.

Bakhtin, Mikhail. 1981 [1975]. "Forms of Time and of the Chronotope in the Novel." edited and translated by Caryl Emerson and Michael Holquist. In *The Dialogic Imagination: Four Essays*, 84–258. Austin: University of Texas Press.

Balcerzak, Scott. 2009. "Andy Serkis as Actor, Body and Gorilla: Motion Capture and the Presence of Performance." In *Cinephilia in the Age of Digital Reproduction*, edited by Scott Balcerzak and Jason Serb, 195–213. London: Wallflower.

Baroni, Raphaël. 2021. "History of Mice as Men: A Transmedial Perspective on Fictionality." *Narrative*, no. 29 (1): 91–113.

Barthes, Roland. 1975 [1970]. *S/Z.: An Essay.* Translated by Richard Miller. Malden: Blackwell.

Barthes, Roland. 1977 [1967]. "The Death of the Author." In *Image, Music, Text*, translated by Stephen Heath, 142–148. London: Fotana.

Baudrillard, Jean. 1983. *Simulations.* Translated by Paul Foss, Paul Patton, and Philip Beitchman. New York: Semiotext(e).

Beach, Lee R. 2010. *The Psychology of Narrative Thought: How the Stories We Tell Ourselves Shape our Lives.* Bloomington: Xlibris.

Beaudoux, Virginia. 2017. "Are Disney Princesses Failing as Role Models?" *World Economic Forum*, July 20. https://www.weforum.org/agenda/2017/07/are-disney-princesses-failing-as-role-models/.

Begley, Sarah. 2015. "Malcolm-Jamal Warner Says the Cosby Show Is Now 'Tarnished.'" *Time*, October 09. https://time.com/4067894/malcolm-jamal-warner-cosby-show-tarnished/.

Bellissimo, Marlene, and John McDermott [Dreamsounds]. 2022. "Disney's Racist Ride." *YouTube*, October 15. https://www.youtube.com/watch?v=1iz4FwBUN2M.

Belson, Ken, and Brian Bremner. 2004. *Hello Kitty: The Remarkable Story of Sanrio and the Billion Dollar Feline Phenomenon.* Singapore: Wiley.

Bennett, Tony. 2017. "The Bond Phenomenon: Theorising a Popular Hero – A Retrospective." *International Journal of James Bond Studies*, no. 1 (1): 1–34.

Berard, Bethany. 2018. "I Second that Emoji: The Standards, Structures, and Social Production of Emoji." *First Monday*, no. 9 (3). https://firstmonday.org/article/view/9381/7565.

Berndt, Jaqueline. 2021. "More Mangaesque than the Manga: 'Cartooning' in the Kimetsu no Yaiba Anime." *Transcommunication*, no. 8 (2): 171–178.

Bertetti, Paolo. 2014. "Toward a Typology of Transmedia Characters." *International Journal of Communication*, no. 8: 2344–2361.

Bertetti, Paolo. 2019. "Buck Rogers in the 25th Century: Transmedia Extensions of a Pulp Hero." *Frontiers of Narrative Studies*, no. 5 (2): 200–219.

Bertetti, Paolo, and Mattia Thibault. 2022. "Towards a Semiotic Theory of Transmedia Characters." *Narrative*, no. 30 (2): 225–239.

Bizzocchi, Jim, and Theresa J. Tanenbaum. 2012. "Mass Effect 2: A Case Study in the Design of Game Narrative." *Bulletin of Science, Technology & Society*, no. 32 (5): 393–404.

Bliss, Gillian E. 2017. *Redefining the Anthropomorphic Animal in Animation.* PhD Thesis. Loughborough: Loughborough University, School of the Arts, English and Drama, 214 pages. https://repository.lboro.ac.uk/articles/thesis/Redefining_the_anthropomorphic_animal_in_animation/9333113.

Blom, Joleen. 2019. *The Dynamic Game Character. Definition, Construction, and Challenges in a Character Ecology.* PhD Thesis. Copenhagen: IT University of Copenhagen, Center for Computer Games Research, 237 pages. https://pure.itu.dk/portal/files/85357319/PhD_Thesis_Final_Version_Joleen_Blom.pdf.

Blom, Joleen. 2022. "Voice Assistants as Characters – or Not." *Narrative: The Journal of the International Society for the Study of Narrative*, no. 30 (2), 170–176.

Bode, Christoph, and Rainer Dietrich. 2013. *Future Narratives: Theory, Poetics, and Media-Historical Moment.* Berlin: de Gruyter.

Bogost, Ian. 2007. Persuasive Games: The Expressive Power of Videogames. Cambridge, MA: MIT Press.

Bolter, Jay D., and Richard Grusin. 2000. *Remediation: Understanding New Media.* Cambridge, MA: MIT Press.

Bolton, Kenneth, and Joe, Feagin. 2004. *Black in Blue: African-American Police Officers and Racism*. New York: Routledge.

Booth, Paul. 2021. *Board Games as Media*. New York: Bloomsbury Academic.

Bordwell, David. 1989. *Making Meaning: Inference and Rhetoric in the Interpretation of Cinema*. Cambridge, MA: Harvard University Press.

Bordwell, David. 2013. "The Viewer's Share: Models of Mind in Explaining Film." In *Psychocnematics: Exploring Cognition at the Movies*, edited by Arthur P. Shimamura, 29–52. Oxford: Oxford University Press.

Bordwell, David. 2015. *The Classical Hollywood Cinema: Film Style & Mode of Production to 1960*. London: Routledge Taylor & Francis Group.

Borlaza, Catherine Regina. 2021. "Binding Threads: The Emotional Structure of Attachment in the Animated Series Demon Slayer." *Transcommunication*, no. 8 (2): 212–233. https://waseda.repo.nii.ac.jp/?action=pages_view_main&active_action=repository_view_main_item_detail&item_id=65471&item_no=1&page_id=13&block_id=21.

Bowman, Sarah L., and Karen Schrier. 2018. "Players and their Characters in Role-Playing Games." In *Role-Playing Game Studies: Transmedia Foundations*, edited by José P. Zagal and Sebastian Deterding, 395–410. London: Routledge.

Branigan, Edward. 1984. *Point of View in the Cinema: A Theory of Narration and Subjectivity in Classical Film*. Berlin: de Gruyter.

Branigan, Edward. 1992. *Narrative Comprehension and Film*. London: Routledge.

Brode, Douglas, ed. 2022. *The DC Comics Universe: Critical Essays*. Jefferson: McFarland.

Brooker, Will. 2012. *Hunting the Dark Knight: Twenty-First Century Batman*. London: Bloomsbury Publishing.

Brooker, Will. 2013. *Batman Unmasked: Analyzing a Cultural Icon*. Reprint. London: Bloomsbury.

Brookey, Robert A. 2010. *Hollywood Gamers: Digital Convergence in the Film and Video Game Industries*. Bloomington: Indiana University Press.

Brown, Jeffrey. 2021. *Panthers, Hulks and Ironhearts: Marvel, Diversity and the 21st Century Superhero*. New Brunswick: Rutgers University Press.

Brown, Tracy. 2019. "In Netflix's 'She-Ra,' Even Villains Respect Nonbinary Pronouns." *Los Angeles Times*, November 6. https://www.latimes.com/entertainment-arts/tv/story/2019-11-05/netflix-she-ra-princesses-power-nonbinary-double-trouble.

Bruner, Jerome S. 1990. *Acts of Meaning*. Cambridge, MA: Harvard University Press.

Bruner, Jerome S. 1991. "The Narrative Construction of Reality." *Critical Inquiry*, no. 18 (1): 1–22.

Bryan, Peter C. 2021. *Creation, Translation, and Adaptation in Donald Duck Comics: The Dream of Three Lifetimes*. Cham: Springer International Publishing.

BT21. 2017. "BT21 UNIVERSE 1 – EP.02." *YouTube*, October 20. https://www.youtube.com/watch?v=jOD7ikz4nXQ&list=PLvteA1S67AOPUmzbpJJCRTVE9YNuaR-Bis&index=3.

BT21. N.d. "Characters." *BT21*. https://www.bt21.com/character.

Buterman, Jan L. 2013. "An Inconvenient Booth: Mistaking Symbol for Both Map and Territory." *Et Cetera*, no. 70 (4): 434–442.

Butler, Jeremy G., ed. 1991. *Star Texts: Image and Performance in Film and Television*. Detroit: Wayne State University Press.

Butler, Judith. 1990. *Gender Trouble: Feminism and the Subversion of Identity*. New York: Routledge.

Butler, Judith. 1997. "Subjects of Sex/Gender/Desire." In *Feminisms*, edited by Sandra Kemp and Judith Squires, 278–810. Oxford: Oxford University Press.

Caïra, Olivier. 2011. *Définir la Fiction: Du Roman au Jeu D'échec*. Paris: Editions de l'EHESS.

Caldwell, John T. 2008. *Production Culture: Industrial Reflexivity and Critical Practice in Film and Television*. Durham: Duke University Press.

Campbell, Joseph. 2008. *The Hero with a Thousand Faces*. Novato: New World Library.

Campbell, Scott. 2020. "Mulan Producer Says they Removed Mushu because of Chinese Audiences." *We Got This Covered*, February 27. https://wegotthiscovered.com/movies/mulan-producer-admits-chinese-audiences-reason-mushu-movie/.

Caracciolo, Marco. 2014. "Experientiality." In *Handbook of Narratology: Volume 1 and Volume 2*, edited by Peter Hühn, Jan C. Meister, John Pier and Wolf Schmid, 149–158. Berlin: de Gruyter.

cardboard boxer. 2014. "Mario Continuity Works Similarly to that of Godzilla." *Reddit*, July 21. https://www.reddit.com/r/FanTheories/comments/2b9wns/mario_continuity_works_similarly_to_that_of/.

Carnicke, Sharon M. 2012. "Emotional Expressivity in Motion Picture Caption Technology." In *Acting and Performance in Moving Image Culture. Bodies, Screens, and Renderings*, edited by Jörg Sternagel, Lesley Stern and Dieter Mersch, 321–338. Bielefeld: transcript.

Carter, Dom. 2019. "Batman and Catwoman Swap Exposes Gender Stereotypes." *Creative Bloq*, November 28. https://www.creativebloq.com/news/batman-catwoman.

Cayla, Julien. 2013. "Brand Mascots as Organisational Totems." *Journal of Marketing Management*, no. 29 (1–2): 86–104.

CBR Staff. 2017. "15 Times a U.S. President Showed up in Marvel Comics." *CBR.com*, January 20. https://www.cbr.com/us-president-appearance-in-marvel-comics/.

Chan, Pauline. 2010. *Narrative Participation within Game Environments: Role-Playing in Massively Multiplayer Online Games*. MA Thesis. Atlanta: Georgia Institute of Technology, School of Literature, Communication, and Culture, 109 pages. https://smartech.gatech.edu/handle/1853/37126?show=full.

Chapman, Llewella. 2021. *Fashioning James Bond: Costume, Gender and Identity in the World of 007*. New York: Bloomsbury Academic.

Chapman, Matt. 2019. "Game of Thrones' Strict Secrecy 'Saw all Cast, Doubles and Stunt People Flown out for the Finale.'" *Digital Spy*, May 20. https://www.digitalspy.com/tv/ustv/a27505590/game-of-thrones-finale-cast-appearances/.

Chatman, Seymour B. 1978. *Story and Discourse: Narrative Structure in Fiction and Film*. Ithaca: Cornell University Press.

Chemers, Michael M. 2007. "'With Your Shield, or on It': Disability Representation in 300." *Reloaded Disability Studies Quarterly*, no. 27 (3). https://dsq-sds.org/article/view/37/37.

Chen, Mark, Riley Leary, Jon Peterson, and David W. Simkins 2018. "Multi-Player Online Role-Playing Games." In *Role-Playing Game Studies: Transmedia Foundations*, edited by José P. Zagal and Sebastian Deterding, 130–158. London: Routledge.

Cheu, Johnston, ed. 2013. *Diversity in Disney Films: Critical Essays on Race, Ethnicity, Gender Sexuality, and Disability*. Jefferson: McFarland.

Child, Ben. 2010. "White Supremacists Urge Thor Boycott over Casting of Black Actor as Norse God." *The Guardian*, December 17. https://www.theguardian.com/film/2010/dec/17/white-supremacists-boycott-thor.

Cho, Sumi, Kimberlé Crenshaw, and Leslie McCall. 2013. "Towards a Field of Intersectionality Studies: Theory, Applications, and Praxis." *Signs: Journal of Women in Culture and Society*, no. 38 (4): 785–810.

Christensen, Ida Broni. 2022. "'Right-hand Pixels': Controlling Companions and Employing Haptic Storytelling Techniques in Single-Player Quest-Based Videogames." *Narrative: The Journal of the International Society for the Study of Narrative*, no. 30 (2): 183–191.

Christian, Alexander. 2017. *Piktogramme: Tendenzen in der Gestaltung und im Einsatz Grafischer Symbole.* Cologne: Herbert von Halem.

Clark, Naeemah. 2015. *Connecting in the Scandalverse: The Power of Social Media and Parasocial Relationships.* New York: Routledge.

Cocca, Carolyn. 2016. *Superwomen: Gender, Power, and Representation.* New York: Bloomsbury.

Cocca, Carolyn. 2020. "Reproducing Inequality and Representing Diversity: The Politics of Gender in Superhero Comics." In *Spaces Between: Gender, Diversity, and Identity in Comics,* edited by Véronique Sina and Nina Eckhoff-Heindl, 1–15. Wiesbaden: Springer.

Cohn, Dorrit. 1999. *The Distinction of Fiction.* Baltimore: Johns Hopkins University Press.

Cohn, Neil. 2013. *The Visual Language of Comics: Introduction to the Structure and Cognition of Sequential Images.* London: Bloomsbury.

Colangelo, BJ. 2013. "Michael Cera Got more than he Bargained for from his Cameo in This Is The End." *Slashfilm,* April 13. https://www.slashfilm.com/830770/michael-cera-got-more-than-he-bargained-for-from-his-cameo-in-this-is-the-end/.

Cole, Helena, and Mark D. Griffiths. 2007. "Social Interactions in Massively Multiplayer Online Role-Playing Gamers." *CyberPsychology & Behavior,* no. 10 (4): 575–583.

Connell, Raewyn W. 2005. *Masculinities.* 2nd ed. Berkeley: University of California Press.

Cook, Roy T. 2013. "Canonicity and Normativity in Massive, Serialized, Collaborative Fiction: Canonicity and Normativity in Massive, Serialized, Collaborative Fiction." *The Journal of Aesthetics and Art Criticism,* no. 71 (3): 271–276.

Cooke, Rachel. 2012. "Guy Delisle: 'The Challenge is not to Explain too Much'." *The Guardian,* May 31. https://www.theguardian.com/books/2012/may/31/guy-delisle-jerusalem-review-interview.

Coplan, Amy. 2004. "Empathic Engagement with Narrative Fictions." *The Journal of Aesthetics and Art Criticism,* no. 62 (2): 141–152.

Coppa, Francesca. 2017. *The Fanfiction Reader: Folk Tales for the Digital Age.* Ann Arbor: University of Michigan Press.

Costikyan, Greg. 2007. "Games, Storytelling, and Breaking the String." In *Second Person: Role-Playing and Story in Games and Playable Media,* edited by Noah Wardrip-Fruin and Pat Harrigan, 5–13. Cambridge, MA: MIT Press.

Coyne, Sarah M., Jennifer Ruh Linder, Eric E. Rasmussen, David A. Nelson, and Victoria Birbeck. 2016. "Pretty as a Princess: Longitudinal Effects of Engagement with Disney Princesses on Gender Stereotypes, Body Esteem, and Prosocial Behavior in Children." *Child Development,* no. 87 (6): 1909–1925.

Crafton, Donald. 2012. *Shadow of a Mouse – Performance, Belief, and World-Making in Animation.* Berkeley: University of California Press.

Creeber, Glen. 2004. *Serial Television: Big Drama on the Small Screen.* London: BFI.

Crenshaw, Kimberlé. 1989. "Demarginalizing the Intersection of Race and Sex: A Black Feminist Critique of Antidiscrimination Doctrine, Feminist Theory and Antiracist Policy." *University of Chicago Legal Forum,* no. 1: 139–167.

Crittenden, Charles. 1991. *Unreality: The Metaphysics of Fictional Objects.* Ithaca: Cornell University Press.

Culler, Jonathan. 1981. "Issues in Contemporary American Criticism." In *American Criticism in the Poststructuralist Age,* edited by Ira Konigsberg, 1–18. Ann Arbor: Oxon Publishing.

Culpeper, Jonathan, and Carolina Fernandez-Quintanilla. 2017. "Fictional Characterisation." In *Pragmatics of Fiction,* edited by Miriam A. Locher and Andreas H. Jucker, 93–128. Berlin: de Gruyter.

Currie, Gregory. 2010. *Narratives and Narrators: A Philosophy of Stories*. Oxford: Oxford University Press.

D'Arcy, Geraint. 2020. *Mise En Scène, Acting, and Space in Comics*. Cham: Palgrave Macmillan.

Daleyna. 2022. "What Netflix's 'Daredevil' Gets Right and Wrong About Blindness." *Incluvie*, January 02. https://www.incluvie.com/articles/what-netflixs-daredevil-gets-right-and-wrong-about-blindness.

Danesi, Marcel. 2017. *The Semiotics of Emoji: The Rise of Visual Language in the Age of the Internet*. London: Bloomsbury Publishing

Data USA. 2022. "Police Officers." *Data USA*. https://datausa.io/profile/soc/police-officers.

David, Margaret. 2021. "Game of Thrones: Why Daario Naharis Was Recast." *CBR.com*, April 02. https://www.cbr.com/game-of-thrones-recast-ed-skrein-daario-naharis/

Davies, Martin, and Tony Stoney, eds. 1995. *Mental Simulation: Evaluations and Applications*. Oxford: Blackwell.

Davis, Lennard J. 2017. "Introduction: Disability, Normality, and Power." In *The Disability Studies Reader*, edited by Lennard J. Davis, 1–16. New York: Routledge.

Davis, Natalie Zemon. 1988. "'Any Resemblance to Persons Living or Dead': Film and the Challenge of Authenticity." *Historical Journal of Film, Radio and Television* 8 (3): 269–283.

Dawkins, Marcia A. 2012. *Clearly Invisible: Racial Passing and the Color of Cultural Identity*. Waco: Baylor University Press.

Declercq, Dieter. 2019. "Drawing Truth Differently: Matt Bors' Fictional Satire and Non-Fictional Journalism." *ImageTexT*, no. 11 (1). https://imagetextjournal.com/drawing-truth-differently-matt-bors-fictional-satire-and-non-fictional-journalism/.

De Dauw, Esther. 2021. *Hot Pants and Spandex Suits: Gender Representation in American Superhero Comic Books*. New Brunswick: Rutgers University Press.

Deleuze, Gilles, and Félix Guattari. 1994 [1968]. *Difference and Repetition*. Translated by Paul Patton. New York: Columbia University Press.

Denson, Shane, and Ruth Mayer. 2018. "Border Crossings: Serial Figures and the Evolution of Media." *NECSUS: European Journal of Media Studies*, no. 7 (2): 65–84. https://necsus-ejms.org/border-crossings-serial-figures-and-the-evolution-of-media/.

Denson, Shane, and Lukas R.A Wilde. 2022. "Historicizing and Theorizing Pre-Narrative Figures: Who Is Uncle Sam?" *Narrative*, no. 30 (2): 152–168.

Derecho, Abigail. 2006. "Archontic Literature: A Definition, a History, and Several Theories of Fan Fiction." In *Fan Fiction and Fan Communities in the Age of the Internet: New Essays*, edited by Karen Hellekson and Kristina Busse, 61–78. Jefferson: McFarland.

Deterding, Sebastian. 2016. "Make-Believe in Gameful and Playful Design." In *Digital Make-Believe*, edited by Phil Turner and J. Tuomas Harviainen, 101–124. Cham: Springer International Publishing.

Dever, Joe, and Gary Chalk. 2018. "Flight from the Dark." *Project Aon*, February 18. https://www.projectaon.org/en/xhtml/lw/01fftd/toc.htm.

Dewey, Donald. 2007. *The Art of Ill Will: The Story of American Political Cartoons*. New York: New York University Press.

Dewey, John A., and Günther Knoblich. 2016. "Representation of Self Versus Others' Actions." *Journal of Experimental Psychology. Human Perception and Performance*, no. 27 (1): 229–240.

Di Filippo, Laurent. 2017. "MMORPG as Locally Realized Worlds of Action." In *World Building. Transmedia, Fans, Industries*, edited by Marta Boni, 231–250. Amsterdam: Amsterdam University Press.

Di Placido, Dani. 2022. "Tucker Carlson Widely Mocked after Criticizing 'Less Sexy' M&Ms." *Forbes,* January 22. https://www.forbes.com/sites/danidiplacido/2022/01/22/tucker-carlson-widely-mocked-after-criticizing-less-sexy-mms/.

Doherty, Thomas. 1999. *Pre-Code Hollywood: Sex, Immorality, and Insurrection in American Cinema 1930–1934.* New York: Columbia University Press.

Doležel, Lubomír. 1995. "Fictional Worlds: Density, Gaps, and Inference." *Style: From Possible Worlds to Virtual Realities: Approaches to Postmodernism,* no. 29 (2): 201–214.

Drummond-Mathews, Angela. 2010. "What Boys will Be: A Study of Shōnen Manga." In *Manga: An Anthology of Global and Cultural Perspectives,* edited by Toni Johnson-Woods, 62–76. New York: Continuum.

Dundes, Alan. 2016. "Folkloristics in the Twenty-First Century." In *Grand Theory in Folkloristics,* edited by Lee Haring, 16–18. Bloomington: Indiana University Press.

Dunniway, Troy. 2000. "Using the Hero's Journey in Games." *Gamedeveloper,* November 27. https://www.gamedeveloper.com/design/using-the-hero-s-journey-in-games.

Dyer, Richard. 1997. *White: Essays on Race and Culture.* London: Routledge.

Eco, Umberto. 1972 [1962]. "The Myth of Superman". Translated by Natalie Chilton. *Diacritics,* no. 2 (1): 14–22.

Eco, Umberto. 1994 [1979]. *The Role of the Reader: Explorations in the Semiotics of Texts.* Bloomington: Indiana University Press.

Eder, Jens. 2008a. *Die Figur Im Film: Grundlagen Der Figurenanalyse.* Marburg: Schüren.

Eder, Jens. 2008b. *Was Sind Figuren? Ein Beitrag Zur Interdisziplinären Fiktionstheorie.* Paderborn: Mentis.

Eder, Jens. 2010. "Understanding Characters." *Projections,* no. 4 (1): 16–40.

Eder, Jens, Fotis Jannidis, and Ralf Schneider. 2010. "Fictional Characters in Literary and Media Studies: A Survey of the Research." In *Characters in Fictional Worlds: Understanding Imaginary Beings in Literature, Film, and Other Media,* edited by Jens Eder, Fotis Jannidis and Ralf Schneider, 3–66. Berlin: de Gruyter.

Edwards, Janis L. 1997. *Political Cartoons in the 1988 Presidential Campaign: Image, Metaphor, and Narrative.* New York: Garland.

El Refaie, Elisabeth. 2009. "Metaphor in Political Cartoons: Exploring Audience Responses." In *Multimodal Metaphor: Applications of Cognitive Linguistics,* edited by Charles Forceville, 173–196. Berlin: de Gruyter.

Elleström, Lars. 2019. *Transmedial Narration: Narratives and Stories in Different Media.* Cham: Palgrave Macmillan.

Erens-Basement. 2019. "Poll: What Is Nanachi's Gender in your Mind?" *Reddit,* March 10. https://www.reddit.com/r/MadeInAbyss/comments/azgjm9/poll_what_is_nanachis_gender_in_your_mind.

ErikLarsen. 2022. "Instead of Changing Punisher's Chest Emblem..." *Twitter,* February 20. https://twitter.com/ErikJLarsen/status/1495267273300271105.

Ernst, Christoph. 2012. "The Medium Sends its Messenger: Mobility beyond the Normative Order in the Television Series 'The Fugitive'." In *Pirates, Drifters, Fugitives: Figures of Mobility in the US and Beyond,* edited by Heike Paul, Alexandra Ganser and Katharina Gerund, 303–329. Heidelberg: Winter.

euromaus_euromausi_travel. 2019. "Ed Euromaus & Edda Euromausi: Fanpage EU." *Instagram.* https://www.instagram.com/euromaus_euromausi_travel/?hl=de.

Europa-Park. 2019. "Ed Euromaus und seine Freunde." *Europa-Park.* https://www.europapark.de/en/ed-euromaus-und-seine-freunde.

Evans, Elizabeth. 2011. *Transmedia Television: Audiences, New Media, and Daily Life.* New York: Routledge.

Evans, Vyvyan. 2017. *The Emoji Code: How Smiley Faces, Love Hearts and Thumbs Up Are Changing the Way we Communicate.* London: Michael O'Mara Books Limited.

Explain XKCD. 2022. "Black Hat." *Explain XKCD*, April 21. https://www.explainxkcd.com/wiki/index.php/Black_Hat.

Fahey, Mike. 2012. "It's not *Star Wars* without Slavery, Torture, and Forced Voyeurism?" *Kotaku*, March 01. https://kotaku.com/its-not-star-wars-without-slavery-torture-and-forced-5872687.

Fawaz, Ramzi. 2011. "'Where no X-Man has Gone before!' Mutant Superheroes and the Cultural Politics of Popular Fantasy in Postwar America." *American Literature*, no. 83 (2): 355–388.

Felski, Rita. 2019. "Identifying with Characters." In *Character: Three Inquiries in Literary Studies*, edited by Amanda Anderson, Rita Felski and Toril Moi, 77–126. Chicago: University of Chicago Press.

Feyersinger, Erwin. 2017. *Metalepsis in Animation: Paradoxical Transgressions of Ontological Levels.* Heidelberg: Winter.

Fischer, David H. 2005. *Liberty and Freedom: A Visual History of America's Founding Ideas.* New York: Oxford University Press.

Fitzpatrick, Kevin. 2019. "The *Avengers: Endgame* Cast was Lied to About the Movie's Most Pivotal Scene." *Vanity Fair,* June 09. https://www.vanityfair.com/hollywood/2019/06/avengers-endgame-funeral-cast-wedding-spoilers.

Fleury, James, Bryan Hikari Hartzheim, and Stephen Mamber, eds. 2019. *The Franchise Era: Managing Media in the Digital Economy.* Edinburgh: Edinburgh University Press.

Fludernik, Monika. 1996. *Towards a 'Natural' Narratology.* London: Routledge.

Fludernik, Monika. 2003. "Natural Narratology and Cognitive Parameters." In *Narrative Theory and the Cognitive Sciences*, edited by David Herman, 243–267. Stanford, CA: CSLI.

Fludernik, Monika, and Mary-Laure Ryan, eds. 2020. *Narrative Factuality.* Berlin: de Gruyter.

Fludernik, Monika, and Stephan Packard, eds. 2021. *Being Untruthful: Lying, Fiction, and the Non-Factual.* Baden-Baden: Ergon.

Forster, E.M. 1927. *Aspects of the Novel.* New York: Harcourt Brace.

Fortune, J.J. 2020. "In the MCU, why couldn't Doctor Strange Do the Whole 'Knocking the Soul out' Thing that The Ancient One Did to him and Hulk but Do it on Thanos?" *Quora*, April 3. https://www.quora.com/In-the-MCU-why-couldnt-Doctor-Strange-do-the-whole-knocking-the-soul-out-thing-that-The-Ancient-One-did-to-him-and-Hulk-but-do-it-on-Thanos.

Fowler, Roger. 1977. *Linguistics and the Novel.* London: Methuen.

Frahm, Ole. 2000. "Weird Signs: Comics as Means of Parody." In *Comics & Culture: Analytical and Theoretical Approaches to Comics*, edited by Anne Magnussen and Hans-Christian Christiansen, 177–191. Copenhagen: Museum Tusculanum Press, University of Copenhagen.

Frank, Allegra. 2017. "Hollywood's Whitewashed Version of Anime never Sells.'" *Polygon*, April 03. https://www.polygon.com/2017/4/3/15142608/hollywood-anime-live-action-adaptations-ghost-in-the-shell.

Frankel, Valerie Estelle. 2017. *Superheroines and the Epic Journey: Mythic Themes in Comics, Film and Television.* Jefferson: McFarland.

Frankel, Valerie Estelle. 2020. *Wonder Women and Bad Girls: Superheroine and Supervillainess Archetypes in Popular Media.* Jefferson: McFarland.

Freeman, Matthew. 2014. "Advertising the Yellow Brick Road: Historicizing the Industrial Emergence of Transmedia Storytelling." *International Journal of Communication*, no. 8: 2362–2381.

Freeman, Matthew. 2016. *Historicising Transmedia Storytelling: Early Twentieth-Century Transmedia Story Worlds*. New York: Routledge.

Freeman, Matthew. 2017. "A World of Disney: Building a Transmedia Storyworld for Mickey and his Friends." In *World Building*, edited by Marta Boni, 93–108. Amsterdam: Amsterdam University Press.

Friedenthal, Andrew J. 2017. *Retcon Game: Retroactive Continuity and the Hyperlinking of America*. Jackson: University Press of Mississippi.

Frow, John. 2014. *Character and Person*. Oxford: Oxford University Press.

Frow, John. 2018. "Character." In *The Cambridge Companion to Narrative Theory*, edited by Matthew Garrett, 105–199. Cambridge: Cambridge University Press.

Fuck DC. 2017. "Our Lord and Savior Kevin Feige". *Facebook*, August 05. https://www.facebook.com/FcukDC/posts/464937090543958.

Funnell, Lisa, and Klaus Dodds. 2017. *Geographies, Genders and Geopolitics of James Bond*. London: Palgrave Macmillan.

Gabilliet, Jean-Paul. 2010. *Of Comics and Men: A Cultural History of American Comic Books*. Jackson: University Press of Mississippi.

Galbraith, Patrick W. 2009. *The Otaku Encyclopedia: An Insider's Guide to the Subculture of Cool Japan*. Tokyo: Kōdansha.

Gallagher, Catherine. 2011. "What would Napoleon Do? Historical, Fictional, and Counterfactual Characters." *New Literary History*, no. 42 (2): 315–336.

Gallagher, Shaun. 2012. "Empathy, Simulation, and Narrative." *Science in Context*, no. 25 (3): 355–381.

Gambarato, Renira R. 2019. "Transmedia Journalism: The Potentialities of Transmedia Dynamics in the News Coverage of Planned Events." In *The Routledge Companion to Transmedia Studies*, edited by Matthew Freeman and Renira Rampazzo Gambarato, 90–98. London: Routledge.

Gambarato, Renira R., and Geane Alzamora, eds. 2018. *Exploring Transmedia Journalism in the Digital Age*. Hershey: IGI Global.

Garber, Marjorie. 2020. *Character: The History of a Cultural Obsession*. New York: Farrar, Straus and Giroux.

Gardner, John. 1984. *The Art of Fiction: Notes on Craft for Young Writers by John Gardner*. New York: Alfred A. Knopf.

Garland-Thomson, Rosemarie. 2005. "Disability and Representation." *PMLA*, no. 120 (2): 522–527.

Garretson Folse, Judith A., Richard G. Netemeyer, and Scot Burton. 2012. "Spokescharacters." *Journal of Advertising*, no. 41 (1): 17–32.

Garretson, Judith A., and Ronald W. Niedrich. 2004. "Spokes-Characters: Creating Character Trust and Positive Brand Attitudes." *Journal of Advertising*, no. 33 (2): 25–36.

Gauthier, Philippe. 2019. "Social Media as Interface, or how Characters Enter our Everyday Reality." In *Screening Characters: Theories of Character in Film, Television, and Interactive Media*, edited by Johannes Riis and Aaron Taylor, 160–173. New York: Routledge.

Geertz, Clifford. 2006. *The Interpretation of Cultures: Selected Essays*. New York: Basic Books.

Giannoulis, Elena, and Lukas R.A. Wilde. 2020. "Emoticons, Kaomoji, and Emoji: The Transformation of Communication in the Digital Age." In: *Emoticons, Kaomoji, and Emoji: The Transformation of Communication in the Digital Age*, edited by Elena Giannoulis and Lukas R.A. Wilde, 1–22. London: Routledge.

Gifreu-Castells, Arnau, Richard Misek, and Erwin Verbruggen. 2016. "Transgressing the Non-fiction Transmedia Narrative." *View: Journal of European Television History and Culture*, no. 5 (10): 1–3.

Giles, D.C. 2002. "Parasocial Interaction: A Review of the Literature and a Model for Future Research." *Media Psychology*, no. 4 (3), 279–305.

Girina, Ivan. 2021. "On Agency and Interactivity in The Stanley Parable." In *Agency Postdigital: Verteilte Handlungsmächte in Medienwissenschaftlichen Forschungsfeldern*, edited by Berenike Jung, Klaus Sachs-Hombach and Lukas R.A. Wilde, 116–144. Cologne: Herbert von Halem.

Goffman, Erving. 1976. *The Presentation of Self in Everyday Life*. Harmondsworth: Penguin Books.

Goldberg, Michelle. 2019. "The Only TV Show that Gets Life under Trump: 'The Good Fight' Is Entertainment for the Resistance." *The New York Times*, May 03. https://www. nytimes.com/2019/05/03/opinion/the-good-fight-trump.html.

Golding, Dan. 2019. *Star Wars after Lucas: A Critical Guide to the Future of the Galaxy*. Minneapolis: University of Minnesota Press.

Gombrich, Ernst H. 1960. *Art and Illusion: A Study in the Psychology of Pictorial Representation*. New York: Pantheon Books.

Goodrum, Michael, Tara Prescott-Johnson, and Philip Smith, eds. 2018. *Gender and the Superhero Narrative*. Jackson: University Press of Mississippi.

Gordon, Ian. 2016. "Refiguring Media: Tee Shirts as a Site of Audience Engagement with Superheroes." *The Information Society*, no. 32 (5): 326–332.

Gordon, Ian. 2017. *Superman: The Persistence of an American Icon*. New Brunswick: Rutgers University Press.

Gramsci, Antonio. 1971. *Selections from the Prison Notebooks of Antonio Gramsci*. Edited and translated by Quintin Hoare and Geoffrey Nowell Smith. London: Lawrence & Wishart.

Grebey, James. 2022. "Are Netflix's Marvel Shows Canon in the MCU? The Harsh Answer Is it doesn't Matter." *Syfy Wire*, March 18. https://www.syfy.com/syfy-wire/ marvel-netflix-mcu-canon-daredevil-jessica-jones-defenders.

Gregersen, Andreas. 2019. "Owning Our Actions: Identification with Avatars in Video Games." In *Screening Characters: Theories of Character in Film, Television, and Interactive Media*, edited by Johannes Riis and Aaron Taylor, 174–188. New York: Routledge.

Greimas, Algirdas Julien. 1983 [1966]. *Structural Semantics: An Attempt at a Method*, translated by Daniele McDowell, Ronald Schleifer and Alan Velie. Lincoln: University of Nebraska Press.

Greimas, Algirdas Julien, and Joseph Courtés. 1982. *Semiotics and Language: An Analytical Dictionary*, translated by Larry Christ, Daniel Patte, James Lee, Edward McMahonII, Gary Phillips and Michael Rengstorf. Bloomington: Indiana University Press.

Grethlein, Paul. 2015. "Is Narrative 'the Description of Fictional Mental Functioning'? Heliodorus against Palmer, Zunshine & Co." *Style*, no. 49 (3): 257–284.

Gubar, Susan. 1997. *Racechanges: White Skin, Black Face in American Culture*. New York: Oxford University Press.

Guynes, Sean, and Dan Hassler-Forest, eds. 2018. *Star Wars and the History of Transmedia Storytelling*. Amsterdam: Amsterdam University Press.

Guynes, Sean, and Martin Lund, eds. 2020. *Unstable Masks: Whiteness and American Superhero Comics*. Columbus: Ohio State University Press.

Hadler, Florian, and Joachim Haupt, eds. 2016. *Interface Critique*. Berlin: Kulturverlag Kadmos.

Hagener, Malte. 2013. "All about Gena, Myrtle and Virginia: The Transitional Nature of Actress, Role and Character." In *Acting and Performance in Moving Image Culture: Bodies, Screens, Renderings*, edited by Jörg Sternagel, Lesley Stern and Dieter Mersch, 195–210. Bielefeld: transcript.

Hall, Stuart. 1996. "New Ethnicities." In *Stuart Hall: Critical Dialogues in Cultural Studies*, edited by David Morley and Kuan-Hsing Chen, 441–449. London: Routledge.

Hall, Stuart. 1997. *Representation: Cultural Representations and Signifying Practices*. London: Sage Publications.

Hammer, Jessica. 2018. "Online Freeform Role-Playing Games." In *Role-Playing Game Studies: Transmedia Foundations*, edited by José P. Zagal and Sebastian Deterding, 159–172. London: Routledge.

Hanly, Michael, and Elisabeth Rowney, 2020. *Visual Character Development in Film and Television: Your Character is Your Canvas*. New York: Routledge.

Haraway, Donna. 1988. "Situated Knowledges: The Science Question in Feminism and the Privilege of Partial Perspective." *Feminist Studies*, no. 14 (3): 575–599.

Haribo, Deutschland. 2022. "HARIBO TV-Spots im Laufe der Zeit." *YouTube*, January 04. https://www.youtube.com/playlist?list=PL9p6qK4MAxlnFErOxqbX0l7 CQONb_i3kL.

Haribo. 2022. "Die Haribo Roadshow 2022." *Haribo*. https://www.haribo.com/de-de/aktivitaeten/roadshow.

Harrison, Edward, and John Harrison, eds. 2011. *Fuzz and Fur: Japan's Costumed Characters*. New York: Mark Batty Publisher.

Hart, Aimee. 2020. "Can You Be Gay in Assassin's Creed Odyssey?" *Gayming: The Home of Queer Geek Culture*, November 23. https://gaymingmag.com/2020/09/can-you-be-gay-in-assassins-creed-odyssey/.

Harvey, Colin B. 2015. *Fantastic Transmedia: Narrative, Play and Memory Across Science Fiction and Fantasy Storyworlds*. Houndmills: Palgrave Macmillan.

Harvey, William J. 1965. *Character and the Novel*. London: Chatto & Windus.

Harviainen, J. Tuomas, Rafael Bienia, Simon Brind, Michael Hitchens, Yaraslau I. Kot, Esther MacCallum-Stewart, David W. Simkins, Jaakko Stenros, and Ian Sturrock. 2018. "Live-Action Role-Playing Games." In *Role-Playing Game Studies: Transmedia Foundations*, edited by José P. Zagal and Sebastian Deterding, 87–106. London: Routledge.

Haslem, Wendy, Elizabeth MacFarlane, and Sarah Richardson, eds. 2019. *Superhero Bodies: Identity, Materiality, Transformation*. New York: Routledge.

Hassler-Forest, Dan. 2012. *Capitalist Superheroes: Caped Crusaders in the Neoliberal Age*. Winchester: Zero Books.

Hassler-Forest, Dan. 2016. *Science Fiction, Fantasy and Politics: Transmedia World-Building beyond Capitalism*. London: Rowman & Littlefield International.

Haugtvedt, Erica. 2017. "The Victorian Serial Novel and Transfictional Character." *Victorian Studies*, no. 59 (3): 409–418.

Heidbrink, Henriette. 2010. "Fictional Characters in Literary and Media Studies: A Survey of the Research." In *Characters in Fictional Worlds: Understanding Imaginary Beings in Literature, Film, and Other Media*, edited by Jens Eder, Fotis Jannidis and Ralf Schneider, 67–110. Berlin: de Gruyter.

Hellekson, Karen, and Kristina Busse. 2006. "Introduction: Work in Progress." In *Fan Fiction and Fan Communities in the Age of the Internet: New Essays*, edited by Karen Hellekson and Kristina Busse, 5–32. Jefferson: McFarland.

Herbert, Daniel. 2020. *Film Reboots*. Edinburgh: Edinburgh University Press.

Herman, David. 2005. "Events and Event-Types." In *Routledge Encyclopedia of Narrative Theory*, edited by David Herman, Manfred Jahn and Marie-Laure Ryan, 151–152. London: Routledge.

Herman, David, ed. 2011. *The Emergence of Mind: Representations of Consciousness in Narrative Discourse in English*. Lincoln, NE: University of Nebraska Press.

Herman, David, ed. 2017. *Animal Comics: Multispecies Storyworlds in Graphic Narratives*. London: Bloomsbury.

Hibbett, Mark. 2022. "The Agents of Doom: An Empirical Approach to Transmedia Actors." In *Comics & Agency: Actors, Publics, Participation*, edited by Vanessa Ossa, Jan-Noël Thon and Lukas R.A. Wilde, 81–100. Berlin: de Gruyter.

Hickethier, Knut. 1999. "Der Schauspieler als Produzent: Überlegungen zur Theorie des medialen Schauspieles." In *Der Körper Im Bild: Schauspielen – Darstellen – Erscheinen*, edited by Heinz-B. Heller, Karl Prümm and Birgit Peulings, 9–29. Marburg: Schüren.

Hilmer, Brigitte. 2009. "Die Zeit der Figuren als Prinzip Filmischer Fiktion." In *'Es Ist, Als Ob': Fiktionalität in Philosophie Film- Und Medienwissenschaft*, edited by Gertrud Koch and Christiane Voss, 107–126. München: Fink.

Hjorth, Larissa, ed. 2017. *Mobile Media & Communication*, no. 5 (1): *Pokémon GO: Playful Phoneurs and the Politics of Digital Wayfarers*, January 27. https://journals.sagepub.com/toc/mmc/5/1.

Hobbs, Allyson. 2014. *A Chosen Exile: A History of Racial Passing in American Life*. Cambridge, MA: Harvard University Press.

Hocking, Clint. 2007. "Ludonarrative Dissonance in Bioshock." *Click Nothing: Design From A Long Time Ago*, October 7. https://clicknothing.typepad.com/click_nothing/2007/10/ludonarrative-d.html.

Hofer, Roberta. 2011. "Metalepsis in Live Performance: Holographic Projections of the Cartoon Band "Gorillaz" as a Means of Metalepsis." In *Metalepsis in Popular Culture*, edited by Karin Kukkonen and Sonja Klimek, 232–251. Berlin: De Gruyter.

Hogan, Patrick Colm. 2011. "Characters and Their Plots." In *Characters in Fictional Worlds: Understanding Imaginary Beings in Literature, Film, and Other Media*, edited by Jens Eder, Fotis Jannidis and Ralf Schneider, 134–154. Berlin: De Gruyter.

Hookway, Branden. 2014. *Interface*. Cambridge, MA: MIT Press.

Hoover, Sarah, David W. Simkins, Sebastian Deterding, David Meldman, and Amanda Brown. 2018. "Performance Studies and Role-Playing Games." In *Role-Playing Game Studies: Transmedia Foundations*, edited by José P. Zagal and Sebastian Deterding, 213–226. London: Routledge.

Horace. 1972 [19 b.c.]. *Horace on the Art of Poetry*. Translated by C. Smart and by E.H. Blakeney. London: Scholartis Press.

Horton, Robin. 1982. "Tradition and Modernity Revisited." In *Rationality and Relativism*, edited by Martin Hollis and Steven Lukes, 201–260. Oxford: Basil Blackwell.

Hosany, Sameer, Girish Prayag, Drew Martin, and Wai-Yee Lee. 2013. "Theory and Strategies of Anthropomorphic Brand Characters from Peter Rabbit, Mickey Mouse, and Ronald McDonald, to Hello Kitty." *Journal of Marketing Management*, no. 29 (1–2): 48–68.

Hughey, Matthew W., and Sahara Muradi. 2009. "Laughing Matters: Economies of Hyper-Irony and Manic-Satire in South Park & Family Guy." *Humanity & Society*, no. 33 (3): 206–237.

Hühn, Peter. 2008. "Functions and Forms of Eventfulness in Narrative Fiction." In *Theorizing Narrativity*, edited by John Pier and José Angel Garcia Landa, 141–163. Berlin: de Gruyter.

Hühn, Peter. 2014. "Event and Eventfulness." In *Handbook of Narratology: Volume 1 and Volume 2*, edited by Peter Hühn, Jan C. Meister, John Pier and Wolf Schmid, 2nd ed., 159–178. Berlin: de Gruyter.

Hühn, Peter, Wolf Schmid, and Jörg Schönert, eds. 2009. *Point of View, Perspective, and Focalization: Modeling Mediation in Narrative*. Berlin: de Gruyter.

Hutton, Nathan. 2021. "Why Is Tim Drake's Robin Being Bisexual so Controversial?" *Quora*, August 10. https://www.quora.com/Why-is-Tim-Drakes-Robin-being-bisexual-so-controversial-Why-do-so-many-people-love-it-and-others-despise-it.

Huver, Scott. 2018. "Star Wars Rebels Creator Dave Filoni Reveals how Season 4 almost Ended and his Clone Wars Revival Plans." *IGN*, August 13. https://www.ign.com/articles/2018/08/12/star-wars-rebels-season-4-finale-clone-wars-final-season-revival-disney-dave-filoni.

Huver, Scott. 2022. "'Stranger Things': Duffer Brothers on Season 4's Epic Scope; Long-Burning Mythology Questions Answered – Contenders TV." *Deadline*, April 10. https://deadline.com/2022/04/stranger-things-duffer-brothers-winona-ryder-season-4-interview-contenders-tv-1234999174/

Hyslop, Jonathan. 2013. "'Days of Miracle and Wonder'? Conformity and Revolt in Searching for Sugar Man." *The Journal of South African and American Studies*, no. 14 (4): 490–501, December 17. https://www.tandfonline.com/doi/full/10.1080/17533171.2013.841066.

Ignatiev, Noel. 2008. *How the Irish Became White*. New York: Routledge.

IGN Staff. 2012. "Top 10 Movie MacGuffins." *IGN*, June 15. https://www.ign.com/articles/2008/05/20/top-10-movie-macguffins.

IMDB. 2018. "Napoleon Bonaparte Is the Most Portrayed/Referenced Real Life Person to be Captured on Film." *IMDB: The Internet Movie Database*, December 28. https://www.imdb.com/list/ls047344740/.

Ishida, Minori. 2019. "Deviating Voice: Representation of Female Characters and Feminist Readings in 1990s Anime." *IMAGE. Special Issue Recontextualizing Characters*, no. 29: 22–37.

Ito, Mizuko. 2008. "Mobilizing the Imagination in Everyday Play: The Case of Japanese Media Mixes." In *The International Handbook of Children, Media and Culture*, edited by Kirsten Drotner and Sonia M. Livingstone, 397–412. Los Angeles, CA: SAGE.

Jacobs, Preston. 2013–present. "Preston Jacobs." *YouTube*. https://www.youtube.com/c/PrestonJacobstheSweetrobin.

Jacobs, Preston. 2014. "A Song of Ice and Fire: The Dornish Master Plan Part 1." *YouTube*, May 20. https://www.youtube.com/watch?v=6TBfdd_xNVo.

Jacobs, Preston. 2017. "How I would Fix Game of Thrones Season 7, Part 1." *YouTube*, October 16. https://www.youtube.com/watch?v=BFUtVmIIAxM

Jannidis, Fotis. 2004. *Figur und Person: Beitrag zu Einer Historischen Narratologie*. Berlin: de Gruyter.

Jannidis, Fotis. 2014. "Character." In *Handbook of Narratology: Volume 1 and Volume 2*, edited by Peter Hühn, Jan C. Meister, John Pier and Wolf Schmid, 2nd ed., 30–45. Berlin: de Gruyter.

Jenkins, Henry. 1992. *Textual Poachers: Television Fans & Participatory Culture*. New York: Routledge.

Jenkins, Henry. 2004. "Game Design as Narrative Architecture." In *First Person: New Media as Story, Performance, Game*, edited by Noah Wardrip-Fruin and Pat Harrigan, 118. Cambridge, MA: MIT Press.

Jenkins, Henry. 2006. *Convergence Culture: Where Old and New Media Collide*. New York: New York University Press.

Jenkins, Henry. 2009. "The Revenge of the Origami Unicorn: Seven Principles of Transmedia Storytelling (Well, Two Actually. Five More on Friday)." *Confessions of an Aca-Fan: The Official Weblog of Henry Jenkins*, December 12. http://henryjenkins.org/blog/2009/12/the_revenge_of_the_origami_uni.html.

Jenner, Mareike. 2018. *Netflix and the Re-Invention of Television*. Cham: Palgrave Macmillan.

Jensen, Robert. 2011. "Whiteness." In *The Routledge Companion to Race and Ethnicity*, edited by Stephen M. Caliendo and Charlton D. McIlwain, 21–28. London: Routledge.

Johnson, Derek. 2013. *Media Franchising: Creative License and Collaboration in the Culture Industries*. New York: New York University Press.

Jost, François. 2004. "The Look: From Film to Novel. An Essay in Comparative Narratology." In: *A Companion to Literature and Film*, edited by Robert Stam and Allesandra Raengo, 71–80. Malden: Blackwell.

Jung, Berenike, and Lukas R.A. Wilde. 2021. "Unravelling the 'Trump Shock,' or: The Intertwined Threat Communication of 'Post-11/9'." In *Threat Communication and the US Order after 9/11: Medial Reflections*, edited by Vanessa Ossa, David Scheu and Lukas R.A. Wilde, 156–175. London: Routledge.

Juul, Jesper. 2005. *Half-Real: Video Games Between Real Rules and Fictional Worlds*. Cambridge, MA: MIT Press.

Karlsen, Joakim. 2019. "Transmedia Documentary: Experience and Participatory Approaches to Non-Fiction Transmedia" In *The Routledge Companion to Transmedia Studies*, edited by Matthew Freeman and Renira Rampazzo Gambarato, 25–34. London: Routledge.

Kearns, Erin M., and Joseph K. Young. 2018. "If Torture Is Wrong, what about 24?" Torture and the Hollywood Effect." *Crime and Delinquency*, no. 64 (12): 1568–1589.

Keen, Suzanne. 2006. "A Theory of Narrative Empathy." *Narrative*, no. 14 (3): 207–236.

Kelleter, Frank, ed. 2017. *Media of Serial Narrative*. Columbus: The Ohio State University Press.

Kentarō, Takekuma [竹熊健太郎]. 1995. "Koma ni Okeru 'Shutai' to 'kyakutai': Manga no koma wa Nani Kara Dekite iru Kka?" In *Manga no Yomikata*, edited by Fusanosuke Natsume [夏目房之介] and Takekuma Kentarō [竹熊健太郎], 76–77. Tokyo: Takarajima-sha.

Ketchum, Alton. 1959. *Uncle Sam: The Man and the Legend*. New York: Hill and Wang.

Kirkpatrick, Ellen. 2022. "Lost Inside a Monster: The Batman, Fridging, and Some Problems with Hero Stories (Part Three)." *The Break*, March 03. https://ellenkirkpatrick.substack.com/p/storiesmatter?s=r.

Kjørup, Søren. 2004. "Pictograms." In: *Semiotics: A Handbook on the Sign*, vol. 4, edited by Roland Posner, Klaus Robering and Thomas Albert Sebeok, 3504–3510. Berlin: de Gruyter.

Klar, Elisabeth. 2013. "Tentacles, Lolitas, and Pencil Strokes: The Parodist Body in European and Japanese Erotic Comics." In *Manga's Cultural Crossroads*, edited by Jaqueline Berndt and Bettina Kümmerling-Meibauer, 121–142. Hoboken: Taylor & Francis.

Klastrup, Lisbeth, and Susanna Tosca. 2004. "Transmedial Worlds: Rethinking Cyberworld Design." *IEEE Xplore*, https://ieeexplore.ieee.org/document/1366205.

Klein, Amanda Ann, and R. Barton Palmer, eds. 2016. *Cycles, Sequels, Spin-offs, Remakes, and Reboots: Multiplicities in Film and Television*. Austin: University of Texas Press.

Klevjer, Rune. 2006. *What Is the Avatar? Fiction and Embodiment in Avatar-Based Singleplayer Computer Games*. PhD Thesis. Bergen: University of Bergen, Department of Information Science and Media Studies, 230 pages. https://folk.uib.no/smkrk/docs/RuneKlevjer_What%20is%20the%20Avatar_finalprint.pdf.

Klevjer, Rune. 2022. *What Is the Avatar? Fiction and Embodiment in Avatar-Based Singleplayer Computer Games. Revised and Commented Edition*. Bielefeld: transcript.

Kock, Christian. 1978. "Narrative Tropes: A Study of Points in Plots." In *Occasional Papers 1976–1977*, edited by Graham D. Caie, Michael Chesnutt, Lis Christensen and Claus Færch, 202–252. Copenhagen: Akademisk Forl.

Krentz, Christopher. 2018. "Disability Studies." In *A Companion to Literary Theory*, edited by David H. Richter, 348–359. New York: Wiley.

Kukkii. 2019. "All Black and White? Racism and Blackface in Cosplay." *Wigs 101*, October 20. https://wigs101.com/all-black-and-white-racism-and-blackface-in-cosplay.

Kukkonen, Karin. 2009. "Textworlds and Metareference in Comics." In *Metareference Across Media: Theory and Case Studies*, edited by Werner Wolf, 499–517. Amsterdam: Rodopi.

Kukkonen, Karin. 2010. "Navigating Infinite Earths: Readers, Mental Models, and the Multiverse of Superhero Comics." *StoryWorlds: A Journal of Narrative Studies*, no. 2: 39–58.

Kunz, Tobias. 2019. "'It's True, all of it!' Character Identity and Canonicity Management in Star Wars." *IMAGE: Journal of Interdisciplinary Image Science*, Special Issue, no. 29: *Recontextualizing Characters*: 60–80.

Kustritz, Anne. 2016. "'They all Lived Happily Ever After. Obviously.': Realism and Utopia in *Game of Thrones*-based Alternate Universe Fairy Tale Fan Fiction." *Humanities*, no. 5 (2): 43. https://doi.org/10.3390/h5020043.

Labi, Nadya. 2001. "Girl Power." *Time*, June 24. http://content.time.com/time/magazine/article/0,9171,139472,00.html.

Lairucrem. 2019. "So after Ep13 is Nanachi a Boy or a Girl?" *My Anime List*, September 29. https://myanimelist.net/forum/?topicid=1669362&pollresults=1.

LaMarre, Thomas. 2008. "Speciesism, Part I: Translating Races into Animals in Wartime Animation." *Mechademia*, no. 3: 75–95.

LaMarre, Thomas. 2009. *The Anime Machine: A Media Theory of Animation*. Minneapolis: University of Minnesota Press.

Lamerichs, Nicolle. 2018. *Productive Fandom: Intermediality and Affective Reception in Fan Cultures*. Amsterdam: Amsterdam University Press.

Lamerichs, Nicolle. 2019. "Character of the Future: Machine Learning, Data, and Personality." *IMAGE. Special Issue Recontextualizing Characters*, no. 29 (1): 98–117.

Lamerichs, Nicolle. 2021 "Agency in Fan Studies: Materialities, Algorithms, and 'Tiny Ontologies.'" In *Agency Postdigital. Verteilte Handlungsmächte in medienwissenschaftlichen Forschungsfeldern*, edited by Berenike Jung, Klaus Sachs-Hombach and Lukas R.A. Wilde, 66–87. Cologne: Herbert von Halem.

Lamerichs, Nicolle. 2022. "Protagonist to Empathy Machine: Exploring the Interpretive Communities and Affective Reception of Characters." *Narrative: The Journal of the International Society for the Study of Narrative*, no. 30 (2): 198–205.

Langkjær, Birger, and Charlotte Sun Jensen. 2019. "Action and Affordances: The Action Hero's Skilled and Surprising Use of the Environment." In *Screening Characters: Theories of Character in Film, Television, and Interactive Media*, edited by Johannes Riis and Aaron Taylor, 266–283. New York: Routledge.

Laurel, Brenda. 2014. *Computers as Theatre*. 2nd ed. Upper Saddle River: Addison-Wesley Publishing Company.

Leary, Alaina. 2017. "How Disfigured Villains like 'Wonder Woman's' Dr. Poison Perpetuate Stigma." *Teen Vogue*, July 05. https://www.teenvogue.com/story/disfigured-villains-dr-poison-wonder-woman.

Leaver, Tama. 2012. "Artificial Mourning: The Spider-Man Trilogy and September 11th." In *Web-Spinning Heroics: Critical Essays on the History and Meaning of Spider-Man*, edited by Robert M. Peaslee and Robert G. Weiner, 154–164. Jefferson: McFarland.

Leavitt, Alex, Tara Knight, and Alex Yoshiba. 2016. "Producing Hatsune Miku: Concerts, Commercialization, and the Politics of Peer Production." In *Media Convergence in Japan*, edited by Patrick W. Galbraith and Jason G. Karlin, 200–239. Kinema Club.

Lee, Gae. 2021. "The Problem with 'Cripping up' and why Casting Disabled Actors Matters." *ABC News*, December 27. https://www.abc.net.au/news/2021-12-28/cripping-up-and-why-casting-disabled-matters/100705512.

Lefèvre, Pascal. 2007. "Incompatible Visual Ontologies: The Problematic Adaption of Drawn Images." In *Film and Comic Books*, edited by Ian Gordon, Mark Jancovich and Matthew P. McAllister, 1–12. Jackson: University Press of Mississippi.

Lejeune, Philippe. 1989. "The Autobiographical Pact." In *On Autobiography*, edited by Paul John Eakin, translated by Katherine M. Leary, 3–30. Minneapolis: University of Minnesota Press.

Leschke, Rainer. 2010. "Einleitung: Zur Transmedialen Logik Der Figur." In *Formen Der Figur: Figurenkonzepte in Künsten Und Medien*, edited by Rainer Leschke and Henriette Heidbrink, 11–28. Konstanz: UVK.

Lesser, Josh. 2014. *Get Yourself Connected: Time, Space, and Character Networks in David Mitchell's Fiction*. MA Thesis. Chicago: DePaul University, Department of English, 74 pages. https://via.library.depaul.edu/etd/173.

Leverage, Paula, Howard Mancing, Richard Schweickert, and Jennifer M. William, eds. 2011. *Theory of Mind and Literature*. West Lafayette: Purdue University Press.

Levin, Bob. 2003. *The Pirates and the Mouse: Disney's War Against the Counterculture*. Seattle: Fantagraphics.

Liebrand, Claudia. 2012. "Casino Royale: Genre-Fragen und James-Bond-Filme." In *Gattung und Geschichte: Literatur- und Medienwissenschaftliche Ansätze zu einer Neuen Gattungstheorie*, edited by Oliver Kohns and Claudia Liebrand, 293–312. Berlin: de Gruyter.

Life is Strange Blog. 2019. "Everything You Need to Know about Daniel in Life Is Strange 2." *Official Life Is Strange Blog*, December 26. https://lifeisstrange-blog.tumblr.com/post/188836949825/everything-you-need-to-know-about-daniel-in-life.

Limoges, Jean-Marc. 2011. "Metalepsis in the Cartoons of Tex Avery: Expanding the Boundaries of Transgression." In *Metalepsis in Popular Culture*, edited by Karin Kukkonen, 196–212. Berlin: de Gruyter.

Linderoth, Jonas. 2005. "Animated Game Pieces: Avatars as Roles, Tools and Props." *Aesthetics of Play Online Proceedings*, August 26–29. https://www.aestheticsofplay.org/papers/linderoth2.htm.

Loock, Kathleen. 2016. "Retro-Remaking: The 1980s Film Cycle in Contemporary Hollywood Cinema." In *Cycles, Sequels, Spin-offs, Remakes, and Reboots: Multiplicities in Film and Television*, edited by Amanda Ann Klein and R. Barton Palmer, 277–298. Austin: University of Texas Press.

LoProto, Mark. 2022. "Which Metal Gear Games Are Canon?" *Cultured Vultures*, March 25. https://culturedvultures.com/metal-gear-games-canon/.

Lotman, Juri. 2005 [1984]. "On the Semiosphere." Translated by Wilma Clark. *Sign Systems Studies*, 33 (1): 205–229.

LotR Fandom. N.d. "Tolkien vs. Jackson: Differences Between Story and Screenplay". *The One Wiki to Rule Them All*. https://lotr.fandom.com/wiki/Tolkien_vs._Jackson:_Differences_Between_Story_and_Screenplay.

Lucat, Bertrand, and Mads Haahr. 2015. "What Makes a Successful Emergent Narrative: The Case of Crusader Kings II." In *Interactive Storytelling*, edited by Henrik Schoenau-Fog, Luis Emilio Bruni, Sandy Louchart and Sarune Baceviciute, 259–266. Cham: Springer International Publishing.

Lyons, Kate. 2018. "Red Dead Redemption 2: Game Criticised over Killing of Suffragette." *The Guardian*, November 07. https://www.theguardian.com/games/2018/nov/07/red-dead-redemption-2-game-criticised-over-killing-of-suffragette.

Lyotard, Jean Francois. 1993 [1979]. *The Postmodern Condition: A Report on Knowledge*. Translated by Geoffrey Bennington and Brian Massumi. Minneapolis: University of Minnesota Press.

MacIntyre, Alasdair. 1981 *After Virtue: A Study in Moral Theory*. London: Bloomsbury.

MacLeod, Lewis. 2011. "'A Documentary-style Film': 'Borat' and the Fiction/Nonfiction Question." *Narrative: The Journal of the International Society for the Study of Narrative*, no. 19 (1): 111–132.

MackMedia. 2019. "Brands & Licensing." *MackMedia*. https://www.mackmedia.de/en/brands-licensing.

Mail & Guardian. 2013. "Discovering Hippies and Teen Rebellion when 'Searching for Sugar Man.'" *Mail & Guardian*, February 08. https://mg.co.za/article/2013-02-08-00-recognition-is-the-sweetest-sound/.

Malone, Kyle. 2019. "Marvel's Avengers: Why the Game's Characters don't Look Like Their MCU Counterparts." *LRM Online*, June 15. https://lrmonline.com/news/marvels-avengers-why-the-games-characters-dont-look-like-their-mcu-counterparts/.

Manovich, Lev. 2016. "What Is Digital Cinema?" In *Post-Cinema: Theorizing 21st-Century Film*, edited by Shane Denson and Julia Leyda, 20–50. Falmer: REFRAME Books.

Margolin, Uri. 1990a. "Individuals in Narrative Worlds." *Poetics Today*, no. 11 (4): 843–871.

Margolin, Uri. 1990b. "The What, the When, and the How of Being a Character in Literary Narrative." *Style*, no. 24 (3): 453–468.

Margolin, Uri. 1995. "Characters in Literary Narrative: Representation and Signification." *Semiotica*, no. 106 (3/4): 373–392.

Margolin, Uri. 1996. "Characters and Their Versions." In *Fiction Updated: Theories of Fictionality, Narratology, and Poetics*, edited by Calin-Andrei Mihailescu and Walid Hamarneh, 113–132. Toronto: University of Toronto Press.

Margolin, Uri. 2007. "Character." In *The Cambridge Companion to Narrative*, edited by David Herman, 66–79. Cambridge, Ma: Cambridge University Press.

Martínez, Matías, and Michael Scheffel. 2003. "Narratology and Theory of Fiction: Remarks on a Complex Relationship." In *What Is Narratology: Questions and Answers Regarding the Status of a Theory*, edited by Tom Kindt and Hans-Harald Müller, 221–238. Berlin: de Gruyter.

Massumi, Brian. 2015. *Ontopower: War, Powers, and the State of Perception*. Durham: Duke University Press.

Mazowita, Amy. 2022. "Privileged Witnessing and the Graphic Self in Sarah Glidden's How to Understand Israel in 60 Days or Less." *Inks: The Journal of the Comics Studies Society*, no. 6 (1): 26–44.

McCloud, Scott. 1993. *Understanding Comics: The Invisible Art*. New York: Harper Perennial.

McDonell, Neil. 1983. "Are Pictures Unavoidably Specific?" *Synthese*, no. 57 (1): 83–98.

McGuire, Liam. 2022. "Punisher's Controversial New Logo & Role with the Hand Get Closer Look." *ScreenRant*, February 4. https://screenrant.com/punisher-new-logo-controversial-hand-marvel.

McLennan, Rachael. 2013. *American Autobiography*. Edinburgh: Edinburgh University Press.

McNary, Dave. 2020. "'Onward' Banned in Several Middle East Countries Due to Lesbian Reference." *Variety*, March 06. https://variety.com/2020/film/news/onward-banned-lesbian-kuwait-oman-qatar-saudi-arabia-1203526359/.

McVeigh, Brian J. 2000. "How Hello Kitty Commodifies the Cute, Cool and Camp." *Journal of Material Culture*, no. 5: 225–245.

Meslow, Scott. 2018. "Our Cartoon President Makes us Wonder: Why Can't Anyone Make a Decent Donald Trump Satire?" *CQ Magazine*, February 09. https://www.gq.com/story/why-cant-anyone-make-a-decent-donald-trump-satire.

Meyer, Christina. 2019. *Producing Mass Entertainment: The Serial Life of the Yellow Kid*. Ohio: Ohio State University Press.

Mikkonen, Kai. 2017. *The Narratology of Comic Art*. New York: Routledge.

Mikkonen, Kai. 2022. "Character: Response to Joleen Blom." *Narrative: The Journal of the International Society for the Study of Narrative*, no. 30 (2): 177–179.

Miller, Joan. 2020. "Raceplay: Whiteness and Erasure in Cross-Racial Cosplay." In *Fandom, Now in Color: A Collection of Voices*, edited by Rukmini Pande, 65–78. Iowa: University of Iowa Press.

Milvy, Erika. 2019. "Nine Black Hermiones, and 'Harry Potter and the Cursed Child' still Won't Talk Race." *Los Angeles Times*, December 01. https://www.latimes.com/entertainment-arts/story/2019-12-01/black-hermione-harry-potter-cursed-child/.

Missinne, Lut. 2019. "Autobiographical Pact." In *Handbook of Autobiography / Autofiction*, edited by Martina Wagner-Egelhaaf, 222–227. Berlin: de Gruyter.

Mitchell, Timothy. 1998. "Orientalism and the Exhibitionary Order." In *The Visual Culture Reader*, edited by Nicholas Mirzoeff, 293–303. London: Routledge.

Mittell, Jason. 2006. "Narrative Complexity in Contemporary American Television." *The Velvet Light Trap*, no. 58: 29–40.

Mittell, Jason. 2015. *Complex TV: The Poetics of Contemporary Television Storytelling*. New York: New York University Press.

Mochocki, Michal. 2018. "Live Action Role Play: Transmediality, Narrativity and Markers of Subjectivity." *International Journal of Transmedia Literacy*, no. 4: 91–115.

Molotiu, Andrei. 2020. "Cartooning." In *Comic Studies: A Guidebook*, by Charles Hatfield and Bart Beaty, 153–171. New Brunswick: Rutgers University Press.

Montpelier, Rachel. 2020. "2020 Diversity Report: Women and POC Make Strides in Film, Remain Underrepresented." *Women and Hollywood*, February 06. https://womenandhollywood.com/2020-diversity-report-women-and-poc-make-strides-in-film-remain-underrepresented/.

Moss, Emily. 2017. "The Edward/Bella Alternative: Twilight Fanfiction, Transmedia Narratives, & the Robsten Romance". *Emily Moss: Electronic Portfolio*, March 19. https://emilymossportfolio.com/the-edward-bella-alternative-twilight-fanfiction-transmedia-narratives-the-robsten-romance/.

Müller, Wolfgang G. 1991. "Interfigurality. A Study on the Interdependence of Literary Figures." In *Intertextuality*, edited by Heinrich Plett, 101–121. Berlin: de Gruyter.

Mulvey, Laura. 2006. "Visual Pleasure and Narrative Cinema." In *Media and Cultural Studies: Keywords*, edited by Meenakshi G. Durham and Douglas Kellner, 342–352. Malden: Blackwell.

Murdock, Maureen. 1990. *The Heroine's Journey: Woman's Quest for Wholeness*. Boston: Shambhala Pub.

Murray, Janet. 1997. *Hamlet on the Holodeck: The Future of Narrative in Cyberspace*. Cambridge, MA: MIT Press.

Myers, Brian. 2017. "Friends with Benefits: Plausible Optimism and the Practice of Teabagging in Video Games." *Games and Culture*, no. 14 (7–8): 763–780.

Nagel, Thomas. 2016 [1974]. *What Is it like to Be a Bat?* Ditzingen: Reclam.

Nannicelli, Ted. 2019. "Seeing and Hearing Screen Characters: Stars, Twofoldness, and the Imagination." In *Screening Characters: Theories of Character in Film, Television, and Interactive Media*, edited by Johannes Riis and Aaron Taylor, 19–36. New York: Routledge.

Naremore, James. 1988. *Acting in the Cinema*. Berkeley: University of California Press.

Natsume, Fusanosuke [夏目房之介]. 1997. *Manga wa Naze Omoshiroi no ka: Sono Hyōgen to Bunpō*. Tokyo: NHK.

Nelson, Kyra. 2015. "Women in Refrigerators: The Objectification of Women in Comics. A Woman's Experience." *Brigham Young University's Journal for Women's Studies*, no. 2 (9): https://scholarsarchive.byu.edu/awe/vol2/iss2/9/.

Nijdam, Elizabeth. 2020. "Transnational Girlhood and the Politics of Style in German Manga." *Journal of Graphic Novels and Comics*, no. 11 (1): 31–51.

Nozawa, Shunsuke. 2013. "Characterization." *Semiotic Review: Open Issue*, no. 3. https://www.semioticreview.com/ojs/index.php/sr/article/view/16/15.

Nozawa, Shunsuke. 2016. "Ensoulment and Effacement in Japanese Voice Acting." In *Media Convergence in Japan*, edited by Patrick W. Galbraith and Jason Karlin, 169–199. Kinema Klub.

Nussbaum, Emily. 2014. "The Great Divide: Norman Lear, Archie Bunker, and the Rise of the Bad Fan." *New Yorker*, March 31. https://www.newyorker.com/magazine/2014/04/07/the-great-divide-emily-nussbaum.

O'Mathúna, Dónal P. 2010. "What would Jack Do? The Ethics of Torture in 24." *Global Dialogue*, no. 12 (1): 1–14.

obsession_inc. 2009. "Affirmational Fandom vs. Transformational Fandom." *Dreamwidth. org*, June 1. https://obsession-inc.dreamwidth.org/82589.html.

Ocasio-Cortez, Alexandria. 2019. "To quote Alan Moore." *Twitter*, January 11. https://twitter.com/AOC/status/1083759782098583553?s=20&t=QY8PtDCJeQ WCKxqP_pxxuA.

Occhi, Debra J. 2012. "Wobbly Aesthetics, Performance, and Message: Comparing Japanese Kyara with their Anthropomorphic Forebears." *Asian Ethnology*, no. 71 (1): 109–132.

Olson, Dan. 2019. "Minecraft, Sandboxes, and Colonialism | Folding Ideas." *YouTube*, August 23. https://www.youtube.com/watch?v=d6i5Ylu0mgM.

Oltean, Tudor. 1993. "Series and Seriality in Media Culture." *European Journal of Communication*, no. 8: 5–31.

Omry, Keren. 2013. "Quantum of Craig: Daniel Craig and the Body of the New Bond." In *Acting and Performance in Moving Image Culture: Bodies, Screens, Renderings*, edited by Jörg Sternagel, Lesley Stern and Dieter Mersch, 115–128. Bielefeld: transcript.

Ortenau Klinikum. 2019. "Ed Euromaus überrascht kleine Patienten mit Geschenken zur Weihnachtszeit." *Ortenau Klinikum*, October 23. https://offenburg-kehl.ortenau-klinikum.de/aktuelles/d/ed-euromaus-beschenkt-kleine-patienten-der-kinderklinik/

Ōtsuka, Eiji [大塚 英志]. 2003. *Kyarakutā Shōgetsu no Tsukurikata*. Tokyo: Kōdansha.

Outlaw, Kofi. 2019. "Kevin Feige Confirms Two Marvel Cinematic Universe Characters are Actually the Same Person." *Comicbook*, May 16. https://comicbook.com/marvel/news/spider-man-far-from-home-incredible-hulk-mcu-connections-martin-starr-roger-harrington/.

Packard, Stephan. 2015. "Closing the Open Signification: Forms of Transmedial Storyworlds and Chronotopoi in Comics." *Transmedial Worlds in Convergent Media Culture*. Special Themed-Issue of *StoryWorlds: A Journal of Narrative Studies*, no. 7 (2): 55–74.

Packard, Stephan. 2017a. "How Factual Are Factual Comics? Parasitic Imaginations in Referential Cartoons." In *Science Meets Comics: Proceedings of the Symposium on Communicating and Designing the Future of Food in the Antropocene*, edited by Reinhold R. Leinfelder, Alexandra Hamann, Jens Kirstein and Marc Schleunitz, 19–27. Berlin: Christian A. Bachmann.

Packard, Stephan. 2017b. "The Drawn-Out Gaze of the Cartoon: A Psychosemiotic Look at Subjectivity in Comic Book Storytelling." In *Subjectivity Across Media: Interdisciplinary and Transmedial Perspectives*, edited by Maike Sarah Reinerth and Jan-Noël Thon, 111–124. New York: Routledge.

Packard, Stephan. 2018. "The Inventibility of Other Audiences: Thoughts on the Popular Ideology of Fiction in Transnational Comic Books, on the Occasion of Captain Marvel #1." *International Journal of Comic Art IJoCA*, no. 20 (1): 65–80.

Packard, Stephan. 2019. "Which Donald Is this? Which Tyche Is this? A Semiotic Approach to Nomadic Cartoonish Characters." *Frontiers of Narrative Studies*, no. 5 (2): 248–67.

Packard, Stephan, Andreas Rauscher, Véronique Sina, Jan-Noël Thon, Lukas R.A. Wilde, and Janina Wildfeuer. 2019. *Comicanalyse: Eine Einführung.* Stuttgart: Metzler.

Palmer, Alan. 2010. *Social Minds in the Novel.* Columbus: Ohio State University Press.

Pande, Rukmini, ed. 2020. *Fandom, Now in Color: A Collection of Voices.* Chicago: University of Iowa Press.

Pandel, Hans-Jürgen. 2006. "Authentizität." In *Wörterbuch Geschichtsdidaktik*, edited by Ulrich Mayer, Hans-Jürgen Pandel, Gerhard Schneider and Bernd Schönemann, 25–26. Schwalbach: Wochenschau Verlag.

Panofsky, Erwin. 1959. "Style and Medium in the Motion Pictures." In *Film: An Anthology*, edited by Daniel Talbot, 15–32. Berkeley: University of California Press.

Parker, Ryan. 2016. "After YouTube 'Dislikes' Controversy, Sony's New 'Ghostbusters' Trailer Debuts elsewhere First". *The Hollywood Reporter*, May 18. https://www.hollywood-reporter.com/movies/movie-news/youtube-dislikes-controversy-sonys-new-895442/.

Parsons, Terence. 1980. *Nonexistent Objects.* New Haven: Yale University Press.

Pascoe, Peggy. 2010. *What Comes Naturally – Miscegenation Law and the Making of Race in America.* Oxford: Oxford University Press.

Patron, Sylvie, ed. 2021. *Optional-narrator Theory: Principles, Perspectives, Proposals.* Lincoln: University of Nebraska Press.

Pavel, Thomas G. 1986. *Fictional Worlds.* Cambridge, MA: Harvard University Press.

Pearson, Roberta E. 2015. "Sherlock Holmes, the de facto Franchise." In *Popular Media Cultures: Fans, Audiences and Paratexts*, edited by Lincoln Geraghty, 186–205. New York: Palgrave Macmillan.

Pearson, Roberta E. 2018a. "'You're Sherlock Holmes, Wear the Damn Hat!': Character Identity in a Transfiction." In *Reading Contemporary Serial Television Universes: A Narrative Ecosystem Framework*, edited by Paola Brembilla and Ilaria A. De Pascalis, 144–166. New York: Routledge.

Pearson, Roberta E. 2018b. "Transmedia Characters: Additionality and Cohesion in Transfictional Heroes." In *The Routledge Companion to Transmedia Studies*, edited by Matthew Freeman and Renira Rampazzo Gambarato, 148–156. New York: Routledge.

Pearson, Roberta E. 2019. "Transmedia Characters: Additionality and Cohesion in Transfictional Heroes." In *The Routledge Companion to Transmedia Studies*, edited by Matthew Freeman and Renira Rampazzo Gambarato, 148–156. New York: Routledge Taylor & Francis.

Peil, Corinna, and Herbert Schwab. 2013. "Hello-Kitty-Konsum als Kommunikationskultur: Zur Veralltäglichung und Vergegenständlichung eines Cute Characters." In *Nipponspiration: Japonismus und Japanische Populärkultur im Deutschsprachigen Raum*, edited by Michiko Mae and Elisabeth Scherer, 335–353. Cologne: Böhlau.

Perron, Bernard. 2016. "Wandering the Panels, Walking through Media: Zombies, Comics, and the Post-ap." *Journal of Graphic Novels and Comics*, no. 7 (3): 306–318.

Perry, David. 2015. "How Well Does 'Daredevil' Handle Disability Issues?" *Vice*, April 20. https://www.vice.com/en/article/jmaez3/how-well-does-daredevil-handle-disability-issues-320.

Pfister, Manfred. 1977. *Das Drama: Theorie und Analyse.* München: Fink.

Phelan, James. 1987. "Character, Progression, and the Mimetic-didactic Distinction." *Modern Philology*, no. 84: 282–299.

Phelan, James. 1989. *Reading People, Reading Plots: Character, Progression, and the Interpretation of Narrative.* Chicago: The University of Chicago Press.

Phelan, James. 2022. "Character as Rhetorical Resource: Mimetic, Thematic, and Synthetic in Fiction and Non-Fiction." *Narrative: The Journal of the International Society for the Study of Narrative*, no. 30 (2): 256–267.

Pisanty, Valentina. 2015. "From the Model Reader to the Limits of Interpretation." *Semiotica*, no. 206: 37–61.

Plantinga, Carl. 2019. "Ethical Criticism and Fictional Characters as Moral Agents." In *Screening Characters: Theories of Character in Film, Television, and Interactive Media*, edited by Johannes Riis and Aaron Taylor, 191–208. New York: Routledge.

Plantinga, Carl. 2010. "'I Followed the Rules, and They All Loved You More': Moral Judgment and Attitudes Toward Fictional Characters in Film." *Midwest Studies in Philosophy*, no. XXXIV: 34–51.

Plunkett, Luke. 2019. "Blackface Controversy Splits Cosplay Scene Over League of Legends Outfit." *Kotaku*, October 13. https://kotaku.com/blackface-controversy-splits-cosplay-scene-over-league-1838924072.

Polo, Susana. 2019. "The Reason Alan Moore Doesn't Want His Name on HBO's Watchmen." *Polygon*, November 11. https://www.polygon.com/comics/2019/11/11/20931078/alan-moore-watchmen-name-hbo-dc-comics-rights-controversy.

Pomerance, Murray. 2016. "Doing Dumbledore: Actor-Character Bonding and Accretionary Performance." In *Cycles, Sequels, Spin-offs, Remakes, and Reboots: Multiplicities in Film and Television*, edited by Amanda Ann Klein and R. Barton Palmer, 166–183. Austin, TX: University of Texas Press.

Poniewozik, James. 2018. "Review: 'Our Cartoon President' Misses a Huuuge Target." *The New York Times*, February 09. https://www.nytimes.com/2018/02/09/arts/television/our-cartoon-president-review-trump-showtime.html.

Potysch, Nicolas, and Lukas R.A. Wilde. 2018. "Picture Theory and Picturebooks." In *The Routledge Companion to Picturebooks*, edited by Bettina Kümmerling-Meibauer, 439–450. London: Routledge.

Prince, Gerald. 1996. "Remarks on Narrativity." In *Perspectives on Narratology: Papers from the Stockholm Symposium on Narratology*, edited by Claes Wahlin, 95–106. Frankfurt a.M.: Lang.

Prince, Stephen, and Wayne E. Hensley. 1992. "The Kuleshov Effect: Recreating the Classic Experiment." *Cinema Journal*, no. 31 (2): 59–75.

Proctor, William. 2018. "Transmedia Comics: Seriality, Sequentiality, and the Shifting Economies of Franchise Licensing." In *The Routledge Companion to Transmedia Studies*, edited by Matthew Freeman and Renira Rampazzo Gambarato, 52–61. New York: Routledge.

Projansky, Sarah, and Kent A. Ono. 1999. "Strategic Whiteness as Cinematic Racial Politics." In *Whiteness: The Communication of Social Identity*, edited by Thomas K. Nakayama and Judith N. Martin, 149–176. Newbury Park: Sage.

Propp, Vladimir. 1984. *Theory and History of Folklore*, translated by Ariadna Y. Martin and Richard P. Martin, edited by Anatoly Liberman. Minneapolis: University of Minnesota Press.

Putnam, Amanda 2013a. "Mean Ladies: Transgendered Villains in Disney Films." In *Diversity in Disney Films: Critical Essays on Race, Ethnicity, Gender Sexuality, and Disability*, edited by Johnston Cheu, 147–162. Jefferson: McFarland.

Putnam, Amanda. 2013b. "Mean Ladies: Transgendered Villains in Disney Films." In *Diversity in Disney Films: Critical Essays on Race, Ethnicity, Gender Sexuality, and Disability*, edited by Johnston Cheu, 147–162. Jefferson: McFarland.

Rajewsky, Irina O. 2005. "Intermediality, Intertextuality, and Remediation: A Literary Perspective on Intermediality." *Intermédialités/Intermediality*, no. 6: 43–64.

Rajewsky, Irina O. 2020. "Theories of Fictionality and Their Real Other." In *Narrative Factuality: A Handbook*, edited by Monika Fludernik and Marie-Laure Ryan, 29–50. Berlin: de Gruyter.

Rauscher, Andreas. 2018. "Die Cartoon-Modalitäten des Batman-Franchise und die Gemachtheit von Gotham City." In *Ästhetik Des Gemachten: Interdisziplinäre Beiträge Zur Animations- Und Comicforschung*, edited by Hans-Joachim Backe, Julia Eckel, Erwin Feyersinger, Véronique Sina and Jan-Noël Thon, 305–334. Berlin: de Gruyter.

Reinerth, Maike S., and Jan-Noël Thon. 2017. "Introduction: Subjectivity Across Media." In *Subjectivity across Media: Interdisciplinary and Transmedial Perspectives*, edited by Maike S. Reinerth and Jan-Noël Thon, 1–26. New York: Routledge.

Reinhard, CarrieLynn, and Christopher Olson, eds. 2019. *Convergent Wrestling: Participatory Culture, Transmedia Storytelling, and Intertextuality in the Squared Circle*. New York: Routledge.

Reitz, Nikki. 2017. "The Representation of Trans Women in Film and Television." *Cinesthesia*, no. 7 (1): Article 2. https://scholarworks.gvsu.edu/cine/vol7/iss1/2.

Ribó, Ignasi. 2019. *Prose Fiction: An Introduction to the Semiotics of Narrative*. Cambridge: Open Book Publishers.

Richardson, Brian. 2010. "Transtextual Characters." In *Characters in Fictional Worlds: Understanding Imaginary Beings in Literature, Film, and Other Media*, edited by Jens Eder, Fotis Jannidis and Ralf Schneider, 527–541. Berlin: de Gruyter.

Riis, Johannes. 2013. "Actor/Character Dualism: The Case of Luis Buñuel's Paradoxical Characters." In *Acting and Performance in Moving Image Culture: Bodies, Screens, Renderings*, edited by Jörg Sternagel, Lesley Stern and Dieter Mersch, 131–144. Bielefeld: transcript.

Riis, Johannes, and Aaron Taylor, eds. 2019. *Screening Characters: Theories of Character in Film, Television, and Interactive Media*. New York: Routledge.

Rimmon-Kenan, Shlomith. 1993. *Narrative Fiction: Contemporary Poetics*. London: Routledge.

Robinson, Ashley. 2021. "Scarlett Johansson on the Sexualization of Natasha Romanoff and why it Took 10 Years to Make 'Black Widow.'" *Collider*, June 15. https://collider.com/black-widow-movie-scarlett-johansson-interview-sexualization/.

Robinson, Joanna. 2015. "Game of Thrones Absolutely Did Not Need to Go there with Sansa Stark." *Vanity Fair*, May 17. https://www.vanityfair.com/hollywood/2015/05/game-of-thrones-rape-sansa-stark.

Rojek, Chris. 2016. *Presumed Intimacy: Parasocial Relationships in Media, Society and Celebrity Culture*. Chichester: Polity Press.

Roller, Emma. 2016. "The Trump Brand, Win or Lose." *The New York Times*, February 9. https://www.nytimes.com/2016/02/09/opinion/campaign-stops/the-donald-trump-brand-win-or-lose.html.

Romano, Aja. 2021. "'Attack on Titan' Creator Gets the Last Word in Debate over Character's Gender." *Daily Dot*, May 31. https://www.dailydot.com/parsec/fandom/attack-titan-snk-hange-hanji-gender-debate/.

Ronen, Ruth. 1994. *Possible Worlds in Literary Theory*. Cambridge: Cambridge University Press.

Rosa, Don. 2014. "Preface." In *The Don Rosa Library #1*, 6–10. Seattle: Fantagraphics.

Rosen, Jeremy. 2016. *Minor Characters Have their Day: Genre and the Contemporary Literary Marketplace*. New York: Columbia University Press.

Rosenbaum, Richard. 2014. "Rewriting the Future: Retroactive Continuity as Marketing." *Overthinking It*, July 29. https://www.overthinkingit.com/2014/07/29/rewriting-future-retroactive-continuity-marketing/.

Rosendo, Nieves. 2016. "Character-centred Transmedia Narratives: Sherlock Holmes in the 21st Century." *Artnodes*, no. 18: 20–27.

Ross, Edward. 2015. *Filmish: A Graphic Journey Through Film*. London: SelfMadeHero.

Ryan, Mary-Laure. 1991a. "Possible Worlds and Accessibility Relations: A Semantic Typology of Fiction." *Poetics Today*, no. 12 (3): 553–576.

Ryan, Marie-Laure. 1991b. *Possible Worlds, Artificial Intelligence and Narrative Theory*. Bloomington: Indiana University Press.

Ryan, Marie-Laure. 1997. "Postmodernism and the Doctrine of Panfictionality." *Narrative*, no. 5 (2): 165–187

Ryan, Marie-Laure. 2013. "Transmedia Storytelling and Transfictionality." *Poetics Today*, no. 34 (3): 361–388.

Sachs-Hombach, Klaus. 2011. "Theories of Image: Five Tentative Theses." In *What Is an Image?*, edited by James Elkins and Maja Naef, 229–232. University Park: Penn State University Press.

Said, Edward W. 2014 [1978]. *Orientalism: 25. Anniversary Edition with a New Preface by the Author*. New York: Vintage Books.

Salter, Anastasia and Mel Stanfill. 2020. *A Portrait of the Auteur as Fanboy: The Construction of Authorship in Transmedia Franchises*. Jackson: University Press of Mississippi.

Sawant, Drushti. 2020. "Johnny Depp in UK Court Confessed that his Drug Use Began when he Was 11-years-old." *Republic World*, July 08. https://www.republicworld.com/entertainment-news/hollywood-news/johnny-depp-in-uk-court-started-taking-drugs-at-about-11-years-of-age.html.

Schaeffer, Jean-Marie. 2013. "Fictional vs. Factual Narration." *The Living Handbook of Narratology*, September 20. https://www.lhn.uni-hamburg.de/node/56.html.

Schalk, Sami. 2016. "Reevaluating the Supercrip." *Journal of Literary & Cultural Disability Studies*, no. 10 (1): 71–86.

Schedeen, Jesse. 2021. "Dark Nights: Death Metal Ending Explained: The Final Evolution of the DC Multiverse." *IGN*, January 05. https://www.ign.com/articles/dark-nights-death-metal-ending-explained-wonder-woman-batman-dc-future-state-multiverse.

Schiller, Amy and John McMahon. 2019. "Alexa, Alert me when the Revolution Comes. Gender, Affect, and Labor in the Age of Home-based Artificial Intelligence." *New Political Science*, no. 41 (2): 173–191.

Schmid, Wolf. 2003. "Narrativity and Eventfulness." In *What Is Narratology? Questions and Answers Regarding the Status of a Theory*, edited by Tom Kindt and Hans-Harald Müller, 17–33. Berlin: de Gruyter.

Schmidt, Victoria Lynn. 2001. *45 Master Characters: Mythic Models for Creating Original Characters*. New York: F+W Media.

Schneider, Ralf. 2001. "Toward a Cognitive Theory of Literary Character: The Dynamics of Mental-model Construction." *Style*, no. 35 (4): 607–640.

Schröter, Felix. 2021. *Spiel | Figur: Theorie und Ästhetik der Computerspielfigur*. Marburg: Schüren Verlag.

Schröter, Felix, and Jan-Noël Thon. 2014. "Video Game Characters: Theory and Analysis." *Diegesis*, no. 3 (1): 40–77.

Schüwer, Martin. 2008. *Wie Comics Erzählen: Grundriss Einer Intermedialen Erzähltheorie der Grafischen Literatur*. Trier: Wissenschaftlicher Verlag Trier.

Scolari, Carlos, Paolo Bertetti, and Matthew Freeman, eds. 2014a. *Transmedia Archaeology: Storytelling in the Borderlines of Science Fiction, Comics and Pulp Magazines*. New York: Palgrave Macmillan.

Scolari, Carlos, Paolo Bertetti, and Matthew Freeman. 2014b. "Introduction: Towards an Archaeology of Transmedia Storytelling." In *Transmedia Archaeology: Storytelling in the Borderlines of Science Fiction, Comics and Pulp Magazines*, edited by Carlos Scolari, Paolo Bertetti and Matthew Freeman, 1–14. New York: Palgrave Macmillan.

Scott, Suzanne. 2019. *Fake Geek Girls: Fandom, Gender, and the Convergence Culture Industry*. New York: New York University Press.

Scrooge McDuck Wiki. N.d. "2017 Continuum." *Scrooge McDuck Wiki*. https://scrooge-mcduck.fandom.com/wiki/2017_Continuum.

Scrooge McDuck Wiki. N.d. "Barks-Rosa Universe." *Scrooge McDuck Wiki*. https://scrooge-mcduck.fandom.com/wiki/Barks-Rosa_Universe.

Searle, John. 1975. "The Logical Status of Fictional Discourse." *New Literary History*, no. 6: 319–333.

Searle, John. 1992. *The Rediscovery of the Mind*. Cambridge, MA: MIT Press.

Searle, John. 1999. *Mind, Language and Society: Doing Philosophy in the Real World*. London: Weidenfeld & Nicolson.

Shakespeare, Tom. 2006. *Disability Rights and Wrongs*. New York: Routledge.

Silverman, Jason. 2007. "300 Brings History to Bloody Life." *Wired*, February 22. https://www.wired.com/2007/02/300-brings-history-to-bloody-life/.

Šima, Karel. 2021. "From Identity Politics to the Identitarian Movement: The European-isation of Cultural Stereotypes?" In *National Stereotyping, Identity Politics, European Crises*, edited by Jürgen Barkhoff and Joep Leerssen, 75–94. Leiden: Brill.

Simone, Gail. 1999. "Women in Refrigerators." *WiR*, March. https://lby3.com/wir/.

Sina, Véronique. 2016. *Comic – Film – Gender: Zur (Re-)Medialisierung von Geschlecht im Com-icfilm*. Bielefeld: Transcript.

Singer, Matt. 2015. "Welcome to the Age of the Legacyquel." *Screen Crush*, November 23. https://screencrush.com/the-age-of-legacyquels/.

Skotnes-Brown, Jules. 2019. "Colonized Play: Racism, Sexism, and Colonial Legacies in the Dota 2 South Africa Community." In *Video Games and the Global South*, edited by Phillip Penix-Tadsen, 143–154. Pittsburgh: ETC Press.

Skov Nielsen, Henrik, James Phelan, and Richard Walsh. 2015. "Ten Theses About Fictionality." *Narrative*, no. 23 (1): 61–73.

Smith, Murray. 1995. *Engaging Characters: Fiction, Emotion, and the Cinema*. Oxford: Clarendon Press.

Sorg, Jürgen. 2009. "Gemischtes Doppel: Zur Psychologie Narrativer Formen in Digi-talen Spielen." In *It's all in the Game: Computerspiele zwischen Spiel und Erzählung*, edited by Benjamin Beil, Sascha Simons, Jürgen Sorg and Jochen Venus, 91–108. Marburg: Schüren.

Sperb, Jason. 2012. *Disney's Most Notorious Film: Race, Convergence, and the Hidden Histories of Song of the South*. Austin: University of Texas Press.

Spiegel. 2022. "'Blue Fire'-Achterbahn: Europa-Park Stoppt Zusammenarbeit mit Nord Stream 2." *Spiegel*, February 24. https://www.spiegel.de/wirtschaft/unternehmen/rust-europa-park-stoppt-zusammenarbeit-mit-nord-stream-2-blue-fire-umbenannt-a-e617823f-6864-4f44-a0bc-4de155a8cec9.

Spivak, Gayatari C. 1985. "The Rani of Sirmur: An Essay in Reading the Archives." *History and Theory*, no. 24 (3): 247–272.

Stacey, Jackie. 1994. *Stargazing: Hollywood Cinema and Female Spectatorship*. New York: Routledge.

Stein, Louisa Ellen, and Kristina Busse. 2012. "Introduction: The Literary, Televisual and Digital Adventures of the Beloved Detective." In *Sherlock and Transmedia Fandom:*

Essays on the BBC Series, edited by Louisa Ellen Stein and Kristina Busse, 9–26. Jefferson: McFarland.

Steinberg, Marc. 2007. "Translator's Introduction: The Animalization of Otaku Culture." *Mechademia*, no. 2: 175–177.

Steinberg, Marc. 2010. "Translator's Introduction: Ōtsuka Eiji and Narrative Consumption." *Mechademia*, no. 5: 99–104.

Steinberg, Marc. 2012. *Anime's Media Mix: Franchising Toys and Characters in Japan*. Minneapolis: University of Minnesota Press.

Sternagel, Jörg, Lesley Stern, and Dieter Mersch, eds. 2012. *Acting and Performance in Moving Image Culture: Bodies, Screens, Renderings*. Bielefeld: transcript.

Stevens, Dana. 2007. "A Movie Only a Spartan Could Love." *Slate*, March 08. https://slate.com/culture/2007/03/the-battle-epic-300-reviewed.html.

Stewart, Dodai. 2012. "A Character-By-Character Guide to Race in The Hunger Games." *Jezebel*, March 03. https://jezebel.com/a-character-by-character-guide-to-race-in-the-hunger-ga-5896515.

Strausbaugh, John. 2006. *Black Like You: Blackface, Whiteface, Insult & Imitation in American Popular Culture*. New York: Penguin Books.

Strengers, Yolande, and Jenny Kennedy. 2020. *The Smart Wife. Why Siri, Alexa, and Other Smart Home Devices Need a Feminist Reboot*. London: MIT Press.

Stucky, Mark D. 2005. "He Is the One: The Matrix Trilogy's Postmodern Movie Messiah." *Journal of Religion & Film*, no. 9 (2): 1–15.

Suan, Stevie. 2017. "Anime's Performativity: Diversity Through Conventionality in a Global Media-Form." *Animation*, no. 12 (1): 62–79.

Suellentrop, Chris. 2001. "A Real Number: A Beautiful Mind's John Nash Is Nowhere Near as Complicated as the Real One." *Slate*, December 21. https://slate.com/culture/2001/12/a-beautiful-mind-s-john-nash-is-less-complex-than-the-real-one.html.

Sugar Zaza. 2015. "Anime in Real Life!!!!." *YouTube*, August 30. https://www.youtube.com/watch?v=xZLwtc9x4yA.

Sullivan, Caitlin. 2021. "Hey Again, Everyone!" Posting in *Star Wars The Old Republic* forum, April 16. https://www.swtor.com/community/showthread.php?t=992068&page=3.

Surman, Steven. 2015. "Alan Moore's Watchmen and Rorschach: Does the Character Set a Bad Example?" *Steven Surman Writes*, January 20. https://www.stevensurman.com/rorschach-from-alan-moores-watchmen-does-he-set-a-bad-example/.

Sutherland, Annie. 2019. "'The Handmaid's Tale' Costume Is Now the Ultimate Symbol of Women's Rights." *Quartz*, June 13. https://qz.com/quartzy/1643273/the-handmaids-tale-costume-has-become-the-symbol-of-womens-rights.

Tassi, Paul. 2020. "An 'Avengers' Deepfake Puts MCU Actors in the Upcoming Game." *Forbes*, August 27. https://www.forbes.com/sites/paultassi/2020/08/27/an-avengers-deepfake-puts-mcu-actors-in-the-upcoming-game/?sh=64c39ab24955/.

Tavinor, Grant. 2009. *The Art of Videogames*. Malden: Wiley-Blackwell.

Taylor, T.L. 2006. *Play Between Worlds: Exploring Online Game Culture*. Cambridge, MA: MIT Press.

Tellería, Ana S. 2016. "Transmedia Journalism: Exploring Genres and Interface Design." *Trípodos*, no. 38: 67–85

Thaler, Peter. 2004. "Good Bye Kitty, Hello Pooh." *Design Report*, no. 5: 32–35.

The Hawkeye Initiative. 2012–present. *The Hawkeye Initiative*. https://thehawkeyeinitiative.tumblr.com/.

Thompson, Kristin. 2007. *The Frodo Franchise: The Lord of the Rings and Modern Hollywood*. Berkeley: University of California Press.

Thon, Jan-Noël. 2014. "Mediality." In *The Johns Hopkins Guide to Digital Media*, edited by Marie-Laure Ryan, Benjamin J. Robertson and Lori Emerson, 334–336. Baltimore: John Hopkins University Press.

Thon, Jan-Noël. 2016. *Transmedial Narratology and Contemporary Media Culture*. Lincoln: University of Nebraska Press.

Thon, Jan-Noël. 2017. "Transmedial Narratology Revisited: On the Intersubjective Construction of Storyworlds and the Problem of Representational Correspondence in Films, Comics, and Video Games." *Narrative*, no. 25 (3): 286–320.

Thon, Jan-Noël. 2019. "Transmedia Characters: Theory and Analysis." *Frontiers of Narrative Studies*, no. 5 (2): 176–199.

Thon, Jan-Noël. 2022. "Transmedia Characters/Transmedia Figures: Drawing Distinctions and Staging Re-Entries." *Narrative: The Journal of the International Society for the Study of Narrative*, no. 30 (2): 140–147.

Thon, Jan-Noël, and Lukas R.A. Wilde, eds. 2019. *Characters Across Media*. Special Issue of *Frontiers of Narrative Studies*, no. 5 (2).

Tisserand, Michael. 2016. *Krazy: George Herriman, a Life in Black and White*. New York: Harper.

Titlestad, Michael. 2013. "Searching for the Sugar-coated Man." *The Journal of South African and American Studies*, no. 14 (4): 466–470, December 17. https://www.tandfonline.com/doi/full/10.1080/17533171.2013.841061.

Tokyo Files. N.d. "Funny Japanese Street Signs 面白い道路標識." *The Tokyo Files*. https://funnyjapanesestreetsigns.wordpress.com/.

Tomasi, Dario. 1988. *Cinema e Racconto: Il Personaggio*. Torino: Loescher.

Toolan, Michael J. 2001. *Narrative: A Critical Linguistic Introduction*. 2nd ed. London: Routledge.

Toratani, Kiyoko. 2013. "Iconicity in Gotoochii 'Localized Hello Kitty'." In *Iconic Investigations*, edited by Lars Elleström and Olga Fischer: 335–353. Amsterdam: Benjamins.

Tosca, Susana, and Lisbeth Klastrup. 2019. *Transmedial Worlds in Everyday Life: Networked Reception, Social Media, and Fictional Worlds*. New York: Routledge.

Trans Characters. 2018. "Speed-o'-sound Sonic" *Trans Characters*, July 07. https://transcharacters.tumblr.com/post/162712724919/character-speed-o-sound-sonic-fandom-one-punch.

Trent, John F. 2021. "Ethan Van Sciver Speculates Marvel and DC Comics Are Being Funded by the Government to Push Radical Gender and Sexuality Ideology." *Bounding Into Comics*, October 26. https://boundingintocomics.com/2021/10/26/ethan-van-sciver-speculates-marvel-and-dc-comics-are-being-funded-by-the-government-to-push-radical-gender-and-sexuality-ideology/.

Tropedia. N.d. "Applied Phlebotinum." *Tropedia*. https://tropedia.fandom.com/wiki/Category:Applied_Phlebotinum.

Truffaut, François. 2017. *Hitchcock/Truffaut*. With the collaboration of Helen G. Scott. London: Faber & Faber.

Tugendhat, Ernst. 1982 [1975]. *Traditional and Analytical Philosophy: Lectures on the Philosophy of Language*. Translated by P.A. Gorner. Cambridge, MA: Cambridge University Press.

Turner, Graeme. 2004. *Understanding Celebrity*. London: Sage Publications.

TV Tropes. N.d. "Aluminium Christmas Tree." TV Tropes. https://tvtropes.org/pmwiki/pmwiki.php/Main/AluminumChristmasTrees.

TV Tropes. N.d. "Chekhov's Gun." *TV Tropes*. https://tvtropes.org/pmwiki/pmwiki.php/Main/ChekhovsGun.

TV Tropes. N.d. "Cosmic Horror Story." *TV Tropes.* https://tvtropes.org/pmwiki/pmwiki.php/Main/CosmicHorrorStory.

TV Tropes. N.d. "Darkness Equals Death." *TV Tropes.* https://tvtropes.org/pmwiki/pmwiki.php/Main/DarknessEqualsDeath.

TV Tropes. N.d. "Epiphanic Prison." *TV Tropes.* https://tvtropes.org/pmwiki/pmwiki.php/Main/EpiphanicPrison.

TV Tropes. N.d. "Evil Makes You Ugly." *TV Tropes.* https://tvtropes.org/pmwiki/pmwiki.php/Main/EvilMakesYouUgly.

TV Tropes. N.d. "'Groundhog Day' Loop." *TV Tropes.* https://tvtropes.org/pmwiki/pmwiki.php/Main/GroundhogDayLoop.

TV Tropes. N.d. "Hammer Space." *TV Tropes.* https://tvtropes.org/pmwiki/pmwiki.php/Hammerspace/Videogames.

TV Tropes. N.d. "Hannibal Lecture." *TV Tropes.* https://tvtropes.org/pmwiki/pmwiki.php/Main/HannibalLecture.

TV Tropes. N.d. "Hensin Hero." *TV Tropes.* https://tvtropes.org/pmwiki/pmwiki.php/Main/HenshinHero.

TV Tropes. N.d. "Humans Are the Real Monsters." *TV Tropes.* https://tvtropes.org/pmwiki/pmwiki.php/Main/HumansAreTheRealMonsters.

TV Tropes. N.d. "Logic Bomb." *TV Tropes.* https://tvtropes.org/pmwiki/pmwiki.php/Main/LogicBomb.

TV Tropes. N.d. "Monster of the Week." *TV Tropes.* https://tvtropes.org/pmwiki/pmwiki.php/Main/MonsterOfTheWeek.

TV Tropes. N.d. "Nice Day, Deadly Night." *TV Tropes.* https://tvtropes.org/pmwiki/pmwiki.php/Main/NiceDayDeadlyNight.

TV Tropes. N.d. "Perspective Flip." *TV Tropes.* https://tvtropes.org/pmwiki/pmwiki.php/Main/PerspectiveFlip.

TV Tropes. N.d. "'Rashomon'-Style." *TV Tropes.* https://tvtropes.org/pmwiki/pmwiki.php/Main/RashomonStyle.

TV Tropes. N.d. "Sharing a Body." *TV Tropes.* https://tvtropes.org/pmwiki/pmwiki.php/Main/SharingABody.

TV Tropes. N.d. "Snap Back." *TV Tropes.* https://tvtropes.org/pmwiki/pmwiki.php/Main/SnapBack.

TV Tropes. N.d. "Status Quo Is God." *TV Tropes.* https://tvtropes.org/pmwiki/pmwiki.php/Main/StatusQuoIsGod.

TV Tropes. N.d. "Tsundere." *TV Tropes.* https://tvtropes.org/pmwiki/pmwiki.php/Main/Tsundere.

Ubisoft Entertainment. 2021. "Watch Dogs: Legion Gameplay Info." *Ubisoft.* https://www.ubisoft.com/en-gb/game/watch-dogs/legion/game-info.

Underwood, Reed. 2016. "Terra Nullius: The Spectral Colonialism of No Man's Sky." *Entropy,* N.d. https://entropymag.org/terra-nullius-the-spectral-colonialism-of-no-mans-sky/.

Uno, Roberta, and Lucy Mae San Pablo Burns, eds. 2002. *The Color of Theater: Race, Culture and Contemporary Performance.* London: Continuum.

Uricchio, William, and Roberta E. Pearson. 1991. "'I'm not Fooled by that Cheap Disguise.'" In *The Many Lives of the Batman: Critical Approaches to a Superhero and his Media,* 182–213. New York: Routledge.

Varis, Essi. 2019. "The Monster Analogy: Why Fictional Characters Are Frankenstein's Monsters." *Substance,* no. 48 (1): 63–86.

Vella, Daniel. 2015. *The Ludic Subject and the Ludic Self: Analyzing the 'I-in-the-Gameworld.'* PhD Thesis. Kopenhagen: IT University Copenhagen, Center for Computer

Games Research, 451 pages. https://pure.itu.dk/portal/en/publications/the-ludic-subject-and-the-ludic-self-analyzing-the-iinthegameworld(5877eb42-85c2-4795-9ffa-6625d00b3418)/export.html.

Walker, Austin. 2020. "'Watch Dogs: Legion' Promises Revolution, but Mostly Delivers Distraction." *Vice*, October 28. https://www.vice.com/en/article/pkdy5y/watch-dogs-legion-review.

Walton, Kendall L. 1993. *Mimesis as Make-Believe: On the Foundations of the Representational Arts*. Cambridge, MA: Harvard University Press.

Watercutter, Angela. 2020. "John Boyega Is Right about Star Wars." *Wired*, September 04. https://www.wired.com/story/john-boyega-star-wars/?mbid=social_twitter&utm_brand=wired&utm_medium=social&utm_social-type=owned&utm_source=twitter.

Watson, David. 2013. "Letting Go of the Cold Facts." *The Journal of South African and American Studies*, no. 14 (4): 485–490. December 17. https://www.tandfonline.com/doi/full/10.1080/17533171.2013.841066.

Weixler, Antonius. 2020. "Story at First Sight? Bildliches Erzählen Zwischen 'Diachroner Zustandsfolge' und 'Synchroner Zustandshaftigkeit'." In *Einzelbild & Narrativität: Theorien, Zugänge, Offene Fragen*, edited by Andreas Veits, Lukas R.A. Wilde and Klaus Sachs-Hombach, 56–87. Cologne: Herbert von Halem.

Wells, Paul. 1998. *Understanding Animation*. London: Routledge.

Wells, Paul. 2009. *The Animated Bestiary: Animals, Cartoons, and Culture*. New Brunswick: Rutgers University Press.

Wendell, Susan. 1996. *The Rejected Body: Feminist Philosophical Reflections on Disability*. New York: Routledge.

Wikipedia. N.d. "Gorillaz." *Wikipedia* (German). https://de.wikipedia.org/wiki/Gorillaz.

Wikiquotes. N.d. "Cary Grant.'" *Wikiquotes*. https://en.wikiquote.org/wiki/Cary_Grant/.

Wilde, Lukas R.A. 2018a. "Character Street Signs (*Hyōshiki*): 'Mangaesque' Aesthetics as Intermedial Reference and Virtual Mediation." *Manga, Comics and Japan: Area Studies as Media Studies*. Special Issue of *Orientaliska Studier*, no. 156: 130–150.

Wilde, Lukas R.A. 2018b. *Im Reich der Figuren: Meta-narrative Kommunikationsfiguren und die 'Mangaisierung' des japanischen Alltags*. Cologne: Herbert von Halem.

Wilde, Lukas R.A. 2019a. "Kyara Revisited: The Pre-narrative Character-State of Japanese Character Theory." *Frontiers of Narrative Studies*, no. 5 (2): 220–247.

Wilde, Lukas R.A. 2019b. "Recontextualizing Characters: Media Convergence and Pre-/meta-Narrative Character Circulation." *IMAGE*. Special Issue *Recontextualizing Characters*, no. 29 (1): 3–21.

Wilde, Lukas R.A. 2020a. "Digital Pictograms? Emojis between Infantilisation and International Ideography." In: *Die Gesellschaft der Zeichen: Piktogramme, Lebenszeichen, Emojis*, edited by Leopold-Hoesch Museum und Museum für Neue Kunst Freiburg, 236–241. Cologne: Verlag der Buchhandlung Walter König.

Wilde, Lukas R.A. 2020b. "Material Conditions and Semiotic Affordances: Natsume Fusanosuke's Many Fascinations with the Lines of Manga." *Mechademia: Second Arc*, no. 12 (2): *Asian Materialities*: 62–82.

Wilde, Lukas R.A. 2021. "Transmedia Character Studies and Agency: From Representation to Assemblage Theory." In *Agency Postdigital: Verteilte Handlungsmächte in Medienwissenschaftlichen Forschungsfeldern*, edited by Berenike Jung, Klaus Sachs-Hombach and Lukas R.A. Wilde, 42–64. Cologne: Herbert von Halem.

Wilde, Lukas R.A., and Shane Denson. 2022. "Historicizing and Theorizing Pre-Narrative Figures: Who Is Uncle Sam?" In *Narrative: The Journal of the International Society for the Study of Narrative*, no. 30 (2): 152–168.

Williams, Dmitri, Tracy L. M. Kennedy, and Robert J. Moore. 2011. "Behind the Avatar: The Patterns, Practices, and Functions of Role Playing in MMOs." *Games and Culture*, no. 6 (2): 171–200.

Williams, Katherine S. 2009. "Enabling Richard: The Rhetoric of Disability in Richard III'." *Disability Studies Quarterly*, no. 29 (4). http://dsq-sds.org/article/view/997/1181.

Williams, Linda. 2006. "Of Kisses and Ellipses: The Long Adolescence of American Movies." *Critical Inquiry*, no. 32: 288–340.

Witek, Joseph. 2011. "Comic Modes: Caricature and Illustration in the Crumb Family's Dirty Laundry." In *Critical Approaches to Comics: Theories and Methods*, edited by Matthew J. Smith and Randy Duncan, 27–42. New York: Routledge.

Wittgenstein, Ludwig. 1986 [1953]. *Philosophical Investigations*. 3rd ed. Translated by Gertrude E.M. Anscombe. Oxford: Blackwell.

Wolf, Mark J.P. 2012. *Building Imaginary Worlds: The Theory and History of Subcreation*. New York: Routledge.

Wolf, Werner. 2009. "Metareference across Media: The Concept, its Transmedial Potentials and Problems, Main Forms and Functions." In *Metareference Across Media: Theory and Case Studies*, edited by Werner Wolf, Walter Bernhart, Katharina Bantleon and Jeff Thoss, ix–85. Amsterdam: Rodopi.

Woloch, Alex. 2003. *The One vs. the Many: Minor Characters and the Space of the Protagonist in the Novel*. Princeton: Princeton University Press.

Woo, Benjamin. 2018. "Is There a Comic Book Industry?" *Media Industries*, no. 5 (1) (January): 27–46.

Wood, Christopher. 2021. *Heroes Masked and Mythic: Echoes of Ancient Archetypes in Comic Book Characters*. Jefferson: McFarland.

Wookieepedia. N.d. "The Power and Relevance of Wookieepedia". *Wookieepedia*. https://starwars.fandom.com/wiki/User_blog:Brandon_Rhea/The_Power_and_Relevance_of_Wookieepedia.

Yano, Christine R. 2016. "Hello Kitty Is not a Cat?!? Tracking Japanese Cute Culture at Home and Abroad." In *Introducing Japanese Popular Culture*, edited by Alisa Freedman and Toby Slade, 24–34. London: Routledge.

Yassin-Kassab, Robin. 2016. "The Arab of the Future by Riad Sattouf Review: An Emotionally Honest Graphic Memoir." *The Guardian*, March 31. https://www.the-guardian.com/books/2016/mar/31/the-arab-of-the-future-by-riad-sattouf-review#:~:-text=The%20Arab%20of%20the%20Future%20is%20an%20authentic%2C%20emotionally%20honest, cosmopolitan%2C%20bourgeois%20Damascus%20would%20be.&text=Sattouf's%20book%20investigates%20authoritarianism%20as%20a%20cultural%20problem.

Yi, Dennis E. 2020. "Why Chinese Viewers Hate Disney's 'Mulan.'" *SupChina*, September 11. https://supchina.com/2020/09/11/why-chinese-viewers-hate-disneys-mulan/#:~:-text=To%20the%20great%20displeasure%20of,   have%20belittled%20China's%20cultural%20totem.

Zipfel, Frank. 2001. *Fiktion, Fiktivität, Fiktionalität: Analysen zur Fiktion in der Literatur und zum Fiktionsbegriff in der Literaturwissenschaft*. Berlin: Erich Schmidt.

Zipfel, Frank. 2014. "Fiction across Media: Toward a Transmedial Concept of Fictionality." In *Storyworlds across Media: Toward a Media-Conscious Narratology*, edited by Marie-Laure Ryan and Jan-Noël Thon, 103–125. Lincoln: University of Nebraska Press.

Zipfel, Frank. 2020. "Panfictionality/Panfictionalism" In *Narrative Factuality*, edited by Monika Fludernik and Mary-Laure Ryan, 127–132. Berlin: de Gruyter.

Zunshine, Lisa. 2006. *Why We Read Fiction: Theory of Mind and the Novel*. Columbus: Ohio State University Press.

Zunshine, Lisa. 2020. "Mindreading and Social Status." In *Further Reading*, edited by Matthew Rubery and Leah Price, 257–270. Oxford: Oxford University Press.

Index

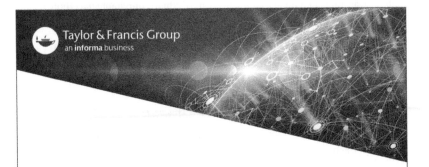

Printed and bound by CPI Group (UK) Ltd, Croydon, CR0 4YY

06/11/2024

01784723-0012